SHAPING TOMORROW'S LAW

Common Law and Modern Society

SHAPING TOMORROW'S LAW

Common Law and Modern Society

Keeping Pace with Change

VOLUME II

MARY ARDEN
Lady Justice of Appeal

OXFORD
UNIVERSITY PRESS

OXFORD
UNIVERSITY PRESS

Great Clarendon Street, Oxford, OX2 6DP,
United Kingdom

Oxford University Press is a department of the University of Oxford.
It furthers the University's objective of excellence in research, scholarship,
and education by publishing worldwide. Oxford is a registered trade mark of
Oxford University Press in the UK and in certain other countries

© M. Arden 2015

First Edition published in 2015

Impression: 1

Published in the United States of America by Oxford University Press
198 Madison Avenue, New York, NY 10016, United States of America

British Library Cataloguing in Publication Data
Data available

Library of Congress Control Number: 2015945826

ISBN 978–0–19–875584–5

Printed and bound by
CPI Group (UK) Ltd, Croydon, CR0 4YY

Contents

Contents

Preface by Justice Ruth Bader Ginsburg and Baroness Hale of Richmond

In this panoramic work, distinguished British jurist Mary Arden brings together her articles and lectures on law shaped by judicial decisions. She describes that law as it exists, and as it is becoming to meet the needs of a changing society. The volume is a companion to the author's earlier-published collection of writings, *Human Rights and European Law*, which looked beyond the UK's borders to examine the currently developing legal orders in Europe. That similarly sweeping work explored the relationship between national and supranational courts and demonstrated the value of a comparative perspective. One can better comprehend, and contribute to the improvement of, one's own law, Mary Arden conveys, by viewing it in light of the legal regimes of other jurisdictions.

Titled *Common Law and Modern Society*, this second volume deals with an array of topics, among them, case law in frontier areas, for example, assisted reproduction and assisted dying, constitutional change, and the respective roles of judges and legislators. Of particular interest in the UK are her thoughts on safeguarding Welsh devolution, where she argues (contrary to the view taken by the UK Supreme Court) that interpreting the statutes devolving legislative power to the Welsh, Scottish and Northern Irish legislatures should not be just like interpreting other statutes, but requires a special approach, in which the UK courts have much to learn from federal jurisdictions in other major legal systems.

For three years, from 1996 until 1999, the author headed the Law Commission of England and Wales, a statutory body set up in 1965 to propose reform of the law. The knowledge and experience Mary Arden gained while leading the Commission's efforts inspired several of her commentaries on law reform, ways to improve the clarity, accessibility and currency of statutes, and prospects for codification, particularly of commercial law and criminal law. She makes a persuasive case for codification, particular in those areas where the common law principles are reasonably well-settled, but by no means clear and accessible. When it comes to the statute book, she draws an interesting distinction between simplicity, which is not necessarily a good thing, and clarity, which is.

In a concluding section, Mary Arden addresses tomorrow's judiciary, persuasively pleading for judgments which are shorter, more user conscious and user friendly, and a bench that better reflects the society that law exists, or should exist, to serve. She wonders why the UK still lags behind other comparable jurisdictions in appointing women to the higher judiciary and tactfully argues that 'great care has to be taken to ensure that the approach to potential women candidates is not through inadvertence inappropriately influenced by the fact that most of the role models...are male...'.

Mary Arden is Head of International Judicial Relations for England and Wales, effectively foreign secretary for the judiciary. Her broad knowledge of the law and belief in its capacity to adjust to changing conditions make her eminently well qualified for that office, which she has held since its creation in 2005.

Throughout the two volumes, Mary Arden aims to stimulate the thinking of current members of the bench and bar, and to encourage and inspire those just embarking on careers in the law. Her companion works will enlighten jurists in her own realm, as well as students, scholars and practitioners of the law in other lands. Throughout, her belief (which is not universally shared) that it is the task of the judiciary, with the help of advocates and academics, to keep the common law up to date shines through. The author's wisdom, fluency and humanity will encourage readers to play a useful part in shaping tomorrow's law.

Ruth Bader Ginsburg,   The Rt Hon Baroness Hale of Richmond,
Associate Justice of the   Deputy President of the Supreme Court
Supreme Court of the United States   of the United Kingdom

Acknowledgements

Anyone who has ever written a book knows how important it is to have the support of colleagues, family, friends, and others whose opinion the writer particularly respects. This work is no exception. It has been a great privilege to receive support from the Rt Hon Baroness Hale, the Honorable Justice Ginsburg, the Rt Hon Beverly McLachlin PC, Chief Justice of Canada, The Rt Hon Lord Mackay of Clashfern, and The Rt Hon Jack Straw. Their Prefaces greatly add to what I have to say and they have done far more than I could ever have asked or contemplated. I am very grateful to them. I also thank my senior colleagues, the Lord Chief Justice of England and Wales, The Lord Thomas of Cymgiedd, and Lord Dyson, Master of the Rolls, for their continued support. I have derived further strength and inspiration from many other colleagues over the years.

I also thank my family, particularly my husband, Jonathan Mance, for all their support and encouragement. At the end of the book, I quote the saying 'it is by walking that we make the road'. It has been extremely helpful to have both family and friends, including non-lawyers, who, like the pilgrims in Chaucer's Canterbury's Tales (of whom one was of course a lawyer), were prepared to share some of the way and to whom I could try to explain the topics. They have shared my enthusiasms, provided their reactions, and inspired new approaches and ways of expression. Among my friends, I mention particularly Alison Donaldson who has somehow constantly found time. I am very grateful to them all. The challenges of the law will continue as long as there is a society for it to serve, and the responses of both lawyers and non-lawyers can be illuminating. The faults, however, remain my own.

I am grateful to Oxford University Press for their thoughtfulness, helpfulness, and high standards of professionalism. I mention in particular Natasha Flemming, Matthew Humphrys, and copy-editor Alison Floyd. I also thank my clerk, Paula Donovan, for her assistance and resourcefulness.

Lady Justice Arden
Member of the Court of Appeal
for England and Wales

1 September 2015
Royal Courts of Justice, Strand, London

Note on references to the law of England and Wales:
I refer in the main to English law but this should be read as meaning the law of England and Wales.

Note on publication dates of original papers:

The chapters contain papers given over what is now a substantial period of time. They are best read as a record of my thinking and of the situation at the time they were first published. Many things have not changed since the papers were written but, where there has been significant change, I have included a footnote updating the position or (occasionally) modified the main text to ensure its continued usefulness to readers.

Why a Second Volume?

Exploring how and when law changes

Law is a lasting social institution, but it must also be able to change. This second volume of my two-part book *Shaping Tomorrow's Law* is about the law's ability and proclivity to change, its capacity for creativity, and, sometimes, its inability to change.

The stimulus for change usually comes from outside the law and is often the result of a change in social needs or thinking. It will be a matter of judgment whether the law should adapt to that change. The change may be made by Parliament or in some cases by the judges. Parliament can enact new legislation, acting on its own initiative or because another body has recommended change. That body might be the Law Commission of England and Wales (the Law Commission), which I have chaired during my time as a judge. At the higher levels, judges have to think hard about changes: they have to be sure the change is sound and will work. Sometimes they explore emerging issues by giving lectures, like the ones reproduced in this work.

The extent or timing of change in the law must be carefully managed lest it create opposition or uncertainty, which leads to instability in society or deters people from entering into business transactions. But, paradoxically, the more successful the law is in absorbing a degree of change the more it contributes to stability in society.

Judges are key players in the task of adaptation. The law is often brought up to date by judges in the process of deciding cases from day to day (applying what we call 'the common law'). But there are limits on what judges can do. They cannot develop the law where legislation is required to make the necessary changes. The process is also generally incremental: judge-made law tends to move slowly. This enables the judges to see how change would work. And judges also play a role in legislative change through the process of interpreting legislation. For instance they may have to 'oil the wheels' of change by giving a liberal interpretation to legislation.

This volume drills down into three of the most important areas of change. It starts by examining how the law has adapted or may need to adapt to three different drivers of change in an evolving society: changing social and economic needs, changes in social values, and changes in the constitution. It then goes on to examine how major projects for simplifying and developing whole areas of the law can best be achieved and, in addition, how legislation can be made generally simpler and more accessible. Lastly, this volume deals with two crucial aspects of the judicial contribution to changing the law: the clear enunciation of judgments and the composition of the judiciary.

Like the first volume, this one mainly brings together previous writings, but it does so with a different perspective from the first volume. There the emphasis was on the international perspective on legal developments: for example, I looked at the impact of human rights and European law on the law of England and Wales. In this second volume, my main concern is to look inwards into our law and legal system. This focus does not exclude appropriate comparisons with other systems—far from it. Those comparisons frequently illuminate our own law. Of course, it remains the case that I am not going to deal with any party-political issue. In addition, if any point discussed in this volume is raised in court, the views I express in this volume would be subject to whatever conclusion was then appropriate.

This volume follows the general pattern I adopted in Volume I. It is divided into three themes. Each section addresses a new theme and contains chapters which record articles that I have written or lectures that I have given, with introductions by distinguished legal figures who give their view of the topic under consideration. There are some general points to make about each of these themes.

Responding to a changing society and a changing constitution

The topics here concern pockets of the law drawn from very different areas that call for change. I have taken examples which show how the law changes in response to social and economic need, such as the case where water law has to change to meet the problem of mill owners abstracting too much water from rivers. There are also changes in social values as may be seen from Chapter 2, on assisted reproduction and assisted dying. And there is constitutional change, a topical subject in 2015, which was the 800th Anniversary of Magna Carta.

Changes in our law are often expressed as pragmatic rather than philosophical. In particular, the common law is not enunciated in abstract terms. This is different from principles of the civil law or codes of rights, such as the European Convention on Human Rights and the EU Charter of Fundamental Rights, which are expressed in very general terms. By contrast, the tradition in English law is to formulate legal rules with relative precision. Also these rules tend to apply to relationships between, say, contracting parties or wrongdoer and victim: thus the problems that English law experiences in deciding to whom a duty to take care is owed are not a cause of problems in continental legal systems. One of the advantages of thinking about the law in terms of relationships is that in many situations it helps refocus the law on people rather than property. The law should be seen in its social context. That helps to increase respect for and confidence in the law and make it more relevant to people in their everyday lives.

Another driver for change has been the call for constitutional change. Constitutional law has become much more prominent in the past few years. When I was a student in Cambridge, we learnt about cases in England with constitutional implications, for instance, cases about stop and search and the powers of the police, as part of a separate subject called constitutional law. I then had the good fortune to study law at Harvard Law School in the United States. My time there made me realize that constitutional law has an impact on almost every area of law. During my judicial career I had an active involvement in constitutional change through being Chairman of the Judges' Working Party on the Constitutional Reform Bill. This was introduced in 2003 and became law in 2005. The overarching aim of the Bill was to enhance the role of the judiciary as a separate branch of the constitution, in particular by establishing the new UK Supreme Court, and to safeguard the independence of the judiciary with protection for its resources and the creation of a new appointments system.

There have been many major constitutional changes in my time as a judge, including devolution, to which I refer in the first section. There are proposals for greater devolution in both Scotland and Wales. As it is often said, the great advantage of an unwritten constitution is that it can develop as need arises.

Simplification and systematic development of the law

In 2015, we have not only the 800th Anniversary of Magna Carta to commemorate: it is also the fiftieth anniversary of the creation of the Law Commission and the Scottish Law Commission. The words 'simplification' and 'systematic development' of the law (used in the title of this section) are taken from the Law Commissions' founding statute, the Law Commissions Act 1965.

I have always been interested in thinking about the overall shape, or 'architecture', of the law on a particular topic, not just the use of the law to solve a current problem. The architecture of the law needs to adapt and change no less than the architecture of buildings. There is a place for innovation, so thinking about the law naturally leads on to thinking about law reform—that is, how the law can be improved or brought up to date. Since there is always some area of the law in need of updating, there is no shortage of problems to think about, and indeed it becomes habitual to think about them. I would encapsulate this discipline by saying: once a law reformer, always a law reformer. Moreover, the discipline of law reform work tends to make the adept interested in what lies over the horizon.

Law reform often takes a long time to achieve and I have had some experience of that in my own career. As part of my master's degree at Harvard Law School, I completed a thesis comparing American and English 'derivative actions'—that is, shareholders' actions to remedy wrongs by directors to their companies. The judge-made law in England and Wales governing these actions, known to generations of lawyers as the Rule in *Foss v Harbottle*,[1] was notoriously ancient, arcane, and complex. I was particularly interested, even at that early stage, in comparing our own law with that of another country, and of course in the United States there are

---

[1] (1843) Hare 461, (1843) 67 ER 189.

some fifty-three jurisdictions from which one can draw inspiration. This must have been one of the earliest occasions on which I had the opportunity to look at foreign law. What I did not then know was that, when I eventually became Chairman of the Law Commission in 1996, I would be able to steer a project which included derivative actions. We produced a report entitled *Shareholder Remedies*,[2] and its recommendations on derivative actions formed the basis of the reforms introduced by the Companies Act 2006. (That statute was and remains the largest statute ever passed by the British Parliament.) In working on the report, I was able to use the knowledge I had gained about how derivative actions had worked in another jurisdiction to help to shape recommendations for reform that was suitable for the different UK environment.

Law which is constantly being updated and added to by judges in the course of deciding cases often becomes unwieldy and inaccessible. One of the ways of addressing this problem is by codifying the law. This section describes the process of codification in a number of different fields with different rates of success. It is often said that the United Kingdom was successful at producing codes of law for its colonies in imperial times while England failed to codify law for itself.

A major project for codification can take years and in that time much thought can be given to it. The same cannot be said of other legislation. The result is that many lawyers in their working lives have to deal with unclear and over-complex legislation. This section therefore concludes with some examination of the ways in which the form of legislation itself can be improved.

Tomorrow's judiciary

This volume concludes with Section C, *Tomorrow's Judiciary*, because in our system much depends on the strength of the judiciary and the way judges, particularly at the higher levels, perform their role. Moreover, recent legislation has also increased their powers and functions.

The judges are often in the public eye but generally there are two particular matters which come to public attention.

The first concerns the way judges articulate and enunciate their judgments. With the advent of the internet and widespread use of social media, it has become increasingly necessary for judges to control the vast amount of available information that relates to the law and to express themselves clearly and concisely in their judgments.

So I start the last Section by discussing judgment writing. Judgments must be readily understood by the parties, and in the case of judgments of the higher courts, by a much wider audience of readers and commentators than ever before. Judgment writing is about the communication between the legal system and the society it serves. Improvements in judgment writing would help ordinary citizens to

---

[2] *Shareholder Remedies* (Law Com No 246, 1997).

understand what the law is. Over-complex and poorly-organized judgments of the higher courts, on the other hand, can add to the cost of getting legal advice in subsequent cases.

There is no one right way of writing a judgment, but the importance of intelligibility, economy, and logical structure are the same for all. I am concerned with how judgments can be made more concise and clear and yet not lose their inherent individuality and, in appropriate situations, their creativity.

The other way in which the judiciary at senior levels commonly comes to public attention is through its lack of diversity. Since the judges are responsible for applying the law and (at the higher levels) for moving it forward in response to change, it is to my mind important that the judiciary should at all levels reflect to some degree the composition of society, and draw on a wide range of talents and experience. There has been some success in relation to both women and ethnic minorities but there is much more to be done. The reasons for the lack of women at senior levels are, as I said in an interview for Woman's Hour of BBC Radio 4 on 15 August 2013, puzzling. We compare poorly with other jurisdictions around the world.

I conclude with two short pieces. The first encourages women and others to take up a legal career and in due course to join the judiciary. The legal system is in good health but can only remain so if the brightest people are prepared to commit themselves to it. The second is addressed to young people doing apprenticeships (or pupillage) at the Bar. Again, the maintenance of the high standards of the English Bar in representing people in our courts is in their hands.

And for the future

In the chapters in this volume I have sought to shine a light in some varied and sometimes ill-lit places. This is work in progress in the sense that some of the engaging issues of the day explored here will continue to evolve and new ones will emerge. An example is the need to find a way of ensuring access to court in civil cases for all those who need it, despite the costs of litigation and cuts in public funding. There is always something new to learn about the law and the justice system. My own thinking will also no doubt continue to evolve. Each of us must find our particular place in the law, and each of us involved in the law must continue on our own journey to find new ways of achieving justice in modern society.

SECTION A

LAW IN A CHANGING SOCIETY

Judges, especially appellate judges, play an important part in updating the general law not laid down in Acts of Parliament. We call this judge-made law 'the common law'. How this works becomes clear here through a number of examples, starting with the law on water, which has evolved over centuries in response to changing needs for water. Or, to take another example, I examine change in the context of assisted reproduction and assisted dying, and consider when judges should leave Parliament to decide on reform of the law on these matters.

Constitutional law is no exception: it, too, evolves in response to social change, as the example of devolution demonstrates. Or new laws may make it necessary to embody previously unwritten constitutional principles, such as the principle of judicial independence and the rule of law, into statute, as when the historic Constitutional Reform Act 2005 was introduced to bring about a formal separation of powers between the judiciary, on the one hand, and Parliament and the executive, on the other.

Preface by The Rt Hon Beverley McLachlin, PC, Chief Justice of Canada

The law cannot stand still. It must keep pace with changes in society. The law provides the framework within which members of society and economic actors operate. It provides guidance for endeavours, public and private, and sets the parameters of lawful behaviour. If the law falls behind the times, it cannot perform these functions properly. At the best, it struggles to find inadequate solutions. At the worst, it falls into desuetude, and is ignored.

It is the task of legislators, lawyers, and judges to keep the law up to date. The role of the legislators is to pass new laws and amend old laws so that the law on the books effectively addresses emerging problems and changing societal views. It is the role of the judges to develop the common law—their home turf—incrementally, in conformity to changing values and needs, and to interpret legislation in a manner that reflects current realities. And it is the role of lawyers to help the legislators and judges 'get it right' by giving wise counsel.

In an age of unprecedented change, the challenge of keeping the law up to date is daunting. Lady Justice Arden examines five aspects of this challenge: (1) water rights; (2) legal problems at the start and end of life; (3) good faith in commercial relations; (4) economic torts; and (5) adapting the law of negligence to modern needs. Her exploration of these subjects affords her and her reader an opportunity to reflect, not only on how the law should adapt in these areas, but on the deeper question of how judges, lawyers, and legislators should approach the task of ensuring that the law serves the needs of modern society.

The Rt Hon Beverley McLachlin, PC,
Chief Justice of Canada

PART I

RESPONDING TO
SOCIAL CHANGE

It is an undoubted fact that societies evolve, and that considerable change has occurred since the 1990s in the economy, technology, medical science, and the constitution. Judge-made law must respond to that change to the extent that it can properly do so, and that raises the question, to what extent do judges actually make the law?

The answer to this question is not straightforward. There is a large body of judge-made law, which we call the common law. Chief Justice Roberts of the United States Supreme Court suggested at one point during his confirmation hearing that a judge was like an umpire, simply applying the rules. However, more generally it is accepted that judges may, within certain constraints, develop the law to meet situations which it does not yet cover or where it needs to be brought up to date to serve society's new needs.

The constraints include proper recognition of the dividing line between legislation and judicial development of the law. This dividing line is a matter of judgment and degree. Judges may develop the law 'interstitially' (just filling in the chinks) but they may not create new law or rewrite existing law when the task ought to be performed by Parliament because of the extent of the change involved. In addition, judges must not develop the law so as to contradict legislation or to be inconsistent with any applicable trend of legislation.

When a new situation governed by the common law arises, and the legal position is uncertain, the common law can be said to have 'run out'. Unsuccessful parties often appeal in these cases in order to seek to persuade an appeal court to decide the new point in their favour. An appeal court may well be better placed to extend or refine existing case law than a judge of a lower court. A lower court may be prevented from doing so by the doctrine of precedent, the principal effect of which is that a court is bound by decisions of a superior court in the judicial hierarchy. The Court of Appeal is also bound by its own decisions.

Any decision to develop the law requires careful thought. It requires the court to identify and articulate the principle that enables the previous rule to be 'distinguished', that is, held inapplicable in some new set of circumstances. Often the process of moving the law on will be done in a way that makes the development appear seamless. It may also be done in a way that leaves scope for further development. The progress has to be measured: it has to be evolutionary and not revolutionary. To use a cricket analogy (and any woman member of the Court of Appeal in earlier times had to follow a conversation about cricket), the common law, as Lord Bingham, the former Senior Law Lord, once put it, moves by hitting single runs rather than by sixes.

Nonetheless, the common law, the body of law created by judges, is now large and enormously important. A single decision on a new point is like a cell in a honeycomb. The bees (other judges) come along and build more cells on its edges until a large honeycomb is created. It does not have to be a large case, or one that involves a large sum of money, to lead to a development in the law, and indeed many of the cases which the Court of Appeal hears are not large cases, nor do they all catch the media's attention.

The theme of this Part, 'Responding to Social Change', encompasses diverse topics, ranging from water rights, through assisted reproduction and dying, and good faith clauses in contracts, to devolution. This variety of material reflects the breadth of the work of the Court of Appeal, since many of my speeches and articles were inspired by cases that I had heard in that court.

The topics covered may seem like pebbles on the seashore: *pace* Newton, I leave much of the great ocean of the law undiscovered before me. However, the papers illustrate what is to me an important point: that judges are privileged to create law that will govern the lives of others. It is a demanding role. And it is to my mind important that as judges we explain what we do and how we see matters, in order to maintain public trust in justice, which is essential to the maintenance of the rule of law.

Chapter 1, *Water Matters*, was originally written as a matter of curiosity. I had had a significant number of cases in the Court of Appeal involving water rights. For example, a person claimed he had acquired ownership of the bed of a canal by mooring his barge in a fixed position for many years. I discovered that water law was both comprehensive and complex. I was intrigued by the fact that water law had developed as society's demands for water had changed. The law has evolved from natural rights theory to appropriation theory, and back to natural rights theory again and then to a modern riparian doctrine. That meant that, at first, everyone was allowed to take as much water as they wanted from a river but later on, when the industrial revolution came, the courts considered that a person should only take a reasonable amount of water from the river so that downstream users would have the water which they needed as well. The United Kingdom presently has enough water, but water law has become increasingly important in many parts of the world adversely affected by global warming and climate change.

Chapter 2, *Legal Problems at the Start and End of Life: The Role of Judges and Parliament*, discusses the effect on the law of problems in the field of IVF, surrogacy, and assisted dying. The challenges here are very recent: there are now many more people who seek to use assisted reproduction than before because developments in medical science (such as the ability to freeze human eggs) have made it attainable by many more people, including gay couples. Assisted dying concerns people who are in the closing stages of life or are facing unbearable pain. But this paper is also of more general interest. Assisted reproduction and assisted dying raise ethical and moral issues as well as legal ones, and this occurs in other areas too. When legal issues raise ethical and moral questions on which people have different views, there is an important question as to the respective roles of judges and Parliament under our constitutional arrangements, and that is the more general question addressed by this paper.

In Chapter 3, *Coming to Terms with Good Faith*, I discuss the controversial question of whether the law of England and Wales should have a principle of good faith. Good faith (which may be a requirement that a party act honestly or deal fairly with the other party) has never been recognized as a generalized concept, though the common law frequently has piecemeal solutions to situations that would be dealt with in other systems under a doctrine of good faith. The chapter was originally written out of a concern that contracts coming before the courts frequently contain clauses stating that the parties will cooperate together or act in good faith towards each other. The question is whether such clauses are without any legal content or whether they should be given legal content. I came to the conclusion that, in line with the principle that the law should give effect to the reasonable expectations of contracting parties, the courts should try to find a meaning for these clauses, particularly in long-term contracts where the parties could not stipulate precisely for everything that was to take place over the term of the contract.

Economic torts are intentional wrongs designed to cause loss, such as conspiracy. They are currently not often encountered. Chapter 4, *Economic Torts in the Twenty-first Century*, addresses the questions: How wide or how narrow should economic torts be? Should they remain individual torts in an 'archipelago' of torts, or should there be some general rationalisation and widening of liability? I emphasized the specific limitations that have to be observed for each of these torts. I was concerned to see that economic torts were not inappropriately used so as to become, so to speak, a 'fashion accessory' to be added to ordinary tort claims, as has happened in other jurisdictions.

I originally wrote Chapter 5, *Duty, Causal Contribution, and the Scope of Responsibility: Does the Law of Negligence Impose Rational Limits?*, in honour of a much-loved Lord Chief Justice, the late Lord Taylor of Gosforth. In it, I attacked the 'dead wood' in the law of negligence and the hangovers in the law from the past. I challenged various aspects of the duty of care, such as whether the courts were truly able to give an informed judgment on whether it was fair, just, and reasonable that there should be a duty of care, where that decision depended on an assessment that to hold otherwise would mean that there would be too many claims.

1

Water Matters

This chapter is based on a paper first published in 2011.[*]

The intricacy of water law

As an island nation surrounded by water, whose favourite pastime is to complain about the weather and whose favourite recreations are frequently washed out, and homes flooded, it is quite surprising how we have failed to produce property lawyers who are intellectually curious about the rights and liabilities attaching to water. It took a gifted Australian academic, Dr Joshua Getzler, to write a fascinating account of the history of water law,[1] and a New Zealand academic, the late Professor Taggart, to write an amusing book[2] on *Bradford Corporation v Pickles*. We owe them an immense debt of gratitude, and I shall draw upon each of their learning. I also draw on the skill of Oliver Pegden, a judicial assistant in the Court of Appeal. When he first heard about my interest in writing about rights related to water, I sensed his disbelief. But, characteristically, he applied himself with great diligence and skill and provided a great deal of research. I hope to demonstrate that water rights is a subject which is full of interest and scope for study. Water rights raise some fundamental issues, and also provide a source of learning for the development of other property rights about resources. Resources will have to be carefully conserved in the years to come.

It goes without saying that water is an essential element of existence: we cannot do without it. It is also untameable. TS Eliot wrote:

> I do not know much about gods; but I think that the river
> Is a strong brown god—sullen, untamed and intractable,
> Patient to some degree, at first recognised as a frontier;
> Useful, untrustworthy, as a conveyor of commerce;
> Then only a problem confronting the builder of bridges.
> The problem once solved, the brown god is almost forgotten

---

[*] 'Water Matters: A Study of Water-Related Problems in Property Law' in Susan Bright (ed), *Modern Studies in Property Law* (Hart Publishing, 2011) 59. Reproduced here by kind permission of Bloomsbury Publishing Plc.

[1] Joshua Getzler, *A History of Water Rights at Common Law* (Oxford University Press, 2004).

[2] Michael Taggart, *Private Property and Abuse of Rights in Victorian England, the Story of Edward Pickles and the Bradford Water Supply* (Oxford University Press, 2002). The case of *Bradford Corporation v Pickles* is reported at [1985] AC 587.

By the dwellers in cities—ever, however, implacable,
Keeping his seasons and rages, destroyer, reminder
Of what men choose to forget . . .[3]

Yet we do try to tame it: people, for instance, try to increase the height of banks of rivers to protect their land. But, if a person is successful at doing this, he may cause harm to those downstream. How are the benefits and burdens of water ownership shared out by the law? This is a question the reader should keep asking throughout this chapter.

This is a remarkable area of law. Let us start with some of the fundamental issues:

(1) Is water a thing?

(2) Can you own water if it is flowing?

(3) What does it mean to own water? Is it enough to have a right to use the water or a right to exclude others from using the water?

(4) Is water ever public property?

There is a treasure house of decided cases on water law. The cases often concern problems arising from the industrialization of Britain. Disputes arose in relation to coal mining, the running of mills, the growth of towns and their need for reservoirs, the development of the United Kingdom's canal system, and the need for water for industrial purposes. For instance, a mill owner may wish to divert a stream so as to use the water for his own mill, and then send the water back into the stream. Can he do this? And what about the landowner who receives decreased supplies of water and himself wants to use it? To take another example, can a water company abstract water not for the benefit of the land it owns, but for the benefit of the inhabitants of a city many miles away?

Such situations may not occur today, thanks to technological developments and the intervention of Parliament. But we have an increasing need to consume water, and that increasing need for water is leading to pressure on global supplies. A single cup of coffee takes 140 litres of water to produce. A glass of beer takes about 45 litres to produce. A hamburger takes about 2,400 litres to produce and a 12oz steak takes a phenomenal 6,000 litres of water to produce.[4]

There are regularly hosepipe bans and water restrictions in the summer. Water has to be allocated between domestic, agricultural, and industrial use. Who should have priority? The shortages which Kent suffers are likely to increase because of the general increase in water usage and because of the programme of building thousands of new houses in the region. And, if it is not enough to think of the problems that may arise domestically, think of the problems around the world, particularly in Africa, India, and the Middle East, where pressure on water resources may well lead to war and civil dissension.[5]

---

[3] *The Dry Salvages*, from Four Quartets, included in *The Complete Poems and Plays, TS Eliot* (Faber and Faber, 1969) 184.

[4] See 'Why Beer Needs Watering Down' (March 2010) 6 *Eureka* 41, which refers to Kent's dryness.

[5] See for example Arundhati Roy, 'The Greater Common Good' at <http://www.narmada.org>.

Nearer to home, if we are going to have water problems, it may fall to the courts to give the lead on how the law should be brought up to date so that we can all share equitably in this essential resource. In my view, the development of case law in this area—in any area—is like promoting sustainable development itself. The courts have to know how to use case law to get the best out of it for today's purposes, and yet leave a body of principled law for future generations to be governed by, and where appropriate develop themselves. So I am promoting the idea of sustainable development of case law in the higher courts, though the development of that idea must await another day.

I would just like to explain how I became interested in this area of law. The fascinating thing about water law is that it arises in the courts in many different contexts and on a regular basis. Let me give some examples from my own period on the Bench:

a. *Seahenge*[6] This may well be the only case where any Chancery judge has been addressed by Druids in full regalia. The case, which arose in 1999, concerned Seahenge, an early Bronze Age timber circle located on the beach at Holme-next-the-Sea. The site was an area of special scientific interest and home to thousands of migratory birds. When Seahenge was laid bare by the movement of sand dunes, a large number of human visitors flocked to the area, including the Druids. Seahenge was within the private ownership of the Le Strange estate, because unusually the beach was owned by it and not the Crown. English Heritage decided that the best way for Seahenge to be preserved was for it to be excavated, and the Le Strange estate gave it a licence to do this. This caused enormous concern to the Druids. The Druids' case was that Seahenge was a cultural gem. They wanted to worship there. They said it was one of the few Druidic places of worship not destroyed by the Romans. One of the respondents said: 'Our ancestors brought the site there to honour all creation, and ownership, therefore, of the site does not come into the matter.' If this dispute had arisen after 2 October 2000 there might have been an issue about how to resolve the conflict between the right to manifest one's religion under Art 9 and the right to property guaranteed by Art 1 of the First Protocol to the European Convention on Human Rights (the 'Convention'). However, despite the submissions of the Archdruid of Britain, private interests prevailed.[7] Seahenge was taken to Lynn Museum, King's Lynn in Norfolk. The case was truly fascinating and there was no forewarning that it would come my way that day, but that is often the case with interlocutory work.

b. *Arscott and others v The Coal Authority and others*[8] concerned the interaction of water rights with the law of nuisance. The homes of the thirty-two claimants had been flooded when the River Taff overflowed its banks in 1998. Before the flood the National Coal Board had deposited colliery spoil on the banks of the Taff

---

[6] See Matthew Champion, *Seahenge, a Contemporary Chronicle* (Barnwell's Timescape Publishing, 2000).

[7] *The Historic Buildings & Monuments Commission for England v Nolan and others*, 6 July 1999 (unreported), Arden J.

[8] [2004] EWCA Civ 892.

up-river from the claimants' homes. As a result the banks were raised and flooding happened around the claimants' homes whereas it would previously have happened further upstream. The claimants sought damages in nuisance, and the National Coal Board sought to defend itself on the basis of the historic 'common enemy principle' by which a person could defend his land from future flooding notwithstanding that it may cause another's land to flood. The Court of Appeal held that acting to defend one's land from future flooding was a reasonable use of land, and thus could not give rise to liability for nuisance. The common enemy principle was upheld. The flood damage for the defendants downstream was not foreseeable. This principle may have very wide implications as river banks have been raised up and down the country to reduce the risk of flooding, but this is liable to increase the risk of flooding to those downstream.

c. *Moore v British Waterways Board*[9] was a recent appeal on a preliminary issue. The case concerned a section of the River Brent which was canalized during the late eighteenth century pursuant to the Grand Junction Canal Act 1793 and which is now called the Grand Union Canal. The claimant, Mr Moore, lived in a houseboat moored by the side of the canal, which he also possessed or owned, but he had been given notice to quit by the British Waterways Board which owned the Grand Union Canal. The claimant said that he had a right to remain by virtue of the common law public right of navigation over the River Brent, which, he said, survived the canalization. One of the issues raised by the case was whether a public right of navigation, or alternatively a private riparian right, included a right to moor.[10]

Water law, therefore, is a living and expanding area of law. I will divide my subject into five sections. I intend to examine: first, some of the legal theories which have underpinned the development of the common law in relation to the use and ownership of water; second, the features of the modern riparian doctrine; third, some of the case law in relation to flooding; fourth, how the modern statutory regime covering water use interacts with common law water rights; and fifth, some possible answers to those fundamental questions which (as previously indicated) water poses.

Different theories

The common law of water rights has a long history and the various theories which have underpinned its development are diverse and complex. It is not possible for me to give a fully-textured picture of the theoretical background. Instead my approach is a simplified one: I want to examine two competing doctrines in

---

[9] [2010] EWCA Civ 42.

[10] This appeal took place before the trial of the action. At the subsequent trial, Hildyard J held that Mr Moore had no right to moor by virtue of either the public right of navigation or his riparian right: see [2012] 1 WLR 3289. The Court of Appeal then upheld the judge's holding on these points, but, reversing the judge's decision in part, held that Mr Moore had not committed any wrong by mooring by the side of the canal: see [2013] Ch 488.

water law. One is the 'appropriation theory', and the other is 'natural rights theory', also known as riparianism. It is accepted that it is natural rights theory which is the doctrine behind modern water law, but, in order properly to understand it, it is important to understand how it differs from its predecessor, appropriation theory. Surprisingly, the common law drew on both American law[11] and civil law in the course of its evolution. This chapter includes a discussion of the great case of *Bradford Corporation v Pickles*, which involved subterranean percolating water.

Appropriation theory

As the name of the doctrine suggests, appropriation theory grants ownership of water to the person who appropriates it. To take a trivial example, if you put water in your bucket it belongs to you. Under this theory water is classified as a form of property. An individual may acquire the ownership of water by using it. Although water in this theory is considered to be property, it is also considered to be 'transient'. Because water is transient it cannot be permanently appropriated. It is only owned whilst it is appropriated. So, to use the words of the old lyric, if there is a hole in my bucket, dear Liza, and the water seeps out, I lose my ownership of it.

Appropriation theory in its modern form may be traced to William Blackstone's *Commentaries on the Law of England*.[12] Dr Getzler reduces Blackstone's expression of the doctrine to five key points. The first three of those points are the most important for current purposes:[13]

(1) Water is a type of corporeal right, a transient element available to the public but subject to a qualified individual property or title during use.
(2) The first appropriator of water wins title under a natural principle defending occupation.
(3) Title subsists only during time of use, as water cannot be possessed or appropriated in the manner of land.

Blackstone drew upon a host of influences, including scripture and Roman law, in the process of defining his appropriation theory of water law, but underpinning the theory are just two key ideas: first, the idea that occupation (in other words, appropriation) is the foundation of title; and, second, the idea that water cannot be occupied in the same way as land because of its fluid nature—in Blackstone's own words: 'For water is a moveable wandering thing and must of necessity continue common by the law of nature so that I can only have a temporary, transient, usufructuary, property therein...'[14] In appropriation theory, unused water remains common property, or one of the *res communes*. There are thus two key Roman law influences on the doctrine: the first is the notion that occupation gives rise to title; the second is the notion that unused water in the natural environment

---

[11] The judge-made law developed by courts in North America after the discovery of America.
[12] Getzler, *A History of Water Rights at Common Law* (n 1) 154.
[13] Getzler, *A History of Water Rights* (n 1) 154.
[14] Getzler, *A History of Water Rights* (n 1) 173–4.

is *publici juris*. Of these two the first has primacy: the essence of appropriation theory therefore is that title in water persists in an individual only for so long as that individual puts the water to use. Although unused water is recognized as public property, in this theory water is not really treated as a communal resource. Instead under appropriation theory the first appropriator may take it all without regard to the fact that he may leave other people short of water in the process. Put another way, there is no concept here of reasonable use.

It is important to note that the upstream user is not necessarily the first appropriator. Where an upstream user increases the amount of water he appropriates, he may deprive an already existing downstream appropriator, and it is that downstream appropriator who, in these circumstances, is the first appropriator.

By the early nineteenth century appropriation theory had become one of the dominant doctrines, if not the dominant doctrine, in English water law. In the case of *Bealey v Shaw*,[15] two mill owners disputed the use of water in the River Irwell. The downstream plaintiff complained that the upstream defendant was diverting more water to his mill than he had done previously, thereby depriving the plaintiff of the flow that he was used to for the purposes of using his own mill. The four judges found in favour of the plaintiff, and two did so on the basis of a pure adherence to the appropriation doctrine. Where an upstream user had hitherto left water unappropriated, that water was left available to be appropriated by successive downstream users. If the upstream user then increased the amount of water that he appropriated, he thereby interfered with the established first appropriation of those below him. That gave rise to an actionable wrong.

Bealey v Shaw can be compared with *Williams v Morland*.[16] In that case, the plaintiff complained that he had lost the benefit and advantage of a stream on his land since the defendant had built a dam upstream. The issue for the Court was whether the plaintiff could simply complain of an interrupted flow without showing some use had been interfered with. The Court rejected the plaintiff's arguments that he had some inherent right to the natural flow of the water on his land, and held that to bring a claim he had to show some injury to the existing appropriation of the water flow. On the facts, the Court held that it was essential that a plaintiff should demonstrate that he had been putting the relevant water to some use. It was not sufficient simply to say that flow had been disrupted. The decision in *Williams v Morland* thus demonstrates the courts' acceptance of the appropriation theory.

Appropriation theory also illustrates the concept of *damnum sine injuria*, meaning that there is no actionable injury despite damage. That is because it was necessary to show actual interference with use. Even if the flow of water had been interrupted, no action was available if there was no use which had been interfered with. I shall have more to say about *damnum sine injuria* later on.

---

[15] (1805) 6 East 208, 102 ER 1266 (KB).   [16] (1824) 2 B&C 910, 107 ER 620.

Natural rights theory

Natural rights theory had been a feature of the English common law of water rights in the seventeenth and eighteenth centuries. It was abandoned in favour of appropriation theory in the early nineteenth century as I have described, but in the mid-nineteenth century it re-established itself and it has persisted since then as one of the foundations of the common law of water rights.

Natural rights theory in essence provides that the right to water is a natural incident to the ownership of the contiguous land. The key difference between natural rights theory and appropriation theory is that in natural rights theory the rights in the relevant water do not depend upon the landowner putting the water to use.

Like appropriation theory, natural rights owes much to Roman law concepts and I wish to emphasize two of those. In the first place, natural rights theory draws upon the Roman law notion of the right to water as a praedial (or property) right.[17] In other words, emphasis was placed upon the right to water being a right arising from and attached to the contiguous land. The right was said to extend from the land abutting the river to the midway point of the river, or the *medium filum*. That had not been a key feature of appropriation doctrine, and although the difference might seem to be academic, by the end of the nineteenth century technological advances had meant that the use (or appropriation) of water was possible without owning adjoining land. Accordingly it became important to define whether the right to water was attached to neighbouring land or not.[18]

The second key Roman influence was water as one of the *res communes*. Whereas this had been a secondary influence under appropriation theory, it was dominant in natural rights theory. This meant that water was residually owned by the public.

The growth of the emphasis upon water as a communal property went hand in hand with a growth in emphasis upon the requirement to use water reasonably, that is with the good of the community in mind. As part of natural rights theory a 'reasonable use' doctrine developed. From an early stage in English law the requirement to limit oneself to 'reasonable use' was explained in terms of the maxim *sic utere tuo ut alienum non laedas* (so use your own property as not to cause injury or nuisance to property of another).

Natural rights theory, unlike appropriation theory, did not accord the first appropriator the right to deprive all others, but rather required that a balance of reasonable use should be struck for the benefit of all. Natural rights theory thus represented not only a distinct set of *legal* principles governing the use of water, but also a distinct set of political and ideological principles. In appropriation theory the absolute right to own property had primacy: it was only water's fluid form that prevented it from being owned outright. On the other hand, natural rights theory provided that water could not be owned because it *should*

---

[17] As to Roman praedial doctrine, see Getzler, *A History of Water Rights* (n 1) 72.
[18] Getzler, *A History of Water Rights* (n 1) 44.

not be owned by individuals, regardless of whether its physical form made this possible.[19]

Natural rights theory was dominant in American law in the early nineteenth century, and by the middle of that century it had become prevalent in England and Wales. The key case in this regard was *Embrey v Owen*,[20] in which the downstream plaintiff sought damages from an upstream defendant for the wrongful diversion of the flow of water, in circumstances where there was no appreciable damage to the plaintiff's use of the river. Parke B, giving the judgment of the Court, held that it was not necessary for there to have been damage for there to be an action for interference with the flow of the river. However, he held that not all interferences with flow would be actionable, since allowance had to be made for the upstream defendant's right to make reasonable use of the river as *publici juris*. Accordingly, only unreasonable use by the upstream user could give rise to an action, albeit that that unreasonable use did not have to cause actual damage. Ultimately the Court found in favour of the defendant on the basis that there had been no sensible diminution of the flow, and that, crucially, his use had been reasonable.

Natural rights theory allowed for instances of *injuria sine damno* or actionable injury without damage. That is because it was only necessary for a plaintiff to show that there had been an interference with the flow, not that he had suffered actual damage or the interference with any particular use.

In *Miner v Gilmour*,[21] the plaintiff complained that the defendant had diverted flow away from his (the plaintiff's) tannery to the defendant's mill. The defendant's defence was that the plaintiff had known about the mill before he bought his property and thus could not complain about it. The Privy Council held that allowance had to be made for everyone's reasonable use of the water. Reasonable use could not give rise to an action even if it caused actual damage. On the facts the defendant's use of the water for his mill was reasonable, given that it was longstanding, and accordingly damage to the plaintiff was not actionable.

In *Miner* the Court explained that although there was no requirement for a plaintiff to show damage, he nevertheless had to show that his right had been materially interfered with. Thus the two requirements for an action were (1) an unreasonable use of the water by the defendant; and (2) a material interference with the plaintiff's right to reasonable use himself.

Chasemore v Richards[22] finally confirmed natural rights theory as the basis of the English common law of water rights. *Chasemore* really concerned the status of underground water (discussed later), but in the process of reaching its decision the House of Lords confirmed that the right to flowing water was a natural right attached to the land over which water flows, and subject to the limit of reasonable use.

---

[19] See Getzler, *A History of Water Rights* (n 1) 43–5.
[20] (1851) 6 Exch 353, 155 ER 579.   [21] (1858) 12 Moo PC 131, 14 ER 861 (PC).
[22] (1859) 7 HLC 349, 11 ER 140 (HL).

Rights to fish and rights in fish: appropriation theory and natural rights theory side by side

A short recreational diversion may help to illustrate appropriation theory and natural rights theory. In the third edition of his work, *The Compleat Angler*, published in 1661, Izaak Walton included a fascinating postscript about seventeenth-century water law in so far as it was relevant to anglers.[23] It represents an interesting juxtaposition of appropriation theory in relation to fish with natural rights theory in relation to water.

In appropriation theory, wild animals, including fish, were treated in much the same way as water. In expounding his understanding of appropriation theory, Blackstone explained that water was to be compared with:

> ... those animals which are said to be *ferae naturae*, or of wild and untameable disposition: which any man may seise upon and keep for his own use or pleasure. ... but if once they escape from his custody, or he voluntarily abandons the use of them, they return to the common stock and any man else has an equal right to seise and enjoy them afterwards.[24]

In the postscript to *The Compleat Angler*, Walton also described the property in fish in appropriation theory terms. He explained that in a river: 'the fish are said to be *ferae naturae*, and the taking of them with an angle is not trespass for that no man is said to have a property in them until he hath caught them, and then it is trespass to take them from him'.[25] What is interesting about the postscript from *The Compleat Angler* is that Izaak Walton proceeds on the basis that fishing rights in a river (as opposed to a pond or several fishery)[26] attach to the land *contiguous* to the water. But, because of the application of appropriation theory to the fish in the river, he concludes that, as long as you have the right to be on that land, you are not abusing your right to be there by taking fish from the river. In the words of the postscript: 'If a man have a licence to enter into a Close or Ground for such a space of time, there though he practise angling all that time, he is not a trespasser because his fishing is no abuse of his licence.'[27] So, *The Compleat Angler* is at one and the same time reflecting both the appropriation theory (in relation to the fish) and also the idea that the ownership of land potentially confers rights in respect of the contiguous water. The latter is an expression of the natural rights theory. As explained, this was the current legal theory in the seventeenth century when *The Compleat Angler* was written.

---

[23] Izaak Walton and Charles Cotton, *The Compleat Angler* (Oxford University Press, 2008) 231–5.

[24] Getzler, *A History of Water Rights* (n 1) 173.

[25] Walton and Cotton, *The Compleat Angler* (n 23) 232.

[26] A several right of fishery is an exclusive right of fishing in a given place. In the postscript cited earlier (Walton and Cotton, *The Compleat Angler* (n 23) 233), Walton stated that the owner of a several fishery also had to own the land over which the several fishery was claimed to exist. However, today a several fishery can exist without ownership of the soil: see James Mackay (ed), *Halsbury's Laws of England*, (5th edn, LexisNexis, 2008) Vol 1(2), para 805.

[27] Walton and Cotton, *The Compleat Angler* (n 23) 232.

Modern riparian doctrine

Key features

The modern riparian doctrine can be summarized as follows:

- riparian rights arise for an owner of water flowing in a defined natural watercourse;
- the riparian owner has a right to the flow of water on to and away from his property regardless of whether he is putting it to use;
- the *prima facie* rule is that his rights in the water extend to the *medium filum*;
- the riparian owner has the right to make reasonable use of the water flow although that may cause damage to another riparian user;
- although a riparian owner need not suffer damage before he can enforce his riparian rights, he must show some interference with his right—this is an application of the *de minimis* principle.[28]

The significance of natural flow in a defined channel

A person who wishes to use water that flows on to his land does not in general have a right as a riparian owner to prevent another landowner from abstracting that water before it reaches his land unless it flows naturally in a defined channel. There are various illustrations of this point in the four subheadings to come, culminating in the notorious case of Mr Pickles, who was sued by Bradford Corporation for abstracting percolating water which the Corporation hoped to use for the city's water supply.

1. Standing surface water

What about standing surface water? The position in relation to standing water was established in *Broadbent v Ramsbotham*.[29] In that case the plaintiff complained that the defendant was draining standing water from the surface of his (the defendant's) land so as to prevent it from reaching a brook into which it had previously flowed. This brook worked the plaintiff's mill, and so the defendant's actions deprived the plaintiff of the flow of water to his mill. The Court held that there was no right to the flow of water beyond the right to the flow of water in the brook itself. Accordingly the defendant was free to treat his standing surface water as he pleased. Flow in a defined channel was essential for an actionable wrong.

---

[28] See generally John Bates, *Water and Drainage Law*, Vol 2, *Rights in Waters and Pipes* (Sweet & Maxwell, loose leaf, last release July 2015). See now also *Moore v British Waterways Board* [2013] Ch 488, see n 10.

[29] (1856) 11 Exch 602; 156 ER 971 (Exch).

In this regard it is important to note that, in relation to ponds and lakes (which do give rise to riparian rights) less emphasis is inevitably placed on the flow, and more on the existence of a defined channel (for example the bed of the lake or pond).[30]

2. Subterranean water in a defined stream

Non-percolating subterranean water, that is, water which forms part of a defined subterranean stream, also attracts riparian rights. This is established by *Dickinson v Grand Junction Canal Co*,[31] in which the Court held that an action could be brought for the diversion of a defined underground watercourse just as it lay for a defined overground watercourse. This was also the approach in *Grand Junction Canal Co v Shugar*.[32]

3. Artificial watercourses

Since the modern riparian doctrine attaches primary significance to *natural* flow in a defined channel, riparian rights do not arise in relation to artificial water courses. That is because although water may flow in artificial watercourses, it is not natural flow. On this issue, Bates on *Water and Drainage Law* cites the decision of the Privy Council in *Rameshur Pershad Narain Singh v Koonj Behari Pattuck*[33] in which Sir Montague Smith held that: 'There is no doubt that the right to the water of a river flowing in a natural channel through a man's land and the right to water flowing to it through an artificial watercourse . . . do not rest on the same principle.'

4. Subterranean percolating water

Similarly, water percolating underground does not give rise to riparian rights.[34] In this regard the courts have often justified their decisions on the basis of practical considerations. The leading nineteenth-century authority on this issue was *Acton v Blundell*.[35] In that case the plaintiff owned mills and in them used water drawn from a well. The neighbouring defendant sank a mine into his own land, and thereby cut off the percolating supply of water to the plaintiff's well. The Court held that the plaintiff had no right to the percolating water in the well. The predominant justification was that underground water is out of sight and there is therefore no means of monitoring changes to the flow. *Chasemore*[36] confirmed that percolating water was not subject to riparian rights, and, again, the justification was practical. The issue was deemed to be evidential: percolating water was out of sight and therefore changes to flow and the causes of any such changes could not be

---

[30] Bates, *Water and Drainage Law* (n 28) paras 1.126–1.134.
[31] (1852) 7 Exch 282, 155 ER 953; see also Getzler, *A History of Water Rights* (n 1) 296.
[32] (1870–1) LR 6 Ch App 483.   [33] (1878) 4 App Cas 121 (PC).
[34] Bates, *Water and Drainage Law* (n 28) paras 1.146–1.150.
[35] (1843) 12 M&W 324, 152 ER 1223.   [36] See n 22.

proved. As I have explained, however, subterranean water in a defined stream *is* subject to riparian rights, and accordingly the underlying basis for the decision in *Chasemore* seems to have been doctrinal rather than practical.

The best known case on the subject of subterranean percolating water is *Bradford Corporation v Pickles*. The facts can be shortly summarized. Bradford was a growing industrial town. It needed water for its inhabitants. Bradford Corporation formed a new statutory company to look for water for the inhabitants of Bradford. They found the perfect place, a gushing spring known as Many Wells. Perfect—or so they thought. They had not reckoned on the fact that Mr Pickles was the owner of a neighbouring farm called East Many Wells farm. The water which emerged at Many Wells collected under Mr Pickles' farm. Mr Pickles wanted to mine the minerals under his land and to achieve this purpose proposed to drain the water under his land and then pipe it back into the river many miles away. Needless to say, this plan caused great consternation in Bradford. Bradford Corporation relied on a private Act of Parliament to prevent Mr Pickles from carrying out his plan, but that only prevented an unlawful diversion of water. Bradford Corporation therefore had to show that Mr Pickles was interfering with its common law water right to percolating water.

The problems which Bradford Corporation faced are immediately apparent. Mr Pickles was operating on his own land and was intercepting percolating water. Since the water was not part of a defined stream, and it was not *publici juris*, he was entitled to do with it as he pleased. The House of Lords relied upon *Chasemore v Richards* for the proposition that Mr Pickles was entitled to the percolating water under his land.

In those circumstances Bradford Corporation sought to establish that Mr Pickles was abusing his rights by acting maliciously and to succeed against him on that basis. The Corporation failed on this argument too. The House of Lords held that, given that Mr Pickles' actions were lawful, his motives were irrelevant. This was neatly expressed by Lord Macnaghten as follows: 'If the act, apart from motive, gives rise merely to damage without legal injury, the motive, however reprehensible it may be, will not supply that element.'[37]

The key point to note from the case is that the reasonable use theory had no application outside the existing parameters of riparian doctrine. If there was no cause of action, then the fact that the defendant had been acting unreasonably was irrelevant. The reasonable use doctrine could not apply. Lord Macnaghten's well-known dictum is one of the high water marks of the rigidity of the common law.

It appears that Scots law offers a much more flexible approach. It contains a useful if little used principle of *aemulatio vicini*. My research in *Stair Memorial Encyclopaedia*[38] suggests that the role of this principle is to provide a remedy in cases where the harm caused is *damnum absque injuria*. Thus this principle can be invoked to qualify the near absolute rights of another to intercept underground percolating

---

[37] [1895] AC 587, 601.
[38] Robert Black, Joseph M Thomson, and Kenneth Miller (eds), *Stair Memorial Encyclopaedia* (LexisNexis, 1991) Nuisance, para 34, *Aemulatio vicini* in modern Scots law.

water. It is true that doubts were expressed by Lord Watson in *Bradford Corporation v Pickles*, but *Stair* considers that Lord Watson did not accurately state the effect of Scots law. The principle has the effect that an act, which is otherwise lawful, is rendered wrongful if done with a malicious intent of injuring a neighbour. Just think what possibilities this principle might offer for insisting on greater neighbourliness throughout property law: suppose that you have a wonderful view over a lake and then the owner of a property between you and the lake decides to plant a woodland of fast-growing Sitka spruce which quickly removes your view. You would have no cause of action in English law. It adopts an absolute rule about motive. It is possible that there would be a different result in Scots law.

Case law on flooding

Actions taken against the infringement of riparian rights most commonly fall within the parameters of the law of nuisance, which protects the enjoyment of real property. But what if you are not seeking to protect the enjoyment of your own right to water? What if you are simply seeking to protect yourself from another's use or misuse of water? A claimant who complains of flooding from a defendant's land, for example, is not seeking to enforce any right that he has to enjoyment of water; on the contrary, he is seeking to be protected from another's water use. This is no longer strictly a question of water rights, but it is still within the broader parameters of water-related nuisance.

The basic rule in relation to the discharge of water is that a lower occupier has no cause of action against the higher occupier for the natural drainage or percolation of water on to his (the lower occupier's) land. Conversely, the higher occupier has no action against the lower occupier if the latter prevents such drainage from the higher land on to his own. This position was confirmed by the Court of Appeal in *Palmer v Bowman*.[39] In this case, the claimant landowners brought an action against the owners of neighbouring land. They claimed that they were entitled to an easement, acquired by lost modern grant[40] for the percolation of water from their land on to their neighbour's land, and that that drainage right had been interfered with by the defendants. At first instance the judge held that, although there had been such an easement, it had since been extinguished. On appeal the defendants sought to uphold that decision, but in the alternative they cross-appealed the judge's finding that there had ever been an easement. The Court of Appeal held that, in order for a claim of lost modern grant to be successful, the subject-matter of the grant had first to be a right capable of existing as an easement. The Court held that natural drainage of percolating and undefined surface water from one piece of land to another, lower, piece of land was not capable of existing as

---

[39] [2000] 1 WLR 842; and see John Bates, 'Flooding and Private Rights' (2007) 18 Water Law 159.
[40] User as of right for at least 20 years.

an easement. There is no right, then, to benefit from natural drainage, nor is there a right to be protected from it.

What if the flow from one piece of land to another is not natural, but artificial or at least artificially increased? The essential distinction to be made here is between flooding that occurs as a result of a defendant's natural use of land, and flooding that occurs as a result of the defendant's non-natural use. The former will not normally be actionable in nuisance, whereas the latter will be.

In relation to waters that have been artificially contained, for example in a reservoir, and which then escape or are released, the well-known rule from *Rylands v Fletcher* [41] may attach strict liability to the occupier of the higher land. The facts of the case were, briefly, that the defendant landowner had built a reservoir over certain disused mineshafts which connected with the plaintiff's mine. Water from the reservoir burst through the disused shafts and flooded the plaintiff's mine. The Court found that the owner of the flooded mine was entitled to damages. Lord Cranworth expressed the ratio succinctly as follows: 'If a person brings, or accumulates, on his land anything which, if it should escape, may cause damage to his neighbour, he does so at his peril.' [42] The essence of the rule in *Rylands* was thus, originally, that the relevant substance needed to have been artificially contained by the defendant. If it then escaped, the defendant would be strictly liable. That conception of the rule, however, not only made the rule in *Rylands v Fletcher* very wide, but it also gives rise to difficulties with regard to determining what is artificially contained and what is not.

These difficulties were partly dealt with when the rule in *Rylands v Fletcher* was considered by the Privy Council in *Rickards v Lothian*. [43] That case concerned the overflow of water from a bathroom sink and the Court determined that the key question in relation to the rule in *Rylands v Fletcher* was not whether the escaping substance had been artificially contained, but whether the damage was caused by the malicious act of a third party. If so, the rule did not apply. Moreover, the land had been put to some non-natural use which brought increased danger to others. The rule did not apply for that reason also. This is a markedly more restricted approach to *Rylands v Fletcher* than the rule in its original form.

These issues were revisited by the House of Lords in 1994 in *Cambridge Water Co Ltd v Eastern Counties Leather plc* [44] and more recently in 2003 in *Transco plc v Stockport Metropolitan Borough Council*. [45] Those cases confirm that the fundamental question is not whether the water is artificially contained, but whether the land is being put to some non-natural use which heightens the risk to others. *Transco* was a claim in respect of damage caused by a large amount of water which escaped from a pipe used to supply a block of flats. The claimant, Transco, sought damages from the defendant authority for loss caused by water flowing from a leak in the pipe. The Court held that the piping of water by the authority was not a non-natural use, and therefore that strict liability could not be attached to the authority.

---

[41] (1868) LR 3 HL 330.   [42] (1868) LR 3 HL 330, 340.
[43] [1913] AC 263, 280.   [44] [1994] 2 AC 264.   [45] [2004] 2 AC 1.

The instances, then, where a defendant may be made strictly liable for flooding his neighbour's land have been restricted by the recent jurisprudence on *Rylands*. In many cases, the use of the land which gave rise to the flooding will not be deemed 'non-natural' and in those circumstances a claimant will have to try to bring his claim within nuisance without the help of the rule in *Rylands v Fletcher*.

It is important to note that the rule in *Rylands* may only apply to flooding where there has been a discharge from one piece of land to another. The Court in *Transco* made clear that, although the key question in *Rylands* was whether the use of the land was natural or non-natural, *Rylands* liability was *only* capable of arising where there had been escape of a substance from one tenement to another.[46]

Rylands thus does not cover circumstances where the defendant's non-natural use of his land causes water to flow on to the claimant's land from another source. In those circumstances, there will be no strict liability and the normal rules of foreseeability will apply.

Arscott[47] was a case in which nuisance was claimed in just those circumstances. The upstream coal authority had raised the banks of the river on its land in such a manner as to cause flooding downstream. By doing so it had in effect displaced the flood from its own land to the claimants' land. But, importantly, there had been no escape of water from the defendant's land to the claimants' land and so *Rylands* could not apply.

As the Court made clear in *Arscott*, the 'common enemy defence' does not apply in circumstances where the flood water has already arrived on to the defendant's land. In other words, a defendant is not able deliberately to transfer flood waters on to his neighbour and in so doing use the common-enemy principle as a defence. In *Whalley v Lancs and Yorks Railway Co*[48] which the Court cited in *Arscott*, the defendant cut channels into his land so as to drain flood water on to his neighbour's land and in those circumstances he was held to be liable. Cases such as this may be seen as instances of 'non-natural' use which, although they concern discharge from one piece of land to another, do not engage *Rylands* because the accumulation is not artificial. Alternatively they may be seen as an example of one of the instances where a defendant may be liable in nuisance notwithstanding that his use of his land was 'natural'—I will briefly discuss such cases now.

Can a defendant be liable in nuisance if his use of his land is 'natural'? In *Smith v Kenrick*,[49] waste water from the defendant's mine was discharged into the plaintiff's mine, and the plaintiff sought damages. The Privy Council held that a mine owner had no obligation to prevent the flow of water from his mine into a neighbour's mine. Modern commentators explain the decision in *Kenrick* on the bases that the mine was not being put to any unnatural use and that the waste water was never artificially accumulated or contained.[50] The Court in *Kenrick* made clear that the

---

[46] See [2004] 2 AC 1, para 9 per Lord Bingham of Cornhill.
[47] [2004] EWCA Civ 892. The case is summarized in the text accompanying n 8.
[48] (1884) 13 QBD 131.   [49] (1849) 7 CB 515.
[50] See for example R Buckley, *Clerk & Lindsell on Torts* (21st edn, Sweet & Maxwell, 2014) para 20–128.

defendant mine owner had the right to work his own mine as he saw fit and thereby cause prejudice to his neighbour 'so long as that does not arise from the negligent or malicious conduct of the party'. On the basis of *Kenrick*, then, no natural use of land will give rise to liability in nuisance unless it is negligent or malicious. That position may be seen as supportive of absolute property rights.

In modern cases, however, the courts have taken a slightly different approach. In *Arscott* the Court held that in nuisance there were two important distinctions to make: (a) the distinction between natural and non-natural use; and (b) the distinction between reasonable and unreasonable use. The Court held that natural use might give rise to liability in nuisance if it was unreasonable, but reasonableness would never be a defence to liability for nuisance for the non-natural use of land.

In summary, the case law that I have described in relation to flooding, like the cases described earlier concerning 'pure' riparian rights, evidences a development of the doctrine of reasonable use. That doctrine appeared in the distinction between 'natural' and 'non-natural' use, but reasonableness is now recognized as a separate concept. Even natural use of land may give rise to liability if it is unreasonable.

The impact of statute: codification of reasonable use doctrine?

The common law position described earlier now operates within an extensive statutory scheme which includes the Water Industry Act 1991, the Water Resources Act 1991, the Statutory Water Companies Act 1991, the Land Drainage Act 1991, the Land Drainage Act 1994, the Environment Act 1995, the Water Industry Act 1999, the Enterprise Act 2002, and the Water Act 2003. I will highlight some of the provisions of the Water Resources Act 1991, which is the most pertinent piece of legislation for our purposes.

Statutory provisions affecting common law on use of water and riparian rights

The Water Resources Act 1991 places significant constraints upon the way water may be used. In broad terms, it provides that no person may 'abstract' or 'impound' water from any inland waters without a licence.[51] The provisions of the 1991 Act ultimately derive from the Water Resources Act 1963 under which, for the first time, the abstraction and impounding of water resources became regulated on a regional basis.

In the context of the terms of the Water Resources Act 1991, to 'abstract' means to remove water from the waterway either temporarily or permanently[52] and to 'impound' means to control water by means of a dam, weir, or other similar works.[53]

---

[51] Resources Act 1991, ss 24 and 25.   [52] Section 221.   [53] Section 25.

The types of waterway covered by these rules are extensive. They include: any river, stream, or other watercourse whether natural or artificial and whether tidal or not; any lake or pond, whether natural or artificial, or any reservoir or dock; and any underground strata. The restriction on abstraction is subject to a *de minimis* exception under s 27 of the 1991 Act. That section essentially provides that no licence is required to abstract water if the volume abstracted in any 24-hour period is less than 20 cubic metres.[54]

An individual may obtain a licence from the Environment Agency, but under s 35 of the 1991 Act his application will not be considered unless (1) he has, or at the time when the proposed licence is to take effect will have, a right of access to land contiguous to the inland waters at that place, or those places; and (2) he will continue to have such a right for a period of at least one year beginning with the date on which the proposed licence is to take effect, or until it is to expire if sooner.[55]

It is to be noted that s 70 of the Water Resources Act 1991 provides that ss 24 and 25 of the Act (that is, those sections that I have described which proscribe abstraction and impounding) are not to be interpreted as conferring a right of action in any civil proceedings (other than proceedings for the recovery of a fine) in respect of any contravention of those restrictions. It is thus envisaged that the statutory scheme should operate alongside the common law and be distinct from it. But the statutory scheme may affect the nature and number of common law actions.

In many ways the statutory scheme preserves the DNA of riparian doctrine. As I have just described, licences may only be granted to those individuals who already have common law riparian rights by virtue of rights in the contiguous land. And, broadly speaking, the regime differentiates between standing or 'discrete' waters and flowing water forming part of a wider network of watercourses.

In other ways, however, the legislation represents a significant departure from riparian doctrine. For example, the regime extends restrictions on the use of water to include artificial watercourses and water percolating in underground strata. Under the common law, a landowner is free to treat those waters as he pleases.

Statutory provisions affecting common law on flooding and nuisance

The Water Resources Act 1991 also contains provisions in relation to flooding and drainage. There are other relevant provisions in the Land Drainage Act 1991. The primary function of those provisions is to create a national infrastructure for dealing with flooding and drainage, in the form of local flood defence committees and drainage boards overseen by the Environment Agency.

The statutory regime also creates public obligations for riparian owners and others to ensure the proper flow of water in watercourses so as to avoid flooding. For example s 23 of the Land Drainage Act 1991 prohibits any person without the written permission of the relevant drainage board from erecting any dam, weir, or

---

[54] Section 27.   [55] Section 35.

other similar obstruction to any ordinary watercourse, or from altering any such obstruction. In this context ordinary watercourses exclude 'main rivers', but similar provisions in relation to main rivers are contained in the Water Resources Act 1991.

Conclusions on the statutory regime

On a broad level, the statutory regime can essentially be viewed as a codification of the doctrine of reasonable use. Matters which would previously have fallen solely within the scope of the common law are now within the scope of the public law statutory provisions. The judgment as to what is reasonable and what is not has to a certain extent been taken out of the hands of the courts, and placed into the hands of an executive agency.

The statutory regime also represents an expansion of the reasonable use doctrine because under it a greater number of instances of water use are subjected to the scrutiny of the state. It is noteworthy that Mr Pickles would probably have fallen foul of the provisions of the Water Resources Act 1991 if it had been in force at the end of the nineteenth century.

Some answers to questions originally posed

At the beginning of this chapter I suggested that water, by its nature, raises the following property law questions:

    (1) Is water a thing?
    (2) Can you own water if it is flowing?
    (3) What does it mean to own water?
    (4) Is water ever public property?

I now propose to offer some short answers to those questions.

Is water a thing?

Yes, water is a thing and it can properly be subject to property law. Nevertheless it is a unique thing from the perspective of property law because of the conjunction of its two important features: first the fact that it is essential to life, and second, the fact that it is a liquid and in its natural state it may be flowing.

Can you own water if it is flowing?

Yes and no. The natural rights theory, which underpins riparianism, provides that no one person owns the actual substance of water which is flowing. Nevertheless riparian rights to water may in some ways result in water being capable of being described as property and therefore of being owned.

What does it mean to own water?

In *National Provincial Bank v Ainsworth*,[56] Lord Wilberforce held that:

Before a right or an interest can be admitted into the category of property, or of a right affecting property, it must be definable, identifiable by third parties, capable in its nature of assumption by third parties, and have some degree of permanence or stability.

These requirements, particularly that of stability, pose difficulties for the ownership of water. Generally speaking, water is not capable of ownership until it is reduced into possession with some element of permanence. You can sell water in tanks. You can sell land with a lake on it. But the right is lost if the water is in a receptacle from which it drains away.

Is water ever public property?

If water is free-flowing, it is not *bonum vacans* (so that anyone may take ownership of it). It has been held that in certain circumstances water is *publici juris*: public property. The courts have explained what this means: for a modern example, see the decision of the High Court of Australia in *ICM Agriculture Property Ltd ABN 32 006 077 765 and others v The Commonwealth of Australia and others*.[57] The plaintiffs had licences to abstract water from aquifers, which were replaced by the state by further licences. The plaintiffs complained that since the licences were for a reduced amount of water the state had acquired property from them for no consideration, contrary to the constitution. However, the majority of the High Court of Australia held that in these circumstances there was no right of ownership in the water until it had been reduced into possession. They applied *Embrey v Owen* and held that water was *publici juris*, not *bonum vacans*. Accordingly, the state could validly be given a statutory right to regulate water without acquiring any property interests of the plaintiffs. The plaintiffs never had a right to water which was taken away from them. This case is particularly interesting because the water was percolating water.

Conclusions

In this study of water rights, we have seen that the common law courts often use theory to develop the law. They have also, unusually, used law from other sources: Roman law, civil law, and American law. We see the conflict between the rights of

---

[56] [1965] AC 1175, 1248.

[57] [2009] HCA 51. In *Embrey v Owen* (n 20) at 369 and 584, Parke B held that:
... flowing water is *publici juris*, not in the sense that it is a *bonum vacans*, to which the first occupant may acquire an exclusive right, but that it is public and common in this sense only, that all may reasonably use it who have a right of access to it, that none can have any property in the water itself, except in the particular portion which he may choose to abstract from the stream and take into his possession, and that during the time of his possession only.

owners and the rights of non-owners being played out. We saw how subterranean percolating water is treated differently. As to the absolute statement in *Bradford Corporation v Pickles* about motive not affecting or invalidating the exercise of rights, the English courts may have to look at that again. For example, in EU law, in claims for damages for breach of member states' obligations, courts have to assess the seriousness of the breach and the good faith of the organ of the state.

We have seen that the law developed different theories of adjusting rights in water.[58] The doctrine of reasonable use is one that creates a great deal of interest. It constitutes an early use of the notion of proportionality. We tend to think that proportionality stems from the European Convention on Human Rights, but the idea may be much older than this. It is interesting to note that reasonable use was part of the weft and weave of water law. It holds out the possibility of an idea that could be used in the future: the development of public rights over private property and a way of securing sustainable use of vital resources.

There are many areas of water law that I have not even touched on—such as the rights to the seashore, fishing, weirs, wharves, and so on. A more modern problem perhaps is the problem of what happens when driving on a beach. Do you have to observe the rule of the road or the rule of the sea? Some of you will remember the AP Herbert story of a road accident on the Chiswick Mall, which was temporarily flooded. Mr Haddock, AP Herbert's favourite character, had been driving on the wrong side of the 'road' and collided with another vehicle making the assumption that it was still the rule of the road which applied. But Mr Haddock pleaded that, as Mall was flooded, the right rule was not the rule of the road but the rule of the sea which meant that he was obliged to drive on the starboard side. The action was dismissed.

I conclude with that improbable story, and express the hope I have said enough to encourage others to study this complex and fascinating area of law.

---

[58] Professor Lon Fuller ('Irrigation and Tyranny' (1965) 17 Stanford Law Review 1021) notes that internationally there was a much greater diversity of legal rules affecting irrigation water.

> In actual practice, over the world and through history, the most diverse rules had been applied to the allocation of irrigation water. These rules expressed every conceivable standard of distributive justice: first-come, come, first served [appropriation theory and Islamic law]; to each according to his contribution [Near East]; to each according to his needs [Persia]; to each according to the needs of society [Persia and Egypt]; to each according to the luck of the throw [British colonial laws in India].

(Words in square brackets added from footnote references given by Professor Fuller.) See also Benjamin N Cardozo, *The Growth of the Law* (Yale University Press, 1924) 118–19, who explains that the arid American states reverted to appropriation theory because of their particular circumstances.

2

Legal Problems at the Start and End of Life

The Role of Judges and Parliament

This chapter is based on a presentation to the South African Institute for Advanced Constitutional, Public, Human Rights and International Law, in the University of Johannesburg, 14 August 2015.

A fine line between making a judicial decision and legislating

In this chapter, I want to look at how the law responds to social change by discussing some legal problems that concern the start of life and end of life. These problems are all recent, and have involved human rights challenges of various kinds. I will concentrate on assisted reproduction—IVF and surrogacy—and assisted dying. These problems usefully highlight the different roles of Parliament and the judges when it comes to developing the law in response to social change.

Sometimes Parliament has put in place a statutory framework, and the responsibility of the courts is then to apply this framework and so far as possible to make it work. In such cases, judges are in general working within given boundaries: from time to time they will have to make choices and exercise their judgment, but within those boundaries. The other type of case is where legal issues require some decision by the courts before Parliament has put a statutory framework in place, or the statutory framework that has been put in place may not have anticipated the challenges that arise.

One major reason for those challenges is the responsibility given to judges by the Human Rights Act 1998. Among other things, this Act imposes on judges obligations to interpret legislation, so far as possible, in a manner that is compatible with human rights, or, if not and the legislation is primary legislation, to make a declaration of incompatibility.

The Human Rights Act 1998 has increased 'rights consciousness' among ordinary citizens who may want to assert their individual rights. Before the Act came into force, the sort of challenges considered in this chapter would not have arisen. Today people naturally want to use the legislation to test restrictions in the law which cause particular hardship to them. Two of the areas which I consider in this chapter, assisted reproduction (including surrogacy) and assisted dying, show how the courts have dealt with human rights challenges.

When judges have to reach a decision, the ultimate question may be whether the courts should develop the law or whether they should leave it to Parliament. Where the policy behind the legislation involves moral or ethical issues, leaving the decision to Parliament may be appropriate.

Assisted reproduction

My first example is *Evans v Amicus Healthcare Ltd.*[1] A woman was no longer able to have her own children because her ovaries had been removed as part of treatment for cancer. She wished to have implanted her embryos which had been harvested before the removal of her ovaries and which had been fertilized by her former partner and frozen. However English statute law required the former partner's consent to implantation of the embryos. He refused to give his consent. Therefore Ms Evans could not have the embryos implanted in her. She complained of a violation of her right to private life under Arts 8[2] and 14[3] of the European Convention on Human Rights (the 'Convention'). The English courts held that the partner's consent was required by statute and that there was no violation of the Convention.

Evans was a case where there was a clear statutory scheme in the Human Fertilisation and Embryology Act 1990. Parliament had thought about the issue in advance and provided a clear framework for the courts. The Court of Appeal (of which I was a member) dealt with the issue of Convention-compatibility quite briefly after a longer study of the domestic statute law. Perhaps a court today would have gone into the Convention issues in much greater detail, and would have gone on to express a view as to what the position ought to be in England and Wales if those rights fell within the margin of appreciation. In the event, however, Ms Evans was refused permission to appeal to the House of Lords and she then made an application to the Strasbourg court. She lost before a Chamber of the Strasbourg court, but the case was remitted to the Grand Chamber. She lost again by a majority. In the opinion of the majority, Art 8 was engaged by the question whether she could become a biological parent but the relevant provisions of the 1990 Act served a number of wider public interests. Since assisted reproduction

---

[1] [2004] EWCA Civ 727, [2005] Fam 1.

[2] European Convention on Human Rights, Art 8:

   1. Everyone has the right to respect for his private and family life, his home and his correspondence.

   2. There shall be no interference by a public authority with the exercise of this right except such as is in accordance with the law and is necessary in a democratic society in the interests of national security, public safety or the economic well-being of the country, for the prevention of disorder or crime, for the protection of health or morals, or for the protection of the rights and freedoms of others.

[3] European Convention on Human Rights, Art 14: 'The enjoyment of the rights and freedoms set forth in the Convention shall be secured without discrimination on any ground such as sex, race, colour, language, religion, political or other opinion, national or social origin, association with a national minority, property, birth or other status.'

gave rise to sensitive moral and ethical issues against a background of fast-moving medical and scientific developments, and there was no consensus between member states, the state had a wide margin of appreciation. So, national law could require, as English law requires, that her former partner, who had fertilized the eggs, should have to consent to implantation.

In the context of assisted dying the Supreme Court has held that, even where domestic legislation falls within the margin of appreciation, the courts must still determine whether it is compatible with Convention rights. In *Evans*, in the Court of Appeal, there was, as I recall, no argument that the statutory rule could violate human rights even though it was within the United Kingdom's margin of appreciation.

Surrogacy

Surrogacy used to be quite rare but it has become more common in recent times with advances in reproductive techniques and more same sex couples wishing to have a family. Surrogacy does not, however, generally come to the attention of the courts because of some surrogacy arrangement made in England. English law prohibits surrogacy arrangements if they are on a commercial basis.[4] Moreover, under English law, all surrogacy arrangements are unenforceable and agencies which make surrogacy arrangements are prohibited in England. Surrogacy comes to the attention of our courts for the reason given in the next two paragraphs.

Parents who are unable to have their own children and who can afford to do so travel abroad to become commissioning parents for another woman to bear the child, who may be the biological child of one or both of them. The child is sometimes adopted by the commissioning parents even before it is born. The parents then bring the child back into the jurisdiction. The surrogacy arrangements will have been made under some foreign law.

Parliament has laid down a tightly drawn statutory scheme for the situation. When the commissioning parents return their newly born child to the United Kingdom, provided the child is the biological child of one of them, they are entitled to apply to the court within six months of a child's birth for a parental order under s 54 of the Human Fertilisation and Embryology Act 2008. The court will then decide whether it is in the best interests of the child to give parental responsibility to the commissioning parents. If not, it may be necessary in the child's best interests for the court to make a placement order for the child to be adopted.

The 2008 Act provides that one of the commissioning parents at least must be domiciled in the United Kingdom at the time of the application. The court has to take into account the commissioning parents' good faith and must consider whether they have committed any offence, such as that of bringing a child into

---

[4] There are some altruistic non-commercial surrogacy arrangements, where, for example, a family member (such as a mother or sister) has a child which is the biological child of a couple in the family who cannot have their own children.

the jurisdiction following a foreign adoption order which they have obtained outside the United Kingdom.[5] The court has held that, where the commissioning parents brought the child into the jurisdiction following an adoption order that was made to meet the local requirements of the court dealing with the surrogacy arrangements, the commissioning parents did not commit the offence in question.

Clearly, the interests of the mother also have to be considered. English law requires the birth mother to give her consent and this is ineffective if it is given less than six weeks after the birth. In some countries the consent can be given even before the birth.

It is also a cardinal feature of English law that, before making a parental order, the court must consider, and if appropriate authorize, any payments which have been made for the surrogacy arrangements which exceed the payment to the birth mother of her reasonable expenses.

In applying this legislation, the courts have applied a liberal interpretation in the best interests of the child. After all, the child has been born and is a fait accompli as far as the court is concerned. The court has even held that it is possible for an application for a parental order to be made outside the six-month period laid down by Parliament.[6]

The approach which English law takes to surrogacy illustrates the complexity of policy making in an area such as this. English law is not driven by any single public policy aim but by several, for example the policy of not permitting commoditization of the human body through commercial arrangements, the policy protecting the child's best interests, and the policy of safeguarding the interests of the birth mother. Parliament has set out a scheme whereby those considerations are balanced and it is for the courts to fulfil their role under this legislation. As mentioned, the courts have had to deal with some challenging situations in interpreting the legislation.

Assisted dying

The legislative position in relation to assisted dying (assisted suicide) is altogether different from that in relation to IVF and surrogacy. There is no legislative scheme in the United Kingdom permitting assisted dying. On the contrary, despite Parliamentary debate over the years, s 2 of the Suicide Act 1961[7] makes it a crime, punishable with up to fourteen years' imprisonment, for a person to assist in another's suicide. I will refer to this as 'the assisted suicide ban'. Suicide itself is no longer a crime.

---

[5] This would constitute an offence under the Adoption and Children Act 2002, s 83 unless the child is to be adopted under a 'Convention adoption order': that is, an order made pursuant to the Hague Convention on Protection and Co-operation in respect of Intercountry Adoption 1993 in accordance with regulations made under the Adoption (Intercountry Aspects) Act 1999, s 1.

[6] *Re X (A Child) (Parental Order: Time Limit)* [2014] EWHC 3135, [2015] Fam 186.

[7] Now as amended by the Coroners and Justice Act 2009, s 177(1), Sch 22, Pt 2.

There have been a series of major challenges to the assisted suicide ban. In the first, Mrs Pretty, who was paralysed and suffering from a degenerative and incurable illness, sought to argue that the ban violated her rights under (among other articles) Arts 2,[8] 3,[9] and 8[10] of the Convention. Her claim was rejected by the House of Lords[11] and subsequently (save with respect to Art 8) by the Strasbourg court.[12] The Strasbourg court held that the assisted suicide ban was within the margin of appreciation and that it was justified, provided that there was some means of reviewing individual cases. It also held that Art 8 was engaged but not violated on the facts of the case. Mrs Pretty therefore failed in her attempt to obtain an undertaking from the Director of Public Prosecutions in advance of her husband committing an offence that he would not be prosecuted under the assisted suicide ban if he helped her to commit suicide in the final stages of her illness (when she was no longer able to do this for herself).

This led to the second case, brought by another appellant with terminal illness. She successfully challenged the absence of a published policy of the Director of Public Prosecutions on deciding whether to prosecute under s 2 of the Suicide Act 1961 (which was replaced by the Coroners and Justice Act 2009). Her case also went to the House of Lords, who granted her an order that the Director of Public Prosecutions should produce guidelines as to when people would be prosecuted for having assisted a person to take his own life.[13]

The third case, which I wish to examine in more detail, is *R (Nicklinson) v Ministry of Justice*.[14] Mr Nicklinson had been an active person but in his early fifties suffered a heart attack which left him with 'locked-in' syndrome: able to move only his head and his eyes, and unable to communicate except laboriously through blinks of the eye and a computer. Mr Nicklinson found his life unbearable and wished to end it but would need assistance to do so. In the Supreme Court, it was explained that a doctor would be able to provide a computer which would provide a lethal injection and which could be operated by the patient with a blink of an eye to enable this to happen. Many of the justices saw an important difference between this method of ending life and that where a person gives the lethal injection. As Lord Neuberger put it:

[94] To my mind, the difference between administering the fatal drug to a person and setting up a machine so that the person can administer the drug to himself is not merely a legal distinction. Founded as it is on personal autonomy, I consider that the distinction also

---

[8] European Convention on Human Rights, Art 2: 'Everyone's life shall be protected by law...'
[9] European Convention on Human Rights, Art 3: 'No one shall be subjected to torture or to inhuman or degrading treatment or punishment.'
[10] See n 2.
[11] *R (Pretty) v Director of Public Prosecutions (Secretary of State for the Home Department intervening)* [2001] UKHL 61, [2002] 1 AC 800.
[12] *Pretty* (n 11).
[13] *R (Purdy) v Director of Public Prosecutions* [2009] UKHL 45, [2010] 1 AC 345.
[14] [2014] UKSC 38, [2015] AC 657. This was heard with the appeal in *R (AM) v Director of Public Prosecutions* [2014] UKSC 38, [2015] AC 657, where the principal issue turned on whether the Court could give directions to the Director of Public Prosecutions to exercise his prosecutorial discretion, but the issues on that appeal are outside the scope of this chapter.

sounds in morality. Indeed, authorising a third party to switch off a person's life support machine, as in *Airedale NHS Trust v Bland* [1993] 1 All ER 821 or *Re B (adult: refusal of medical treatment)* [2002] 2 All ER 449 seems to me, at least arguably, to be, in some respects, a more drastic interference in that person's life and a more extreme moral step, than authorising a third party to set up a lethal drug delivery system so that a person can, but only if he wishes, activate the system to administer a lethal drug.

The case proceeded on the basis that the method involving the computer would be used. Mr Nicklinson sought to challenge the assisted suicide ban by relying on his Convention right to respect for his private life under Art 8. He lost in the High Court and in the Court of Appeal, and then decided to refuse all nourishment. He sadly died before the appeal to the Supreme Court took place, but the Supreme Court allowed the appeal to proceed. At the time of the hearing before the Supreme Court, an Assisted Dying Bill had been introduced in the House of Lords by Lord Falconer, though this would only permit physician-assisted suicide for persons with terminal illness and a prognosis of six months or less.

It is a measure of the importance attached to this case that no fewer than nine Supreme Court justices sat on it in the Supreme Court. They were all of the view that Strasbourg jurisprudence permitted a state to have an absolute ban on assisted suicide provided that it was properly justifiable to protect the vulnerable, but that they still had to consider whether English law complied with the Convention.[15] This was another potential case of what the Supreme Court of Canada, in a case I shall refer to later, memorably called 'overbreadth'.[16]

On this issue, the members of the Supreme Court took different views. The judgments are comprehensive and cover the issues in depth. Space does not permit me to summarize the judgments in any detail, still less can I offer critical comment, as the issues may yet come back to the courts.[17] Lord Neuberger, with whom Lord Mance and Lord Wilson agreed (in addition to giving their own judgments), considered that no declaration of incompatibility should be made when Parliament was about to consider the matter. So they did not provide an answer to the question whether there was a violation of Mr Nicklinson's rights. They indicated that a

[15] Interestingly that point was not taken in *Fleming v Ireland* [2013] IESC 19, a decision of the Supreme Court of Ireland in 2013, which was not cited in *Nicklinson*. This concerned a 59-year-old woman who had advanced multiple sclerosis and who was almost immobile and in severe pain. She wanted a declaration that the assisted suicide ban in Irish law was unconstitutional and/or incompatible with the Convention. As the assisted suicide ban was contained in primary legislation of the Oireachtas (the Parliament of the Republic of Ireland), the presumption of constitutionality applied. The fact that suicide no longer involved the commission of a criminal offence did not mean that there was a right to take one's own life; nor was there any right under the Irish Constitution 'either to commit suicide, or to arrange for the termination of one's life at a time of one's choosing.'(para 114). Likewise the Court was satisfied that the assisted suicide ban was not discriminatory. The Supreme Court then went on to consider compatibility with the Convention. It held that the Strasbourg court in *Pretty* had held that the assisted suicide ban was justified provided that the means of enforcement had regard to the circumstances of a particular case. The Court considered that, as the Oireachtas had approved the assisted suicide ban, there was no incompatibility.

[16] It explained the meaning of this term in the opening sentence of para 85 of its judgment, set out later in this chapter.

[17] Because Parliament has not yet produced a definitive answer to this legal issue.

declaration of incompatibility might be made if the matter was not resolved by Parliament. Lord Neuberger foresaw the possibility that persons with locked-in syndrome might be vulnerable and need protection too.[18]

Lord Sumption, with whom Lord Clarke, Lord Reed, and Lord Hughes agreed, held that this was a classic case where the issue should be left to Parliament, though they (the judges) might intervene if Parliament chose not to debate the issue.[19] Lord Sumption gave three main reasons for this:

... The first is that, as I have suggested, the issue involves a choice between two fundamental but mutually inconsistent moral values, upon which there is at present no consensus in our society. Such choices are inherently legislative in nature. The decision cannot fail to be strongly influenced by the decision makers' personal opinions about the moral case for assisted suicide. This is entirely appropriate if the decision makers are those who represent the community at large. It is not appropriate for professional judges. The imposition of their personal opinions on matters of this kind would lack all constitutional legitimacy.

[231] Secondly, Parliament has made the relevant choice. It passed the Suicide Act in 1961, and as recently as 2009 amended s 2 without altering the principle. In recent years there have been a number of Bills to decriminalise assistance to suicide, at least in part, but none has been passed into law.... As Lord Bingham observed in *R (on the application of the Countryside Alliance) v A-G* [2007] UKHL 52 at [45], [2008] 2 All ER 95 at [45], '[t]he democratic process is liable to be subverted if, on a question of moral and political judgment, opponents of the Act achieve through the courts what they could not achieve in Parliament'. Cf *AXA General Insurance Ltd v Lord Advocate (Scotland)* [2011] UKSC 46 at [49], [2012] 1 AC 868 at [49] (Lord Hope).

[232] Third, the parliamentary process is a better way of resolving issues involving controversial and complex questions of fact arising out of moral and social dilemmas. The legislature has access to a fuller range of expert judgment and experience than forensic litigation can possibly provide. It is better able to take account of the interests of groups not represented or not sufficiently represented before the court in resolving what is surely a classic 'polycentric problem'. But, perhaps critically in a case like this where firm factual conclusions are elusive, Parliament can legitimately act on an instinctive judgment about what the facts are likely to be in a case where the evidence is inconclusive or slight: see *R (on the application of Sinclair Collis Ltd) v Secretary of State for Health* [2012] QB 394, especially at [239] (Lord Neuberger), and *Bank Mellat v HM Treasury* [2013] UKSC 39 at [93]–[94], [2013] 4 All ER 533 at [93]–[94] (Lord Reed). Indeed, it can do so in a case where the truth is inherently unknowable, as Lord Bingham thought it was in *R (on the application of the Countryside Alliance) v A-G* [2008] 2 All ER 95 at [42].

It is important to note the point that it would be constitutionally illegitimate for judges to express views on moral issues. In no part of this chapter will I consider such issues.

The majority made it clear that the decriminalization of suicide did not mean that there was a Convention right to commit suicide: the issue is whether the state

---

[18] *R (Nicklinson) v Ministry of Justice* [2014] UKSC 38, [2015] AC 657, para 85.

[19] Though Lord Clarke (para 293) stated that he would expect the courts to intervene if Parliament failed altogether to address the matter, and Lord Sumption accepted that that might be a different case (para 233).

has violated Art 8 by interfering with respect for a person's private life. As Lord Mance said:

[159] It would be wrong in my view to deduce from this that the Strasbourg jurisprudence accepts that those capable of freely reaching a decision to end their lives, but physically incapable of bringing that about by themselves, have a prima facie right to obtain voluntary assistance, which is now the issue in this case, to achieve their wish. Article 8(1) is, on the authority of *Pretty v UK* (2002) 12 BHRC 149, engaged in this area. But it does not by itself create a right. A right only exists (at least in any coherent sense) if and when it is concluded under art 8(2) that there is no justification for a ban or restriction.[20]

The minority view was that of Lady Hale DP and Lord Kerr. They considered that the Supreme Court should make a declaration immediately. Lady Hale approached the matter through the rule that a person who is adult and mentally competent may decide to end medical treatment.[21] She attached particular weight to a person having autonomy over their own body.[22] While she accepted that it did not follow that a person with locked-in syndrome has a right to demand help from another person, in her view, for the state to criminalize the actions of a person in these circumstances goes beyond the minimum interference which the law should authorize.[23]

The declaration of incompatibility which she would have made would declare that the assisted suicide ban was incompatible with the Convention if a person has made a free and fully informed decision to end his life and is competent to make that decision but requires help to do so.[24] She considered that a legislative scheme could be put in place providing for judges to make decisions. She took the view that these decisions would be no more difficult than the decisions which courts are now required to make in any event as to whether the continuation of medical treatment is in the best interests of a person who no longer has capacity to make decisions on his own behalf. As Lady Hale, with whom Lord Kerr on this point agreed (in addition to delivering his own judgment), put it:

[314] It would not be beyond the wit of a legal system to devise a process for identifying those people, those few people, who should be allowed help to end their own lives. There would be four essential requirements. They would firstly have to have the capacity to make the decision for themselves. They would secondly have to have reached the decision freely without undue influence from any quarter. They would thirdly have had to reach it with full knowledge of their situation, the options available to them, and the consequences of their decision: that is not the same, as Dame Elizabeth pointed out in *Re B (adult: refusal of medical treatment)* [2002] 2 All ER 449, as having first-hand experience of those options. And they would fourthly have to be unable, because of physical incapacity or frailty, to put that decision into effect without some help from others. I do not pretend that such cases would always be easy to decide, but the nature of the judgments involved would be no more difficult than those regularly required in the Court of Protection or the Family Division when cases such as *Aintree University Hospitals NHS Foundation Trust v James* [2013] UKSC

---

[20] See also *Nicklinson* (n 18) para 216 per Lord Sumption and para 264 per Lord Hughes.
[21] *Nicklinson* (n 18) paras 302–303.   [22] *Nicklinson* (n 18) para 311.
[23] *Nicklinson* (n 18) paras 313–314.   [24] *Nicklinson* (n 18) para 321.

67, [2014] 1 All ER 573 or *Re B (adult: refusal of medical treatment)* [2002] 2 All ER 449 come before them.

Lady Hale did not consider that there was evidence that to permit assisted suicide in these circumstances would impose pressure on the vulnerable and the elderly.[25]

After the Supreme Court decided *Nicklinson*, the House of Lords debated the Assisted Dying Bill, which had already been presented, but the Bill did not complete its stages in the House of Lords before Parliament was dissolved for the 2015 election. Parliament has to consider two other similar Bills introduced since the election. Meanwhile, the Scottish Parliament considered an Assisted Suicide (Scotland) Bill for similar purposes, but this fell on 27 May 2015 following the Stage 1 debate on the principles in the Bill.[26]

Deferring to Parliament—the approach in other jurisdictions

So the majority in *Nicklinson* did not consider that the courts should decide the issue in this case, at least before Parliament had considered whether to pass legislation on assisted dying.[27]

Not all common law courts adopt the same approach to assisted dying as the majority in *Nicklinson* did by deferring to Parliament. In February 2015, the Supreme Court of Canada gave its momentous decision in *Carter v Canada*[28] in which it unanimously held that two provisions of the Canadian Criminal Code unjustifiably infringed the right to life in s 7 of the Canadian Charter of Rights and Freedoms ('the Canadian Charter').[29] The first provision was s 241(b), which is similar to the English assisted suicide ban, and s 14 invalidates a person's consent to

---

[25] *Nicklinson* (n 18) para 316.

[26] The Scottish Parliament's website stated that the aim of this Bill was to enable people with terminal or life-shortening illnesses or progressive conditions which are terminal or life-shortening and who wish to end their own lives to obtain assistance in doing so. It did this by removing criminal and civil liability from those who provide such assistance, provided that the procedure set out in the Bill was followed. This procedure for accessing a lawful assisted suicide was designed to ensure that the individual seeking it meets the Bill's eligibility criteria, has made his or her own informed decision to end his or her life, and has had the opportunity to reflect before moving forward at key stages.

[27] Other common law courts have declined to accept assisted dying for different reasons: see the decision of the Supreme Court of Ireland (see n 15). On 4 June 2015, Collins J in the High Court of New Zealand refused to grant a declaration that a doctor would not commit a criminal offence if he were to give a lethal dose to a terminally ill patient at her request (*Seales v Attorney General* [2015] NZHC 1239). Mrs Nicklinson applied to the Strasbourg Court contending that the UK courts had violated Art 8 by leaving the matter to Parliament. On 23 June 2015, the Strasbourg Court ruled her application inadmissible. Art 13 of the Convention (right to an effective remedy) did mean that a person had to be able to challenge a law on the ground that it was contrary to the Convention: 'If the domestic courts were to be required to give a judgment on the merits of such a complaint this could have the effect of forcing upon them an institutional role not envisaged by the domestic constitutional order.' (para 84). The assisted suicide ban fell within the state's margin of appreciation, and national law could determine whether the law should be developed by the judges or Parliament (*Nicklinson & Lamb v United Kingdom* App nos 2478/2015 and 1787/15).

[28] 2015 SCC 5.

[29] This provides: 'Everyone has the right to life, liberty and security of the person and the right not to be deprived thereof except in accordance with the principles of fundamental justice.'

having death inflicted on him. Unlike the position in the United Kingdom, the Supreme Court of Canada did not have to go through a two-stage approach of considering what the Strasbourg court had held, and then, if the question fell within the state's margin of appreciation, the nature of the right for the purposes of English law. The Supreme Court of Canada had to consider, and consider only,[30] the position under the Canadian Charter.

Carter is also not on all fours with *Nicklinson* because the trial judge had in that case made extensive findings of fact as to whether, for instance, 'a permissive scheme with properly designed and administered safeguards was capable of protecting vulnerable people'. The Supreme Court of Canada rejected an application for further evidence on the way in which the issue was operating in Belgium.

The judgment of the Supreme Court of Canada requires comprehensive study, which is outside the scope of this chapter. A major point was its conclusion on what was called 'overbreadth':

[85] The overbreadth inquiry asks whether a law that takes away rights in a way that generally supports the object of the law, goes too far by denying the rights of some individuals in a way that bears no relation to the object: *Bedford*, at paras. 101 and 112–13. Like the other principles of fundamental justice under s. 7,[31] overbreadth is not concerned with competing social interests or ancillary benefits to the general population. A law that is drawn broadly to target conduct that bears no relation to its purpose 'in order to make enforcement more practical' may therefore be overbroad (see *Bedford*, at para. 113). The question is not whether Parliament has chosen the least restrictive means, but whether the chosen means infringe life, liberty or security of the person in a way that has no connection with the mischief contemplated by the legislature. The focus is not on broad social impacts, but on the impact of the measure on the individuals whose life, liberty or security of the person is trammelled.

[86] Applying this approach, we conclude that the prohibition on assisted dying is overbroad. The object of the law, as discussed, is to protect vulnerable persons from being induced to commit suicide at a moment of weakness. Canada conceded at trial that the law catches people outside this class: 'It is recognized that not every person who wishes to commit suicide is vulnerable, and that there may be people with disabilities who have a considered, rational and persistent wish to end their own lives' (trial reasons, at para. 1136). The trial judge accepted that Ms. Taylor was such a person—competent, fully-informed, and free from coercion or duress (para. 16). It follows that the limitation on their rights is in at least some cases not connected to the objective of protecting *vulnerable* persons. The blanket prohibition sweeps conduct into its ambit that is unrelated to the law's objective.

Having given judgment, the Supreme Court of Canada ruled that:

[127] The appropriate remedy is therefore a declaration that s. 241(*b*) and s. 14 of the *Criminal Code* are void insofar as they prohibit physician-assisted death for a competent

---

[30] Canada is not party to any relevant regional human rights instrument, unlike the UK which is a party to the Convention.

[31] The Canadian Charter of Rights and Freedoms, s 7 which provides: 'Everyone has the right to life, liberty and security of the person and the right not to be deprived thereof except in accordance with the principles of fundamental justice.'

adult person who (1) clearly consents to the termination of life; and (2) has a grievous and irremediable medical condition (including an illness, disease or disability) that causes enduring suffering that is intolerable to the individual in the circumstances of his or her condition. 'Irremediable,' it should be added, does not require the patient to undertake treatments that are not acceptable to the individual. The scope of this declaration is intended to respond to the factual circumstances in this case. We make no pronouncement on other situations where physician-assisted dying may be sought. . . .

The Supreme Court of Canada then suspended the declaration for twelve months. That period was to enable Parliament to devise an appropriate statutory scheme. Subject to that delay, the declaration no doubt gave the appellant all that he could have hoped for.

Of interest for the purposes of this chapter is that there was little discussion in the Supreme Court of Canada's judgment of the position of Parliament. The tenor of the judgment suggests that the Supreme Court of Canada had little expectation that the Canadian Parliament would give further consideration to the issue. The Supreme Court of Canada effectively concluded that less weight should be given to the views of Parliament as expressed in the Criminal Code:

[96] Here, the limit is prescribed by law, and the appellant concedes that the law has a pressing and substantial objective. The question is whether the government has demonstrated that the prohibition is proportionate.

[97] At this stage of the analysis, the courts must accord the legislature a measure of deference.

[98] On the one hand, as the trial judge noted, physician-assisted death involves complex issues of social policy and a number of competing societal values. Parliament faces a difficult task in addressing this issue; it must weigh and balance the perspective of those who might be at risk in a permissive regime against that of those who seek assistance in dying. It follows that a high degree of deference is owed to Parliament's decision to impose an absolute prohibition on assisted death. On the other hand, the trial judge also found—and we agree—that the absolute prohibition could not be described as a 'complex regulatory response' (para. 1180). The degree of deference owed to Parliament, while high, is accordingly reduced.

In many systems, the doctrine of Parliamentary sovereignty does not apply. A notable example is the United States, where the Supreme Court has a constitutional mandate to interpret the constitution. That does not always make the role of the legislature totally irrelevant. In *Washington v Glucksberg*,[32] O'Connor J, with whom Breyer and Ginsburg JJ agreed, held in her concurring opinion that there was no reason to think that the democratic process will not strike a proper balance between the competing interests:

The parties and *amici* agree that in these States a patient who is suffering from a terminal illness and who is experiencing great pain has no legal barriers to obtaining medication, from qualified physicians, to alleviate that suffering, even to the point of causing unconsciousness and hastening death. . . . In this light, even assuming that we would recognize such an interest, I agree that the State's interests in protecting those who are not truly competent

---

[32] (1997) 521 US 702, 117 S Ct 2538.

or facing imminent death, or those whose decisions to hasten death would not truly be voluntary, are sufficiently weighty to justify a prohibition against physician-assisted suicide.... There is no reason to think the democratic process will not strike the proper balance between the interests of terminally ill, mentally competent individuals who would seek to end their suffering and the State's interests in protecting those who might seek to end life mistakenly or under pressure. As the Court recognizes, States are presently undertaking extensive and serious evaluation of physician-assisted suicide and other related issues.

Why leave matters to Parliament?

Judges down the centuries have asked themselves whether they can develop the law or must leave the question to Parliament. In a democracy it is a question of vital importance whether unelected judges or democratically appointed legislators should decide what the law should be. In an oft-cited passage, Lord Goff once observed that, while he was well aware of the boundary, he was never quite sure where to find it.[33] It would be impossible to draw up a definitive list of the circumstances when a court should leave Parliament to amend the law, but Lord Bingham, writing extra-judicially, has provided much useful guidance by giving examples of circumstances in which judges should leave matters to Parliament.

Lord Bingham wrote:

Adherents of the third, currently majoritarian, school[34] would acknowledge that a range of different road signs may in different situations be appropriate, ranging from 'No entry' and 'Stop' to 'Give way' and 'Slow'. The debate is as to which of these injunctions applies in differing circumstances, and with what degree of compulsion. There are, however, various situations in which most Judges, even of the reformist, majoritarian tendency, would regard one or other of these signs as apposite. Such situations would include the following:

(1) Where reasonable and right-minded citizens have legitimately ordered their affairs on the basis of a certain understanding of the law. As Lord Reid put it:[35]
    'And there is another sphere where we have got to be very careful. People rely on the certainty of the law in settling their affairs, in particular in making contracts or settlements. It would be very wrong if Judges were to disregard or innovate on what can fairly be regarded as settled law in matters of this kind.'

(2) Where, although a rule of law is seen to be defective, its amendment calls for a detailed legislative code, with qualifications, exceptions and safeguards which cannot feasibly be introduced by judicial decisions. Such cases call for a rule of judicial

---

[33] *Woolwich Equitable Building Society v IRC* [1993] AC 70, 173.
[34] Lord Bingham divided judges into four different schools of thought and considered that most modern judges belonged to the third group. This group regarded making new law as entirely appropriate within certain limits. The other groups were (1) judges who would hold that judges have no role as lawmakers; (2) judges who acknowledge that judges do make law but urge that this role should be so far as possible covert and imperceptible to the general public; and (4) judges who like Lord Denning assert a right to make law whenever established law impedes the doing of justice in an individual case.
[35] (1972) 12 Journal of the Society of Public Teachers of Law 22, 23.

abstinence, particularly where wise and effective reform of the law calls for research and consultation of a kind which no Court of law is fitted to undertake.

(3)　Where the question involves an issue of current social policy on which there is no consensus within the community. As Lord Reid again put it:[36]

'When public opinion is sharply divided on any question—whether or not the division is on party lines—no Judge ought in my view to lean to one side or the other if that can possibly be avoided. But sometimes we get a case where that is very difficult to avoid. Then I think we must play safe. We must decide the case on the preponderance of existing authority. Parliament is the right place to settle issues which the ordinary man regards as controversial. On many questions he will say: "That is the lawyers' job, let them get on with it." But on others he will say: "I ought to have my say in this. I am not going to accept dictation from the lawyers." Family law is a good example. It is not for Judges to say what changes should be made on big issues.'

(4)　Where an issue is the subject of current legislative activity. If Parliament is actually engaged in deciding what the rule should be in a given legal situation, the Courts are generally wise to await the outcome of that deliberation rather than to pre-empt the result by judicial decision. Lord Radcliffe thought the Judges should walk warily in fields where Parliament regularly legislated or had recently done so.[37] Cardozo thought the Judge should 'legislate only between gaps. He fills the open spaces in the law.'[38]

(5)　Where the issue arises in a field far removed from ordinary judicial experience. This is really another way of saying that whereas the Judges may properly mould what is sometimes called lawyers' law, they should be very slow to lay down far-reaching rules in fields outside their experience. They should be alert to recognize their own limitations. Even where a Judge recognizes that a change in the law is called for, he is well advised to walk circumspectly. On the whole, the law advances in small steps, not by giant bounds. Many judges will seek to adopt the approach of Bacon, in his declaration that 'The work which I propound tendeth to pruning and grafting the law, and not to ploughing up and planting it again.'[39]

As always, it is difficult to improve on what Lord Bingham says. Moreover, all but the first of the situations he lists are relevant to the question 'Why leave matters to Parliament?' and all but the first are relevant to *Nicklinson*, where (a) a detailed legislative code was required, (b) there was no consensus in society on what the law should be, (c) there was current legislative activity, and (d) judges did not have expertise in all the specialist fields involved.

In *Nicklinson*, Lord Sumption, in the passage I have already cited, gave thoughtful reasons why the courts should leave assisted dying to Parliament. His first two reasons accord with the third and fourth situations given by Lord Bingham. His third reason is not directly within Lord Bingham's categories and may now usefully be added to the list. Souter J made a similar point in the US Supreme Court in *Washington v Glucksberg*.[40] This case held that the prohibition on assisted suicide

---

[36] Lord Reid (n 35) 23.

[37] Lord Radcliffe, *Not in Feather Beds* (Hamish Hamilton, 1968) 216.

[38] Benjamin N Cardozo, *The Nature of the Judicial Process* (Yale University Press, 1921).

[39] Tom Bingham, 'The Judge as Lawmaker' in *The Business of Judging, Selected Essays and Speeches: 1985–1999* (Oxford University Press, 2011) 31–2.

[40] 521 US 702, 117 S Ct 3258.

was not unconstitutional in the United States. Souter J considered that the legislature would be in a superior position to the court to determine whether assisted suicide should be allowed:

Legislatures ... have superior opportunities to obtain facts necessary for a judgment about the present controversy. Not only do they have more flexible mechanisms for fact finding than the Judiciary, but their mechanisms include the power to experiment, moving forward and pulling back as facts emerge within their own jurisdiction.[41]

I do not read Justice Souter as suggesting that the legislature will enact new law in this area as an experiment, but simply that if a problem emerges after enactment, which could not have been foreseen, the legislature can move quickly to pass amending legislation. The legislature does not, like a court, have to wait until the next suitable case comes. The legislature can, as Souter J points out, investigate a much wider range of issues. As hinted at by O'Connor J, in the case of assisted suicide, those issues might include whether sufficient palliative or other medical care is available to persons who might otherwise wish to commit suicide.

Effect of changing social attitudes on judicial law-making

There are other matters which have an impact on whether it is right to leave a change in the law to Parliament. Attitudes may matter. This is an age which is sceptical about the past and has less faith in certainties or how things have traditionally been done. People have higher expectations about control over their own bodies and lives. Changing attitudes and expectations may make judges more inclined to develop the law.[42] This is not in principle a new phenomenon. Earlier generations had analogous challenges to overcome. In the eighteenth century, Lord Mansfield, possibly assisted by his experience in politics before becoming a judge, sensed that the commercial world wanted the law to break away from its feudal approach and be more responsive to commercial needs. He brought about considerable change in the law, in particular so that it was better fitted for the country's expansion of trade.

Much may also depend on the precise issue in question. It may be easier to develop the law if the question falls within a narrow compass and has no repercussions on other aspects of the law.

Calling for the Law Commission to be involved is yet another option to courts when law reform is required but the courts are not able to deal with the matter. When a court reaches the conclusion that there is a need for law reform on which there is consultation and a comprehensive set of changes, judges can suggest that the Law Commission be asked to undertake a project. Parliament can no doubt

---

[41] *Washington v Glucksberg* (n 40) 788.
[42] See generally, Benjamin N Cardozo, *The Paradoxes of Legal Science* (Columbia University Press, 1928) 55: 'A judge is to give effect in general not to his own scale of values, but to the scale of values revealed to him in his readings of the social mind.' This applies only where the judges find that Parliament has left it to the judges to determine the issue.

invite a minister to do the same. In a field such as medical science, the project might have to be focused on a legal issue on which recommendations can be made.

A South African example is pertinent here. In the recent case of *Stransham-Ford v Minister of Justice and Correctional Services*,[43] the High Court of South Africa (North Gauteng High Court) made an order permitting physician-assisted suicide for a terminally ill cancer patient who was in great pain. It is evident from the report that the Court was greatly assisted by a report of the South African Law Commission.

Importance of judicial explanation

The fact that the question is not an appropriate one for the court does not mean the court has no function. The court may be required to explain the position in greater detail than it would have done before. In *Nicklinson* the Supreme Court seems to have spelt out the issues with great clarity and depth in order to assist the debate that was likely to happen in Parliament and no doubt elsewhere. That suggests that there is in some circumstances a special role for the Supreme Court and a special type of judgment required.[44] A measure of Parliamentary debate has now taken place and it was no doubt the richer for the range of views expressed by the Supreme Court.

Conclusion

As I indicated at the start of this chapter, in some areas Parliament has already laid down a statutory scheme and the judges must apply that scheme and move within the boundaries established by Parliament. I contrasted that case with the situation where Parliament has not yet laid down a scheme, or the scheme meets unforeseen challenges, as where there are human rights challenges to legislation passed before the Human Rights Act 1998 came into force. These categories are not watertight. Even where a statutory scheme has been laid down, it may not fit all cases that arise under it.[45] Judges must courageously try to adjudicate on claims to individual rights against the state and, where appropriate, uphold individual rights, as the 1998 Act requires.

As Lord Bingham wrote and recent case law shows, there will be some situations where it is inappropriate for judges to rule on claims to individual rights, for example where to do so would be inconsistent with the constitutional role of judges. In that situation, judges may have a new role, as is shown by the judgments of the Supreme Court in *Nicklinson*, of providing careful explanation of their response to the issues that concern judges. This will help to ensure that both the issues and the approach of the courts are clear to all concerned in the public debate which follows.

---

[43] (27401/15) [2015] ZAGPPHC 230 (4 May 2015).

[44] See, eg, in *Nicklinson*, Lord Wilson's provisional views on the considerations relevant to determining whether a person had given appropriate consent to another assisting him to end his life. Similar dialogue between the courts and Parliament might usefully take place on the Convention-compatibility of any conditions imposed on modifying the assisted suicide ban.

[45] At least without some liberal interpretation: see for example the case cited at n 6.

3

Coming to Terms with Good Faith

This chapter is based on a Distinguished Speaker's Lecture given to the Singapore Academy of Law on 26 April 2013 by invitation of the Chief Justice of Singapore, Justice Menon.*

Increasing reference to good faith in contracts

The title of this chapter, *Coming to Terms with Good Faith*, was chosen for two reasons. First, it came to my notice that, rightly or wrongly, parties are increasingly inserting obligations to do things in good faith into their contracts governed by English law. Second, I wanted to try to take stock of the state of the law in relation to express contractual terms of good faith in England and Wales and also in Singapore.[1] I shall be referring to normal commercial contracts, and not contracts such as employment contracts, to which special principles may apply. In addition, at the end of this chapter, I want to get out my crystal ball and offer some ideas about where English law, at least, may be heading. First, to make good the point that parties are increasingly using good faith obligations, I give two examples: derivatives and construction contracts.

Derivatives

The International Swaps and Derivatives Association (ISDA) Master Agreement[2] contains a number of good faith duties. In particular, cl 6(f) provides for good faith in reaching agreement on the valuation of a rate of exchange; cl 9(h)(i)(2) provides for good faith in reaching agreement on fair market value; the following definitions in cl 14 refer to good faith: the definition of 'Applicable Deferral Rate' provides the duty to select a bank in good faith; the definition of 'Close-out Amount' provides for good faith in reaching agreement on the valuation of the close-out amount; the

---

* This paper was first published in (2013) 30 Journal of Contract Law 1999 and is reproduced with the kind permission of LexisNexis.

[1] I would like to express my thanks to Ekaterina Finkel, then my Judicial Assistant in the Court of Appeal, for her excellent research into this subject, and to Kirsty Tan, partner, Allen and Gledhill, who kindly assisted me in relation to Singapore. However, the views expressed in this chapter remain my own.

[2] The first standardized terms of business for derivative transactions were issued by the ISDA (in 1992). The terms as to the consequences of early termination were revised in 2002.

definition of 'Termination Currency Equivalent' provides a duty to select a foreign exchange agent in good faith; and the definition of 'Unpaid Amount' provides for good faith in reaching agreement on fair market value. All of these references to good faith raise the question: if good faith is such an uncertain and unruly concept, why is it used in ISDA contracts? They govern transactions of a ruthlessly competitive and fast-moving kind.

Construction contracts

This is a very different example. Good faith clauses are now a feature of a number of standard form construction contracts, and they have been adopted as part of an attempt to move away from an adversarial approach to contract law. Importantly, in this context the parties agree to cooperate. Thus, for example, the third edition of the standard form New Engineering Contract (NEC) states: 'The Employer, the Contractor, the Project Manager and the Supervisor shall act as stated in this contract and in the spirit of mutual trust and co-operation.' More significantly, the Joint Contracts Tribunal incorporated an express obligation of good faith: 'The Parties shall work with each other and with other project team members in a co-operative manner, in good faith and in a spirit of trust and respect.'

What is required to show good faith in a particular term will be a matter of the construction of the contract. The expression 'good faith' has several meanings. Contracting parties who choose to use this expression would do well to specify the meaning that they intend to apply in their contract. I am going to assume for the purposes of this chapter that it has both a subjective and an objective meaning: that is, to comply with the obligation of good faith, a contracting party must act in a manner which the contracting party reasonably believes is honest, and his or her conduct must be such as would be considered to be fair and reasonable by right-thinking people engaged in the same business. So, on this basis, good faith has both a subjective and an objective meaning. Conduct which is fair and reasonable will, of course, in some cases have to take the position of the other contracting party into account. That is, as they say, the rub. It is a theme to which I will return towards the end of this chapter.

The growing use of good faith clauses struck me as altogether surprising because, as is well known, in recent times English law has been very resistant to a general or overarching concept of good faith. This was not always the position.

English law's longstanding preference for piecemeal solutions

In 1766, Lord Mansfield sought to broaden the application of the principle of good faith (in insurance contracts) to all contracts. He declared:[3]

The governing principle is applicable to all contracts and dealings. Good faith forbids either party by concealing what he privately knows, to draw the other into a bargain, from his

---

[3] *Carter v Boehm* (1766) 3 Burr 1905, 1910.

ignorance of that fact, and his believing the contrary. But either party may be innocently silent, as to grounds open to both, to exercise their judgment upon.

However, this approach did not survive. The general attitude of the courts and legislators in England in the nineteenth and twentieth centuries was one of laissez-faire, freedom of contract and party autonomy.

This development was paralleled in civil law countries, such as France, as well as in the United States.[4] The sanctity of contract gave priority to the values of predictability and foreseeability. The primary approach to the interpretation of contracts was also one of determining the meaning of contracts by reference to the ordinary meaning of words, abstracted from their context.

However, the emphasis on freedom of contract led on occasions to harsh results. In some countries, but not the United Kingdom, legislators sought to restore the balance by adopting a general duty of good faith in contracts. The idea was that it would allow sufficient discretion to the courts to intervene if justice so required. Good faith would serve two functions: first, as an interpretative tool in order to enforce the *real* bargain of the parties, and second (perhaps less accepted at the time), as a substantive duty to cooperate.

However, England did not follow such an approach. Rather, unfair situations called for targeted interventions. In 1989, Bingham LJ (later Lord Bingham) famously observed:[5]

In many civil law systems, and perhaps in most legal systems outside the common law world, the law of obligations recognises and enforces an overriding principle that in making and carrying out contracts parties should act in good faith. This does not simply mean that they should not deceive each other, a principle which any legal system must recognise; its effect is perhaps most aptly conveyed by such metaphorical colloquialisms as 'playing fair', 'coming clean' or 'putting one's cards face upwards on the table'. It is in essence a principle of fair and open dealing ... English law has, characteristically, committed itself to no such overriding principle but has developed piecemeal solutions in response to demonstrated problems of unfairness.

So there is no general duty of good faith but rather a series of piecemeal solutions. We can find many instances in contract law where, while not using the concept of an obligation to act in good faith, the law often comes to the same sort of conclusions it would have reached if English law recognized a general duty to act

---

[4] The French Code Civil, art 1134 states that between the parties 'contract is law'. In the US, the Restatement of Contracts (1932) adopted by the American Law Institute embodied a formalistic approach to contract interpretation and gap-filling. Indeed at the heart of the formalistic approach to contract interpretation was 'the plain meaning' rule and the 'parol evidence rule'. It was said then that 'commercial stability requires that parties to a contract may rely upon its express terms without worrying that the law will allow the other party to change the terms of the agreement at a later date': Harold Dubroff, 'The Implied Covenant of Good in Contractual Interpretation and Gap-filling: Reviling a Revered Relic' (2006) 80(2) St John's Law Review, Article 3, <http://scholarship.law.stjohns.edu/lawreview/vol80/iss2/3>, 569 citing the case of *Baker v Bailey* 782 P 2d 1286, 1288 (Mont 1989). Cf the principle of *aemulatio vicini* in Scots law, explained on p 24 of this volume.

[5] *Interfoto Picture Library Ltd v Stiletto Visual Programmes Ltd* [1989] 1 QB 433, 439 per Bingham LJ.

in good faith. For instance, a party may only recover losses attributable to a breach of contract. This rule is commonly, but inaccurately, referred to as a duty to mitigate.[6] In a system which recognizes a duty of good faith, a rule limiting the losses that may be claimed may be regarded simply as an instance of the duty to act fairly towards the other party, contrary to the normal common law rule that a party is entitled to exercise his or her rights as he or she thinks fit in his or her own interests. Likewise we have a principle that onerous and unusual terms in a contract must be fairly and reasonably drawn to a party's attention before they can be incorporated into a contract.[7] This, too, is contrary to the normal common law approach that a contract once signed is binding.

As I have said, substantially the same result may be achieved in these situations as if there were an obligation to act in good faith. So we can agree with Lord Hope that: 'The preferred approach in England is to avoid any commitment to over-arching principle, in favour of piecemeal solutions in response to demonstrated problems of unfairness.'[8]

Agreement to negotiate in good faith rejected

So where is the present hostility of English law to a general concept of good faith to be found? The best example is the decision of the House of Lords in *Walford v Miles*,[9] decided in 1992. This rejects the idea that there can be an implied duty of good faith and seems to throw rather a lot of cold water generally on the subject of good faith.

The essential fact in *Walford v Miles* was that the defendants had entered into an exclusivity agreement with the plaintiffs; that is, they had agreed to negotiate with them for the sale of the business on an exclusive basis. The defendants subsequently broke off negotiations and the question was whether they were liable for damages for breach of an implied term to negotiate in good faith. It was argued that the defendants could not terminate the negotiations unless they honestly believed that they had a good reason to do so.

There was one reasoned speech, that of Lord Ackner, with which the other members of the House agreed. The House effectively rejected a dictum of Lord Wright in *Hillas v Arcos Ltd*[10] that there could be a contract to negotiate. Lord Ackner held:[11]

The reason why an agreement to negotiate, like an agreement to agree, is unenforceable, is simply because it lacks the necessary certainty. The same does not apply to an agreement to use best endeavours. This uncertainty is demonstrated in the instant case by the provision

---

[6] *The Sorholt* [1983] 1 Lloyd's Rep 605.

[7] See *Interfoto* (n 5). A further example would be the situation where the court grants rectification because the parties made a common mistake as to the terms or effect of their agreement: see *Ahmad v Secret Gardens (Cheshire) Ltd* [2013] EWCA Civ 1005.

[8] *R (European Roma Rights) v Prague Immigration Office* [1995] 2 AC 1, 59.

[9] [1992] AC 128.   [10] 1932 147 LT 505, 515.   [11] *Walford* (n 9) 138.

which it is said has to be implied in the agreement for the determination of the negotiations. How can a court be expected to decide whether, *subjectively*, a proper reason existed for the termination of negotiations? The answer suggested depends upon whether the negotiations have been determined 'in good faith.' However the concept of a duty to carry on negotiations in good faith is inherently repugnant to the adversarial position of the parties when involved in negotiations. Each party to the negotiations is entitled to pursue his (or her) own interest, so long as he avoids making misrepresentations. To advance that interest he must be entitled, if he thinks it appropriate, to threaten to withdraw from further negotiations or to withdraw in fact, in the hope that the opposite party may seek to reopen the negotiations by offering him improved terms. Mr. Naughton, of course, accepts that the agreement upon which he relies does not contain a duty to complete the negotiations. But that still leaves the vital question—how is a vendor ever to know that he is entitled to withdraw from further negotiations? How is the court to police such an 'agreement?' A duty to negotiate in good faith is as unworkable in practice as it is inherently inconsistent with the position of a negotiating party. It is here that the uncertainty lies. In my judgment, while negotiations are in existence either party is entitled to withdraw from those negotiations, at any time and for any reason. There can be thus no obligation to continue to negotiate until there is a 'proper reason' to withdraw. Accordingly a bare agreement to negotiate has no legal content.[12]

This is a robust decision. As a result of *Walford v Miles*:

- A mere agreement to negotiate is too uncertain to be enforceable.
- A mere agreement to negotiate in good faith is no better. It is also too uncertain to be enforceable. The good faith relied on was purely subjective. The courts cannot determine when a person is acting in subjective bad faith in terminating negotiations since he is always free to exercise the power to withdraw from negotiations as he thinks fit. The right of a party to act in his own interests makes the duty to act in good faith meaningless and deprives it of any content.

However, the House of Lords was not saying that every agreement to negotiate was unenforceable. It would be enforceable if it was, for example:

- an agreement to negotiate for a particular period; or
- an agreement to use reasonable endeavours to come to an agreement as a result of the negotiations.

The latter is likely to be indistinguishable in practice from an agreement to negotiate in good faith. However, one part of the reasoning of Lord Ackner if taken literally would rule out any kind of obligation of good faith because the duty to negotiate in good faith is described as inherently repugnant to the adversarial position of the parties when involved in negotiations. That amounts to saying that the right to withdraw from negotiations, or, it would follow, any other right, could not be qualified by a good faith obligation because the right is one which is always exercisable by a contracting party in his own interests. That would rule out any restriction on the rights of a party as to how he or she exercises some particular right.

[12] *Walford* (n 9) 138C–G.

In my view, to read *Walford v Miles* in that way is to go far too far. We now know from a number of subsequent cases that if a party has some unilateral right under a contract, the court may find that he or she must exercise the rights in a particular way, whether it be reasonably or not perversely or honestly. Freedom of contract is also freedom to qualify the way contractual rights may be exercised. I will come to those cases shortly but for now the point I make is that the decision in *Walford v Miles* is driven by two things: the need for enforceable contractual obligations to be certain, and the right of a party to a contract to exercise his rights in his own best interests.

Turning point in the law in cases of contractual discretion

The next question is this: would the answer in *Walford v Miles* have been different if the obligation had not been one simply to negotiate but to exercise some contractual right and if the agreement expressly or by implication required this right to be exercised in a particular manner which takes into account to a greater or lesser extent the interests of the other contracting party?

The answer in terms of principle is that there is an important difference between the case in *Walford v Miles* and the case where there is a clause in the parties' agreement and it is this: for the court to say that such an agreement is unenforceable would be to frustrate the purpose of the agreement and that is a matter to which I want to return. The answer in the authorities (and these are the cases I alluded to a moment ago) is that there are cases where a contracting party has a right and the courts have imposed an obligation on him to exercise that right in an honest or not unreasonable way.[13] I will give three examples.

My first example is the decision to which I was a party in *Lymington Marina Ltd v MacNamara*.[14] This was an unusual case because it concerned licences for berths for boats on a marina. The first defendant held a ninety-eight-year licence. He wanted to execute sublicences in favour of his brothers for two successive periods. The approval of the landlord was necessary. We held that the landlord could only refuse to grant its approval to the grant by a tenant of a sublicence on grounds that related to the third party and his suitability to use the berth.

There was then a question whether there was any further restriction. Another subclause of the same clause of the licence enabled the landlord to refuse permission to assign in its absolute discretion—that is, without having to give any particular reason for its refusal. Those words did not apply to the power to grant or withhold approval to a sublicence for a limited period.

We held that the power to grant or withhold approval was, therefore, not one which the landlord could exercise at its sole discretion. We further held that, on the true interpretation of the licence, the power was required to be exercised honestly

[13] For a further analysis of these cases, see Richard Hooley, 'Controlling Contractual Discretion' (2013) 72 CLJ 65.
[14] [2007] Bus LR Digest D29.

and not arbitrarily. We preferred not to say, as the judge had done, that the landlord had also to act in a manner which was not unreasonable in the *Wednesbury* sense as this would import notions of public law into contract law. This raises a separate issue on which views may differ but which I do not have space to discuss here. The landlord had also an obligation to consider the application placed before it. These obligations, therefore, qualified the landlord's contractual obligation to approve sublicences.

Lymington Marina followed two earlier decisions, *The Product Star*[15] and *Gan Insurance Co Ltd v Tai Ping Insurance Co Ltd (No 2)*.[16] *The Product Star* contains an important dictum by Leggatt LJ recognizing that contractual discretions must be exercised in good faith and for a proper purpose. However, I take the *Gan* case as my second example. In that case, the Court of Appeal held that, where a reinsurer had a contractual discretion to withhold approval to a proposed settlement by the reinsured, a term was to be implied preventing the reinsurer from acting arbitrarily and requiring him to act in good faith. He also had to consider the facts giving rise to the particular claim, and to act without reference to factors which were extraneous to the subject-matter of the reinsurance. This case, too, is inconsistent with the idea that a party can always exercise his contractual rights solely in his own interests and as he thinks fit.

My third example is *Socimer International Bank Ltd v Standard Bank London Ltd*.[17] The facts were that on closing out forward exchange contracts, the seller had to value, and give credit for, securities belonging to the buyer which it held. The Court of Appeal held that the discretion was limited as a matter of necessary implication 'by concepts of honesty, good faith, and genuineness, and the need for the absence of arbitrariness, capriciousness, perversity and irrationality'.[18] All the further qualities mentioned by the Court of Appeal may in fact be encompassed within the concept of good faith.

These cases to my mind represent a turning point in our understanding of the impact of good faith in contract. They demonstrate that there is nothing inherently unenforceable or inherently impossible in law about an obligation to act in good faith.

However, they are all examples of unilateral rights. They are not cases where the parties' performance of their contractual obligations has been subjected to a duty to act in good faith. For authorities where the courts have had to consider whether parties' performance obligations were subject to any requirement to act in good faith, we have to look at two recent cases. These disclose different trends.

Two cases with opposing approaches to good faith

The first of these two cases is *Compass Group UK and Ireland Ltd v Mid-Essex Hospital Services NHS Trust Ltd*.[19] In this case, an NHS hospital trust ('the Trust')

---

[15] [1993] 1 Lloyd's Rep 397.   [16] [2001] 2 All ER (Comm) 299.
[17] [2008] 1 Lloyd's Rep 558.   [18] *Socimer* (n 17) para 66 per Rix LJ.
[19] [2012] EWCA Civ 781.

and a supplier of cleaning and other services entered into a contract for the provision of catering services. Under the contract the Trust had the right to award service failure points and make deductions from its monthly payments accordingly. The Trust had awarded itself an extraordinary number of service failure points for trivial failures, including an award of service failure points which led to a deduction of £84,540 for one-day old chocolate mousse which had passed its sell-by date. At trial the case for the supplier turned (so far as is relevant) on two issues. The first was whether the Trust was under an implied obligation not to exercise its contractual discretion to award service failure points in a manner which was 'arbitrary, irrational or capricious'. The second was whether, on its true construction, cl 3.5 of the contract imposed upon the parties a general duty of good faith.

Clause 3.5 obliged the parties to: 'co-operate with each other in good faith and to take all reasonable action as was necessary for the efficient transmission of information and instructions and to enable the Trust or any beneficiary to derive the full benefit of the contract'.[20]

The trial judge, Cranston J, was impressed by this clause. He reviewed a number of authorities, including Australian cases, which I do not have space to discuss in this chapter. The judge also held that the contractual discretion could not be exercised in a manner which was arbitrary, irrational, or capricious. With regard to the duty to cooperate in good faith in cl 3.5, the judge held that 'good faith' bore an objective, as well as a subjective, meaning and that the duty primarily encompassed faithfulness to the common purpose of the contract. He added that fair dealing, and acting consistently with the parties' justified expectations, were 'in a sense, corollaries of that'.

The Trust appealed. The Court of Appeal came to a different view on both of these points.[21] The Court of Appeal held that the contractual discretion to award service points was free from any obligation not to exercise it arbitrarily, capriciously, or irrationally, as this line of authority (in cases like *Gan* and *Socimer* which I have already discussed) could only apply if there was a discretion which involved an assessment or choosing from a range of options rather than having to decide whether to exercise an absolute right, which they considered the discretion to be. I have difficulty with this distinction because it does not sit easily with *Lymington Marina* which was not cited to the Court. As explained in that case, there was no range of options, simply a yes/no decision to approve the grant of a sublicence.

However, the Court also expressed the view that it would be difficult to exclude the obligation to exercise a discretion other than arbitrarily, capriciously, or irrationally. That may revive the argument that a good faith obligation is inherent in a contractual relationship in any event, but discussion of this point is beyond the scope of this chapter.

---

[20] *Compass Group UK and Ireland Ltd (trading as Medirest) v Mid Essex Hospital Services NHS Trust* [2012] EWHC 781 (QB), [2012] 2 All ER (Comm) 300, para 23.

[21] [2013] EWCA Civ 200.

As to the meaning of cl 3.5, the Court of Appeal came to a different conclusion from that of the trial judge. It held that the obligation of good faith was not an independent obligation but one focused on the two stated purposes, namely the efficient transmission of information and instructions and enabling the Trust or any beneficiary to derive the full benefit of the contract.[22] Accordingly, it did not apply to the award of service failure points. In reaching this conclusion the Court re-emphasized the point that there is 'no general doctrine of good faith in English contract law'.[23] As it happened, the award of excessive service failure points was caught by another provision in the contract.

The second of the two recent cases about good faith and performance obligations is the decision of the High Court in *Yam Seng Pte v International Trade Corporation Ltd*.[24] This was decided between the trial and the appeal in *Compass*. The facts were that a Singaporean distributor brought a claim for breach of contract against its English supplier. Leggatt J (not the Leggatt LJ in *The Product Star*) held that the parties had a number of implied obligations under a distribution agreement, for example not knowingly to give false information. He further held that these obligations were aspects of an implied obligation to perform the contract in good faith. He described English law as 'swimming against the tide':[25] civil law, like the law of the United States, Canada, New South Wales, and Scotland, recognizes a general doctrine of good faith.

This decision has attracted a great deal of attention in the United Kingdom. It goes into the previous cases in greater detail than is possible here. I propose simply to pull out certain points in it.

The judge addressed the relationship between good faith and implied terms. He observed that the modern case law on the construction of contracts has emphasized that contracts, like all human communications, are made against a background of unstated shared understandings which inform their meaning.[26] That 'background' consists of shared values,[27] norms of behaviour,[28] and expectations of honesty.[29]

In the course of this discussion, the judge particularly referred to relational contracts, that is, agreements to govern a long-term relationship such as distribution agreements. The judge took the view that these contracts involve high expectations of loyalty which are not legislated for in the express terms of the contract but which can be implied as a matter of business efficacy. The judge also referred to cases on contractual discretion. The judge concluded, perhaps surprisingly, that 'there is in my view nothing novel or foreign to English law in recognizing an implied duty of good faith in the performance of contracts'.[30]

The judge went on to make observations about the hostility of English law to the duty of good faith. In particular he saw the duty as case-sensitive, and that that was consistent with the common law method. In his view it would create no more

---

[22] *Mid Essex* (n 21) para 106 per Jackson LJ.　　[23] *Mid Essex* (n 21) para 105 per Jackson LJ.
[24] [2013] EWHC 111 (QB), [2013] 1 All ER (Comm) 1321.
[25] *Yam Seng* (n 24) para 124.　　[26] *Yam Seng* (n 24) para 133.
[27] *Yam Seng* (n 24) para 134.　　[28] *Yam Seng* (n 24) para 134.
[29] *Yam Seng* (n 24) para 135.　　[30] *Yam Seng* (n 24) para 145.

uncertainty than was inherent in the process of contractual interpretation. For my own part, that treats somewhat too lightly the problems of diminished certainty or the amount of time that might have to be spent in some cases in resolving disputes as to the application of the good faith clause.

Nonetheless, this decision is undoubtedly a welcome tour de force on good faith, and an important case to watch. It is not clear whether it will be appealed,[31] as the critical terms were in fact specific terms which could be implied in any event under the general principles applying to the implication of contractual terms. The Court of Appeal in *Compass* mentioned the decision in *Yam Seng*, but did not discuss it in any detail.

Before I turn to my concluding section, I shall consider some recent developments in the law of Singapore.

Law of Singapore

I am interested to see that Singapore contract law has also been undergoing change in recent years in the context of good faith clauses. First, in *Ng Giap Hon v Westcomb Securities Pte Ltd and Others*,[32] the Singapore Court of Appeal refused to imply a general duty of good faith. The case involved an agency agreement under which a stockbroking company authorized its agent to trade and deal in securities in return for a commission. The agent sued the company for commissions which he stated were due to him for certain clients but which the company had intercepted. He stated that in doing so the company breached its duty to act in good faith, a duty that he said was implied.

Phang JA, giving the judgment of the Court, analysed separately the possibility of a term implied in law and the possibility of a term implied in fact.[33] He held that 'implying a "term implied in law" into a contract involved broader policy considerations. It also established a precedent for the future. Put simply, the implication of such a term into a contract would entail implying the same term in the future for all contracts of the same type.'[34] This required extreme caution. As he held that the 'doctrine of good faith is very much a fledgling doctrine in English and (most certainly) Singapore contract law', he did not endorse an implied duty of good faith.

Phang JA also refused on the facts to imply a term that the company would not do anything to prevent the agent from earning his commission. He applied the usual test for implying a term in a particular factual matrix, namely necessity. The threshold for necessity is a high one. Insisting on the principle that judges will not rewrite contracts on the basis of their own sense of justice, Phang JA found that an implied term of good faith was not necessary in this case.

The decision was a disappointment to some who thought that there was a missed opportunity to introduce the doctrine of good faith into Singapore law.[35]

---

[31] No judgment on appeal had been given by July 2015.   [32] [2009] 3 SLR (R) 518.
[33] *Ng Giap Hon* (n 32) paras 35–40.   [34] *Ng Giap Hon* (n 32) para 46.
[35] See for example Louis Joseph, 'A Doctrine of Good Faith in Singapore?' [2012] Singapore Journal of Legal Studies 416.

Second, and most recently, Singapore courts have upheld an express duty to negotiate in good faith. *HSBC Institutional Trust Services (Singapore) Ltd (Trustee of Starhill Global Real Estate Investment Trust) v Toshin Development Singapore Pte Ltd*[36] concerned a rent review mechanism in a lease agreement under which the rent for each new rental term after the first rental term had to be determined by agreement between the landlord and tenant, or failing agreement, by designated valuers. The clause provided that parties 'shall in good faith endeavour to agree on the prevailing market rental value of the Demised Premises' prior to the appointment of the designated valuers. VK Rajah JA, giving the judgment of the Court, held:[37]

In our view, notwithstanding Lord Ackner's statement in *Walford* (at 138) that '[a] duty to negotiate in good faith is . . . unworkable in practice', that case does not have the effect of invalidating an express term in a contract which employs the language of good faith (see [40]–[41] below). As a preliminary observation, we are of the view that a valid distinction can be drawn between the pre-contractual negotiations in *Walford* and the 'negotiations' between the Parties under the Rent Review Exercise in the present case.

The Singapore Court of Appeal upheld the good faith clause. Interestingly, it considered the broader impact of upholding a principle of good faith in contracts:[38]

In our view, there is no good reason why an express agreement between contracting parties that they must negotiate in good faith should not be upheld. First, such an agreement is valid because it is not contrary to public policy. Parties are free to contract unless prohibited by law. Indeed, we think that such 'negotiate in good faith' clauses are in the public interest as they promote the consensual disposition of any potential disputes. We note, for instance, that it is fairly common practice for Asian businesses to include similar clauses in their commercial contracts . . . We think that the 'friendly negotiations' and 'confer in good faith' clauses . . . are consistent with our cultural value of promoting consensus whenever possible. Clearly, it is in the wider public interest in Singapore as well to promote such an approach towards resolving differences. The second reason why we are of the view that 'negotiate in good faith' clauses should be upheld is that even though the fact that one party may not want to negotiate in good faith (for whatever reason) will lead to a breakdown in negotiations, no harm is done because the dispute can still be resolved in some other way.

Thus the Singapore Court has expressly sought to integrate the concept of good faith into Singapore's legal and cultural framework. In the result, this case develops the law in a not dissimilar way to that in which it has been developed in some of the more recent English cases to which I have referred.

What does the future hold?

In the eleventh century, Canute, the King of England, set his throne by the seashore and commanded the tide to halt and not wet his feet, but of course the tide failed to stop. In fact this was a subtle ploy to show his courtiers that they

---

[36] [2012] 4 SLR 738. [37] *HSBC* (n 36) para 37. [38] *HSBC* (n 36) para 40.

were fools to think he was all powerful and that he was well aware of their flattery. However, the story is usually cited as an example of the failure to face reality.

The story has some resonance as English law engages with external influences and considers whether to make changes or hope to ride out the forces of change. The strategy of trying to ride out the forces of change has sometimes been successful but sometimes it has led to a retreat of stout party, as in the recent unsuccessful battle in the Supreme Court over the reception of Art 8 jurisprudence in the context of social housing. The Supreme Court decided in the end that it had to accept the principle of Convention case law that a person, who was about to be evicted in accordance with the landlord's rights under domestic law, had to have an opportunity to be able to pursue a serious defence in court that the eviction would interfere *in a disproportionate way* with his right to respect for his home.[39]

English law is these days subject to global influence, particularly new legislation coming from the European Union. The requirement of good faith is prevalent in the majority of the civil law systems of the European Union. Unsurprisingly therefore, the duty of good faith has been incorporated into legislation of the European Union itself. Most notable (and controversial at the time) is the example of the Unfair Terms in Consumer Contracts Regulation 1999. Regulation 5(1) states that a contractual term will be 'unfair' if 'contrary to the requirement of good faith, it causes a significant imbalance in the parties' rights and obligations arising under the contract, to the detriment of the consumer.' Recital 16 of the preamble to the directive giving rise to these regulations states that the requirement of good faith is satisfied where the consumer is equitably and fairly dealt with. Fairness is to be determined by reference to the subject-matter, the circumstances of the case, and other terms of the contract. The good faith requirement here relates to the conduct of the parties, rather than being an interpretative principle, and the House of Lords has confirmed that it requires both procedural and substantive fairness in contracting.[40]

A further example is the Commercial Agents Directive[41] which sets the standard of the agents' duties to their principals according to which an 'agent must...act dutifully and in good faith'.[42] The Court of Justice of the European Union ('Luxembourg Court') has also referred to 'good faith' as a 'principle of civil law'.[43]

Most recently, Art 2 of the proposed Common European Sales Law imposes a duty on each party to act in accordance with good faith and fair dealing; a duty which cannot be excluded.[44] Good faith and fair dealing is also used in clauses on

---

[39] *Manchester City Council v Pinnock* [2011] 2 AC 104.

[40] *Director General of Fair Trading v First National Bank plc* [2001] UKHL 52, [2002] 1 AC 481.

[41] 1986/653/EEC.

[42] See also Financial Services Distance Marketing Directive 2002/65/EU referring to 'principles of good faith in commercial transaction' in setting information which a supplier must provide to a consumer before concluding the contract; and Unfair Commercial Practices Directive 2005/29/EU which defines 'unfair commercial practice' by (indirect) reference to good faith.

[43] C-489/07 *Messmer v Kruuger* [2009] ECR I-7315, para 26.

[44] Proposal for a Regulation of the European Parliament and of the Council on a Common European Sales Law Com (2011) 635 final, Annex I, CESL Proposal, Annex I, Art 2 CESL.

the duty to provide information in commercial contracts, mistake, fraud, contractual interpretation, the implication of terms, and unfair contract terms.

The negative side of EU legislation is that it may, in a worst case scenario, require us to abandon some of the principles of the common law. One of the ways of countering this risk is indeed to develop our own body of case law which can be used to influence the development of new laws in the European Union. There is probably little that we can say about the requirements of good faith in English law at the present time because we have no coherent body of law to offer. Developing some principles of good faith would, therefore, strengthen the influence of the common law in the development of EU law but those principles would of course have to be consistent with the ethos of the common law.

On the positive side I would add that it should not be supposed that the influence of the laws of other member states is always negative: there are matters which we can learn from civil systems, and ideas that we can borrow, such as the concept of proportionality, which is now being used in many areas of English law.

Comparative study of legal systems and laws can help us to widen our horizons as to what makes for good law. It is like learning new languages. As Goethe said, 'A man who has no acquaintance with foreign languages knows nothing of his own.'[45]

The principal objection to introducing a concept of good faith into English law is that it would bring with it uncertainty, delay, and expense if the question of what the concept meant in any given case had to be litigated. But I have only been considering the question of contracts where parties have opted for an obligation of good faith. Where they do so expressly, they have really only themselves to blame if they do not provide sufficient guidance to enable them to work out when there has been a breach.

There is also the principled answer to this point, namely that certainty is not a trump card that defeats all other principles in contract law. Of course certainty and predictability are qualities of English commercial law but they are not the be-all and end-all of contract law. In the *Golden Strait* case,[46] the issue was whether in the assessment of damages the Court could take into account matters reducing the loss but occurring after the renunciation of the contract. The majority thought that the 'breach date rule', which excluded subsequently occurring events, had to give way to the principle that damages should simply compensate the claimant for his loss. Lord Scott, giving the leading speech, rejected the argument that this would render the law uncertain in these trenchant terms: 'Certainty is a desideratum and a very important one, particularly in commercial contracts. But it is not a principle and must give way to principle.'[47] Likewise, in the field of good faith clauses, certainty may have to yield in appropriate cases to the principle of giving effect to the parties' agreement in accordance with the principle of party autonomy.

---

[45] Johann Wolfgang Von Goethe, *Maxims and Reflections*, Bailey Saunders (trans) (The MacMillan Company, 1906) 154.
[46] *Golden Strait Corp v Nippon Yusen Kubishika Kaisha* [2007] 2 AC 353.
[47] *Golden Strait* (n 46) 384.

Fundamentally I consider that the law is already slowly developing in a way which can accommodate the concept of good faith within contract law. Take, for example, the law of contractual interpretation. Until recently, documents were interpreted without reference to the background of fact against which they were made. Now, following the decision of the House of Lords in *Investors' Compensation Scheme Ltd v West Bromwich Building Society*,[48] courts are required to interpret documents against the background of material facts. They do this in order to ascertain the meaning which a reasonable person in the position of the parties and having the knowledge of the background which they had, or ought to have had, would give to them. Thus, in the field of interpretation of contractual documents, the courts have come to recognize, if they had not already done so, that there is another important principle, alongside certainty and party autonomy, which underlies contract law, namely the need for the court where possible to give effect to the parties' reasonable expectations. This is properly regarded as a principle. The same point can be made about the implication of terms, which has been subsumed within the scope of interpretation of contracts.[49]

I would apply the principle of giving effect to the reasonable expectations of the parties to the debate on good faith clauses in the following way. If the parties have agreed that contractual obligations should be performed in good faith, the court should, so far as it can, give effect to that agreement and, by doing so, to the parties' reasonable expectations.

There is strong support for this approach from one of our most outstanding commercial judges, Lord Steyn. Lord Steyn stressed the view in his Azlan Shah lecture in 1996 that, if the point in *Walford v Miles* arose again for decision, it should not be rejected out of hand. He considered that respect for the reasonable expectations of the parties made it unnecessary to adopt any general concept of good faith:[50]

As long as our courts always respect the reasonable expectations of parties our contract law can satisfactorily be left to develop in accordance with its own pragmatic traditions. And where in specific contexts duties of good faith are imposed on parties our legal system can readily accommodate such a well-tried notion. After all, there is not a world of difference between the objective requirement of good faith and the reasonable expectations of the parties.

That is very strong support indeed for the development of the concept of good faith or its equivalent, and for doing so, as I would myself wish to do, within the values and traditions of the common law. There are other very eminent judges who have also supported the introduction of good faith.

I would go further. We have long since ceased to believe that there is one approach to contract law which will suit all sets of contracting parties. Where, for

---

[48] [1998] 1 WLR 896.

[49] *Attorney General v Belize Telecom Ltd* [2009] 3 LRC 577, [2009] UKPC 10.

[50] Lord Steyn, 'Contract Law: Fulfilling the Reasonable Expectations of Honest Men' (1997) 113 LQR 433, 439.

instance, there is an inequality of bargaining power, the courts and the legislature have now intervened and adopted or developed principles to redress the balance.

As we have seen, we have also already come part way down the path we need to follow in the context of contractual discretions. The English courts now recognize that there is no inalienable right for the party entitled to the discretion to exercise the discretion in his own best interests: see the *Lymington Marina* and other cases.

We need to recognize more generally that there are some contracting situations where the parties expressly do not want to give each other the right to take decisions exclusively in their own interests. We saw this in the building contracts to which I referred at the start of this chapter. The types of contract that I have in mind are likely to be long-term contracts where the parties cannot, or do not wish to, prescribe in stone all their requirements at the date the contract is made.[51]

Parties in these cases, as we have seen, now sometimes and maybe often expressly agree to cooperate in how they will perform the contract or indeed in how they will reach agreement during the course of the contract, for example for a revised price structure over the term of the contract. These parties are not, therefore, looking for a model of contract law which will enable them to take advantage of the other— quite the opposite. They are not expecting to be told that their agreement to cooperate is meaningless and that either party is free to exercise his contractual rights as he or she thinks fit.

This reasoning provides a suitable normative framework for the development of good faith. Reasonable certainty will have to be provided for in the contract. Thus the parties will probably have to provide the court with benchmarks which it can apply to determine whether there has been cooperation of the type which they desire to have.

As I see it, there could also be economic advantages in providing a more appropriate structure for cooperative arrangements. It would lead to stability in these arrangements and this may produce cost benefits as well as more secure employment. Our relatively new statutory codification of directors' duties requires directors to have regard to the long-term consequences of their actions. This is some confirmation of the economic desirability of long-termism. The new principle was called 'enlightened self-interest' to replace what was previously seen as the naked self-interest of companies. *Walford v Miles* was a case where great value was set on the principle of contractual law of freedom to act in accordance with naked self-interest.

The time has therefore come to recognize that, while these are not vulnerable parties, there are parties who agree on good faith clauses or their near cousin, cooperation clauses, and who seek a different principle to apply to their contracts.

---

[51] For an example in this category, see *McKillen v Misland (Cyprus) Investments Ltd* [2013] EWCA Civ 781, [2013] 2 BCLC 583. This judgment, which was delivered after the lecture on which this chapter is based, illustrates three possible functions of an express term to act in good faith: as an interpretative tool, as a substantive obligation, and as a provision filling gaps in what the parties have agreed. These various functions of a good faith clause are helpfully analysed in Howard O Hunter, 'The Growing Uncertainty about Good Faith in American Contract Law' (2004) 20 Journal of Contract Law 50.

We should recognize this expressly. We should seek to develop a body of law which will deliver this. To do so will give our law a new option, a new flexibility, which will make it more, not less, attractive in the global marketplace for commercial law.

I also attach considerable importance to the role of the independent judiciary. It is crucial for judges to seek to develop the law in line with evolving commercial and social need. It is part of their responsibility to have a vision of the law as a dynamic, not a static, set of principles and rules, to see the big picture and overall trends, and to have a sharp eye for what is coming over the horizon rather than simply that which has served us well in the past.

To develop the law incrementally along the lines I have suggested in this chapter will also deliver on the role and responsibility of the independent judiciary as I see it to be.

4

Economic Torts in the Twenty-first Century

This chapter is based on a lecture given to the Association of Law Teachers on 14 October 2005.*

Recognizing the contribution of academics and legal theory

Although the subject of economic torts is arcane, it is well worth discussing, as recent case law suggests that it is a field ripe for development, and indeed it is in the course of development. In this chapter I cannot hope to cover all of the battlefield, but I hope I will leave you with some food for thought.[1]

I would like to begin by paying tribute to the work of scholars in this field. There are many who have contributed but those best known are Hazel Carty, who has written a brilliant monograph, *An Analysis of the Economic Torts*,[2] Peter Cane, who wrote *Tort Law and Economic Interests*,[3] and Tony Weir, who has given a series of lectures on Economic Torts, published as *Economic Torts*.[4] Others have written passages in text books and notes in learned journals. I have not by any means read them all. However, I would like to express my debt to these scholars. Development of the law in this area is undoubtedly assisted by their work. That is not to say that the courts can simply adopt ideas wholesale. As in any field, the courts will simply use that part of an idea which in their judgment reflects the law. In the same way, it is my view that the analysis of problems in commercial law can on occasions

---

* Published as Mary Arden, 'Economic Torts in the Twenty-first Century' (2006) 40(1) Law Teacher 1. Reproduced here by kind permission of Taylor & Francis Ltd.

[1] While, as explained in this chapter, some changes have occurred since this text was written, it continues to provide food for thought concerning the background to those changes and so it remains relevant to any further development.

[2] Hazel Carty, *An Analysis of the Economic Torts* (Oxford University Press, 2001). A second edition of this work was published by Oxford University Press in 2010, but references to the first edition are retained in this chapter. Carty's view remains that economic torts should be narrowly defined in the interests of commercial certainty, and that their role is to police excessive competitive behaviour. In an even more recent publication, she has criticized the decision of the House of Lords in *Total Network SL v Revenue and Customs Commissioners* [2008] UKHL, [2008] 1 AC 1174 (see n 14), which in her view has led to the tort of unlawful means conspiracy having a wider role for reasons which are obscure: see Hazel Carty, 'The Modern Functions of Economic Torts: Reviewing the English, Canadian, Australian, and New Zealand Positions' (2015) 74 CLJ 261.

[3] Peter Cane, *Tort Law and Economic Interests* (2nd edn, Clarendon Press, 1996).

[4] Tony Weir, *Economic Torts* (Clarendon Press, 1997).

be enriched by reference to law and economics. Legal rules affect behaviour. For example, an employer who is about to recruit an executive working for someone else will probably consult his lawyers in case he becomes liable to the old employer. But, if liability is too easily imposed on the prospective employer, then mobility of the workforce may be impeded. This is because employers do not want to undertake the risk of liability to the old employer or to incur the costs of taking legal advice on the occasion of every hiring. On the other hand, if there is no liability in any circumstances, prospective employers may act without regard to generally accepted standards of behaviour. The imposition of legal liability can in appropriate circumstances provide an incentive to observe proper standards of conduct. But it would not be possible to adopt the theory of law and economics wholesale or to use it otherwise than as a supplementary means of analysis.

Putting names to economic torts

As anyone who reads any of the leading academic texts on economic torts will quickly discover, there is a great deal of debate about the function, and ingredients, of economic torts. There is also debate about which torts fall into this category. Among the torts usually given this description are conspiracy, inducement of breach of contract, intimidation, unlawful interference with trade, deceit, passing off, and malicious falsehood. Economic torts such as conspiracy are torts of intention. Some economic torts are not torts of intention, such as passing off. In this chapter I consider the following economic torts: (1) inducing breach of contract, (2) conspiracy, (3) intimidation, and (4) unlawful interference with trade. Indeed most of my discussion will relate to inducing breach of contract. I shall therefore not be dealing with deceit, malicious falsehood, or passing off. Economic torts are often compared and discussed in combination with torts involving an abuse of power such as malicious prosecution and misfeasance in public office, but I will not be dealing with these save in passing.

Characteristics of this group

My selection of the group which I have mentioned is based on convenience not on the view that these torts necessarily form a coherent group. In some cases, they contain inconsistent requirements. They also contain areas of uncertainty. I prefer to present these torts, to use an expression recently used by Tony Weir in relation to the economic torts as a whole,[5] as an archipelago rather than as a continent, that is, as a series of specific torts developed to deal with particular situations. I would just like to repeat that word 'specific' because it is a word that I shall be using again in relation to the requirement for intention in relation to these torts. These torts are not there simply to fill the gaps thought to be left by other torts. On my approach,

---

[5] Tony Weir, 'An Analysis of the Economic Torts' (2002) 118 LQR 164.

there is no generalized tort of injury to economic interests. There are simply pockets of liability within these particular areas.

But, to go back to Tony Weir's metaphor, even islands in an archipelago tend to have features which they share in common. So it is with the economic torts which I have chosen. There are common threads between them and one of the questions that this area of law raises is whether there ought to be more common threads running between them.

The function of economic torts

I have of course to outline each of the torts with which I am concerned but before I do so it may help if I make some attempt to describe the function of these torts in the law of tort. Hazel Carty says in chapter 1 of her work, that 'the economic torts, as their name suggests, have as their primary function the protection of economic interests'. I am happy to adopt that statement of function for the purpose of this lecture. Of course it would be an over-generalization to say that economic torts are always concerned with the protection of economic interests or that all economic interests are protected. That could not be. If all economic interests were given the same level of protection, individual freedoms would be restricted and there would be liabilities attaching to the normal conduct of business transactions.

Let me give a simple example of what I mean. Suppose Tom makes an oral offer to buy a flat which Dick the seller accepts, Tom has an economic interest in Dick entering into a binding contract with him to sell that flat to him at the price which they have agreed. But as a matter of law that contract is not binding until a written contract is signed complying with s 2 of the Law of Property (Miscellaneous Provisions) Act 1989. If Harry comes along before they sign the necessary contract and makes a higher offer, the seller must be free to accept it, and it would be limiting the seller's freedom of contract if the position were otherwise. Indeed, it would undermine the legislative policy behind s 2 of the 1989 Act if Harry had to pay damages to Tom if Dick enters into a contract with Harry simply because he (Harry) knows of the prior offer by Tom, or even if he made his offer specifically intending to harm Tom's interests. So economic torts do not protect all economic interests. They do not in general compensate a party for disappointed expectations. There have to be limits on the protection of economic interests.

Now in speaking of the function of economic torts in this way, I should make it clear that I am taking no account of the long history which these torts have had in labour law. Anyone who wants to know about that area should read, for instance, the contribution on labour law by the late Professor Otto Kahn-Freund in *Law and Opinion in England in the Twentieth Century*.[6]

---

[6] Otto Kahn-Freund, 'Labour Law' in Morris Ginsberg (ed), *Law and Opinion in England in the Twentieth Century* (Stevens & Sons, 1959).

Ingredients of the economic torts selected

In order to make clear what I want to say about the economic torts which I have selected I have to describe them in relatively simple terms. I am not promising anything more than a thumbnail sketch.

Inducing breach of contract

I shall have to qualify virtually everything I say about the ingredients of this tort as I go through them because it has been the subject of considerable expansion and debate, but I have to start somewhere. There are two forms of this tort, namely direct inducement of a breach of contract and indirect inducement of a breach of contract. An inducement is said to be direct when one of the contracting parties is procured or persuaded to breach his contract. An inducement is said to be indirect where a person who is not a party to that contract is induced or procured to act in a particular way so as to have an effect on the claimant's contracting party or contract. The classic example is where the defendant induces employees to break their contracts so that the employer of those employees cannot fulfil his contract with the claimant. This is the form of economic tort in issue in *D.C. Thomson v Deakin*.[7]

Here is the first qualification: Hazel Carty argues that the indirect form of tort should be treated as part of the tort of interference with business. Tony Weir has taken the same view. There is much force in the argument that the indirect form of the tort is really a form of the tort of unlawful interference with a trade or business. However the distinction is well known and it would be confusing not to treat it as part of the tort of inducing breach of contract in this chapter. The importance of the distinction is that where the inducement is indirect, unlawful means have to be shown. This form of the tort was crystallized in *D.C. Thomson v Deakin*, mentioned earlier, in which Upjohn J was the first instance judge. A trade union called for employees of Bowaters to go on strike. The employees then told Bowaters that that they might not be able to deliver paper due to be delivered to the plaintiff. The paper was not delivered. The plaintiff sought damages from the officials of the trade union. The Court of Appeal set out the requirements for the indirect inducement of a breach of contract but held that the union was not liable on the facts because they had not procured the employees to breach their contracts with Bowaters, which would have been unlawful means for this purpose.

There is a certain amount of lack of clarity about what conduct constitutes unlawful means for this purpose. It may be that unlawful means are limited to means which are tortious and to breaches of contract procured by the defendant and not other unlawful acts which could constitute unlawful means for the purpose of the tort of conspiracy.

---

[7] *Thomson (D.C.) & Co Ltd v Deakin* [1952] Ch 646.

For the purposes of the tort of inducing breach of contract there has to be actual persuasion or procurement by words or conduct. The mere provision of advice or information or the facilities for the commission of a breach is not enough. Persuasion, inducement, or procural of the breach is needed. I am going to call this the 'inducement' point and I will refer to it later.

The defendant has to know of the contract and that his persuasion will cause a breach. This is illustrated by *British Industrial Plastics v Ferguson*.[8] In that case, the ex-employee of the plaintiffs approached the defendants with some trade secrets. The defendants knew that they were trade secrets belonging to the plaintiffs but 'illogically and muddle-headedly' considered that they would be entitled to use them if they were patentable. They were mistaken in this view, but, because of their lack of knowledge that what they proposed would involve a breach of the obligations owed by the ex-employee to his employer, they were not liable for the tort of inducing breach of contract. It did not matter that their view was wholly unreasonable in this regard.

There has to be an intention to cause harm. I will be coming to what this entails later. Harm for this purpose is a breach of contract. In the case of direct inducement, the relevant contract is the contract between the person induced and the claimant. In the case of indirect inducement the relevant contract is the contract between the claimant and the person whose actions were driven by the person induced. As we shall see, there has been an issue as to whether this is 'targeted' harm, that is, whether the claimant has to show that the defendant had a specific intention to cause him harm. I will be illustrating this issue later by reference to *Millar v Bassey*.[9]

I need to make yet another qualification. I have called this tort 'inducing breach of contract'. There are other forms of civil wrongs which can be induced and give rise to liability, for example breach of statutory or fiduciary duty. Moreover the contract need not always be breached. How far this goes is a matter of debate but certainly, in *Merkur Island Shipping Corporation v Laughton*,[10] the House of Lords held that the tort of inducing breach of contract was committed even where no actual breach of contract resulted from the inducement because there was a clause in the contract exempting the plaintiff from liability. In this case a trade union was sued by the owners of a ship for having persuaded the employees of a tug owner not to tow the plaintiff's ship out of port. The ship was subject to a charter. The terms of the charter provided that the ship was to proceed with the utmost despatch but that there should be no liability in the circumstances which arose. The question was whether the trade union was liable for interfering with the performance of the charter. Lord Diplock, with whom all the other members of the House agreed, referred to *Torquay Hotel Co v Cousins*.[11] He continued:

That was a case in which the contract the performance of which was interfered with was one for the delivery of fuel. It contained a force majeure clause excusing the seller from liability for non-delivery if delayed, hindered or prevented by, inter alia, labour disputes. Lord Denning MR stated the principle thus:

---

[8] [1940] 1 All ER 479.   [9] [1994] EMLR 44.
[10] [1983] 2 AC 570.   [11] [1969] 2 Ch 106.

'...there must be *interference* in the execution of a contract. The interference is not confined to the procurement of a breach of contract. It extends to a case where a third person prevents or hinders one party from performing his contract, even though it be not a breach.' (Lord Denning's emphasis)

In inducing breach of contract, justification may be a defence. Thus, in the well-known case of *Brimelow v Casson*,[12] it was held that the defendant was not liable for damages for inducing breach of contract where he induced the proprietors of theatres not to employ chorus girls employed by the plaintiff who were so poorly paid that they might be driven to supplement their earnings by prostitution. But this was a very exceptional case and it is unlikely that justification can often be shown.

Conspiracy

There are two kinds of conspiracy. First there is the tort of what one can call simple conspiracy constituted by two ingredients: (1) an agreement between two or more persons to cause harm to the claimant in a way that does not involve any unlawful means; and (2) damage caused by the actions of the conspirators pursuant to that agreement. A heightened form of intent is required here, namely a sole or predominant intention to cause harm to the claimant. The fact no unlawful means has to be shown is often said to be anomalous. One of the reasons given by the courts for the imposition of liability in the case of simple conspiracy is that 'a combination may make oppressive or dangerous that which if it proceeded from a single individual would be otherwise, and the very fact of combination may show that the object is simply to do harm, and not to exercise one's own just rights'.[13] If we return to the example of Tom, Dick, and Harry, the effect of the law on conspiracy is that if there was an agreement between Dick and Harry, that Harry should make an offer which by its acceptance would mean that Tom would lose the flat, the tort of conspiracy might be committed, but if and only if Dick and Harry had as their sole or predominant intention the intention of harming Tom as opposed to serving some interest of their own.

The other kind of conspiracy is a conspiracy to cause harm by unlawful means. Here again there must be an agreement between two or more persons which causes damage to the claimant, but there is no requirement here to show that the conspirators had as their sole or predominant aim an intention to harm the claimant. However, unlawful means must be used and this means that there must probably be tortious conduct or a breach of contract actionable by the claimant. In this context, the unlawful means may include the commission of a crime, but it may be that the crime has to be one which gives rise to a civil remedy actionable by the claimant.[14]

---

[12] [1924] 1 Ch 302.

[13] *Mogul Steamship Co v McGregor, Gow & Co* (1889) 23 QBD 598, 616 per Bowen LJ.

[14] In *Total Network SL v Revenue and Customs Commissioners* (n 2), the House of Lords held criminal conduct, at common law or by statute, could constitute unlawful means for the purposes of unlawful means conspiracy, provided that it was the means of intentionally inflicting harm, rather than being merely incidental to it. This may extend the rationale and scope of economic torts.

Interference with trade or business

This tort is constituted where the defendant uses unlawful means to interfere with the claimant's trade or business falling short of an actual breach of contract. The conduct must cause harm to the claimant. As Hazel Carty says in her work: 'The magic of the tort of unlawful interference is to allow the claimant, though indirectly attacked via a third party, to sue on his own behalf.'[15]

Intimidation

The tort of intimidation occurs where the defendant threatens to do something which is unlawful as against the person to whom the threat is delivered as a result of which that person takes steps which he is entitled to take and causes damage to himself or another party. The remarkable thing about this tort is that liability stems from the making of threats. The leading case on this tort is *Rookes v Barnard*.[16]

Limits on the protection of economic interests

I have already made the point that there cannot be absolute protection of economic interests. In the torts with which I am concerned, limits are placed on the protection of economic interests in a variety of ways, for example by requiring the claimant to show that the conduct of the defendant was of a particular kind or that the defendant had an intention of a particular nature. The defence of justification also limits the scope of these torts.

One specific requirement imposed by the courts which limits the protection which the law gives to economic interests is a requirement that the claimant must show that the defendant should have an intention to harm the claimant. For many years there has been a question mark here as to the type of intention required. For example at page 105 of her work, Hazel Carty notes that there are 'competing views' on the proper definition of intention for the purposes of unlawful interference with trade. On one view, a wide definition of intentional harm would include foresight of inevitable or even probable consequences. Another view would favour a narrow definition requiring deliberate harm, with the defendant targeting the claimant. A question mark has also hung over the tort of inducing breach of contract. Must the claimant show that the defendant knew of the contract and sufficient about its terms to anticipate a breach and that his conduct induced the breach of contract? Or must a claimant go further and show that the defendant specifically intended that that breach should occur?

---

[15] Carty, *An Analysis of Economic Torts* (n 2) 103.   [16] [1964] AC 1129.

The problem about intention is best illustrated by examining the oft-cited case of *Millar v Bassey*. The case concerns the well-known singer Shirley Bassey. She had a contract to make a recording with a recording company which employed the plaintiffs, who were musicians. Before the recording was made, Shirley Bassey received an invitation for a lucrative engagement which made it impossible for her to continue with her contract to make a recording and so she terminated her contract with the recording company. The recording company in turn broke its contracts with the plaintiff musicians and they brought an action for damages against Shirley Bassey for inducing breach of contract. The issue was whether the claim disclosed a cause of action. The pleadings did not allege that she had acted with an intention to cause damage to the musicians or that her actions were directed to them.

The Court of Appeal by a majority declined to strike out as disclosing no cause of action a statement of claim against Shirley Bassey. The judges were three former Chairmen of the Law Commission of England and Wales: Beldam, Ralph Gibson, and Peter Gibson LJJ. The Court left for trial the question whether it had to be shown that Miss Bassey intended to damage the plaintiffs or whether it was enough that she had acted deliberately and that she knew that the probable consequence of her acts was that the recording company could not perform its contract with the plaintiffs. Beldam LJ held that it was unnecessary for the plaintiffs to assert that Miss Bassey had any specific intention to interfere with the plaintiffs' contracts with the second defendant. However, Peter Gibson LJ, in his famous dissenting judgment, held that the plaintiffs had to assert that Miss Bassey intended to interfere with the plaintiffs' contracts with the recording company, not merely that such interference would result from her actions. He contrasted deliberate interference with a contract with a view to bringing about its breach, which was conduct targeted at the claimant, with interference with a contract which was merely an incidental consequence of the defendant's conduct. The third member of the court, Ralph Gibson LJ, considered that the point about intention had not been clearly decided and for that reason the proceedings should not be allowed to go to trial and not be struck out summarily.

So the crucial issue on which the judges divided was whether, to induce a breach of contract, the defendant had merely to have known of the breach or must have had a specific intention of harming that contract by his persuasion.

I would like to add that Hazel Carty makes the point that the 'inducement' point might also have arisen if the case had gone to trial since it was not by any means clear that Shirley Bassey had procured the recording company to break the plaintiffs' contracts. The problem of what constitutes inducement is a problem which arises in this tort generally and needs clarification by the courts.

The issue of the intention required in economic torts, raised in the context of inducing breach of contract by *Millar v Bassey*, was considered in a decision of the Court of Appeal handed down in May 2005, namely *Douglas v Hello! Ltd*.[17] This

---

[17] [2005] EWCA Civ 595 (Lord Phillips MR and Clarke and Neuberger LJJ).

very important decision has helped to clarify the issue of intention for the purpose of the torts which I am discussing.

Douglas v Hello!

This decision concerned the question of the liability of Hello! magazine for the use of photographs of the wedding of the celebrities Michael Douglas and Catherine Zeta-Jones (whom I will call the Douglases). The Douglases had sold the exclusive right to use photographs of their wedding to the magazine OK! But Hello! obtained some unauthorized photographs which they were able to publish first. So far as material the Court of Appeal held that the publication of these photographs was a breach of confidence vis-à-vis the Douglases.[18] The question then arose whether on the facts as found by the trial judge, Hello!, the publisher of the photographs taken in breach of confidence, was liable for the economic torts of conspiracy and interference with the economic or other interests between the Douglases and OK!. I need not summarize any of this Court's holdings on breach of confidence, save that this Court concluded that Hello! was not liable to OK! for damages for breach of confidence[19] but that the breach of confidence vis-à-vis the Douglases could constitute unlawful means for the purposes of an action for conspiracy by unlawful means, or unlawful interference with business brought by OK!.

Paragraphs 152 to 236 of the judgment of the Court, however, are concerned with OK!'s claim based on the economic torts of unlawful interference with business and conspiracy by unlawful means.

In these paragraphs, the Court of Appeal conducted an overview of the case law on intention in all economic torts. At paragraph 159, the Court noted that there were several contenders for intention to injure in the context of the tort of unlawful interference:

a) an intention to cause economic harm to the claimant as an end in itself;
b) an intention to cause economic harm to the claimant because it is a necessary means of achieving some ulterior motive;
c) knowledge that the course of conduct undertaken will have the inevitable consequence of causing the claimant economic harm;
d) knowledge that the course of conduct will probably cause the claimant economic harm;
e) knowledge that the course of conduct undertaken may cause the claimant economic harm coupled with reckless indifference as to whether it does or not.

The Court explained that a course of conduct undertaken with an intention that satisfies test a) or b) can be said to be 'aimed', 'directed', or 'targeted' at the claimant. Causing the claimant economic harm will be a specific object of the conduct in question. A course of conduct which only satisfies test c) could not of itself be said to be so aimed, directed, or targeted, because the economic harm, although inevitable, would be no more than an incidental consequence, at least from the defendant's perspective. The Court nonetheless recognized that, the fact

---

[18] *Douglas* (n 17) paras 122–137.   [19] *Douglas* (n 17) paras 226–236.

that the economic harm was inevitable (or even probable) might well be evidence to support a contention that test b), or even test a), is satisfied.

The Court held that, on the judge's findings, an intention within a) and b) was not shown. The conduct of Hello! was not targeted at OK! and Hello! had no specific intention to cause economic harm. Nor was intention within test c) shown on the judge's findings, as the judge had found only that Hello! knew that its conduct might cause economic harm to OK!. However, the judge had found intention within test e). OK!'s case was that knowledge within both tests d) and e) was sufficient in law to satisfy the requirement of intention in the tort of economic interference with business.

In the course of its wide-ranging review of the case law, the Court referred to the judgment of Evershed MR in *D.C. Thomson v Deakin*, recording that in that case it was conceded that the defendant to a claim for damages for inducing breach of contract must have acted with the intention of doing damage to the person damaged and that he must have succeeded in his efforts. Having considered these and other authorities the Court concluded that the position, prior to the decision of this court in *Millar v Bassey*, was as follows:

[199] Thus far, judicial statements in relation to intention are wholly consistent with those in relation to the tort of unlawful interference. There is no requirement of a predominant intention to harm the claimant, but such harm must nonetheless be an object of the defendant's conduct, albeit aimed at achieving an ulterior purpose.

The Court then considered *Millar v Bassey* and drew the following conclusion about that case:

[205] Since the decision in *Millar v Bassey*, it is the approach of Peter Gibson LJ, rather than that of Beldam LJ, that has found judicial favour. In *Issac Oren v Red Box Toy Factory Ltd* [1999] FSR 785, Jacob J considered the tort of interfering with contractual relations, which requires an intention to interfere, and expressly followed the approach of Peter Gibson LJ, saying at p 799 that the unlawful conduct must 'in some real sense be "aimed at" the contract.' In *OBG Ltd v Allen* [2005] EWCA Civ 106, at paragraphs 43 and 82–3 respectively, Peter Gibson LJ himself (with whom Carnwath LJ agreed) and Mance LJ (who dissented in the result) adopted the approach of Peter Gibson LJ, in preference to that of Beldam LJ, in *Millar v Bassey*. Indeed, they expressed the view that Peter Gibson LJ's approach was that of the majority in *Millar v Bassey*.

Next the Court considered the authorities on intention for the purposes of the tort of misfeasance in public office. It drew together its conclusions on intention as follows:

[214] However, in all cases of alleged unlawful interference and unlawful means conspiracy where liability has been established, the necessary object or purpose of causing the claimant economic harm has not been made out unless the conduct can be shown to have been aimed or directed at the claimant....

[216] Cases on other economic torts appear to us to have approached the question of intention in the same way. For example, in the context of inducement, in the passage quoted above from *Allen v Flood*, Lord Watson referred to 'the use of illegal means directed against a third party'. In her book, at p 101, Hazel Carty traces the tort of unlawful interference back

to the assertion of Lord Lindley in *Quinn v Leathem* at p 495, by reference to *Lumley v Gye* (1853) 2 E & B 216, that the underlying principle was 'wrongful acts done intentionally to damage a particular individual and actually damaging him'.

[217] The relevant conduct was as much directed at the claimant in the *Kuwait Oil Tanker* case as in all the others. Only by diverting income that should have gone to the claimants could the defendants have enriched themselves. In other words test b) was satisfied, because the very act of diverting the money to the defendants required and involved (as opposed to merely resulted in) diverting the money away from the claimant. Indeed, it may be said that the wrongful act of diverting the money from the claimant in a sense preceded the ulterior motive, namely the receipt of the money by the defendant. However, in some situations an unlawful act will have adverse financial consequences to third parties, which are foreseeable and foreseen, but which are not consequences that the defendant desires or has any interest in bringing about. The statement from *Bourgoin* cited in the *Kuwait Oil Tanker* case might suggest that foresight of consequences must always be equated with intention to cause them—i.e. that satisfying test c) will suffice to establish the necessary intention. However, as we have explained in a paragraph 208 above, looked at the context in which the statement was made, it does not carry that inference.

[218] The authorities that we have considered indicate that it is of the essence of the torts of unlawful means conspiracy and unlawful interference that the conduct that causes the harm is aimed or directed at the claimant, and that in such cases the courts have inferred that the requisite intention, that is the purpose or object of causing the claimant economic loss, is present. The one discordant voice is that of Woolf LJ in *Lonhro v Fayed*. He postulated that foresight by a defendant of harm to a plaintiff was sufficient to satisfy the mental element in the tort of unlawful interference even though there was no desire to bring about that consequence in order to achieve what he regarded as his ultimate end. If by this Woolf LJ meant that foresight of an incidental consequence of unlawful action sufficed to constitute the mental element of the tort, even though achieving that consequence was no part of the defendant's design, we consider that his statement was contrary to the weight of the authority that we have summarised.

[219] As to the cases on interference with contractual rights, Tony Weir in his published lectures on Economic Torts (1997) reacted strongly against the decision in *Millar v Bassey*. At p 19 he said this:
'Admittedly it was a striking-out action, but what nonsense that it should go to trial, that Miss Bassey should have to defend herself against five people she had never contracted with and did not aim to harm just because she changed her mind about making a recording. Must I perform my contract with you just because a third party may, to my knowledge, suffer if I don't? Suppose that I agree to buy goods from you knowing that if the sale goes through, your agent will receive a hefty commission: am I liable to him for refusing to accept delivery? In such a case there is only one third party: in *Millar v Bassey* the defendant looked to be liable to a whole orchestra plus the electronic bank. Dear me! Privity come back!—almost all is forgiven. It is easy to see how wrong this decision is, and we shall see later how it came to be possible.'

[220] Other commentators have expressed similar, although more moderate, views. We consider that the conclusions of Peter Gibson LJ are to be preferred to those of Beldam LJ. It is often the case that failure to perform one contract will lead to a series of consequent breaches of contracts to which the original contract breaker is not party. To render him liable for these breaches simply because they are consequences which he foresaw would be to undermine the doctrine of privity of contract.

[221] Professor Weir and most other writers, including Hazel Carty and Messrs Sales and Stilitz, are of the view that the gist of all the economic torts is the intentional infliction of economic harm. We consider that this is a fair and satisfactory conclusion to draw from the authorities, difficult as some of these are to reconcile. Intention to inflict harm on a claimant is not the same as a wish to harm him. It is, however, very different from knowledge that economic harm will follow as a result of incidental consequences of conduct, when those consequences are not necessary steps in achieving the object of the conduct and are unsought.

[222] *Three Rivers District Council v Bank of England (No 3)* [2003] 2 AC 1 establishes that foresight of probable injury or subjective recklessness as to whether such injury is caused is the mental element required in relation to the consequences of abuse of power, if the cause of action of misfeasance in public office is to be made out. This is a developing tort, as is the tort of unlawful interference. Is there a case for equating the mental element in the two torts? The House of Lords did not so suggest in *Three Rivers*, and Clarke J, who sat at first instance in *Three Rivers*, did not consider that there was—see at [1996] 3 All ER 558 at p 583. We do not consider that there is. The gist of the tort of misfeasance in public office is the deliberate abuse of power. The mental element in the first form of the tort, namely targeted malice, bears strong echoes of the mental element required for unlawful interference, particularly in the early days of the development of that tort. The same is not true of the alternative requirements of foresight of consequences or subjective recklessness. These are not the gist of the tort; they are closer to control mechanisms limiting the liability that flows from the wrongful conduct.

[223] The gist of the tort of unlawful interference is the intentional infliction of economic harm. In other words, it must be shown that the object or purpose of the defendant is to inflict harm on the claimant, either as an end in itself, or as a means to another end. If foresight of probable consequences or subjective recklessness sufficed as the mental element of the tort, this would transform the nature of the tort. This, in effect, is what Mr Browne sought to persuade us to do when he advanced tests d) and e) as sufficient to satisfy the mental element in the tort of unlawful interference. Indeed, we take the view that satisfaction of test c) would not be sufficient to establish the requisite mental element. However, as mentioned in paragraph 159 above, establishing that the defendant knew that the claimant would suffer economic loss may well be evidence which can support a contention that test b) or even test a) is satisfied.

[224] It might be possible to envisage a case in which an intention satisfying test a) or b) could be established even though the unlawful act was not aimed, targeted or directed at the claimant. Equally it might be possible to envisage a case in which the relevant intention was not established, even though the unlawful conduct was in some way directed at the claimant. These are, however, unlikely scenarios and the decided cases do not provide an example of either. In principle we agree with Hazel Carty, and what she describes as 'most commentators', that it is necessary to prove targeted or directed harm. The essence of the tort is that the conduct is done with the object or purpose (but not necessarily the predominant object or purpose) of injuring the claimant or, which seems to us to be the same thing, that the conduct is in some sense aimed or directed at the claimant.

There are a number of points which I would like to make about this case, although much of what it said about intention is strictly obiter.

First, the Court took what might be described as a holistic approach to intention in the economic torts of unlawful interference with trade and inducing breach of contract and unlawful means conspiracy. The Court's view was that the intention required in these cases is a specific intention to cause harm to the claimant. It was not enough that the harm resulted from the defendant's act. In taking this holistic approach the Court has identified a common thread, a golden thread, running through all these torts. The Court expressly answers a question raised by Hazel Carty in her book[20] on the requirement for intention, and this elucidation is extremely welcome.

It is to be noted that the Court drew no distinction for this purpose between direct or indirect inducement of a breach of contract. The Court refers to *Millar v Bassey*, which was of course a case of direct inducement. The Court did not refer to the possibility that the intention required for direct inducement might be somewhat less than that for indirect inducement of breach of contract as suggested by some scholars in this field, but likewise the Court did not suggest that the intention was any less specific in the case of direct inducement.

It is worth taking a moment to consider that outspoken comment by Tony Weir: he said in his criticism of *Millar v Bassey*: '[Shirley Bassey] looked to be liable to the whole orchestra . . . Dear me! Privity come back!' The point is that the plaintiffs would, if they succeeded, obtain a remedy for the breach of their contracts from a person who was not a party to them and indeed who took no benefit under those contracts. That situation has led scholars to treat the liability for inducing breach of contract as a form of secondary liability. True it is that the liability is parasitic on the breach of contract, or the interference with the contract, and those acts are a precondition of liability, but the liability is not ancillary in the sense of a default liability. Inducing a breach of contract, or interfering with the performance of a contract, is an independent wrong. Because liability is being imposed on a person for breach of or interference with a contract to which he is not a party, the law imposes stringent requirements about specific intention and procurement.

As I explained earlier, there are therefore good reasons why economic torts should be limited in scope. I should add that some other common law jurisdictions have taken a very different line. For instance, in California the law has been extended in two particular ways at least. First, the tort can be committed where no contract has yet been made. So, in my example of Tom's contract to buy a flat Tom might have a remedy in California. Second, the law has been extended so that the tort is committed if the third party acts negligently. He need not therefore have acted with the specific intention of harming the claimant.

In a recent case note on *Douglas v Hello!*,[21] Roderick Bagshaw argues that the purpose of the tort of interference with business by the use of unlawful means is the regulation of competition and that if unlawful means are simply determined by what is unlawful in other fields of law then behaviour is determined to be unlawful for reasons quite separate from whether such behaviour is unacceptable in competition. However, the courts have never taken it upon themselves to determine what is fair competition. As Fry LJ said in the *Mogul Steamship* case in the Court of Appeal, 'to draw a line between fair and unfair competition passes the power of the

---

[20] See for example Carty, *An Analysis of Economic Torts* (n 2) 103.
[21] [2005] 121 LQR 550.

courts', or as Lord Macnaghten put it in *Trego v Hunt*,[22] 'the common law has always been jealous of any interference with trade'. The only tools which the courts have for expressing their disapproval of conduct is to hold that it is unlawful by reference to some tort or possibly some crime already recognized in law.

There have been two more cases in the Court of Appeal this year on inducing breach of contract. One was *Mainstream Properties Ltd v Young*.[23] As it was a decision to which I was a party I do not propose to comment on it. I simply draw attention to certain passages from the judgment and invite you to read it in full.

As to the background, Mainstream Properties Ltd ('Mainstream') was a property development company, owned by a Mr Moriarty. Mr Young was a director of Mainstream and Mr Broad was an employee. Mr Young and Mr Broad formed two companies, one of which undertook two developments as joint ventures with a Mr De Winter. Both were on sites identified by Mr Young and Mr Broad as suitable for Mainstream's purposes and therefore Mr Young and Mr Broad acted in breach of their duties to Mainstream in diverting them to their own company. When Mr Moriarty discovered the position, he dismissed them. Mainstream then sued them for loss of the opportunity to develop one of the sites. Mainstream also sought damages against Mr De Winter on the ground that he had induced a breach of Mr Young's and Mr Broad's contracts with Mainstream. At trial the claims against Mr Young and Mr Broad succeeded but that against Mr De Winter failed. Mr De Winter had provided finance for the acquisition of the relevant site. There was no issue on appeal as to whether there had been sufficient procurement of a breach by the provision of funding.

As regards the claim against Mr De Winter, the judge held:

123. I accept the submissions of Mr Lomas QC. I have found that Mr De Winter knew sufficient of the contracts to spot the conflict problem. I have found that he raised the conflict issue. I have found that he genuinely believed that the participation of Mr Young and Mr Broad in the Findern venture would not occasion a conflict between their duty and their interest. What a reasonable man ought to have known or done or intended is not relevant. The tort is one of deliberately inducing breach of contract: not carelessly or negligently inducing such a breach. It follows that I must hold that Mainstream has not established that Mr De Winter intended to procure a breach of or to interfere with the performance of the employment contracts. It follows that I dismiss the claim against Mr De Winter.

The issue on appeal was as to the intention required to found liability for inducing breach of contract. The Court referred to the judgment of the Court of Appeal in *Douglas v Hello!*. It held that there had to be a specific intention to cause harm. The Court held that the case raised a question of law very similar to that which would have arisen if *Millar v Bassey* had gone to trial and the pleaded case had been proved. All that has been found is that Mr De Winter knew that Mr Young and Mr Broad were a director and employee respectively of Mainstream. He knew that his funding of the site would prevent Mainstream from developing the site

---

[22] [1896] AC 7, 24.   [23] [2005] EWCA Civ 861.

itself but he did not consider that there was any conflict of interest because of the assurance he had been given. Just as in *Millar v Bassey*, no specific intention to harm the other contracting party was pleaded, so in the Mainstream case no specific intention to cause harm was shown. The Court also rejected the argument that recklessness would suffice for the purposes of the tort of inducing breach of contract.

The other case is also a case where the majority considered that there should be no extension of the scope of application of the tort of inducing breach of contract. This case was decided before *Douglas v Hello!* but I have referred to it after *Douglas v Hello!* because the facts are more complex:

OBG Ltd v Allan

This case[24] arose out of the invalid appointment by a debenture holder of receivers. I can say from my experience in the Chancery Division that this is not the first time that this has happened. The receivers go in and they dismiss the employees and sell the company's stock and so on. Then it becomes clear that the receivers were trespassers. So far as tangible assets and land are concerned, no problem arises because the receivers can be sued for interference with goods or trespass. Where the realization is at an undervalue the receivers may also be held liable for damages in negligence. But in *OBG* the facts were rather special. The receivers took possession of contracts. The company was a civil engineering company which had various construction contracts. The receivers did not realize these contracts negligently but they did realize them for a smaller sum than the company would have achieved. If Lord Upjohn had been with us he might have asked why the company did not sue the receivers for an account in equity for the value of all the assets of which they wrongly took possession. Perhaps if Tony Weir had been here he would have said: 'Dear me! *Equity* come back!' But as Peter Gibson LJ points out, the company did not pursue its equitable claims. The company instead brought a claim for interference with its contractual relations.

The majority (Peter Gibson and Carnwath LJJ) rejected this claim. Peter Gibson LJ noted that the tort of inducing breach of contract had been extended to interference with the performance of a contract. He went on, however, to hold:

47. I am not aware of any case where the tort has been held to apply to an act of a third party who, although aware of a contract between the contracting parties, was not intending to procure a breach of the contract or other actionable wrong or to prevent or hinder the performance of the contract nor would the act have been a breach of contract if performed by a party. The decided cases are concerned with interference with the performance of a contract where such interference was aimed at procuring a failure to comply with some obligation imposed by a term of the contract: see Cane, *Tort Law and Economic Interests*, 2nd ed (1996), p 119. As is said in *Clerk & Lindsell on Torts*, 18th ed (2000), para 24-05 an interference with contractual performance that causes no breach of contractual obligation on principle cannot be tortious. It is powerfully argued by Hazel Carty in *An Analysis of the*

---

[24] [2005] QB 762, and see Hazel Carty, 'The Need for Clarity in the Economic Torts' [2005] King's College Law Journal 165.

Economic Torts (2001), pp 63 and 271 that there must be an actionable wrong sought to be procured by the alleged tortfeasor for this tort to arise. That, as it seems to me, was the essence of the tort, but cases such as *Torquay Hotel* and *Merkur Island* breach that purist principle. However, the present case would extend that breach even further. The fact that the tort has been extended to include prevention of the due performance of a primary obligation even though no secondary obligation to make monetary compensation came into existence does not justify a further extension of the tort to circumstances where the alleged tortfeasor was not intending to prevent the performance of any primary obligation of the contract. That would be to change the nature of the tort which hitherto has had as an essential ingredient the intention to procure a breach, or the non-performance of an obligation, of a contract or a breach of duty. Such intention is lacking in a case such as the present, where the interference is not directed at preventing or hindering the performance of any obligation imposed by a contract. The objection to the interference goes only to who should be managing the contractual rights of one party. No doubt the receivers did intend to manage the contractual rights of the claimants, but, whilst that was an intention to interfere with the claimants' business (though without intending to cause loss or damage), it does not seem to me to amount to an interference with contractual relations in any relevant sense. Accordingly, I would respectfully disagree with the judge in his holding that the tort of interference with contractual relations was committed. I would allow the appeal on this point.

He held that this form of interference was not interference in any relevant sense for the purpose of the economic tort of inducing breach of contract. The receivers had in effect undertaken to provide a service of 'running off' the contracts, not interfering with their performance.

There was a dissenting judgment by Mance LJ (as he then was). He considered that the receivers should be liable for interfering with the contract. He considered that a central question was whether the tort was 'capable of covering the situation of an unauthorised agent, who takes over the handling of a contract with a view to its performance by settlement of mutual rights and obligations but with the result the "principal" suffers a loss which he would not otherwise have suffered'.[25] He held that the tort covered the situation where a person's pre-existing legal position was altered, even though this did not involve any breach or non-performance of any obligation to a third party.[26]

The decision left the company with no claim in the action for loss of the contracts. The decision produced a situation where a different result was reached as regards the company's tangible and intangible assets. The Court rejected a solution which would have extended the tort of inducing breach of contract.

Conclusions

The Court of Appeal decided three important cases involving economic torts in the space of five years. In anticipation of further appeals, this is an opportune moment to try to identify what has been achieved and what still needs to be clarified in this field.

[25] *OBG* (n 24) para 86.   [26] *OBG* (n 24) para 91.

I will start my conclusions with some general observations.

My first point is that there needs to be a principled basis for the group of economic torts that I have been discussing. If there is no well understood principled basis for them, the courts will constantly be faced with pressure to extend the torts into areas not covered by their true rationale. Hazel Carty says: 'The sounder the tort's conceptual basis, the nearer we are to establishing cosmos from chaos.'[27] The issue at the heart of the debate about economic torts is their function in modern society. I have suggested previously that their primary function is to protect economic interests. I think that that statement is useful because it expresses a recurring theme in the torts I have been discussing. However, that statement of the function of economic torts is expressed at a very high level of abstraction. Scholarly discourse needs to dig deeper. Is it the primary function of economic torts to protect economic interests in order to ensure appropriate standards of commercial conduct? Or is it the purpose of economic torts to provide compensation for unfair competition? Or is it both purposes? Do all economic interests merit the same level of protection? In *Douglas v Hello!*, the economic interest at stake was in confidential information. Is confidential information generally or in particular cases worthy of greater protection than other economic interests? Is there a need for an additional layer of common law in the form of economic torts in areas where there is already considerable regulation providing civil remedies for breach? In all these issues, I suggest that it will generally be found that the marketplace is a very sensitive eco-system where what seem obvious extensions as a matter of law can provide perverse incentives, or lead to unfortunate second order effects. Carnwath LJ expressed this point in *OBG* thus: 'the boundaries of economic torts are a sensitive area in which it is difficult to anticipate the consequences of redefinition'. Moreover, the common law provides other remedies for improper behaviour apart from remedies for economic torts, such as remedies for duress and, in the case of public authorities, for misfeasance in public office.

Furthermore, the encouragement of excessive litigation is not in the public interest. That consideration might be a supplementary reason why economic torts should be tightly defined. They should not be allowed to become a fashion accessory, for instance as an alternative claim to any claim for breach of contract, as economic torts have become in some jurisdictions.

Academic discourse also needs to consider the role of human rights in this field. If a pressure group asks people going into a hairdresser to make an appointment for hair colouring not to use hair tints because they are tested on animals, the right to freedom of expression is engaged. There may also be a question of the right to freedom of assembly and association.

With those general observations, I now move to some specific points for further consideration.

It could be said that there is quite a shopping list of points which the House of Lords may have to consider. They include the following. First, there is the 'inducement' issue. Some writers have taken the view that a very broad interpretation

---

[27] Carty, *An Analysis of Economic Torts* (n 2) 128.

should be given to what constitutes inducement for the purposes of breach of contract. It may include hiding the tools of an employee so he cannot perform his contract for his employer. Does it include the termination of a contract without any persuasion of the other party to take any step in relation to this contract with the claimant? Does it include providing funds which enable a breach of contract to take place? Or must the inducement be, as Jenkins LJ expressed it, in *D.C. Thomson v Deakin* 'unequivocal'? Hazel Carty in particular attaches considerable importance to the 'inducement' point. Looking at the various authorities, it does not seem to me that the courts have always given clear guidance on what constitutes inducement.

Second, there is the question of unlawful means. Hazel Carty regards this as the key issue. We now know from the decision in *Douglas v Hello!* that breach of an obligation of confidence owed to another person can constitute unlawful means, one of the areas of lack of clarity noted by Hazel Carty in her book. But there are other questions. Should unlawful means be the same for all the economic torts? Should the commission of a crime constitute unlawful means in any of these torts, and, if so, should crimes constitute unlawful means even though they do not give rise to any civil liability actionable by the claimant?[28]

Third, there is the question of the tort of indirect inducement, namely whether it should be part of the tort of inducing breach of contract and whether it should more properly be classified as part of the tort of unlawful interference with trade or business. I referred to this debate earlier.

I close with these observations. In this field, all I can do is give an introduction to the complexities of the law. As I am a judge, I am asking questions rather than giving answers today as some of these questions may in due course come before me. I much welcome the decision of the House of Lords to grant permission to appeal in three cases. There is a role for the House of Lords to consider the various ingredients of these economic torts in the light of modern conditions. But there is also a role for academic commentators to produce articles and case notes which will guide the courts. I am not suggesting that is the only reason for scholarship in the law but I can say from my experience that it is one of its many valuable features.[29]

---

[28] See now nn 14 and 2 earlier.

[29] The appeals in *OBG*, *Douglas v Hello! Ltd*, and *Mainstream Properties* were heard together and the judgments of the House of Lords are reported at [2008] 1 AC 1. In line with the conclusions in this chapter, the House established the principled basis of these torts and defined them narrowly in important respects. The House rejected the idea of a 'unified' tort and clarified the elements of the two torts of causing loss by unlawful means and inducing breach of contract. For causing loss by unlawful means, there had to be unlawful means, that is actionable conduct, and an intention to cause loss. For inducing breach of contract, the defendant had to know that there would be a breach of contract and to intend to procure a breach of that contract. In addition, there had to be a breach of contract in fact. In the result, the House affirmed the decisions of the Court of Appeal in *OBG* and *Mainstream Properties*, and reversed its decision in *Douglas v Hello! Ltd*. The House also disapproved the decision in *Millar v Bassey*. The House rejected the idea of a distinction between direct and indirect inducements of breach of contract. The true question was whether there was sufficient causal interference with the contract. It also held that unlawful means should be limited to wrongful acts which were connected with the damage inflicted on the claimant. There are several references in the judgments to academic writings, including Carty, *An Analysis of Economic Torts* (n 2). However, the more recent article by Carty, 'The Modern Functions of Economic Torts' (n 2), shows that aspects of economic torts remain fluid and controversial.

5

Duty, Causal Contribution, and the Scope of Responsibility

Does the Law of Negligence Impose Rational Limits?

This chapter is based on a lecture given to the Professional Negligence Bar Association in honour of Lord Taylor on 12 April 2005.

Legal hangovers and the law of negligence

Those who worked closely with Lord Taylor, or knew him well, speak of his sense of humour and his ability, even when holding the highest office, to maintain a sense of balance and occasionally even to be irreverent to authority. It was those characteristics that inspired the title and theme of this chapter. What I intend to do is to cast a critical eye over certain aspects of the law of negligence.

Professor David Ibbetson starts the final chapter of his book, *A Historical Introduction to the Law of Obligations*, with this sentence 'The common law has many virtues; tidiness is not among them.'[1] He also says that the common law suffers from hangovers; not hangovers in the sense that you will immediately think of but what he calls legal hangovers: although the common law is capable of casting off outdated rules that have ceased to be appropriate in contemporary conditions, it is much less good at losing doctrines or whole bodies of ideas. One example he gives is of the doctrine of consideration in contract. My purpose in this lecture is to demonstrate that there are concepts in the law of negligence that are really legal 'hangovers'. They are there for historical reasons, they do not serve an essential purpose today and they can obscure the task of analysing a problem. At the same time I will look at some of the more controversial areas of this field of the law and suggest that, contrary to the common view, they are useful and worthwhile.

The law of negligence is vast and thus I will have to focus on a few discrete areas, namely:

(1) the duty question, that is, when will a duty be regarded as arising?—*Caparo Industries plc v Dickman*;[2]

---

[1] David Ibbetson, *A Historical Introduction to the Law of Obligation* (Oxford University Press, 1999).
[2] [1990] 2 AC 605.

(2) the assumption of responsibility—*Williams v Natural Life*;[3]

(3) the scope of the duty—*SAAMCO*;[4]

(4) causal contribution—*Fairchild*[5] and *Chester v Asfar*.[6]

I have radically to cut down the number of cases that could be cited. The choice is accordingly a somewhat eclectic one, but I have sought to use cases that will be familiar or whose facts follow a pattern that lawyers will meet in the course of their professional negligence practices. I have therefore left whole areas of law which I could have dealt with untouched, including, for instance, psychiatric injury.

The duty question

Courts find it necessary to ask whether there was a duty owed. This is really a legal hangover from *Donoghue v Stevenson*,[7] the ground-breaking decision that manufacturers of consumer products were responsible to consumers if they put into circulation defective goods. The manufacturers of ginger beer were liable for having put in circulation ginger beer containing a noxious element, namely a dead snail. The contemporary equivalent might be the production of a carton of orange juice with a syringe in it—as happened recently. *Donoghue v Stevenson* enunciated the neighbour test. You owe a duty of care to avoid acts or omissions which you can reasonably foresee would be likely to injure your neighbour. Since then, factual situations have arisen where the relationship of the parties was not as obvious. In those situations, the law has had difficulty in determining exactly where a duty of care lies. Foreseeability has been found not to be a test that of itself answers the question: when does a duty of care exist?

The process to be undertaken when determining whether a duty of care exists was examined in *Anns v Merton London Borough Council*.[8] That case appeared to establish that little more than foreseeability of harm was needed. Foreseeability of harm to the claimant or a class of persons including the claimant would give rise to a prima facie duty of care. This could be negatived by sufficiently weighty policy arguments. But the approach in *Anns* was found in practice to be flawed.

The duty question was reconsidered in *Caparo v Dickman*.[9] In that case the question was whether the auditors of a public company owed a duty of care to shareholders and investors who, without the prior knowledge of the auditors, bought shares in the company in reliance on the audited accounts and thereby suffered economic loss. The shareholders' and investors' claim for this loss was rejected. The House of Lords recognized that there was a distinction between negligently produced goods like ginger beer and negligent misstatements. To

---

[3] [1998] 1 WLR 830.
[4] *South Australian Asset Management Corp v York Montague Ltd* [1997] AC 191.
[5] *Fairchild v Glenhaven Funeral Services Ltd* [2003] 1 AC 32.
[6] [2005] 1 AC 134.　　　[7] [1932] AC 562.　　　[8] [1978] AC 728.
[9] [1990] 2 AC 605.

borrow the famous phraseology of Cardozo CJ in *Ultramares Corporation v Touche*,[10] the latter can, if liability is not properly limited by the law, lead 'to a liability in an indeterminate amount for an indeterminate time to an indeterminate class'. The House of Lords laid down that the correct test to establish whether one person owed another a duty of care was not just foreseeability but whether there was a sufficient relationship of proximity (or neighbourliness) and whether it was fair, just, and reasonable to impose a duty. The courts should approach the question of whether a duty exists on an incremental basis. What this means is that the law will be developed gradually. The concept of neighbourliness or proximity does no more than tell you that, on the facts considered as a whole, the courts may find that a duty arises. See, for example, Lord Jauncey in *Caparo v Dickman* at 655:

As Bingham LJ observed in the present case, the concept of proximity is somewhat elusive, extending as it does beyond mere physical proximity. It might be described as the circumstances in which the law considers it proper that a duty of care should be imposed on one person towards another.

Proximity would appear to be a requirement that the courts should look at the relative position of the parties before the act or omission said to constitute negligence in fact happened. Even, however, where proximity exists, the courts still ask—is it fair, just, and reasonable for liability to be imposed?

I have two criticisms of the law of negligence to make at this stage. First, I suggest that to have to establish a duty of care is unnecessary. The real question is whether there should be liability for doing something. It is to be noted that in the American Restatement of the Law of Torts (Second) (1965) there is no complex discussion of when a duty of care exists. All that is necessary, subject to causation, is that the wrongdoer should have invaded an interest of the claimant which is legally protected against invasion, and that the conduct of the wrongdoer should have been negligent with respect to the claimant or a class of persons which includes the claimant. There is usually no need to construct the notion of a duty of care and then decide whether the conduct of the wrongdoer breached that duty. The Restatement in general goes straight to the second and third stages: negligent conduct and causation.[11]

---

[10]   255 NY 170, 179–80, 174 NE 441 (1931).

[11]   Thus for example para 324A contains the following statement of the circumstances in which a person comes under a liability to a third party for the negligent performance of an undertaking to render services to that party:

One who undertakes, gratuitously or for consideration, to render services to another which he should recognize as necessary for the protection of a third person or his things, is subject to liability to the third person for physical harm resulting from his failure to exercise reasonable care to protect his undertaking, if (a) his failure to exercise reasonable care increases the risk of such harm, or (b) he has undertaken to perform a duty owed by the other to the third person, or (c) the harm is suffered because of reliance of the other or the third person upon the undertaking.

The Restatement of the Law of Torts (Third): Liability for Physical and Emotional Harm (The American Law Institute, 2012) uses the language of duty. However, it also recognizes that courts often use the language of duty or no duty inappropriately, for example 'when all that is meant is the application of the negligence standard to a particular factual situation' or 'where there was insufficient evidence of causation' (Vol 1, p 95).

My next criticism is this. The requirement that the imposition of a duty of care should be fair, just, and reasonable presupposes that the courts will be able, under our adversarial system, to know whether the imposition of a duty of care in a particular context will be desirable or not. However, the courts will not have evidence showing the economic consequences or socio-legal consequences of imposing a duty in particular circumstances. In those circumstances, how can the courts know, for instance, whether the recognition of new duties in a particular sphere will, or will not, lead to a flood of new claims? This is the floodgates argument, which is often wheeled out as a reason for not imposing a duty of care. In my days at the Law Commission, it was considered desirable that no new liability would be imposed unless it was shown to be fair and desirable on the basis of research. Sometimes that research would take the form of analysing the responses of consultees. Sometimes, there would be empirical or economic research. The Law Commission had to try to produce a research-based assessment of the effect of imposing or not imposing liability on future behaviour. Courts cannot perform that sort of exercise. Of course fairness to the defendants is sometimes a sufficient condition for the imposition of liability. But more often it is a question of competing fairnesses and of an assessment of the second order effects of imposing liability.

All these considerations amply reinforce Lord Bingham's famous phrase: on the whole the law advances in small steps and not by giant bounds, or (as it is sometimes put) he who would extend the common law should do so by single runs and not by sixes. That is particularly true in many aspects of the law of negligence. The experience of law reform which I had at the Law Commission makes me sceptical that a court can always make a valid decision as to the strength of the policy reasons for imposing or not imposing a duty of care.

What I would suggest, therefore, is that, while courts should certainly not impose a liability which can be seen not to be fair, just, or reasonable, it is difficult for them convincingly to conclude that the imposition of liability in a new situation will always in fact be fair, just, and reasonable. I have already mentioned the floodgates argument. Another danger is the perception of a compensation culture. Many people feel that there is a compensation culture and that damages are too often and too generously awarded. But certainly the experience of the Law Commission was that in the field of personal injury the level of general damages was not high enough. That led to the reconsideration of the law with the benefit of a Law Commission report[12] in *Heil v Rankin*.[13] It is a factor which should cause concern that the *Caparo* test confers such a broad, unstructured discretion on the courts and that a deserving claimant may be deprived of a remedy because of factors such as an unquantifiable risk of floodgates or a perception of a compensation culture.

Moreover, in the interests of legal certainty, the imposition of a duty of care should be predictable. This would suggest that less weight should be given to factors such as whether the imposition of liability is fair, just, and reasonable than to

---

[12] *Damages for Personal Injury: Non-Pecuniary Loss* (Law Com No 257, 1999).
[13] [2001] QB 272.

other factors, such as proximity, to which legal meaning can be given. The notion of proximity is inherently a fairer guide as to whether there should be liability since it turns on factors specific to the parties before the courts, whereas when the court asks whether it is fair, just, and reasonable to impose a duty of care, it is making a judgment about factors outside the case in hand or about things that might have happened but did not happen in the particular case under consideration, such as whether it was reasonable for the claimant not to have obtained other advice. Take *X v Bedfordshire County Council*.[14] In that case the claimants suffered very serious personal injury as a result of the negligence of the local authority, which was held not to owe a duty of care to them. One of the claimants was so traumatized by his experiences that he could not lead a normal life or form relationships.[15] If, as Lord Bingham has said, the rule of public policy which has first claim on the loyalty of the law is that wrongs should be remedied, it is difficult to explain why it is the law that there was no duty of care for reasons which have nothing to do with the facts of the individual case. Indeed it could be said that it is the logical consequence of Lord Bingham's observation, and indeed of the traditional role of the courts, that, if there is to be a question of any class of defendants being effectively immune from liability, that should be a matter for Parliament.

The criticisms which I am making of the fair, just, and reasonable test can be demonstrated by considering what has happened in the field of auditors' liability. The decision of the House of Lords in *Caparo* has not led to claims against auditors being kept within manageable bounds. So much so that the government—representing the public interest—has been persuaded by the profession that statutory reform is necessary. Thus the government has in principle accepted the idea that shareholders and auditors should be able to agree that the liability of auditors should be limited to the amount which the court considers just and equitable having regard to the auditors' responsibility for the loss incurred. This is called 'proportionate liability by contract'. Similarly, the government is presently considering whether to alter the law so as to enable a company and a director to agree by contract to limit or exclude the liability of the director for negligence,[16] but it has reached no decision yet on this issue. The latter proposal would not enable a director to contract out of his duty of loyalty but would enable, say, a non-executive director to agree to become a director on the basis that his liability for negligence was limited to some amount for which he was able to afford insurance.[17]

However, despite these criticisms, the *Caparo* test is certainly an improvement on the previous law. It is the system we have, and I think the best that we can devise.

---

[14] [1995] AC 633.   [15] See *Z v United Kingdom* [2001] 1 FLR 612.

[16] Such agreements are generally void but there are exceptions for insurance and certain indemnities (Companies Act 2006, ss 232–235 amending the Companies Act 1985, s 310).

[17] This proposal was rejected, though the Companies Act 2006, ss 534–536 now permits auditors to enter into agreements which limit their liability for audit work. These agreements are subject to a number of conditions, including conditions that the limit be agreed once a year, that the company approves any limitation agreement by ordinary resolution before the parties enter into it, and that the limit is fair and reasonable.

Duty of care and words

Thus far I have said nothing about negligent misstatement. For a long time, English law took the view that there was a fundamental difference between carelessness in acts and carelessness in words: see the famous dissenting judgment of Denning LJ in *Candler v Crane Christmas & Co.*[18] The great step forward was made in *Hedley Byrne & Co Ltd v Heller & Partners Ltd.*[19] Inevitably, however, the House of Lords concentrated on the distinction between words and deeds, rather than on the nature of the loss. Thus, for instance, Lord Devlin held that it was difficult to see why liability should depend on the nature of the damage and that any distinction between words and deeds was unworkable. Lord Pearce, on the other hand, recognized that 'Words are more volatile than deeds. They travel fast and far afield. . . . They are dangerous and cause vast financial damage.'

Hedley Byrne in reality started a new strain of negligence liability. As Lord Reid and Lord Pearce both said, *Donoghue v Stevenson*[20] could not be relied upon as authority justifying the imposition of liability in that case. Accordingly the House had to identify the circumstances in which the new liability for careless words would arise. The essential conditions were that there was an assumption of responsibility by the maker of the statement and that there was reasonable reliance on this statement by the recipient—because, for example, the maker of the statement had some special skill. The duty would not arise where liability was disclaimed or where the words were spoken on a purely social occasion. The House has more recently gone on to hold that, if the court is satisfied that there was an assumption of responsibility, there was no need to ask whether it was fair, just, and reasonable to impose a duty of care for the purposes of the *Caparo* test.[21]

Unquestionably the *Hedley Byrne* decision was one of the great turning points in the law. However, I question whether it was right to draw the line between words and deeds rather than between physical harm and economic harm. Given the special features of economic loss, the line could I think more logically have been drawn there. You can have a case in which a misstatement causes physical harm and the problems of economic loss do not arise. Likewise you can have a case of property damage which leads to a claim by the owner of the property or third party to economic loss: such a case gives rise to the same policy considerations as arise in relation to economic loss caused by a misstatement. Furthermore the *Hedley Byrne* case contains a few of the hangovers to which I referred earlier. For instance, Lord Devlin held that liability would arise only in circumstances 'equivalent to contract'. This may have eased the passing (if that is the right phrase to use in the context of Lord Devlin) from liability for misstatement where there is a fiduciary or contractual relationship to liability in circumstances where there was no such pre-existing relationship. It is not, however, a concept which can be sensibly invoked as the touchstone of liability today. It suggests a formal pre-existing relationship.

---

[18] [1951] 2 KB 164.   [19] [1964] AC 465.   [20] [1932] AC 562.
[21] *Henderson v Merrett Syndicates Ltd* [1995] 2 AC 145.

There is also, I think, another more visible hangover here, and that is the notion of assumption of responsibility. We shall look at that next. In a nutshell, it is difficult to see how the assumption of responsibility differs from asking whether it is a proper case in which to impose a duty of care on *Caparo* principles.

The assumption of responsibility

What does the concept of assumption of responsibility mean? In *Williams v Natural Life Health Foods Ltd*[22] Lord Steyn emphasized the importance of the interaction between the adviser and the advisee:

> The touchstone of liability is not the state of mind of the defendant. An objective test means that the primary focus must be on things said or done by the defendant or on his behalf in dealings with the plaintiff. Obviously the impact of what a defendant says or does must be judged in the light of the relevant contextual scene. Subject to this qualification the primary focus must be on the exchanges (in which term I include statements and conduct) which cross the line between the defendant and the plaintiff.

It is clear that it is not necessary for the wrongdoer subjectively to have intended to undertake responsibility. The test is objective. It does not therefore help to ask whether the wrongdoer intended to assume responsibility.

The courts have devoted some time to discussing whether assumption of responsibility means assumption of responsibility for the task in hand or an assumption of responsibility for liability if a statement is negligently made. I do not find this enquiry helpful, particularly if responsibility means responsibility for liability where the statement is negligently made. There are not many commercial parties who think about what should happen if the advice is wrong. The whole concept of assumption of responsibility is suggestive of a voluntary process, whereas we know from the cases that liability will be imposed in appropriate circumstances on an objective basis. Tort after all is about the imposition of liability for wrongs. The concept of the assumption of responsibility is simply not meaningful in situations where the parties were not in a relationship of adviser and client. What then is the court looking for?

In a recent case, the question arose whether a firm of actuaries had assumed a duty of care by providing information to a third party who made an offer for the shares of their client. It was said to be the first case at that level involving actuaries. In that case, *Précis (521) Ltd v Mercer*,[23] in order to determine whether the actuaries owed a duty of care to a third party to whom they had supplied information, the Court of Appeal applied the criteria (for determining whether there has been an assumption of responsibility) laid down in the well-known judgment of Neill LJ in *BCCI v Price Waterhouse*[24] in 1998. In that case, Neill LJ held that the criteria to be

---

[22] [1998] 2 All ER 577, 582. [23] [2005] EWCA Civ 114, The Times, 24 February 2005.
[24] [1998] PNLR 564.

used for the purpose of determining whether there was an assumption of responsibility included the following:

(1) the precise relationship between the adviser and the advisee;

(2) the precise circumstances in which the information or advice came into existence;

(3) the precise circumstances in which the information or advice was communicated to the advisee, and here I quote: 'the degree of reliance which the adviser intended or should reasonably have anticipated would be placed on its accuracy by the advisee, *and the reliance that was in fact placed on it*' (emphasis added);

(4) the presence or absence of other advisers on whom the advisee could rely;

(5) the opportunity given to the adviser to issue a disclaimer.

Putting aside the odd man out (number 3, 'reliance') in Neill LJ's immensely useful list of illustrative factors that can be used to determine whether there has been an assumption of responsibility, what can we deduce from this list as a whole? I suggest that what it shows is that all the factors generally used to determine assumption of responsibility are really factors which would go to the question whether there was proximity or whether it was fair, just, and reasonable to impose a duty of care, that is, the *Caparo* test. I do not think that there is anything in the point that the concept of assumption of responsibility is useful and meaningful because it directs one to the issue of whether it would be reasonable to recognize responsibility. Liability for misstatements, as we know, is imposed on a party on an objective basis and irrespective of whether a person thought he was assuming a duty of care. In my view, if one was able to start again, the more rational approach for the law would surely be to abandon the concept of 'assumption of responsibility' altogether and apply the *Caparo* test to all cases. The latter test was after all enunciated in order to deal with cases of economic loss and it must therefore be apt for this purpose. Indeed it would be difficult to believe that the *Caparo* test would lead to any different result than that which would be achieved by application of the assumption of responsibility test.

Moreover, it is difficult to see why a court should be concerned with an assumption of responsibility in a three-party case—the sort of case where a professional adviser is asked by his client to provide some information to, or do something for, a third person. The adviser may never have met the third person. He may deal with him only indirectly through the client or the third party's own advisers. Why should an assumption of responsibility be the touchstone of liability in such a case? Furthermore, the client and the professional adviser may have agreed on a limitation of liability between themselves. That makes it even more difficult to think in terms of an assumption of responsibility. In fact, in the *Précis* case, there was a contract between the client and third party for a limitation on liability for the negligent provision of information by the client or any of his professional advisers. The actuaries sought to rely on this clause, of which they were unaware at the time they provided information. The Court of Appeal held that, since the question was one of the assumption of responsibility, this clause could not have the effect of preventing a duty of care from arising. The question did not have to be answered whether there would have been a different approach to this clause under the *Caparo* test. While the analysis of the problem might have been different having regard to the limitation of liability, the result would in my view have been the same. The clause could only have been a factor in the defendant's favour and, in any event, the defendants won on the assumption of responsibility point.

Another situation which shows the inaptness of the assumption of responsibility test is the case where the claimant seeks to say that there was a duty of care owed to him by a professional adviser and he (the claimant) was in fact the party on the opposite side of the transaction to the professional adviser's own client. That a duty of care can be owed in such a situation is shown by the Court of Appeal's decision in *Dean v Allin & Watts*,[25] a case where the claimant was a party who had not had his own lawyer and who succeeded in his claim to make the other party liable for failing to draw up effective security documentation. However, to say that there has been an assumption of responsibility in such a case is generally inappropriate because professional advisers acting for one party do not generally assume responsibility to parties on the other side of the transaction and who therefore have interests which conflict with those of their own clients.

Furthermore, if you look closely at the factors identified by Neill LJ they nearly all concern the relative position of the parties—that is, proximity—or factors which are relevant to the question whether it is fair, just, and reasonable to impose a duty of care. So I would suggest a properly organized law of negligence would not use the concept of assumption of responsibility. It would apply the same requirement for proximity, and the rest of the *Caparo* test, as in the context of the duty of care generally.

The scope of the duty

I now turn to a concept which in my view is far more useful in the context of professional negligence and that is the scope of the duty: the *SAAMCO*[26] approach. This could be placed either under the heading of duty or under the heading of causation. It is of great importance in the field of professional negligence because as between client and adviser there is usually no question but that a duty is owed. The issue is the extent of the adviser's liability.

The *SAAMCO* principle has its critics: there are those who say it is not difficult to understand but it is difficult to apply. There are others who will say that that is rubbish: it is neither easy to understand nor easy to apply: see the difficulty which the House of Lords had in deciding how the principle should be applied in *Aneco Reinsurance Underwriting Ltd v Johnson & Higgins Ltd.*[27] (The issue here was to

---

[25] (2001) 2 Lloyd's Rep 249.
[26] *South Australian Asset Management Corp v York Montague Ltd* [1997] AC 191.
[27] [2001] 2 All ER (Comm) 929.

define the scope of the duty undertaken by the brokers—was it to place reinsurance of £11 million or was it to advise on the market's assessment of the primary layer of £35 million to which the underwriter would otherwise not have committed itself?)

The basic principle is that for loss to be recoverable, the defendant must have owed a duty to the claimant in respect of the type of loss suffered. The problem, as you will recall, that arose in *SAAMCO* (and a number of similar cases) was that a valuer of property made a negligent valuation on the basis of which the claimant lent money. After the loan was made, the transaction went pear-shaped for a number of reasons, including the fall in the market, and the bankruptcy of the borrower. The claimant bank sought to say as against the valuer that it would never have gone into the transaction but for the negligent valuation. Therefore the negligent valuer was liable for all the loss it suffered as a result of entering into the transaction, including the loss due to the fall in the property market, etc. Lord Hoffmann (with whom the remainder of the House agreed) analysed *Caparo* as being a scope of the duty case. (The auditors owed a duty of care to the shareholders in their capacity as members of the company being audited but not as investors in the company.) Lord Hoffmann reached this conclusion because in *Caparo* the House of Lords concluded that there was no duty of care in these circumstances by looking at the statutory scheme for the appointment of the auditors, their duties, etc. Lord Hoffmann in *SAAMCO* drew an interesting analogy with the law on breach of statutory duty: the duty there depends on the purpose of the rule imposing the duty. So, too, in negligence at common law:

The scope of the duty, in the sense of the consequences for which the valuer is responsible, is that which the law regards as best giving effect to the express obligations assumed by the valuer: neither cutting them down so that the lender obtains less than he was reasonably entitled to expect, nor extending them so as to impose on the valuer a liability greater than he could reasonably have thought he was undertaking.

Lord Hoffmann continued, at 213:

Rules which make the wrongdoer liable for all the consequences of his wrongful conduct are exceptional and need to be justified by some special policy. Normally the law limits liability to those consequences which are attributable to that which made the act wrongful. In the case of liability in negligence for providing inaccurate information, this would mean liability for the consequences of the information being inaccurate.

Lord Hoffmann then gave his famous example of the mountaineer:

I can illustrate the difference between the ordinary principle and that adopted by the Court of Appeal by an example. A mountaineer about to undertake a difficult climb is concerned about the fitness of his knee. He goes to a doctor who negligently makes a superficial examination and pronounces the knee fit. The climber goes on the expedition, which he would not have undertaken if the doctor had told him the true state of his knee. He suffers an injury which is an entirely foreseeable consequence of mountaineering, but has nothing to do with his knee.

On the Court of Appeal's principle, the doctor is responsible for the injury suffered by the mountaineer because it is damage which would not have occurred if he had been given correct information about his knee. He would not have gone on the expedition and would have suffered no injury. On what I have suggested is the more usual principle, the doctor is not liable. The injury has not been caused by the doctor's bad advice, because it would have occurred even if the advice had been correct.

The Court of Appeal summarily rejected the application of the latter principle to the present case, saying ([1995] 2 All ER 769 at 840, [1995] QB 375 at 404):
'The complaint made and upheld against the valuers in these cases is ... not that they were wrong. A professional opinion may be wrong without being negligent. The complaint in each case is that the valuer expressed an opinion that the land was worth more than any careful and competent valuer would have advised.'

I find this reasoning unsatisfactory. It seems to be saying that the valuer's liability should be restricted to the consequences of the valuation being wrong if he had warranted that it was correct, but not if he had only promised to use reasonable care to see that it was correct. There are, of course, differences between the measure of damages for breach of warranty and for injury caused by negligence, to which I shall return. In the case of liability for providing inaccurate information, however, it would seem paradoxical that the liability of a person who warranted the accuracy of the information should be less than that of a person who gave no such warranty but failed to take reasonable care.

Your Lordships might, I would suggest, think that there was something wrong with a principle which, in the example which I have given, produced the result that the doctor was liable. What is the reason for this feeling? I think that the Court of Appeal's principle offends common sense because it makes the doctor responsible for consequences which, though in general terms foreseeable, do not appear to have a sufficient causal connection with the subject matter of the duty. The doctor was asked for information on only one of the considerations which might affect the safety of the mountaineer on the expedition. There seems no reason of policy which requires that the negligence of the doctor should require the transfer to him of all the foreseeable risks of the expedition.

I think that one can to some extent generalise the principle upon which this response depends. It is that a person under a duty to take reasonable care to provide information on which someone else will decide upon a course of action is, if negligent, not generally regarded as responsible for all the consequences of that course of action. He is responsible only for the consequences of the information being wrong. A duty of care which imposes upon the informant responsibility for losses which would have occurred even if the information which he gave had been correct is not in my view fair and reasonable as between the parties. It is therefore inappropriate either as an implied term of a contract or as a tortious duty arising from the relationship between them.

The principle thus stated distinguishes between a duty to provide information for the purpose of enabling someone else to decide upon a course of action and a duty to advise someone as to what course of action he should take. If the duty is to advise whether or not a course of action should be taken, the adviser must take reasonable care to consider all the potential consequences of that course of action. If he is negligent, he will therefore be responsible for all the foreseeable loss which is a consequence of that course of action having been taken. If his duty is only to supply information, he must take reasonable care to ensure that the information is correct and if he is negligent, will be responsible for all the foreseeable consequences of the information being wrong.

In a nutshell, what Lord Hoffman is saying in the mountaineering example is that it would be wrong to transfer to the doctor all the foreseeable risks of the expedition. There is a distinction between giving information and advice. The doctor in his famous example did not advise on the merits of the expedition in general, only whether the knee was in a satisfactory condition for the expedition. Therefore on his example the doctor was not liable if an accident occurred which, while wholly foreseeable, had no connection with the knee. It is not enough for the patient to say: 'I would not have gone on this expedition if you had given me the correct advice about my knee.' The doctor was only liable for the consequences of the information about the knee being wrong: for example if the patient could not complete the expedition because of his knee. The contrary conclusion would mean that whenever a person gives access to goods or services by the provision of incorrect information, he becomes liable for everything that happens even if what happens is not the result of information being untrue. There will be myriad reasons for a person wanting access to goods or services, and loss may well be attributable to those other reasons.

The *SAAMCO* principle is of great importance in the field of professional negligence. This is illustrated by the unreported decision of the Court of Appeal in *Johnson v Gore Wood (No 2)*.[28] This was the appeal from judgment following the trial of the action which followed the decision of the House of Lords on reflective loss,[29] which Lord Justice Chadwick discussed in a 2007 lecture.[30] You will recall the basic facts of this case. The solicitors to Mr Johnson, Gore Wood & Co, gave him and his company negligent advice as to whether, and within what time frame, he would be able to enforce an option granted to his company to acquire land which he planned to develop at a large profit. The option price was a mere £175,000 and the value of the land was said to be £600,000. The solicitors gave what the Court of Appeal for shorthand called the 'six month no lose advice'—you will win the specific performance application or obtain damages (in fact on the basis of breach of warranty of authority) within six months. On the faith of that advice, Mr Johnson made all sorts of financial commitments: he acquired (with some small professional involvement by way of advice from Gore Wood) businesses which needed cash injections; he borrowed money from acquaintances which he could not repay; he ran up a large overdraft with his bank; he was unable to make a contribution to his own pension fund; and he incurred tax liabilities which he could have avoided if the company had had more cash and could have paid the salary voted to Mr Johnson. His company secured a settlement of £1.5 million from the solicitors. Mr Johnson's damages were said to be £4.3 million. At trial he was awarded a mere £88,791. To what extent were the solicitors liable? There was detailed evidence about the extent to which Gore Wood knew about his financial position. In particular there was a memorable letter which he wrote to his solicitor and in which he said that he had had to sell some investment properties and his wife's car which he said was 'not as funny as it may sound to some' and which noted

[28] [2003] EWCA Civ 1728.   [29] *Johnson v Gore Wood* [2002] AC 1.
[30] Chadwick LJ put forward an alternative analysis of reflective loss in his Annual Lecture for the Chancery Bar Association, given on 19 March 2007, entitled 'Complementary Duties: a Solution to Problems of Double Liability and Double Recovery?', available on the CBA website <http://www.chba.org.uk>. Chadwick LJ also gave the Peter Taylor Memorial Lecture in 2004, which may also have discussed the same subject in more detail but I have been unable to find any record of that lecture.

that Gore Wood 'had cheerfully reminded him that situations like this were character-building'.

The case is worth looking at in detail. The Court emphasized that it was not the scale of the losses that mattered but whether they were the kind of loss in respect of which a duty was owed. The Court drew attention to the extraordinarily robust nature of the advice. Gore Wood were not formally asked to advise on most of the new investments which Mr Johnson entered into on the strength of the 'six month no lose' advice. The Court of Appeal said that the scope of the duty had to encompass anything which Mr Johnson could be expected to do on the basis of the advice. The Court of Appeal then went through the heads of the damages item by item claimed, and awarded damages on a rather more generous basis than the trial judge, including for example, the cost of the personal borrowing which he could not repay because the 'six month no lose' advice was incorrect down to the date when the solicitors ceased to act.

Causal contribution

Professor Jane Stapleton has argued that factual cause and scope of liability must be kept separate.[31] I agree with her that this is in general a helpful approach. The fact that an accident occurs and would not have happened but for the negligence of the defendant does not of course mean that the defendant caused the accident for legal purposes, or that the defendant must be liable: the scope of the duty principle which we have just examined shows that. Take the example of the garage attendant who fails to tell a car owner to turn off his engine while filling with petrol. The purpose of the duty is to prevent an explosion. Suppose what happens is not an explosion but an accident due to the car rolling down the hill on which the garage is located because the engine is still on and the handbrake is not engaged? Is the garage proprietor liable? If the purpose of his duty is to prevent explosions, then his omission is outside the scope of the duty imposed on him.

I have there taken the example of an omission to make a statement. You will recall that a special rule applies to failures to give information. The authority usually cited is that of Millett LJ in *Bristol & West v Mothew*:[32]

In the present case the society's claim is not for misrepresentation. Accordingly, questions of inducement and materiality are not relevant. Its claim lies in negligence, and the relevant concept is reliance. In considering the issue of causation in an action for negligence brought by a client against his solicitor it appears from *Downs v Chappell* that it is necessary to distinguish between two different kinds of case.

Where a client sues his solicitor for having negligently failed to give him proper advice, he must show what advice should have been given and (on a balance of probabilities) that if such advice had been given he would not have entered into the relevant transaction or would not have entered into it on the terms he did. The same applies where the client's complaint

---

[31] See 'Cause in Fact and the Scope of Liability for Consequences' (2003) 119 LQR 388.
[32] [1998] Ch 1.

is that the solicitor failed in his duty to give him material information. In *Sykes v Midland Bank Executor and Trustee Co Ltd* [1970] 2 All ER 471, [1971] 1 QB 113, which was concerned with a failure to give proper advice, the plaintiff was unable to establish this and his claim to damages for negligence failed. In *Mortgage Express Ltd v Bowerman & Partners (a firm)* [1996] 2 All ER 836, which was concerned with a failure to convey information, the plaintiff was able to establish that if it had been given the information it would have withdrawn from the transaction and its claim succeeded.

Where, however, a client sues his solicitor for having negligently given him incorrect advice or for having negligently given him incorrect information, the position appears to be different. In such a case it is sufficient for the plaintiff to prove that he relied on the advice or information, that is to say that he would not have acted as he did if he had not been given such advice or information. It is not necessary for him to prove that he would not have acted as he did if he had been given the proper advice or the correct information.

This principle was applied by Hobhouse LJ (as he then was) in *Downs v Chappell*.[33] The principle has been criticized. Why should it be more difficult to show causation where there was a failure to give any advice than where there was advice given but it was incorrect? If there is a requirement to show that you would have acted differently if given the right advice, then surely, under any coherent system of tort law, that principle should apply both where wrong advice is given and where no advice is given? In many cases it is, of course, difficult to say whether the situation is one in which no advice was given or one in which the wrong advice was given.

In my view the distinction, which at first sight is of the 'now you see it now you don't' kind, is logically correct. It shows the importance of distinguishing legal from factual causation. If no advice was given, you cannot show that the omission was causative of the loss unless you can show that as a matter of fact you would have acted on the advice if given. There is no need to do this if incorrect advice was given, since as a matter of fact loss ensues if you act on the wrong advice. The principle established by Millett LJ is a rational one in addition to being a useful one in the context of professional negligence.

One of the joys of the Bench is that no two days and no two cases are the same and my recollection is that life was much the same at the Bar. We had a professional negligence appeal[34] in 2004 which involved an alleged omission by a solicitor to advise his client of the effect of a notice to quit. The judge found that, if the solicitor had given the right advice, the client (the claimant) would not have acted any differently from the way that he did in fact act. You may think that that looks like a pretty good answer on causation in the light of the principle in *Mothew*. The case came on appeal just after the House of Lords handed down their decision in *Chester v Asfar*.[35] The unrepresented litigant made an immediate connection between that case and his own.

You will recall the basic facts of *Chester*: a patient was not advised of a serious but remote side effect of surgery which eventuated through no fault of the surgeon in performing the surgery. The claimant could not show that she would not have had

---

[33] [1997] 1 WLR 426.   [34] *White v Paul Davidson & Taylor* [2004] EWCA Civ 1511.
[35] [2005] 1 AC 134.

the operation if she had been told of the side effect though she would have taken a second opinion so that the operation would have been delayed. She was held entitled to recover the whole of the damages caused by having the operation. This was a case[36] in which there would be no remedy for the defendant's failure (in this case, to warn) unless the claimant could recover damages. Moreover, the claimant had as a result of the operation lost the right to make her own fully-informed decision as to whether to have the operation. In the circumstances it was held that there was sufficient causation for legal purposes. There was a difference of view in the House as to whether the risks of the injury occurring would have been any less if the operation had been performed at a later date. The case is one where the desire to achieve distributive justice triumphed over the desire to do corrective justice. What is interesting is whether this decision marks the start of a new direction in the jurisprudence of the House of Lords—or now the Supreme Court—in cases where there was a clear duty and a clear breach of duty but causation cannot be shown on conventional principles. We shall have to wait and see. The door is definitely open but we cannot yet see in.

In the solicitors' negligence case to which I referred, the unrepresented appellant submitted that it was in the public interest that a solicitor should compensate his client if he acted negligently and so the Court of Appeal should hold, applying *Chester*, that the failure by a solicitor to provide advice was itself enough to found liability.

I think that we would all now recognize that in any legal system there has to be room for exceptional cases where liability exists even though the claimant cannot show on a balance of probabilities that the defendant's wrongful conduct resulted in the claimant's injury, that is, causation on conventional principles. This is now established by *Fairchild v Glenhaven*.[37] Here the defendants had materially contributed to the risk of their employees catching asbestosis—a single indivisible injury. It was not possible, in the light of current medical knowledge, for the employees to show that any defendant's wrongful act caused the asbestosis from which they suffered—the disease might have been caused by a single fibre or by a cumulative exposure to asbestos. (Over time, they had each had several employers.) An analogy can be drawn with the Canadian case about two hunters—both fire a shot. The victim is killed or injured with a single shot but it cannot be shown from which gun the shot came. If causation has to be proved on a conventional basis, neither hunter would be liable. So too, in *Fairchild*, if the claimant had not succeeded, all the defendants would have escaped liability. As we all know, the House of Lords held that all the employers were held liable for the whole injury: the employees could 'leap over' the evidentiary gap.[38]

I note that the employers did not ask for the damages to be apportioned between them. It may not be possible for the courts to apportion damages under the Civil Liability (Contribution) Act 1978 because it cannot be shown that the other alleged

---

[36] Like *Fairchild*, as to which see later.   [37] [2003] 1 AC 32.

[38] A phrase borrowed from Professor Jane Stapleton, 'Lords a'Leaping over Evidentiary Gaps' (2002) Torts Law Journal 276.

wrongdoer was necessarily liable in respect of the same damage. That problem, however, was not addressed in the House of Lords decision.[39]

Fairchild was clearly a welcome decision on the facts but, once you admit the principle that there should be times when a defendant is liable because otherwise the claimant will have no remedy against anyone, it is difficult to see where it should stop. It has, for instance, been argued by academics that special principles of causation should apply to cases where there has been a breach by the employer of his duty of mutual trust and confidence in the way the business is run but the employee cannot show that his employment prospects elsewhere were diminished as a result.[40] In *Chester v Asfar*, the House of Lords did not lay down rules for applying different principles of causation. It will, I think, be difficult to define the circumstances. There may be anomalies—why should the claimants in *Fairchild* recover everything while the claimant in *Gregg v Scott*[41] received nothing? Those are difficult issues which I propose to leave for another day.

In case you were wondering, the Court of Appeal did not apply *Chester v Asfar* in the solicitors' negligence case to which I have referred but held that it was bound by the holdings of Millett LJ in the *Mothew* case. The Court distinguished the *Chester* case as turning on policy considerations related to the sanctity of informed patient consent, and referred to the Charter of Fundamental Rights and Freedoms in the proposed European Constitution.[42]

Conclusion

I hope that I have convinced you that there is some unnecessary dead wood in the law of negligence—concepts which Professor Ibbetson in the passage I started with called legal hangovers. There, the great challenge for advocates is to help the courts to cut away the dead wood and help to make the law of negligence more modern and more transparent, and the limits on liability more rational in their operation. The great mission of an advocate is of course to win his or her case for the client. But the chances of winning are far greater the more attractive you make the legal principle involved. If you can cut a way through the veritable forest of authorities on negligence and make the way plain to the court, you will not only have done the best for your client, you will have contributed to the development of the law and in particular to making it more accessible for future generations.

At the present time there is evidence of new growth as in the *Fairchild* and *Chester* principles. Who knows where they will go? The law must lay down rational limits and try to avoid hangovers of the kind I referred to at the start of this chapter.

---

[39] The problem arose, however, in the later case of *Barker v Corus* [2006] 2 AC 572, where the employers were held responsible according to their relative contribution to the risk that the employee would contract mesothelioma, but that decision was reversed by the Compensation Act 2006.
[40] See *Husain v BCCI* [2002] EWCA Civ 82.   [41] [2005] 2 WLR 268.
[42] This was ultimately not ratified by the EU member states, and was replaced by the Lisbon Treaty.

PART II

ABSORBING THE IMPACT OF CONSTITUTIONAL CHANGE

The special feature of the UK constitution is that even today it is largely unwritten. People act on the basis of usage and understanding rather than on the basis of written law. The usages and understandings have been built up over our long history, step by step. In my view, the execution of Magna Carta at Runnymede in 1215 was an important step not just because of what it said but because of the way in which the ideas in it were developed. That is the subject of the first chapter in this Part, *Magna Carta and the Hidden Wiring of the Common Law*. The ideas reflected in Magna Carta facilitated a change in social and political behaviour which might not otherwise have occurred.

As Chairman of the Judges' Working Party on Constitutional Reform from 2004 to 2006, I worked on the Bill that became the historic Constitutional Reform Act 2005. This Act instituted a separation of powers between Parliament and the executive, on the one hand, and the judiciary, on the other. For instance, it removed the Lord Chancellor as the head of the judicial system in England and Wales (placing the Lord Chief Justice of England and Wales in that role instead) and set up a new process of independent judicial appointments. Provisions of the Bill had to set out or at least be consistent with elements of our constitution that were previously unwritten. For example, the Bill had to set out the responsibilities of the Lord Chancellor in relation to the judiciary that would remain after he ceased to be its head. It also imposed an obligation on the Lord Chancellor, ministers of the Crown, and all with responsibility for the administration of justice to respect judicial independence.

The next chapter, *Independence of the Judiciary and the Role of Parliaments*, was originally written following the passing of the Constitutional Reform Act 2005. It describes the principle of judicial independence and the impact of the new legislation.

Judicial independence has at least two components. The first is the individual independence of the judge in the particular cases in which they are sitting, and the second is the independence of the judiciary as an institution.

The independence of the judiciary from the legislature and the executive is a constitutional principle of cardinal importance. It ensures that the individual will receive justice, however powerful the government of the day. It also underpins the point that I have made throughout this work that the role of the judiciary is to keep judge-made law up to date.

The Constitutional Reform Act 2005 also enacted for the first time that there should be a statutory scheme for complaints against the judiciary. These can be complex and the Working Party that I chaired went on to oversee the drafting of the lengthy regulations to set up the new scheme.

The final chapter, *What is the Safeguard for Welsh Devolution?*, deals with the legal implications of another major constitutional change. I argue that devolution is a form of federalism. This is a significant conclusion in itself, because it requires an analysis of what constitutes federalism. In Volume I,[1] I expressed some brief, tentative views about the principles that should apply to the interpretation of legislation that sets out the powers of devolved institutions as against those of the Westminster Parliament or the government of the United Kingdom. I develop those thoughts further in Chapter 8 of this Part, as devolution constitutes what I call federalism 'in fact'.

My further concern in Chapter 8 is that the courts should draw on the case law of courts that have dealt with issues between state and federal powers in federal systems. Recent decisions of the Supreme Court have not drawn any distinction between devolution and other legislation. It is perhaps early days yet in terms of problems arising from devolution legislation in the United Kingdom, so the Supreme Court may revisit its approach. In that event, the ideas discussed here may indeed beat the path to tomorrow's law.

---

[1] 'The Changing Judicial Role: Human Rights, Community Law and the Intention of Parliament' in *Shaping Tomorrow's Law*, Volume I, *Human Rights and European Law: Building New Legal Orders* (Oxford University Press, 2015) ch 8, 112–29.

6

Magna Carta and the Hidden Wiring
of the Common Law

This chapter is based on papers given at the Howard and Smith Law Seminar, Lady Margaret Hall, Oxford, on 29 May 2015, and at the seminar comparing the Declaration of the Rights of Man and Magna Carta, organized by the Franco-British Council and held at Lancaster House, London, on 11 June 2015.

Influence and constitutional importance of Magna Carta

To mark the 800th anniversary of Magna Carta in 2015, much has been written about its influence on the making of modern Britain. In my view, the argument for Magna Carta as an important constitutional event in our history is a strong one, and my aim here is to demonstrate why I call it the 'hidden wiring of the common law'.[1]

Inevitably there are those who say that Magna Carta's influence is a myth and that its contribution to the growth of our constitution was much less than some like to think. There is insufficient space to answer all their points, but I shall try to address some of them.

It is well known that the United Kingdom does not have a written constitution in the sense of a single document adopted by an approved mechanism which sets out what rights we have and how the United Kingdom is governed. The United Kingdom gave many colonies and dominions written constitutions when they gained independence but it has never had one of its own: apparently we felt that the protection of a written constitution was unnecessary at home. Magna Carta— or rather, as I shall explain later, the use made of it—may be one of the reasons why this is so. Quite simply, over time, the values in Magna Carta became hard-wired in our law.

In recent years, the balance between written and unwritten has somewhat changed. A number of statutes in areas that would normally be covered by a written

---

[1] This volume examines Magna Carta in two separate chapters. In this, the first, I discuss its constitutional implications. The second, Ch 18, *Magna Carta and the Judges: Realizing the Vision*, explores the contribution which Magna Carta has made to the establishment of an independent judiciary.

constitution have been passed since 1998, including the Human Rights Act 1998, the Scotland Act 1998, the Northern Ireland Act 1998, the Freedom of Information Act 2000, the Government of Wales Act 2006, and the Fixed-term Parliaments Act 2011. But the reality remains that there are still significant areas which are not defined in any enactment, such as the fundamental concepts of independence of the judiciary, ministerial responsibility,[2] the rule of law, and the procedure for changing our constitutional arrangements. The truth is that the UK constitution is not static but constantly evolving. It follows that, if constitutional change is made by legislation, it is at least possible that it will need amendment, as has happened already with some of the statutes that I have mentioned. Moreover, if there is legislation, the courts have the responsibility for interpreting that legislation in accordance with its language and purpose.

In terms of content, Magna Carta was the early ancestor of a modern constitution. It was a long document, containing some sixty-three clauses. The best known among them are cls 39 and 40, which provide:

(39) No free man shall be seized or imprisoned, or stripped of his rights or possessions, or outlawed or exiled, or deprived of his standing in any way, nor will we proceed with force against him, or send others to do so, except by the lawful judgment of his equals or by the law of the land.

(40) To no one will we sell, to no one deny or delay right or justice.[3]

These two clauses are still in force today. The only other clauses still in force are cl 1, which provides that the English Church shall be free,[4] and cl 13, which preserves 'the ancient liberties' of the City of London and states that other cities, boroughs, towns, and ports shall also all have their liberties and free customs.

Magna Carta was sealed by King John in an age when many monarchs executed royal charters[5] apparently giving rights and liberties. The best known is perhaps the Golden Bull of Hungary 1222.[6] Magna Carta was not a wholly original document. It drew on earlier documents, such as the Charter of Liberties, signed by Henry I on his coronation in 1100. This had sought to protect the property of the Church and the barons from the depredations of the monarch but it had been widely disregarded. Hence the drafters of Magna Carta saw the need for it to be reaffirmed by the monarch: there was as yet no parliament and it was a pretty lawless world.

---

[2] There is, however, a very important and comprehensive ministerial code, to be found on the Cabinet Office website, which sets out the standards of conduct expected of ministers and how they discharge their duties.

[3] This is taken from the translation of the 1215 version of Magna Carta used by the British Library in connection with the celebrations for its 800th Anniversary: See more at <http://www.bl.uk/magna-carta/articles/magna-carta-english-translation>. The original Magna Carta was in Latin and is said to have been translated into English in 1300. These clauses became cl 29 of the 1225 version of Magna Carta.

[4] A point which Magna Carta, cl 63 repeats.

[5] The word 'carta' is Latin for 'charter', and so it became known in English as the Great Charter of Liberties.

[6] The Golden Bull was also confirmed on several occasions in the 13th and 14th centuries. Among other matters, it confirmed liberties, such as that of a landowner not to be seized or brought to ruin unless first summoned and convicted by judicial procedure.

Magna Carta was a remarkable document. It was drawn up on the basis that a seemingly autocratic king could be subjected against his will to a document which he sealed. Indeed, the version of Magna Carta that was sealed in 1215 contained a mechanism for its enforcement against the King. Clause 61, often called 'the security clause', provided for a council of twenty-five barons to adjudicate on whether the King had breached Magna Carta, whereupon the King was to rectify the matter. Even though the security clause did not appear in later versions of Magna Carta, it was a very important early recognition of the rule of law. Even sovereign power is subject to the law.

Criticisms of Magna Carta as a significant document

The fact that King John executed Magna Carta against his will had a number of repercussions, which are at the heart of the argument of those who say that the influence of Magna Carta is a myth. First, the King was able to persuade Pope Innocent III to issue on 24 August 1215 a papal bull to the effect that it was not binding. The exact legal basis on which the Pope was acting is not clear.[7] Be that as it may, the Pope's action meant that, so far as the King was concerned, Magna Carta was in force for less than 100 days. The very next year King John died, so further confrontation was avoided. But that was not the end of Magna Carta. King John's heir was his 9-year-old son, who became Henry III. On the advice of his sapient regent, William Marshall, Earl of Pembroke, Henry III reissued most of Magna Carta and in 1225 he promised to abide by it.[8] As we shall see, Magna Carta was reissued (with some changes) on several occasions.[9]

Critics of Magna Carta also like to point out that it largely benefited classes who were privileged anyway, namely the barons, the free men, the Church, and the City of London. On that basis it was never intended to be a statement of the liberties of all citizens, but only of that smaller class of persons. It contained no clause directed to alleviating the burdens on those who were not free men, for example by enabling them to work for other lords.[10] The only mention of 'villeins' (peasants bound to the lord of the manor in feudal times) was in cl 20, which states that a villein's husbandry tools shall not be taken from him[11] and that fines will only be imposed

---

[7] See GB Adams, 'Innocent III and the Great Charter' in Henry Malden Smith (ed), *Magna Carta Commemoration Essays* (Royal Historical Society, 1917).

[8] It had also been reissued by his regent and the Papal emissary on his behalf on earlier occasions.

[9] The clauses which remain in force today have done so because they formed part of Magna Carta when it was reissued in 1225. They subsequently became part of Magna Carta as issued in 1297, which became a statute of the Westminster Parliament. The parts of Magna Carta as issued in 1297 which remain in force, being the four clauses mentioned in the text, can be viewed on <http://www.legislation.gov.uk>, the official database for UK legislation enacted since 1267.

[10] See generally Edward Jenks, 'The Myth of Magna Carta' (1902) 4 Independent Review 260; and Lord Sumption, 'Magna Carta Then and Now', Address to the Friends of the British Library, 6 March 2015 <https://www.supremecourt.uk/docs/speech-150309.pdf>.

[11] Presumably by way of a fine.

on him on the testimony of reputable men of the neighbourhood. There is a popular misconception that cl 39 secured the right to trial by jury. This was a later interpretation.[12] Furthermore, the only means specified in Magna Carta for the enforcement of the rights granted by it was the security clause (see earlier). Thus, in the view of the critics, the beginnings of a real constitutional settlement only came when Parliament was first convened by Simon de Montfort in 1264 and then by Edward I later in the thirteenth century.

A document before its time

In evaluating these criticisms, some allowance has to be made for the fact that Magna Carta was the product of a mediaeval society. It made little use of the word 'right'. Even so, it did assume the sanctity of property and provided protection for property rights. Magna Carta has to be seen in the context of the common law which developed many of the rights now reflected in modern statements of rights. As Sir John Baker QC has written:

Human rights were not invented in the 1940s and they certainly did not emanate from the Continent.... There is inevitably a difference between principles, which are normative rather than descriptive, and what people—including governments—actually do. But that does not invalidate the principles.

With that caveat in mind, it is possible to see that most of the main items in our modern lists of human rights—no slavery, the right to a fair trial, no punishment without law, and the protection of property or possessions—were part and parcel of the common law from an early date.[13]

Moreover, although Magna Carta addressed some current or relatively mundane grievances, such as fish-weirs and bridges, some of the provisions were written in open-textured terms which were in part visionary. Thus, for example, in 1215, cl 1, which as I have explained provides that the English Church 'shall be free', had nothing to do with the Reformation, but with the idea of freedom from interference with Church property. Nonetheless, the germ of a wider idea about independence of the Church in terms of freedom of conscience was there.

Many of the other similar contemporary royal charters were forgotten as time passed but Magna Carta's provisions lived on. Today nearly all the clauses of Magna Carta have been superseded over time or repealed, so that only four remain in effect, but Magna Carta is not to be regarded as simply a dead letter.

---

[12] On its face, cl 39 applied only to free men. This was, however, clarified in the 14th century by legislation which made it clear that it applied to all men whatever their estate or condition: 28 Edw III c 3.

[13] Robin Griffith-Jones and Mark Hill QC (eds), *Magna Carta, Religion and the Rule of Law* (Cambridge University Press, 2015) 81–3. Footnotes in the original text have been omitted.

Understanding the reasons for Magna Carta's longevity

So, how did Magna Carta survive? There were, it seems, three particular explanations for the fact that Magna Carta was kept alive through the corridors of history despite the fact that the rights for which it provided were overtaken by other legislation or events. The first explanation is that, when Magna Carta was reissued in 1265, an order was given for it to be read twice-yearly in county courts, and when it was reissued in 1297, an order was given that it had also to be read out in cathedrals up and down the land at least twice a year. In an age when we have a vast range of public entertainment, it is difficult to think that the reading out of Magna Carta was much of an attraction, but in the later Middle Ages it did no doubt draw in the crowds, and acted as a means of reminding or telling people for many generations of the important things that Magna Carta said.[14]

The second explanation is that it was reissued (with some, but for present purposes immaterial, differences) and thereby confirmed by monarchs on several occasions, often in order to be able to raise taxation. In addition, on at least one occasion when Magna Carta was reissued, it was made enforceable on pain of excommunication. It is not known how often this sanction was enforced but the fact that it was capable of being enforced is an indication of the lasting importance which Magna Carta was considered to have.

The third explanation was perhaps the most important. When Magna Carta was clarified and reissued again in 1297, it was made clear that, although it had not contained any provisions about enforcement (except in the security clause in the case of breaches by the Crown), it could be enforced through the courts.

I can give a small example of enforcement by the courts in a case which I found in the law reports called *Claygate v Batchelor*,[15] decided by the entire bench of the Court of Common Pleas on New Year's Day in 1600, the penultimate year of the reign of Queen Elizabeth I. The report is very short. It appears that Mr Batchelor had a son, Robert, who had been apprenticed as a haberdasher to Mr Claygate, and Mr Claygate had exacted from Mr Batchelor (no doubt as the price of teaching Robert the skills of a haberdasher, which would enable him to earn a living) a bond for £30. This bond was payable if two conditions were satisfied if: (1) his son, Robert, took up the haberdashery trade in any capacity in Canterbury or Rochester within the period of four years after the date of the bond, and (2) Mr Batchelor had not paid Mr Claygate the sum of £20.[16] So it was effectively a covenant in restraint of trade with financial penalties attached.

The Court held that the covenant was against the law: 'for it is against the liberty of a free-man, and against the statute of Magna Carta cap. 20. and is against the

---

[14] With each reissue, an official charter was written, sealed, and sent out from the Royal Chancellery to each county, and this was another way of reminding people about Magna Carta.

[15] (1600) Owen 143; 74 ER 961. Also reported as *Colgate v Bacheler* (1600) Cro Eliz 872; 78 ER 1097.

[16] This condition seems to have been a discount for voluntary payment.

commonwealth. 2 H. 5. & 5.'.[17] There is no reason to think that the reference to Magna Carta was anything out of the ordinary or a flash in the pan: the reference to '2H 5. & 5.' is to *Dyer's* case in the yearbooks, which was decided in 1414 on similar points and also referred to Magna Carta. The brief report of *Claygate v Batchelor* goes on to record that one of the judges held that Mr Batchelor might as well bind himself that he would not go to church. In other words, the judges treated the restraint on personal freedom as objectionable in the eyes of the law as if it had been a promise not to practise one's religion. Accordingly, Mr Batchelor was found not liable on the bond and judgment was given against the plaintiff.

In due course, the judges developed the common law in response to the needs of commerce. Thus, in the eighteenth century with the growth in commerce and the need, for example, for enforceable covenants in restraint of trade when businesses were sold, the courts held that, where the area and period of time were reasonable, such a covenant would be enforced.[18] These cases illustrate how the common law used the provisions of Magna Carta and built on them as society developed.

One can only admire the creative genius of mediaeval law. Nothing was expressly said in Magna Carta about freedom from servitude. Society was feudal. There were barons, free men, and villeins, and the last group were anything but free. Mr Batchelor and his son, Robert, were obviously free men though in a relatively ordinary way of life. The court clearly regarded the bond as an unacceptable restriction on the liberty of Robert. Even though Magna Carta said nothing about personal freedom from servitude, what *Claygate v Batchelor* illustrates is that Magna Carta is being used to support the proposition that a person should be free not simply in the ordinary sense of being free from wrongful imprisonment, but in the more sophisticated sense of not being bound by a covenant preventing him from working at a particular time or place. That more sophisticated approach to freedom was, I suggest, a significant step. It marked the beginnings of a system of law which could respond over time to the development of commerce, social mobility, and political rights and freedoms. Political rights would in due course include important rights not contemplated at the time of Magna Carta, such as the right of freedom of religion and freedom of expression.

In public life, Magna Carta would be used in the seventeenth century to fortify the position of Parliament against the Crown. It is in this context that Sir Edward Coke made his famous remark in Parliament on 17 May 1628: 'Magna Charta is such a fellow, that he will have no "Sovereign".'[19]

The interpretation of Magna Carta in the courts and in public life has become wired into the social and political psyche of the nation, so that Magna Carta is now symbolic of our appreciation of freedom. Magna Carta was seamlessly extended by

---

[17] This is the 1297 version of Magna Carta. There appear to be two minor errors: 'cap. 20.' should be 'cap. 29.' and '2 H.5. & 5.' should be a reference to '2 H.5.5.'. The reference to Magna Carta does not appear in the year book report of this case, which refers instead to the common law.

[18] That development happened in the eighteenth century: see *Mitchell v Reynolds* (1711) 1 P Wms 181, as the House of Lords recognized in the landmark 19th-century case on covenants in restraint of trade, *Nordenfelt v Maxim Nordenfelt* [1894] AC 535.

[19] See Anthony Arlidge and Igor Judge, *Magna Carta Uncovered* (Hart, 2014) 134.

interpretation and usage and made responsive to the needs of a developing society. In assessing the legacy of Magna Carta 800 years on, it matters not that its provisions are not all contained in statute law which is in force today nor that the courts now rarely refer to Magna Carta. It is indeed part of the 'hidden wiring' of our constitution.

Influence overseas

Undoubtedly Magna Carta had a considerable influence on the constitutions of the newly independent American colonies, which in many cases made specific reference to the two great clauses of Magna Carta, cls 39 and 40. When the Constitution of the United States was drafted, one of the purposes of the drafters was to ensure that the people of America had the same rights as Englishmen. The famous clauses of Magna Carta were evident in the Fifth Amendment—the due process clause— which provides: 'Nor shall any person be deprived of life, liberty or property, without due process of law.' This clause led to a flowering of jurisprudence about due process, both procedural and substantive, which is of great importance in US constitutional law. Procedural due process ensures, for instance, that before depriv- ing a person of his property, the government follows the correct procedure: this may involve giving notice and an opportunity to speak. Substantive due process is a more radical doctrine. It enables the courts to assess the justification for an exercise of official power, and to impose substantive limits on such exercise.

There were, however, some important differences between Magna Carta and the Bill of Rights in the US Constitution. In particular, in contrast to Magna Carta, which secured the rights and liberties of the English Church, the First Amendment to the Bill of Rights in the US Constitution precludes Congress from making laws on the establishment of religion.

The Bill of Rights in the US Constitution was one of the influences which led to the adoption of the Declaration of the Rights of Man and the Citizen in the French Constitution. However, the French document is very different from Magna Carta. It is also difficult to compare with Magna Carta because it comes at a much later point in time—it was finally approved in 1791—and is the product of different circumstances. Nevertheless, certain points can be made. By the time it was adopted, France was a republic. The Declaration proceeds not upon the basis of the grant of rights by a king but on the basis that the rights of man were inherent, natural, universal, and inalienable. The Declaration was adopted after the French Revolution and marked the beginnings of an entirely new society. In contrast, Magna Carta did not bring about an end to feudal society in mediaeval Britain. If anything it enhanced the rights of the barons, the Church, and the City of London, and not those of everyday citizens.

There was another specific difference in relation to freedom of religion and freedom of expression. The Declaration of the Rights of Man and the Citizen guaranteed freedom of religion and contained the germ of the thinking that led ultimately to the separation of religion from the state as found in the current French constitution (*laïcité*). That means that religion can play no part in public life organized by the state. This is a totally different approach from Magna Carta but the difference is understandable since Magna Carta was a pre-Reformation and pre-Enlightenment document. Other differences include the fact that, unlike the Declaration of the Rights of Man and the Citizen, Magna Carta contained a mixture of provisions, some public law, and some private law. Magna Carta was not, therefore, a document which looked like a modern bill of rights.

Nonetheless, we can see some echoes of Magna Carta in the Declaration of the Rights of Man and the Citizen. For example, cl 7 of the Declaration provides that 'no person shall be accused, arrested, or imprisoned except in the cases and according to the forms prescribed by law'.

Returning to the United Kingdom, a point not often made is that Magna Carta did not apply in Scotland, which was a separate Kingdom. Nor did it apply in Wales, which at the time had its own legal system. There were some incidental provisions which were meant to apply in relation to those countries, but in general Magna Carta applied only to England. That does not mean, however, that it has not since or cannot now be embraced by the whole of the United Kingdom.

Continuing use and value of Magna Carta

Magna Carta has been used over the centuries to support liberal causes. It was even argued by suffragettes in the early twentieth century that it was a breach of Magna Carta to deny women the vote. Space does not permit me to go into the use made of it, particularly in the seventeenth century, in the struggles against the Crown. However, looking back, we can see how it has helped social and political change to take place in this country and has encouraged our appreciation of liberty to grow. It encouraged the development of the common law, and the common law became one of the mechanisms within our unwritten constitution for controlling the exercise of political power.

Moreover, the name of Magna Carta is revered in many parts of the world. In the fanfare of celebration, Magna Carta's most important role on the occasion of its 800th anniversary may be in the promotion of the rule of law and democracy throughout the world.

Today some of what Magna Carta stands for is emblematic: we treat it as a synonym for a statement of fundamental rights even though those rights were quite rudimentary and have undergone much further development since. Magna Carta has become so hard wired into our national life and culture that we take it for granted and no longer appreciate its contribution. But, like any hidden wiring, it has a strong influence on our thinking and values. It is also an important reminder of the virtues of our unwritten constitution and the common law as tools for reflecting social and political development over time. Its legacy may therefore be to continue to provide inspiration for further constitutional development.

7

Independence of the Judiciary
and the Role of Parliaments

This chapter is based on a paper given at a conference organized by the Institute of European and Comparative law at the University of Oxford in September 2004 and published in 2007.*

Two kinds of independence to be distinguished

What do we mean by independence of the judiciary? Section 3 of the Constitutional Reform Act 2005[1] provides that the Lord Chancellor and Ministers of the Crown shall uphold the continued independence of the judiciary. As I see it, this involves at least two things. First, it involves the judge in any individual case being free to reach the decision which he considers to be in accordance with the law, free from any influence. Second, judicial independence means institutional independence, that is, it involves the notion that respect is given for the judiciary as an institution.

The latter meaning of judicial independence is discussed in a recent case in the Supreme Court of Canada. In *An Application under Article 83.28 of the Criminal Code*,[2] legislation passed by the Canadian Parliament was challenged as being in contravention of the constitutional principle of independence of the judiciary. The Crown sought to invoke powers conferred on them by the Canadian Anti-terrorism Act 2001. The Crown wanted to examine under oath an uncooperative witness in the then ongoing trial of two persons charged in connection with the explosion of an Air India jet in 1985. The Crown wanted to examine the witness in private and in the absence of the accused. The witness would not be entitled to decline to answer.

The judge who heard the application (who was not the trial judge) made the order sought by the Crown. Counsel for the accused became aware of the order,

---

* 'Independence of the Judiciary' in Katja Ziegler, Denis Baranger, and Anthony Bradley (eds), *Constitutionalism and the Role of Parliaments* (Hart Publishing, 2007) 191. Reproduced here by kind permission of Bloomsbury Publishing Plc.

[1] Constitutional Reform Act 2005, s 3(1) (which resulted from the almost identical Constitutional Reform Bill, cl 1(1)) provides: 'The Lord Chancellor, other Ministers of the Crown and all with responsibility for matters relating to the judiciary or otherwise to the administration of justice must uphold the continued independence of the judiciary.'

[2] [2004] Supreme Court of Canada 42.

and challenged it on constitutional grounds. On appeal, the order was varied so that counsel for the accused could attend but on terms that he should leave if information unrelated to the trial was elicited. No information obtained in the course of the examination was to be given to the accused.

The case went to the Supreme Court of Canada. Applying a presumption of constitutionality and a purposive approach, the majority held that it was implicit in the statutory power that counsel for the accused should be able to participate in the examination of the witness. As to the threshold test for relevance and admissibility, the Supreme Court held (applying a purposive approach) that the proceedings were criminal proceedings. Thus, for example, the privilege against self-incrimination would apply. The witness would also have immunity from extradition and deportation proceedings arising from use of the evidence against him.

Like the United Kingdom, Canada has no formal separation of powers, and thus the role of the judiciary under the constitution is a matter of inference rather than express provision. The defendants sought to challenge the constitutionality of the new powers on the grounds that they infringed judicial independence. They argued that the judge was co-opted into performing an executive function. The Supreme Court of Canada held that judicial independence was an unwritten principle of the Canadian constitution. However, by a majority, it rejected the appellants' challenge. The judge's role when the witness was being examined was the traditional role of ensuring that the investigation was conducted fairly. The purpose of the investigation was to investigate a terrorist offence. There was a presumption that such hearings should be held in public, but in the present case the hearing would be in private and the evidence would not be released until later.

Judicial independence was protected by the constitution and the common law. The role of the judiciary was not simply to adjudicate on disputes, but also to uphold constitutional protections. In the present case, the presence of the judiciary at the examination of the witness served as a check on state excess. The judge was empowered to ensure that the questioning was fair and relevant.

However, two judges of the Supreme Court, Le Bel and Fish JJ, who dissented, thought that the statute infringed judicial independence and should be declared constitutionally invalid. The dissenting judges distinguished individual judicial independence from institutional judicial independence. The former attaches to judges as individuals, the latter to the courts as an institution. If a reasonable, well-informed person would conclude that the judiciary had become allies of the executive branch, judicial independence was infringed. In the case under appeal it was institutional judicial independence that was violated. The appearance of separation of powers had to be preserved. The investigation of offences was a matter for the executive. The judge was not given the necessary tools to protect the constitutional rights of the witness. The dissenting judges were also sceptical about the judge's ability to exclude irrelevant evidence. In their view, the legislation used the judicial function, not to obtain a legal ruling or an adjudication on a question of fact, but as a form of coercion to compel information in the advancement of the executive function. The distinction between the judicial and executive branches of government had thus become blurred.

The significance of this case for present purposes is that, in the view of the dissenting judges, the principle of judicial independence could be used to strike down legislation under Canadian law. As to English law, there is a very difficult question, which is outside the scope of this chapter, whether under s 3(1) of the Constitutional Reform Act 2005 the duty to which I have referred is a 'target' duty only[3] or whether the courts might seek to give it some legal force in some way.

The House of Lords, in its legislative capacity, has considered an amendment to the Constitutional Reform Bill to make cl 1(1),[4] and indeed a similar proposed clause dealing with the maintenance of the rule of law, a kind of fundamental law. The amendment would have required judges to construe other legislation, so far as possible, as not violating judicial independence or the rule of law. It would also have empowered judges to make declarations of incompatibility where they could not so construe legislation. However, these amendments were rejected as unnecessary, or alternatively, as giving judges too much power. The government did not want the provision to be enforceable through the courts but through ministerial account-ability to Parliament. It is to be noted that s 3 of the Constitutional Reform Act 2005 does not impose any duty on judges to be independent. It is taken for granted that they will be independent, as indeed they are bound to be, both as a matter of the common law and by virtue of Art 6 of the European Convention on Human Rights (the 'Convention').

Relationship between the judiciary and Parliament

Turning from judicial independence to the relationship between the judiciary and Parliament, I want to put forward a theory. The theory is that the constitution contains a number of moving parts. These parts are the three arms of the consti-tution: the legislature, the executive, and the judiciary. These three parts are constantly changing in shape and size and are constantly rubbing against each other. I contemplated calling these moving parts tectonic plates, but, had I done that, a reader might have thought they would give rise to earthquakes when they rub together. That would be the wrong analogy.

Writing the *Law of the Constitution* in the late nineteenth and early twentieth century, Professor AV Dicey did not discuss the position of the judiciary under the constitution at all. By contrast, *The Commonwealth Principles on the Accountability and Relationship between the Three Branches of Government*, approved by the Heads of Government of the Commonwealth, including the United Kingdom, in December 2003 in Nigeria, refers in terms to the judiciary as a branch of government.[5] This demonstrates the point that the three branches of government

---

[3] See for example *R v Inner London Education Authority, ex p Ali* (1990) 2 Admin LR 822.

[4] See now Constitutional Reform Act 2005, s 1 and Lord Bingham, 'The Rule of Law' (2006) 15(3) Commonwealth Lawyer 22; and see also *FP (Iran) v Secretary of State for the Home Department* [2007] EWCA Civ 13.

[5] Available for download at <http://www.cmja.org/downloads/latimerhouse/commprinthreearms. pdf> and other websites.

are moving parts. They are constantly changing in shape and size and, of course, rubbing against each other.

What is the function of the judicial branch of government under the Commonwealth Principles? In para II, headed 'Parliament and the Judiciary', the judiciary's responsibilities are stated to be 'the interpretation and application of the law'. Thus the Principles appear to be promoting the view that the judiciary's function is limited to adjudication, and interpretation of the law. But the Principles also recognize that the function of the judiciary these days goes beyond simply deciding disputes between private parties. At para VII(c) there is a passage headed 'Judicial Review'. This states that: 'Best democratic principles require that the actions of government are open to scrutiny by the courts, to ensure that decisions taken comply with the Constitution, with relevant statutes and other law, including the law relating to the principles of natural justice.' Thus, this provision gives judges a role under the constitution: they are given the role of monitoring compliance with the constitution. As Professor Vernon Bogdanor points out, even though the United Kingdom may not have a written constitution, it, too, certainly has a constitution, and it is undergoing a process of considerable change at the present time.

Judicial review where Convention or other fundamental rights are engaged

It is beyond the scope of this chapter to trace the history of judicial review in the United Kingdom in great detail. In the second half of the twentieth century, there was undoubtedly an explosion in judicial review. This was brought about by a number of factors, most recently the Human Rights Act 1998 and the development of fundamental common law rights. The 1998 Act requires judges to construe legislation so far as possible in accordance with the Convention rights. If they cannot do so, they may declare the legislation incompatible with those rights. In other words, Parliament is clearly making judges the arbiters of whether laws comply with Convention rights. The significance of the powers given to the court by the Human Rights Act 1998 can be seen, for example, from *A v Secretary of State for the Home Department*.[6] The first question in that case was whether there was 'a public emergency threatening the life of the nation', giving rise to the power to derogate from the Convention for the purpose of creating a power in the Anti-terrorism Crime and Security Act 2001 to detain suspected terrorists who were aliens. The further questions in that case were whether that power was a proportionate response to the emergency and whether it was open to Parliament, when creating that power, to draw a distinction between aliens, who could be detained indefinitely or until they chose to leave the jurisdiction, and other persons in the United Kingdom, who were not subject to the power. The first question was

---

[6] [2005] 2 AC 68.

resolved in the government's favour but the House of Lords held for the detainees on the second and third questions.[7]

Fundamental common law rights are at an early stage of development. One of those rights is the right of access to court. There are some disputes which a citizen must be capable of bringing before a court and his right to do so must be effective. Where a fundamental common law right exists, Parliament can only take it away by clear language.

The introduction of the Human Rights Act 1998 and the development of common law rights is only the start of a journey, and we do not know where this journey will end. Recently, the Home Secretary promoted an amendment to insert into legislation an 'ouster clause', that is, a clause which purported to oust the jurisdiction of the court, on every conceivable known ground, to review decisions of the new Asylum and Immigration Tribunal. The amendment was subsequently withdrawn. It must be a question for speculation whether the judges would have found a way around that particular provision.[8] It has been said that the doctrine of parliamentary sovereignty is a creation of the judges.[9] Moreover, many now contend that in reality Parliament can qualify its own sovereignty, as it did when the United Kingdom entered the European Community.

Some Convention rights, such as those conferred by Arts 8 and 10 are of a qualified nature. This means that, when determining whether a Convention right has been violated, the courts have to decide whether the restriction on the Convention right is necessary in a democratic society, serves a legitimate aim, and is proportionate. Thus, if the executive has formulated a particular policy, or the legislature has enacted a particular law, and that policy or law protects the majority at the expense of the minority for reasons which seem to the executive or the legislature to be valid, the courts may now, under the Human Rights Act 1998, have to assess whether that decision of the executive or legislature, as the case may be, was a legitimate aim or was proportionate or is necessary to a democratic society The courts clearly have this function. They may start from the position that the decision or legislation in question is justified for good reasons. But does this mean that the executive or legislative act can only be set aside if it is manifestly unreasonable? It is clearly not enough that the court would have acted differently. It may be that the courts should give the executive or the legislature latitude where the executive or the legislature, as the case may be, is better placed as an institution under the constitution to make the decision. This may be the case where the decision relates to the allocation of resources raised by taxation or the policy concerns education, planning, or national security. But, even if those are examples of situations where the executive is better placed to make decisions, where does that leave decisions on other matters, such as good taste and decency,[10] and the evidential

---

[7] For a fuller discussion of this case, see Vol I of this work, especially at 149–61.

[8] See generally Anthony Lester 'Beyond the Powers of Parliament' (2004) 9 Judicial Review 95.

[9] See *R (Jackson) v Attorney General* [2006] 1 AC 262, para 102 per Lord Steyn and para 104 per Lord Hope; see also Conrad Russell, 'Thomas Cromwell's Doctrine of Parliamentary Sovereignty' (1977) *Transactions of the Historical Society* 235.

[10] See *R (ProLife Alliance) v British Broadcasting Corporation* [2004] 1 AC 185.

basis for security decisions?[11] The proper scope of the area of discretionary judgment of the executive or the legislature is a very difficult question, and the law is in a state of development.[12]

In certain areas, the legislature has sought to remove questions from the courts. I have already mentioned the ouster clause, but that was withdrawn and so never became law. A further example is the creation of the Sentencing Guidelines Council by the Criminal Justice Act 2003. It has power to commission research and to lay down guidelines which judges must take into account. Before the legislation setting up the Sentencing Guidelines Council was passed, there were criticisms of the courts. It was said that sentencing was poorly targeted, leading to sentencing drift and an increase in the prison population. It was also said that there were wide disparities between different courts leading to the so-called 'postcode justice', and that sentencers did not have sufficient information. So Parliament has now taken away what to many is a traditional role of the judiciary, that is, to decide on sentencing policy. Putting it another way, Parliament is intruding into a judicial area. However, for my own part, I do not consider that this infringes judicial independence. The courts must still take the decision in a particular case. The court which sentences an individual offender is only obliged to take the guidelines into account. It is not obliged to follow them in every case. I am well aware from my experience as a former Chairman of the Law Commission of England and Wales that there are some areas of law where judges are not well placed to know how best to apply, or develop, the law. There may need to be, for instance, economic, sociological, empirical or other research. The Sentencing Guidelines Council, if properly resourced, will be able to conduct such research or obtain such information.

So I will turn to my theory that the constitution contains these three moving parts. I have sought to show that those plates are shifting and rubbing against each other. We have not heard the end of the story. The process is one of ongoing development.

---

[11] *Secretary of State of the Home Department v Rehman* [2003] 1 AC 153.
[12] See, eg, the discussion in Vol I of this work at 73–4, 93–5.

8

What is the Safeguard for
Welsh Devolution?

This chapter is based on a keynote speech given at the Welsh Legal Services
Conference on 9 October 2013.*

The importance of statutory interpretation

Devolution has been described as a process and not an event. It is an ongoing
process. Any ongoing process needs to be kept in good running order. Therefore,
devolution needs to be safeguarded. It is for Parliament and the people of Wales to
decide how it should be developed, but the potentiality for its development already
existing in the law must be preserved.

Hence the question discussed in this chapter is: What is the safeguard for Welsh
devolution? I shall focus on the role of the courts in the interpretation of the
statutory provisions that set out the competence of the Welsh Assembly.

My thesis is this. The safeguarding of Welsh devolution has many facets but in
part the preservation of the potentiality for the development of Welsh devolution
depends on the informed interpretation of the Government of Wales Act 2006.
That is a matter for the courts. Therefore one essential safeguard is the presence of
an independent judiciary to perform that task.

I go on to argue that that is not enough in itself. A well-informed approach
to statutory interpretation is needed. A devolution statute is not, as I see it, to be
interpreted in exactly the same way as any other statute. The principles of interpretation need to be informed by relevantly similar constitutional arrangements in other
parts of the world. The courts need to build up knowledge and expertise around
constitutional arrangements of this nature. When an issue arises as to who has the
power to decide on a matter for the people of Wales, the courts will then have the
special skills that they need for the statutory interpretation of a devolution statute.
They will thereby create an institutional memory and sensitivity for such issues. They
will then be better able to safeguard Welsh devolution in appropriate cases.

* This paper was first published as Mary Arden, 'What is the Safeguard for Welsh Devolution?' in
[2014] PL 189, © Sweet & Maxwell Ltd. It is reproduced here with kind permission of the publisher
Sweet & Maxwell Ltd.

I have a considerable interest in constitutional matters and this has caused me to look at federalism in other parts of the world. The insights which I wish to convey in this chapter stem from those interests.

I have also always been interested in statutory interpretation. Statutory interpretation is one of the traditional roles of the courts. Moreover, the courts have in the first instance a near monopoly: statutes mean what judges say they mean, though of course judges must apply formulated principles. If Parliament disagrees with the judges' interpretation, it can amend the legislation. This is an example of our constitutional checks and balances. But in the first instance, the legislature is bound by the courts' decisions on matters of statutory interpretation. The courts are in the driving seat.

The starting point is, of course, a few words of introduction to the statutory framework for devolution in Wales.

Assessment of the statutory framework for Welsh devolution

Prior to the Government of Wales Act 2006, the only legislative powers devolved by the Westminster Parliament to Wales were powers to make secondary legislation. The 2006 Act provided for primary legislative powers to be conferred on the Welsh Assembly in two stages. Under the first stage, powers were conferred, in advance of a referendum, on the Welsh Assembly to pass Assembly Measures containing provisions that could be included in an Act of Parliament, but these Measures were subject to approval by Order in Council. Under the second stage, the Government of Wales Act 2006 provided that primary legislative powers should be conferred on the Welsh Assembly in some twenty specific matters if there was a referendum in favour of that outcome. A referendum was held and there was a vote in favour of giving the Welsh Assembly primary legislative powers, which were then conferred. This was the first ever referendum in British history that was binding.

So the present position is that the Welsh Assembly has the power to pass primary legislation applying to Wales in relation to twenty specified matters, such as health and health services.

There are some restrictions and exceptions. In particular, the Welsh Assembly cannot remove or add to any 'pre-commencement function' of a Minister of the Crown, that is, any function exercisable by a Minister of the Crown before the Assembly acquired primary legislative powers,[1] unless (in the case of the removal or

---

[1] See Sch 7, Pt 2, para 1 which provides:

    (1) A provision of an Act of the Assembly cannot remove or modify, or confer power by subordinate legislation to remove or modify, any pre-commencement function of a Minister of the Crown.

    (2) A provision of an Act of the Assembly cannot confer or impose, or confer power by subordinate legislation to confer or impose, any function on a Minister of the Crown.

    (3) In this Schedule 'pre-commencement function' means a function which is exercisable by a Minister of the Crown before the day on which the Assembly Act provisions come into force.

modification of a function) the Minister consents, or the provision is merely incidental to, or consequential on, some other.[2]

In addition, the Welsh Assembly cannot pass legislation which is contrary to EU law, or which is incompatible with the rights conferred by the European Convention on Human Rights (the 'Convention').[3] This ensures, for instance, that Westminster can intervene to ensure that devolution legislation does not result in a breach of the United Kingdom's obligations to the European Union or to ensure that such legislation observes human rights.

The Welsh model is very different from that in Scotland. As Lady Hale put it in her speech to Legal Wales in 2012, under the Scottish model, a matter is *in unless it is out* whereas under the Welsh model, it is *out unless it is in*.[4] The Welsh model is often called a 'conferral powers' model.

The Welsh solution can also be seen as reflecting the interdependence of the two jurisdictions. England and Wales share many resources, such as healthcare, water, and the environment. A defining feature of Anglo-Welsh devolution is that there is that interdependence.

It is to be noted that the Welsh Assembly does not have exclusive competence to make laws. Accordingly, it is not (for instance) possible for a person to obtain from a court an order judicially reviewing an enactment of the Westminster Parliament

---

[2] See Sch 7, Pt 3, para 6(1) which reads:

Part 2 [general restrictions on Acts of the Welsh Assembly] does not prevent a provision of an Act of the Assembly removing or modifying, or conferring power by subordinate legislation to remove or modify, any pre-commencement function of a Minister of the Crown if—
  (a) the Secretary of State consents to the provision, or
  (b) the provision is incidental to, or consequential on, any other provision contained in the Act of the Assembly.

[3] See s 108(6), which provides:

  (6) But a provision which falls within subsection (4) or (5) is outside the Assembly's legislative competence if—
    (a) it breaches any of the restrictions in Part 2 of Schedule 7, having regard to any exception in Part 3 of that Schedule from those restrictions,
    (b) it extends otherwise than only to England and Wales, or
    (c) it is incompatible with the Convention rights or with [EU] law.

[4] See s 154 which provides:

  (1) This section applies to—
    (a) . . .
    (b) any provision of an Act of the Assembly, or a Bill for such an Act, which could be read in such a way as to be outside the Assembly's legislative competence, and
    (c) any provision of subordinate legislation made, or purporting to be made, under an Assembly Measure or Act of the Assembly which could be read in such a way as to be outside the powers under which it was, or purported to be, made.
  (2) The provision is to be read as narrowly as is required for it to be within competence or within the powers, if such a reading is possible, and is to have effect accordingly.

The UK government announced in March 2015 that legislation would be introduced to make Wales a 'reserved powers' model like Scotland. The Welsh Assembly had already been given additional powers by the Wales Act 2014. As far as Scotland is concerned, the main political parties agreed in June 2014 that further legislative power should be devolved to Scotland, including in the areas of fiscal responsibility and social security. In May 2015, a new Scotland Bill was introduced into Parliament for this purpose.

on the grounds that it relates to matters on which only the Welsh Assembly can legislate.

Section 154(2) of the Government of Wales Act 2006 confers an obligation on the courts, when an issue of statutory interpretation arises, to 'read down' Welsh legislation, that is, to adopt a restrictive interpretation of it, if it is possible to do so, to enable it to come within the devolved powers of the Welsh Assembly. This is a significant provision. It goes further than a presumption of validity. Such a presumption could be rebutted and would not have the effect that the courts had to read down a statute if that course were possible. In my view, one can safely assume that, if all s 154 did was to replicate some existing common law rule of interpretation, it would not have been inserted into the statute. It is a well-established convention that Parliament does not enact provisions that are unnecessary. Furthermore, s 154(2) is a strong indication that Parliament wanted to uphold the Acts of the Welsh Assembly. It follows that, in enacting the 2006 Act, to quote a Canadian judge in another context, Parliament was 'sensitive to the freedom of action which must be allowed to the Legislatures to safeguard their legitimate interests as in their wisdom they see fit'.[5]

Section 112 of the 2006 Act states that the Attorney General for England and Wales may refer to the Supreme Court the question whether any Bill of the Welsh Assembly that has been passed but not yet received Royal Assent is within the competence of the Welsh Assembly. As yet, there is one decided case where the Attorney General has exercised this power.[6]

Reasons for devolution

There are many reasons given for devolution. It reflects the fact that the United Kingdom has several different nations within it. It also allows for the decentralization of powers. It reflects the political theory that there are advantages to solving local problems at the local level. It helps to resolve the historical difficulty that the Westminster Parliament did not give sufficient priority to Welsh affairs: see, for example, the fifty years that it took to disestablish the Church of Wales and remove the burden of paying tithes and so on.[7]

It perhaps also reflects one of the effects of the European Union. The institution of an international organization of European states—to do collectively that which is

---

[5] *Canadian Industrial Gas & Oil Ltd v Saskatchewan* [1978] SCR 545, 573–4 per Dickson J in the context of the presumption that the Supreme Court of Canada makes in favour of the constitutional validity of provincial statutes.

[6] *Attorney General v National Assembly for Wales Commission and others* [2013] 1 AC 792. Others have now followed: *Re Agricultural Sector (Wales) Bill: Attorney General for England and Wales v Counsel General for Wales (Attorney General for Northern Ireland Intervening)* [2014] UKSC 43, [2014] 1 WLR 2622. The Government of Wales Act 2006, s 112 also enables the Counsel General for Wales to refer the question whether a Bill is within the legislative competence of the Welsh Assembly to the Supreme Court, and the Counsel General exercised this power in *Recovery of Medical Costs for Asbestos Diseases (Wales) Bill: Reference by the Counsel General for Wales* [2015] UKSC 3, [2015] AC 1016.

[7] See Kenneth O Morgan, *Wales in British Politics 1868–1922* (University of Wales Press, 1991).

better so done than done individually—challenges the idea that governmental action is necessarily best done at the level of the state. If it can be better done at a supranational level, it follows that logically it can also, in an appropriate case, be better done at the level of constituent parts of the state.

There are other ways of analysing devolution and seeing its function. It is a way of reflecting the unity of the United Kingdom as well as keenly appreciating the strength of its diversity. In the case of Wales, it is a diversity that astonishingly survived the assimilation of Wales's political and legal institutions into Anglo-Saxon traditions. In terms of constitutional theory, devolution can also be seen as a means of building in new checks and balances and of achieving more limited central government. Without any disrespect to the importance of diversity in national terms in the United Kingdom, it is therefore possible to see devolution as a form of limited government. It would be surprising if this major change has no effect on the function of the courts when devolution issues arise.

Effect of devolution on the role of the courts

Devolution has brought about major constitutional change in the United Kingdom. It has given the courts a new role. They will have to decide conflicts between central and devolved governments, and for that purpose to decide on the constitutionality of enactments of the devolved legislatures. Often, these are problems of statutory interpretation, but the courts will have to perform their traditional task of interpretation in the wholly new context of devolution. If one stopped there, it would, I think, be surprising if this new context did not lead to some change in the way the courts perform their traditional role.

Now, the United Kingdom has no history of the sort of arrangements involved in devolution. We have no case law in UK constitutional law. We need a new vocabulary. In addition, judges need to have an open and inquiring mind as to whether the law should develop a new set of principles. In the new constitutional environment of devolution, the courts need to build up a new legal lexicon and to create an institutional memory of devolution issues.

Can jurisprudence from federal systems assist?

But where do we go to look for this new vocabulary and for this new set of principles? In my view, we need to look at other jurisdictions to find principles that might help us in matters of statutory interpretation. The jurisdictions I have in mind are in federal states. There are numerous federal systems throughout the world with developed legal orders, such as those of the United States, Germany, Canada, South Africa, and Australia. There is considerable jurisprudence in these countries on federal questions. Moreover, in earlier times, appeals from many of these countries, save the United States and Germany, went to the Privy Council. The Privy Council was then the final appellate court of these federal states. The

Privy Council built up an invaluable jurisprudence on constitutional issues, including federal issues. Appeals from those countries stopped some years ago. However, we have that rich pool of jurisprudence readily available.

But is devolution something quite separate from federalism, so that we can learn nothing from these federal systems? My answer is no. I shall explain why. Federalism is normally defined in a way that requires sovereignty to be shared. Writing in 1951, Professor KC Wheare stated that 'the term "federal government" is used very loosely in political discussion and it is seldom given a meaning which is at once clear and distinct'.[8] According to Professor Wheare, the modern idea of federalism is often attributed to the United States of America—even though the words 'federal' and 'federalism' do not appear even once within the US Constitution. On this basis, the essential principle is that powers are divided between a general government and governments of the associated states, both of which operate on the citizen. One is not subordinate to the other but, rather, both are coordinate.

Could a state in which local or general government is subordinate be classed as a 'federal state'? Wheare believed that the history of the United States itself provided the answer. He concluded that only a state in which general and local government is coordinate can truly be classed as 'federal'. The historical answer lay in the distinction between the United States Articles of Confederation of 1777 and the United States Constitution of 1787. Under the Articles of Confederation the states appointed delegates to the Congress, which only had one chamber (the Senate), and was very much subordinate to the states. Under the Constitution of 1787,[9] a coordinate structure was adopted. In due course, the Constitution was amended to provide for the direct election of Senators.

Wheare's classic definition of the federal principle is: 'the method of dividing powers so that the general and regional governments are each, within a sphere, co-ordinate and independent'. He drew on numerous examples of federations in history, but he had no experience, of course, of the United Kingdom's devolution arrangements.

Devolution arrangements are not federalist in the 'Wheare' sense because the Westminster Parliament can always decide to revoke the powers given to the Welsh Assembly, just as the UK government brought to an end the government of Northern Ireland in 1972.

Devolution can be described as *quasi*-federalism. However, I baulk at that expression because it tells us very little except that devolution is not federalism in the full sense. It does not tell us how devolution differs from federalism, so we cannot assess whether that difference is a material one.

I would prefer to say that devolution is in reality or, in fact, federalism. The actual label is not important. It means a stable relationship under which, in fact, two sets of political institutions exercise mutually exclusive power in the same territory. This was the approach that I took in *R (Horvath) v Secretary of State for the*

---

    [8] KC Wheare, *Federal Government* (2nd edn, Oxford University Press, 1951) 1.
    [9] Following efforts of Hamilton, Jay, and Madison, who published the famous series of papers known as *The Federalist Papers*.

Department of Environment, Food and Rural Affairs.[10] The importance of this case is that it ultimately established that EU measures could be implemented in the United Kingdom in different ways. That is sometimes called the differential implementation of EU measures by the devolved administration.

Before this case was resolved, it was thought that the EU principle of non-discrimination might prevent differential implementation. The principle of non-discrimination in EU law in general prevents a member state from discriminating between different groups of its subjects when it implements an EU measure. Membership of the European Union is confined to states, and our membership is as the United Kingdom. It may seem obvious that differential implementation should be permitted, because that is what devolution involves, but it was not obvious in EU law. There was no authority directly on this point.

The facts of *Horvath* demonstrate how easily this problem could arise post-devolution. The applicant was an English farmer. He saw that the conditions for obtaining agricultural subsidies out of EU money administered by member states were more burdensome in England than in other parts of the United Kingdom, where these conditions were laid down in devolved legislation. He contended that the more burdensome conditions contravened EU law. The trial judge held that there should be a reference to the Court of Justice of the European Union (the 'Luxembourg Court') for its interpretation of the EU treaties. The Court of Appeal dismissed an appeal by the Secretary of State against the judge's order. One can well understand why the Secretary of State might have opposed such a reference. Even if the policy decisions are taken in Brussels, significant issues can arise at the stage of implementation. If differential implementation was not possible, devolution was of limited value to Scotland, Wales, and Northern Ireland. Any policy on the important topic of implementing EU measures would have to be decided nationally for the United Kingdom as a whole and not by each devolved government separately.

In my judgment I expressed the view that the devolution arrangements in the United Kingdom should be treated for EU law purposes in the same way as the constitutional arrangements in a federation. Differential implementation appeared to be permitted for federal member states. I devoted my judgment to describing the arrangements for devolution. I argued that the arrangements for devolution were stable and that they were effectively the same as a federal system. I held:

57 The United Kingdom devolution arrangements lack some of the characteristics of a federal system. The Westminster Parliament has not given up its sovereignty over the devolved administrations and that means that in theory, subject to constitutional conventions, it could restrict or revoke the powers that it has given to the devolved administrations. Furthermore, there is no provision for judicial review of legislation passed by the Westminster Parliament on the grounds that it deals with devolved matters. The only qualification to that principle is if the court decides that the legislation of the Westminster Parliament violates Community law. If any such question arises, the courts of any part of the United

---

[10] [2007] EWCA Civ 620 (May, Arden, Scott Baker LJJ).

Kingdom can refer a question to the Court of Justice for a preliminary ruling. In addition, there is no separate legislative body for England as opposed to Wales, Scotland or Northern Ireland. The judicial systems for England and Wales are not separate. There is no dual system of courts in any part of the United Kingdom. Moreover, the United Kingdom ministers have, as I have described, a reserve power with respect to the implementation of Community law.

58 However, the important point is that for Scotland, Wales and Northern Ireland there are political structures now in place that have stability. In addition, the legislation of the devolved administrations is subject to judicial review. The stability of the devolution arrangements will be enhanced over time by the operation of constitutional conventions. Constitutional conventions play a large part in the United Kingdom where the constitution is uncodified. For example, conventions developed in the nineteenth and early twentieth century so that the Westminster Parliament would take no step to amend the Canadian constitution except at the request of the Canadian government approved by a resolution of the Canadian Parliament, even though the Canadian Parliament, like the Scottish Parliament, was a body to which the Westminster Parliament had transferred powers in the past (see Monaghan, Constitutional Law, 3 ed. 2006, page 162–4). Irrespective of the question of whether a convention exists at the present time, the Devolution [Memorandum of Understanding] affirms the intention of the United Kingdom government to 'proceed in accordance with the convention that the UK Parliament would not normally legislate with regard to devolved matters except with the agreement of the devolved legislature.'

When the matter was before the Luxembourg Court, the United Kingdom's Advocate General referred to my judgment. The Court of Justice came to the view that where the directive did not exclude differential implementation it was consistent with EU law for the member state to implement an EU measure differentially, following its own internal constitutional arrangements. That was a major advance but another major advance was achieved by silence. The Court of Justice made no point that devolution was different from federalism because it (devolution) did not involve co-sovereignty. It simply assumed that devolution was on a par with the more usual federal arrangements. In other words, it drew no distinction between the possible types of internal constitutional arrangements. The Court of Justice's approach therefore supports the idea of 'in fact' federalism.

Strasbourg jurisprudence may also support the idea of 'in fact' federalism. It seems that the Strasbourg Court may also take the pragmatic line that, although only the state is a contracting party to the Convention, there can be different arrangements within a member state for giving effect to Convention rights where there are constitutionally separate parts of the state, even if there is no federalism in the 'Wheare' sense.[11]

Furthermore, in my view, the analogy with federalism does not have to be dismissed because a devolved legislature is not sovereign. There are other features, including the stability of the arrangements, that put it on the same level for all practical purposes as a federal legislature.

It is also sometimes said that the asymmetry between Scotland, Wales, and Northern Ireland on the one hand and England on the other, in terms of matters

---

[11] See *Magee v United Kingdom* (2000) 8 BHRC 646; *Dudgeon v United Kingdom* (1981) 4 EHRR 149; and (Application no 71503/01) *Assanidze v Georgia* (2004) 39 EHRR 653, para 147.

such as physical area and population, is a reason why devolution cannot constitute federalism. But on my definition asymmetry is not a deciding factor. Likewise, in my view, nothing turns on the distinction in devolution models in Scotland (*in unless it is out*) and Wales (*out unless it is in*). The fact is that there are different models of federalism to meet different circumstances.

Sometimes the threat is of encroachment by the states on the central power. In those circumstances, the central power may be given all the residual powers and the states may be given a list of specified powers. When the risk of encroachment is the other way around, the states may be given the residual powers and the central power may be given a list of powers, as in the case of Scotland. In some situations, a mixture of both types of federalism is used according to the nature of the subject-matters. However, these variations are not of great importance at the end of the day because under the UK model of devolution each devolved legislature shares the feature that it lacks sovereignty, which is retained by the Westminster Parliament. The point for my purposes is that both the Scottish model and the Welsh model are consistent with federalism and qualify as 'in fact' federalism.

Separation of powers in federalism and in fact federalism

What, then, is the critical feature which federalism and 'in fact' federalism share? As I see it, the fundamental requirement of federalism and 'in fact' federalism is that both the central power and the state power are themselves subject internally to a separation of powers. It follows that the main feature of Welsh devolution that enables it to be compared with federalism is the separation of powers in the Welsh devolution arrangements. There is a separate legislature and a separate executive for Wales. Separate from them is an independent judiciary to determine conflicts between the UK central government and Wales. Under the UK model the role of the executive and the legislature are not mutually exclusive: for instance, Ministers of the Crown, who are members of the executive, sit in the legislature.

Normally, in a federal system, there is one judiciary for each constituent part and another for federal matters. But that is not a necessary part of a federal system. Nor am I going to enter into the controversy as to whether the English and Welsh legal systems should be separated. The only point I make is that the critical question is whether the judiciary of England and Wales is independent of both the central and the devolved institutions, and it is. In those circumstances it can properly determine conflicts between the devolved institutions in Wales and the Westminster institutions. It follows that it is a key element which safeguards Welsh devolution.

That is not to say that it is the only necessary part of the new constitutional settlement. There have to be detailed provisions dealing with such matters as elections and appointments, and so on. We can find those provisions in the Government of Wales Act 2006. There has also to be an acceptance of the rule of law, but in the UK context I take that as read. There are in addition other officers and institutions, apart from an independent judiciary, which safeguard Welsh devolution. However, an independent judiciary is an essential safeguard without which the other arrangements could not properly safeguard Welsh devolution. An independent judiciary is needed to uphold and enforce the constitutional settlement, including the devolution arrangements.

If we concentrate on the judiciary for a moment, we can ask a further question: is it enough that the judiciary is independent of the government of the United Kingdom as well as that of Wales? It is to that question that I now turn. That question has a connection with the point I have just made about the relationship between devolution and federalism.

Potential legal impact of the federalism analogy

The great advantage of analysing the association with other systems of constitutional arrangements, as we have just done, is that we can start to open the door and look at the experience in other jurisdictions, and obtain from them assistance in formulating the special principles that guide the interpretation of devolved legislation.

What would we find if we opened this door? One can start with the doctrine of pith and substance, which is applied to determine the essential character of legislation when an issue arises as to the interpretation of federal and state powers. For instance, a question may arise as to whether a piece of state legislation enacted by a member of a federation encroaches on a power reserved to the federal power. The courts have to identify the true nature of the legislation under challenge. They do this by identifying the essential character of the law and disregarding that which is purely incidental.

The doctrine of pith and substance has some important implications. In federal matters, a legislature, whether at the state or federal level, may be unable to legislate effectively without seeming to encroach on the powers of another legislature. The effect of the pith and substance doctrine is that one level of government may lawfully legislate on matters apparently outside its powers. That legislation may indeed have a significant impact on those matters.

The doctrine of pith and substance can be found in Privy Council jurisprudence.[12] The Appellate Committee of the House of Lords has also applied it in relation to the powers conferred on the Parliament of Northern Ireland by the Government of Ireland Act 1920.[13] The Supreme Court referred to the doctrine in *Martin v Most*[14] but without any elaboration.

Overseas courts have considered the doctrine in more detail in recent years, notably the Supreme Court of Canada in its recent split decision in *Attorney General of Canada v Attorney General of Quebec (Reference re Assisted Human Reproduction Act)*.[15] The issue here was whether the federal legislature, in

[12] See for example *Attorney General for Alberta v Attorney General for Canada* [1943] AC 356.
[13] *Gallagher v Lynn* [1937] AC 863.   [14] [2010] UKSC 10.   [15] 2010 SCC 61.

exercise of its competence in criminal law, could control certain activities in the field of assisted reproduction or whether the provincial legislatures had exclusive competence to legislate in exercise of their competence in health matters.

Furthermore, as I read it, the Government of Wales Act 2006 specifically invites the courts to use some aspects of the doctrine of pith and substance. Section 108 lays down a special rule about interpreting the devolved powers. When the court is considering the question whether an Act of the Welsh Assembly 'relates' to one of the subjects listed in Pt 1 of Sch 7 to the Government of Wales Act 2006, it is to determine that question 'by reference to the purpose of the provision, having regard (among other things) to its effect in all the circumstances'.[16] In other words, the 2006 Act contains a specific direction to look at the purpose and effect of the provision.

That is a special principle for federal/state legislation.[17] To find the purpose or effect, a court interpreting federal/state legislation is not restricted to evidence admissible on a question of statutory interpretation under the usual rules. It can look at any relevant evidence. The courts normally only look at statutory history in limited circumstances.[18] The statutory direction to have regard to the effect of legislation when determining the scope of a devolved or reserved power is particularly important. The court may find it relevant to consider evidence about the way the statute was working in practice. The court might need to look at its effect in conjunction with other legislation, whether state or federal. Again these are ramifications of the pith and substance doctrine which have no analogue in normal statutory interpretation.

Another ramification of the pith and substance doctrine is that a federal or state legislature may be held by implication to have ancillary powers. In the Government of Wales Act 2006 there are express powers for the Welsh Assembly to pass legislation on ancillary matters. Thus it has express power to pass legislation for the enforcement of an Act of the Welsh Assembly and on incidental matters.[19] This is another indication that the special principle of pith and substance is to apply to devolution legislation.

A further ramification of the pith and substance doctrine is that it is the court that decides what the purpose of legislation is. It does so by an objective process of

---

[16] Section 108(7) reads:

> (7) For the purposes of this section the question whether a provision of an Act of the Assembly relates to one or more of the subjects listed in Part 1 of Schedule 7 (or falls within any of the exceptions specified in that Part of that Schedule) is to be determined by reference to the purpose of the provision, having regard (among other things) to its effect in all the circumstances.

[17] See *Attorney General for Alberta* (n 12).
[18] See *Pepper v Hart* [1993] AC 593.
[19] See s 108(5) which reads:

> (5) A provision of an Act of the Assembly falls within this subsection if—
> (a) it provides for the enforcement of a provision (of that or any other Act of the Assembly) which falls within subsection (4) or a provision of an Assembly Measure or it is otherwise appropriate for making such a provision effective, or
> (b) it is otherwise incidental to, or consequential on, such a provision.

evaluation, and not simply by accepting what the legislation asserts its purpose to be.[20] A number of jurisdictions have case law dealing with the determination of the true purpose of legislation.[21]

Other jurisdictions have also considered whether, when a statute is partially within the competence of a devolved legislature and partly outside it,[22] the appropriate remedy is to sever the good from the bad (upholding the validity only of the good part), or whether the remedy of severance should be refused since it would alter the nature of the legislation. I do not consider that s 154(2) of the 2006 Act precludes the possibility of refusing to read down a statute, since the court is only required so to do where it is possible. The court would have to consider what the word 'possible' means in this context.

Moreover, the Appellate Committee of the House of Lords has recognized that the principles of interpretation to which I am referring are special principles which apply to the powers of subordinate or federal parliaments. It has treated both sorts of parliament on the same footing. As Lord Atkin held in *Gallagher v Lynn*:

> These questions affecting limitation on the legislative powers of subordinate parliaments or the distribution of powers between parliaments in a federal system are now familiar, and I do not propose to cite the whole range of authority which has largely arisen in discussion of the powers of Canadian Parliaments. It is well established that you are to look at the 'true nature and character of the legislation': *Russell v. The Queen* (7 App 839) 'the pith and substance of the legislation.' If, on the view of the statute as a whole, you find that the substance of the legislation is within the express powers, then it is not invalidated if incidentally it affects matters which are outside the authorized field. The legislation must not under the guise of dealing with one matter in fact encroach upon the forbidden field. Nor are you to look only at the object of the legislator. An Act may have a perfectly lawful object, e.g., to promote the health of the inhabitants, but may seek to achieve that object by invalid methods, e.g., a direct prohibition of any trade with a foreign country. In other words, you may certainly consider the clauses of an Act to see whether they are passed 'in respect of' the forbidden subject.[23]

The speeches of Lord Bingham and Lord Hoffmann in the more recent case of *Robinson v Secretary of State for Northern Ireland*[24] also support the view that special principles apply to devolution legislation. Mr Robinson contended that the appointments of the First Minister (Mr David Trimble) and Deputy First Minister (Mr Mark Durkan) were invalid because they fell two days outside the period of six weeks prescribed by ss 16 and 32 of the Northern Ireland Act 1998. These sections, when read together, required that the appointments be made within six weeks of Mr Trimble's earlier resignation as First Minister. The Secretary of State for Northern Ireland had seemingly extended the deadline to allow discussions to take place and an agreement to be reached. Mr Robinson contended that the Secretary of State had no power to grant such an extension with the result that the Secretary of State had to dissolve the Northern Ireland Assembly and call fresh elections. However, the House

[20] See *Attorney General for Alberta* (n 12)
[21] See the colourability doctrine in Canadian law and the pretext doctrine in US law.
[22] See for example *Hodge v R* (1883) 9 App Cas 117, 130.
[23] *Gallagher v Lynn* [1937] AC 863, 870.   [24] [2002] UKHL 32.

of Lords held, by a majority, that he had such a power by implication. The minority adopted a more literal approach to interpretation and determined that the statutory phrase 'six weeks' should be interpreted as just that.

The approach adopted by the majority in *Robinson* was a purposive approach, giving weight to the background to the Northern Ireland Act 1998 and what it was intended to achieve. Lord Bingham held:

10 The [Northern Ireland Act 1998], as already noted, was passed to implement the Belfast Agreement, which was itself reached, after much travail, in an attempt to end decades of bloodshed and centuries of antagonism. The solution was seen to lie in participation by the unionist and nationalist communities in shared political institutions, without precluding (see s 1 of the Act) a popular decision at some time in the future on the ultimate political status of Northern Ireland. If these shared institutions were to deliver the benefits which their progenitors intended, they had to have time to operate and take root.

11 The 1998 Act does not set out all the constitutional provisions applicable to Northern Ireland, but it is in effect a constitution. So to categorise the 1998 Act is not to relieve the courts of their duty to interpret the constitutional provisions in issue. But the provisions should, consistently with the language used, be interpreted generously and purposively, bearing in mind the values which the constitutional provisions are intended to embody. Mr Larkin submitted that the resolution of political problems by resort to the vote of the people in a free election lies at the heart of any democracy and that this democratic principle is one embodied in this constitution. He is of course correct. Section 32(1) and (3) expressly contemplate such elections as a means of resolving political impasses. But elections held with undue frequency are not necessarily productive. While elections may produce solutions they can also deepen divisions. Nor is the democratic ideal the only constitutional ideal which this constitution should be understood to embody. It is in general desirable that the government should be carried on, that there be no governmental vacuum. And this constitution is also seeking to promote the values referred to in the preceding paragraph.

12 It would no doubt be possible, in theory at least, to devise a constitution in which all political contingencies would be the subject of predetermined mechanistic rules to be applied as and when the particular contingency arose. But such an approach would not be consistent with ordinary constitutional practice in Britain. There are of course certain fixed rules, such as those governing the maximum duration of parliaments or the period for which the House of Lords may delay the passage of legislation. But matters of potentially great importance are left to the judgment either of political leaders (whether and when to seek a dissolution, for instance) or, even if to a diminished extent, of the Crown (whether to grant a dissolution). Where constitutional arrangements retain scope for the exercise of political judgment they permit a flexible response to differing and unpredictable events in a way which the application of strict rules would preclude.

13 All these general considerations have a bearing, in my opinion, on the statutory provisions at the heart of this case . . . [25]

When Lord Bingham here says 'generously', in my view he means 'without undue technicality'.

---

[25] [2002] NI 390, 398.

Lord Hoffmann also placed considerable emphasis on the context of the statutory provisions. He drew an analogy with the interpretation of constitutional documents in the United States. He held:

The long title of the Act is 'to make new provision for the government of Northern Ireland for the purpose of implementing the agreement reached at multi-party talks on Northern Ireland...'. According to established principles of interpretation, the Act must be construed against the background of the political situation in Northern Ireland and the principles laid down by the Belfast Agreement for a new start. These facts and documents form part of the admissible background for the construction of the Act just as much as the Revolution, the Convention and the Federalist Papers are the background to construing the Constitution of the United States.[26]

Neither Lord Bingham nor Lord Hoffmann drew a distinction between the interpretation of the competence of a devolved legislature and the interpretation of the constitution of a sovereign state. It will be remembered that the point that I made in *Horvath* was in effect that, at the level of practical reality, no such distinction can be drawn so long as the sovereign Parliament respects the arrangements for devolution.

The jurisprudence of the Privy Council confirms the approach that constitutional provisions should be liberally interpreted. Thus, in *Edwards v Attorney General for Canada*,[27] Lord Sankey, giving the advice of the Privy Council, held:

The British North America Act planted in Canada a living tree capable of growth and expansion within its natural limits. The object of the Act was to grant a Constitution to Canada. 'Like all written constitutions it has been subject to development through usage and convention': Canadian Constitutional Studies, Sir Robert Borden (1922) p.55.

Their Lordships do not conceive it to be the duty of this Board... to cut down the provisions of the Act by a narrow and technical construction, but rather to give it a large and liberal interpretation so that the Dominion to a great extent, but within certain fixed limits, may be mistress in her own house, as the Provinces to a great extent, but within certain fixed limits, are mistresses in theirs. 'The Privy Council, indeed, has laid down that Courts of law must treat the provisions of the British North America Act by the same methods of construction and exposition which they apply to other statutes. But there are statutes and statutes; and the strict construction deemed proper in the case, for example, of a penal or taxing statute... would be often subversive of Parliament's real intent if applied to an Act passed to ensure the peace, order and good government of a British Colony': see Clement's Canadian Constitution, 3rd ed., p. 347.

I now turn to the recent case law of the Supreme Court. It has yet to confront many of the issues which the Privy Council and overseas courts have had to decide, but the question is whether the Supreme Court has reserved itself room to consider jurisprudence on federal questions in the future.

---

[26] *Robinson* (n 25) para 33.
[27] [1930] AC 124. This is the famous 'persons' case, so-called because it decided, on an appeal by five women in public office, that the word 'persons' in the British North America Act 1867, s 24 included women, so that they could be senators in the Canadian Parliament.

Two recent cases of the Supreme Court—a critique

In two recent cases, the Supreme Court has expressed the view that there are no special principles of statutory interpretation that apply to provisions setting out the competence of the devolved legislatures, including the Welsh Assembly. The Government of Wales Act 2006 and the Scotland Act 1998 are, therefore, to be interpreted like any other statute and the fact that they are statutes of constitutional significance does not alter the application of the rules of interpretation.

In *Attorney General v National Assembly for Wales Commission*,[28] the Attorney General used his powers under s 112 of the Government of Wales Act 2006 to refer to the Supreme Court the question whether the Local Government Byelaws (Wales) Bill 2012, the first Bill passed by the Welsh Assembly under its new powers in the 2006 Act, exceeded the legislative competence of the Welsh Assembly. The issues revolved around cls 6 and 9 of the Bill, which removed the need for the byelaws listed in Pt 1 of Sch 1 to the Bill to be confirmed by Welsh ministers or by the Secretary of State. Clause 6 contained a list of enactments currently requiring such confirmation, and cl 9 allowed Welsh ministers to add to that list.

The Supreme Court held that cl 6 was incidental to or consequential upon the purpose of the legislation, which was to streamline the process by which local authorities made byelaws. Thus it fell within the ancillary powers of the Welsh Assembly.[29]

There was a major issue about the constitutionality of cl 9 in the light of para 1(1) of Pt 2 of Sch 7 to the 2006 Act.[30] The Supreme Court held that in the context of the Bill this provision was not outside the Welsh Assembly's legislative competence. It could be read as limited to the confirmatory powers of Welsh ministers acting alone and confirmatory powers of the Secretary of State whose removal was consequential on or incidental to the achievement of the purposes of the Bill. Alternatively, it could be read down under s 154(2) of the Government of Wales Act 2006.[31]

As the Counsel General explained in his keynote address to the Welsh Government Legal Services Conference, this was an important case in the development of the United Kingdom's constitutional law and structure. However, there is a possible fly in the ointment so far as my approach to the interpretation of the legislative competence of the Welsh Assembly is concerned. Lord Hope, with whom all the other Justices agreed on this point, held that this was a pure question of statutory interpretation and that there were no special rules of interpretation applying to the interpretation of devolution legislation. He held:

General principles
78 It may be helpful to restate, in the Welsh context, some principles of general application that have guided the court when dealing with issues about the legislative competence of the Scottish Parliament.

---

[28] [2012] UKSC 53, [2013] 1 AC 792.
[29] See the Government of Wales Act 2006, Sch 7, Pt 3, para 6(1)(b), set out in n 2.
[30] See n 1.   [31] See n 4.

79 First, the question whether a Bill of the Assembly is within its legislative competence is a question of law which, if the issue is referred to it, the court must decide. The judicial function in this regard has been carefully structured. It is not for the judges to say whether legislation on any particular issue is better made by the Assembly or by the Parliament of the United Kingdom at Westminster. How that issue is to be dealt with has already been addressed by the United Kingdom Parliament. It must be determined according to the particular rules that section 108 of the 2006 Act and Schedule 7 have laid down. Those rules, just like any other rules, have to be interpreted. It is for the court to say what the rules mean and how, in a case such as this, they must be applied in order to resolve the issue whether the measure in question was within competence.

80 Second, the question whether the Bill is within competence must be determined simply by examining the provisions by which the scheme of devolution has been laid out. That is not to say that this will always be a simple exercise. But, as Lord Walker of Gestingthorpe JSC observed in *Martin v Most* 2010 SC (UKSC) 40, para 44 when discussing the system of devolution for Scotland, the task of the United Kingdom Parliament in relation to Wales was to define the legislative competence of the Assembly, while itself continuing as the sovereign legislature of the United Kingdom. It had to define, necessarily in fairly general and abstract terms, permitted or prohibited areas of legislative activity. The aim was to achieve a constitutional settlement, the terms of which the 2006 Act was designed to set out. Reference was made in the course of the argument in the present case to the fact that the 2006 Act was a constitutional enactment. It was, of course, an Act of great constitutional significance, and its significance has been enhanced by the coming into operation of Schedule 7. But I do not think that this description, in itself, can be taken to be a guide to its interpretation. The rules to which the court must apply in order to give effect to it are those laid down by the statute, and the statute must be interpreted like any other statute. But the purpose of the Act has informed the statutory language, and it is proper to have regard to it if help is needed as to what the words mean.

81 Third, the question whether measures passed under devolved powers by the legislatures in Wales, Scotland and Northern Ireland are amenable to judicial review, and if so on what grounds, was considered in *AXA General Insurance Co Ltd v HM Advocate* [2012] 1 AC 868. The court in that case had the benefit of submissions by the Counsel General. It was common ground that, while there are some differences of detail between the 2006 Act and the corresponding legislation for Scotland and Northern Ireland, these differences do not matter for that purpose. The essential nature of the legislatures that the devolution statutes have created in each case is the same. But it has not been suggested that the Bill is the result of an unreasonable, irrational and arbitrary exercise of the Assembly's legislative authority. This case is concerned only with the question whether the Bill is outside competence under the provisions laid down by the statute.

Of course, the interpretation of devolution legislation by the courts must be objective and impartial as between those who support the devolution of powers and those who support the opposite result. The principles which I have been discussing are neutral as to these two points of view. I can also see that, if it is possible to reach the answer to a question of interpretation by a process of straightforward interpretation, it is right to do so. It is also clear that a devolution statute is like any other statute in the sense that Parliament can at any time amend it or repeal it. However, in my view, it is unhelpful to say that devolution statutes must be interpreted like any other statute, since this might be read as suggesting that devolution statutes are not regarded in law as having similar constitutional significance to federal constitutions or as attracting special principles of interpretation. For the reasons that I have given already, I consider that that conclusion would be wrong. Moreover, the exclusion of wider principles of interpretation may impede the determination of future cases.

There are always distinctions to be made in the interpretation of statutes depending on the type of enactment. A statute dealing with the regulation of the water industry would be likely to be interpreted differently from open-textured legislation setting out people's rights. Courts are more ready to give a liberal interpretation to the latter kind of legislation, and to minimize the significance of shortcomings, in favour of promoting the purpose of the legislation despite changes in social conditions.[32] Justice Kirby of the High Court of Australia once said, quoting an 'anonymous sage', that if you interpret a constitution like a last will and testament, that is what it will become.[33]

The task of the court when interpreting a statute is to find the intention of Parliament as best it can, and to do that it needs to take account of the context of the enactment. This means looking at the subject-matter and deducing from it the likely intention of Parliament as to how it is to work, just as Lord Bingham did in *Robinson*. Of course, in some cases the courts cannot find any guide of this kind, in which case they can only find support for interpretation in the language used. But in my experience there are very few cases in that category. As so often in the law, context is everything.

The Supreme Court took a similar approach to the interpretation of the provisions of the Scotland Act 1998 dealing with the legislative competence of the Scottish Parliament in *Imperial Tobacco Ltd v Lord Advocate*.[34] Lord Hope, with whom Lord Walker, Lady Hale, Lord Kerr, and Lord Sumption agreed, held:

12 ... [It] it may be helpful to summarise, quite briefly, three principles that should be followed when undertaking the exercise of determining whether, according to the rules that the 1998 Act lays down, a provision of an Act of the Scottish Parliament is outside competence.

13 First, the question of competence must be determined in each case according to the particular rules that have been set out in s 29 of and Schs 4 and 5 to the 1998 Act...

14 Second, those rules must be interpreted in the same way as any other rules that are found in a UK statute. The system that those rules laid down must, of course, be taken to have been intended to create a system for the exercise of legislative power by the Scottish Parliament that was coherent, stable and workable. This is a factor that it is proper to have in mind. But it is not a principle of construction that is peculiar to the 1998 Act. It is a factor that is common to any other statute that has been enacted by the legislature, whether at Westminster or at Holyrood. The best way of ensuring that a coherent, stable and workable outcome is achieved is to adopt an approach to the meaning of a statute that is

---

[32] See Ch 12, *Modernizing Legislation*.

[33] Michael Kirby, *Judicial Activism* (Sweet & Maxwell, 2004) 40.

[34] [2012] UKSC 61. As the Counsel General explained in his keynote address to the Welsh Government Services Conference, the case of *AXA General Insurance Ltd v The Lord Advocate* [2011] UKSC 46 [2012] 1 AC 868 importantly establishes that Acts of the Scottish Parliament are not subject to judicial review at common law on the grounds of irrationality, unreasonableness, or arbitrariness and this principle applies also to the Welsh Assembly.

constant and predictable. This will be achieved if the legislation is construed according to the ordinary meaning of the words used.

15 Third, the description of the Act as a constitutional statute cannot be taken, in itself, to be a guide to its interpretation. The statute must be interpreted like any other statute. But the purpose of the Act has informed the statutory language. Its concern must be taken to have been that the Scottish Parliament should be able to legislate effectively about matters that were intended to be devolved to it, while ensuring that there were adequate safeguards for those matters that were intended to be reserved. That purpose provides the context for any discussion about legislative competence. So it is proper to have regard to the purpose if help is needed as to what the words actually mean . . .

Usefulness of pith and substance doctrine

History has the habit of repeating itself, and it may be that it will do so again. In 1887, the Privy Council held that there were no special principles to be applied to questions of interpreting federal constitutions. They were to be interpreted as other statutes. Lord Hobhouse giving the judgment of the Privy Council held:

Their Lordships have been invited to take a very wide range on this part of the case, and to apply to the construction of the Federation Act the principles laid down for the United States by Chief Justice Marshall. Everyone would gladly accept the guidance of that great judge in a parallel case. But he was dealing with the constitution of the United States. Under that constitution, as their Lordships understand, each state may make laws for itself, uncontrolled by the federal power, and subject only to the limits placed by law on the range of subjects within its jurisdiction. In such a constitution Chief Justice Marshall found one of those limits at the point at which the action of the state legislature came into conflict with the power vested in Congress. The appellant invokes that principle to support the conclusion that the Federation Act must be so construed as to allow no power to the provincial legislatures under sect. 92, which may by possibility, and if exercised in some extravagant way, interfere with the objects of the Dominion in exercising their powers under sect. 91. It is quite impossible to argue from the one case to the other. Their Lordships have to construe the express words of an Act of Parliament which makes an elaborate distribution of the whole field of legislative authority between two legislative bodies, and at the same time provides for the federated provinces a carefully balanced constitution, under which no one of the parts can pass laws for itself except under the control of the whole acting through the Governor-General. And the question they have to answer is whether the one body or the other has power to make a given law. If they find that on the due construction of the Act a legislative power falls within sect. 92, it would be quite wrong of them to deny its existence because by some possibility it may be abused, or may limit the range which otherwise would be open to the Dominion parliament.[35]

The passage in which this paragraph occurs gave rise to difficulties in later cases. In due course, in *Attorney General of Alberta v Attorney General of Canada*[36] the Privy Council held that this case established only that a proviso preventing abuse of a

---

[35] *Bank of Toronto v Lambe* (1887) 12 App Cas 575, 587.
[36] [1939] AC 117, 134.

legislative power could not be implied into legislation. That was indeed an application of standard rules of interpretation. But the Privy Council was careful to add that that did not mean that 'if such a use was attempted to be made of a provincial power as materially to interfere with Dominion power, the action of the Province would be intra vires'. This was a reaffirmation of the doctrine of pith and substance, which as we have seen is a special rule applying to the interpretation of federal and state legislation.

Conclusions

Devolution is of enormous constitutional significance. It can be analysed as a form of federalism. The common feature of devolution, in which sovereignty is retained by the Westminster Parliament, and federal systems that share sovereignty is that both systems involve the separation of powers between the legislature, the executive, and the judiciary. The boundaries between these institutions are, however, to some extent porous. The British constitution favours checks and balances, and does not make each power entirely separate from the other.

The courts have taken on a new role of seeing that the rules that regulate the new devolution arrangements are followed. The independence of the judiciary is thus essential to the maintenance and development of devolution.

However, leaving aside the Privy Council, the courts of the United Kingdom have no history of this sort of constitutional arrangement to call upon. The UK courts should enrich their understanding of the courts' interpretive role in this new situation by looking to see what courts have done in federal jurisdictions in other major legal systems. They should recognize that their new role in devolution calls for a special approach to statutory interpretation. As I see it, this would strengthen the way in which the courts perform their important role of safeguarding devolution.

So, the answer to the question in the title to this chapter—What is the safeguard for Welsh devolution?—is that the maintenance and development of devolution requires an independent judiciary to decide conflicts between the central and devolved institutions in an impartial way. In addition, the maintenance and development of devolution needs a judicial approach to devolution issues involving statutory interpretation that is informed by case law from courts in other jurisdictions with experience of federal systems. Much can be learnt from studying the leading decisions of these courts.

SECTION B

SIMPLIFICATION AND SYSTEMATIC DEVELOPMENT OF THE LAW

To keep the law up to date, there is a need for systematic development and improvement in certain areas. We see here how the Law Commission reviews the law for this purpose, employing rigorous research and analysis. A primary aim is to simplify or modernize the general law, and also to make statutes more accessible. To date, the Law Commission has accomplished these tasks in a number of ways: primarily by making recommendations for reform after a thorough examination of the law and the needs of those affected by it. This is done by preparing consolidation bills and identifying redundant statutory provisions for repeal; by recommending the codification of areas of law, for example in the case of directors' duties; and by preparing reports which may one day lead to the codification of the criminal law. This Section examines the history of the codification of the law in different fields, and other recent steps taken or proposed to modernize and simplify statute law, for example the work of the Tax Law Rewrite.

Preface by The Rt Hon Lord Mackay of Clashfern

In recent times the volume of legislation, both primary and secondary, has become so great that it regulates our lives almost completely, and in consequence most of the cases that come before the courts depend for their decision on an application of statute to the facts of the case. The ordinary citizen depends on finding the relevant statutory material and then understanding how it applies to the circumstances with which he or she has to deal. This indicates the central importance of the statute book today.

Since statute is a text, interpretation is crucial. Clarity is vital. Moreover, it must be relatively easy to access the relevant text. In this respect, modern information technology makes the task easier.

Good preparation of the law is the groundwork for this vital clarity but it is also necessary to consider, in that preparation of the law, its relevance to present conditions and the form in which it is presented.

Lady Justice Arden's great experience equips her to help us see at once what should go into this preparation, the width of material that requires to be considered, and how it should be marshalled. The machinery for making law in a democracy such as ours is through the legislature, and she has important insights to give us on this process and suggestions for its improvement.

In this connection her experience as Chairman of the Law Commission of England and Wales is particularly important. She draws attention to many aspects of this work of law reform that are interesting and stimulating. There are also less exciting tasks such as deleting from the statute book obsolete provisions and the consolidation of a succession of statutes dealing with a particular field of law to produce one comprehensive statute, with its attendant difficulty of securing a period when Parliament is not active in that field and ensuring that the relevant assistance required for the task from the policy department concerned is available.

It is now fifty years since the Law Commissions were set up. Their institution was not without controversy. Among the opponents was my predecessor as Lord Advocate of Scotland, but the stature of Lord Gardiner, the Lord Chancellor, was sufficient to ensure that his proposal reached the statute book. The first Chairman of the Law Commission was Lord Scarman, and of the Scottish Law Commission it was Lord Kilbrandon.

Although the statute set out the functions of the Commissions and their relation-ships with the government, it fell to the first Chairmen and their colleagues to develop the way in which they should work. The Commission charged with considering a particular branch of the law laid out in a paper its understanding of the present state of that branch. The paper then went on to consider to what extent that branch of the law was unsatisfactory and finally made suggestions on how it might be reformed. The paper was then issued as a green paper for consultation. The Commissioners and their staff made themselves available to stimulate the consultation. On the conclusion of the consultation and after consideration of the responses, if a sufficient degree of consen-sus emerged for reform, the Commission went on to prepare a report and append a draft Bill to implement the proposed reform.

This process has proved successful although often it has been difficult for parliamentary time to be found to enact the Bill when the government has accepted the Report. During my time as Lord Chancellor a special committee procedure was adopted (see Author's Notes on Law Commission Bills, Note 1).

I believe that over the years the Commissions have proved their utility in the enactment of good legislation and that their authoritative studies of existing areas of the law have been useful to the public as well as to the legal profession and to the courts.

It is my impression also that the success of the Commissions' way of working has assisted in the government's development of consultation (see Author's Notes on Law Commission Bills, Note 2).

One area of the law of England that should be mentioned is criminal law and the call for codification. A Bill for this purpose would be a massive undertaking and the number of changes that are made by Parliament in every session on this branch of the law has so far put this call beyond achievement. An excellent example of achieved codification is recounted by Lady Justice Arden and my hope is that the extent to which the Law Commissions have contributed in their first fifty years to improvement in our laws will be crowned in their second fifty years by their contribution to the criminal law of England.

I commend these studies to all with an interest in this important subject.

The Rt Hon Lord Mackay of Clashfern

Author's Notes on Law Commission Bills

Note 1

Over the past two decades, new procedures have been introduced for non-controversial Law Commission Bills:

(1) Committee stage: to ease the problem of finding Parliamentary time for Law Commission Bills, Lord Mackay encouraged the use of the Special Public Bill Committee procedure, known as the Jellicoe procedure, in the House of Lords (where Law Commission Bills are often introduced) for non-controversial Law Commission Bills, including the Bill that became the Private International Law (Miscellaneous Provisions) Act 1995. This enabled

the committee stage to be taken in Grand Committee, rather than in the Chamber. All members of the House can attend proceedings in Grand Committee, which take place in the Moses Room of the House of Lords.

(2) Second reading: the aforementioned procedure was extended on a trial basis to the second reading stage, when in 2008 the House of Lords introduced special arrangements enabling the second reading debate on non-controversial Law Commission bills to take place in Grand Committee. This procedure for second reading was made permanent in 2010 (see *Report of the Procedure Committee*, HL Paper 63, adopted on 7 October 2010). It involves a motion for the second reading itself to take place in the Chamber but the associated debate to take place in the Moses Room. (The committee stage is then generally conducted under the Jellicoe procedure, as described earlier.)

(3) The report and third reading stages: these take place in the Chamber, as with other Bills. One of the Bills for which the newer procedures for non-controversial Law Commission bills was used was the Bill leading to the Insurance Act 2015. This implemented most of the recommendations in the Law Commissions' *Report on Insurance Contract Law: Business Disclosure; Warranties; Insurers' Remedies for Fraudulent Claims; and Late Payment* (Law Com No 353, Scot Law Com No 238, 2014).

Note 2

Since a Law Commission Bill is not automatically presented to Parliament, a minister must first accept the recommendations and decide to introduce a Bill. By the time this happens, it may be necessary for the government to make changes to the recommendations of the Law Commission. Alternatively it may wish to make minor changes to those recommendations in any event. So there will often be further consultation. But the process is frequently made easier by the thorough public consultation which the Law Commission has already carried out.

PART III

SYSTEMATIC DEVELOPMENT AND REFORM OF THE LAW

In 1965, Parliament created the Law Commission of England and Wales and the Scottish Law Commission as independent and permanent institutions dedicated to reform of the law.[1] The function which Parliament gave to these new bodies was breathtaking in its width: it was to review all the law with which they are respectively concerned with the overall aim of its simplification and modernization. All areas of law were potentially open to Law Commission review: Parliament did not limit the areas of law to be considered. However, Parliament specified the type of law reform projects on which the Law Commissions were expected to focus, namely projects for (1) the 'systematic development and reform' of the law; (2) codifying the law; (3) eliminating statutory anomalies; and (4) rationalizing the statute book[2] by preparing Bills for consolidating statute law in a given field or for repealing statute law that was obsolete or no longer required.[3]

---

[1] See the Law Commissions Act 1965.

[2] By 'statute book' I mean the whole body of statute law. The term denotes either the physical (or now the digital) record or its substantive provisions (or both).

[3] Thus the Law Commissions Act 1965, s 3 (as amended) provides:

(1) It shall be the duty of each of the Commissions to take and keep under review all the law with which they are respectively concerned with a view to its systematic development and reform, including in particular the codification of such law, the elimination of anomalies, the repeal of obsolete and unnecessary enactments, the reduction of the number of separate enactments and generally the simplification and modernisation of the law, and for that purpose—

   (a) to receive and consider any proposals for the reform of the law which may be made or referred to them;

   (b) to prepare and submit to the Minister from time to time programmes for the examination of different branches of the law with a view to reform, including recommendations as to the agency (whether the Commission or another body) by which any such examination should be carried out;

   (c) to undertake, pursuant to any such recommendations approved by the Minister, the examination of particular branches of the law and the formulation, by means of draft Bills or otherwise, of proposals for reform therein;

   (d) to prepare from time to time at the request of the Minister comprehensive programmes of consolidation and statute law revision, and to undertake the preparation of draft Bills pursuant to any such programme approved by the Minister;

One critical feature of the Law Commission was that Parliamentary counsel were assigned to it, and so it was able not only to make recommendations as to law reform but also to produce a draft Bill. This would show how the changes could be implemented and enabled steps for enacting the legislation to be taken without delay.

2015 marks the fiftieth anniversary of the Law Commissions.[4] There is much to celebrate: many important Acts of Parliament, such as the Mental Capacity Act 2005, the Bribery Act 2010, and the Land Registration Act 2002, are the result of Law Commission recommendations.

I have been involved in law reform since virtually the start of my professional career. I sat on the Law Society's Company Law Committee for about twenty years starting in 1976. This Committee included many eminent solicitors in the field. It met regularly and responded almost continuously with great expertise and care to proposals for reform from the government department with responsibility for company law. Later, I was a member of the Financial Law Panel (now the Financial Markets Law Committee). The primary purpose of this body was to identify changes in law or practice that might pose risks to the conduct of financial services or banking business in the City of London.

In 1996, three years after becoming a High Court judge, I was appointed Chairman of the Law Commission of England and Wales by Lord Mackay of Clashfern, then Lord Chancellor. I held that office until the end of January 1998. In that time I had led the Law Commission's project, *Shareholder Remedies*, and taken the project—which was a joint project with the Scottish Law Commission's *Company Directors: Regulating Conflicts of Interests and Formulating a Statement of Duties*—to an advanced stage. In due course both were implemented by the Companies Act 2006.

      (e) to provide advice and information to government departments and other author-
           ities or bodies concerned at the instance of the Government of the United
           Kingdom or the Scottish Administration with proposals for the reform or amend-
           ment of any branch of the law;
     (ea) in the case of the Law Commission, to provide advice and information to the
           Welsh Ministers;
      (d) to obtain such information as to the legal systems of other countries as appears to
           the Commissioners likely to facilitate the performance of any of their functions.
(2) The Minister shall lay before Parliament any programmes prepared by the Commission and approved by him and any proposals for reform formulated by the Commission pursuant to such programmes.
(3) Each of the Commissions shall make an annual report to the Minister on their proceedings, and the Minister shall lay the report before Parliament with such comments (if any) as he thinks fit.
(3A) Subsections (2) and (3) of this section shall have effect in relation to the Scottish Law Commission with the substitution of 'the Scottish Parliament' for 'Parliament'.
(4) In the exercise of their functions under this Act the Commissions shall act in consultation with each other and the Northern Ireland Law Commission.

[4] Many Commonwealth countries have followed the UK in setting up law reform bodies on the lines of the Law Commission. However, the Law Commissions set up by the Law Commissions Act 1965 were not the first Law Commissions. Other Law Commissions had already been set up. For instance, the first Law Commission of India was set up in 1834 under the chairmanship of Lord Macaulay, and it recommended codification of criminal law and criminal procedure and a few other matters.

It is a great advantage for a judge to have experience of law reform. First, the judge has the valuable experience of examining the whole of the law on a particular subject, rather than concentrating on particular points in order to advise clients. Second, the judge is exposed to a much wider range of subject-matter than he or she is likely to have met in practice. Third, the judge also discovers how in practice lay people who have to use a particular area of law find it to be. A fourth benefit—and this is mainly obtained through Law Commission work—is that the judge sees how policy behind legislation is formed and how statutes are drafted to give effect to that policy. The insight gained provides experience of how government actually works and makes for informed interpretation of statute law generally when sitting in a judicial capacity.

During my term as Chairman, I gave the paper which forms the basis of Chapter 9, *The Work of the Law Commission*, which reviews the methodology and achievements of the Law Commission during my time in office. The work of the Law Commissions has many facets. To my mind the great advantage of this permanent, dedicated institution is that it has built up experience on carrying out law reform projects and has an established institutional memory of the most effective way of proceeding. Bodies set up to perform one particular law reform task have to go through the process of deciding how their task will be best performed without the benefit of the experience or institutional memory that a Law Commission has. That can be a serious disadvantage.

One characteristic feature of Law Commission work is that it analyses the existing law extremely thoroughly before making any recommendations for reform. In addition, before it makes any recommendations, it will often seek to set out the principles that should govern the area of law in question.

Very little has changed in principle with regard to the way the Law Commission discharges its role since I wrote this paper save in two particular respects. First as a result of the Law Commissions Act 1989, there is now a formal protocol in place between the Lord Chancellor and the Law Commission about its working methods. Second, and significantly, this change has now been extended by the Wales Act 2014 to the Welsh Ministers,[5] and the Welsh Ministers may now ask the Law Commission for advice and assistance. In addition, the Law Commission now has a Welsh Advisory Committee to help it to act as an effective law reform body for Wales.

The usual criticism of Law Commission work is that the recommendations are rarely adopted by the government or enacted by Parliament. However, the figures are to the contrary: since the creation of the law Commission in 1965, around 69% of its law reform projects have been implemented in whole or part.[6] One change which should reduce delays in implementation is the new system for dealing with

---

[5] By virtue of the Government of Wales Act 2006, s 45(2) the Welsh Ministers are the First Minister and the ministers appointed by him under s 48 of that Act.
[6] *The Work of the Law Commission incorporating the Twelfth Programme*, published by the Law Commission, February 2015, p 2. This points out a recent fall in implementation rates, but sets out steps taken to redress that point.

Law Commission bills which I described in the Author's Notes[7] to Lord Mackay's Preface.

In Chapter 10, *Improving the Statute Book 1: A Law Reformer's Viewpoint*, I have set out the first part of a paper also given during my term of office as Chairman of the Law Commission. It focuses on the Law Commission's work in relation to statute law, principally the consolidation of statutes and statute law revision. Both of these areas of work are highly skilled and painstaking: for example, thorough research is likely to be necessary before the Law Commission can conclude that a provision in a statute is obsolete or no longer necessary. I have included the rest of this paper in the next Part (Part IV, Chapter 11), as it explains other ways, apart from Law Commission work, in which the accessibility of statutes can be improved.

---

[7] See Preface to Section B by The Rt Hon Lord Mackay of Clashfern, Author's Notes on Law Commission Bills, n 1.

9

The Work of the Law Commission

This chapter is based on the Hind Lecture, given to the University of Nottingham Law School in February 1999.*

The need for law reform

To be involved in the law, whether as a student or a teacher or a practitioner, and not to have an interest in law reform is like having a car without headlights—in some situations you have no vision.

Law and law reform go hand in hand. Why is this? Laws get out of date. For instance there is technological innovation. We need to have laws dealing with electronic signatures, electronic filing, determining when a contract is made and so on.

There is the added problem in the common law world—we are used to judges developing the law on a case-by-case basis. Cases decided by the higher courts create binding precedents. Sometimes the law cannot develop fast enough, or the highest court takes the wrong turn. Then it is time to call in the Law Commission and ask it to do a review of the law and make recommendations as to how it should be reformed. I will be giving an example of this later in relation to liability for psychiatric illness.

The contribution of the Law Commissions

The Law Commission was set up in 1965, along with the Scottish Law Commission. Its primary function is to review the law with a view to its systematic reform.[1] The English and the Scottish Law Commissions were among the first Law Commissions to be set up. There are numerous similar bodies throughout the Commonwealth.

---

* The author was Chairman of the Law Commission from January 1996 to the end of January 1999. This chapter describes the activities and methodology of the Law Commission at the time, which have not since fundamentally changed. The footnotes provide updating on events since 1999 on projects and other matters, where appropriate. This chapter is based on a paper first published in (2000) 53 Current Legal Problems 559 (Oxford University Press), reproduced here with kind permission of the publishers.

[1] Law Commissions Act 1965, s 3(1).

The Law Commission is a non-departmental government body. It is funded by the government, but the commissioners are not members of the civil service and they form their views independently of government. While I was Chairman, there were five commissioners, two academics, one barrister, one solicitor, and myself. To begin with, all the staff, other than support staff, are lawyers, although at least one economist was subsequently appointed. Each commissioner, other than the Chairman, has a team, consisting of one or two government lawyers and then two or three research assistants, who are graduates who have not yet entered practice. There is great competition for the post of research assistant and often it provides a useful bridge between university and practice or doctoral research, as the case may be.

The Law Commission only does a very small part of the law reform being undertaken in government at any one time. Other law reform matters include bringing our law into line with European Community requirements and dealing with matters like asylum. The Law Commission aims to deal with areas which are not party political and which are predominately legal. The legal system is like a car. It needs to be serviced from time to time.

The government White Paper, *Modernising Justice*,[2] contains the following passage on law reform:

Law Reform
1.14 Clear, up-to-date law allows legal transactions to be completed, and legal disputes to be resolved more effectively, by ensuring that people are aware of their rights and responsibilities from the beginning. The Government intends to keep the law up to date, relevant and useable. To take one current example, we are carefully considering recently published proposals[3] to modernise the law governing land registration, which dates from 1925. These would streamline the system for transferring land, and establish clear principles to underpin it.

1.15 Law reform is concerned with modernising existing law. It is also necessary to ensure that, where the law on a particular subject has become fragmented as a result of piecemeal amendment over the years, it is brought together from time to time into a single piece of coherent legislation. Also law which has become obsolete or redundant needs to be removed from the statute book. Otherwise, the statute book can become unclear, distracting users and possibly adding to legal costs. The Government recognises the importance of the consolidation and revision of the statute law, and will pursue this as part of our overall programme of modernization.

That final passage refers to other work which is done by the Law Commission, apart from law reform. The Law Commission also undertakes statute law revision. The statute law revision team identifies enactments which are no longer necessary and prepares a Bill which is then introduced into Parliament to repeal the spent legislation. The team has produced a chronological table of local legislation from 1797 to 1993 which contains details of some 26,500 local Acts of Parliament

[2] *Modernising Justice* (Cmd 4155, 1998).
[3] Law Commission and HM Land Registry, *Land Registration for the Twenty-First Century: A Consultative Document* (Law Com No 254, 1998).

passed between those dates. This was the product of some twenty years' work. The Law Commission is also about to produce a chronological table of personal and private Acts over the same period. This will contain details of some 11,000 Acts.[4] Without these tables there would be no complete list of statutes which have been passed.

The Law Commission also undertakes the consolidation of statutes. For instance, in relation to sentencing powers, there are now some fifteen Acts of Parliament, which cover in whole or part sentencing, and in many cases these statutes amend Acts previously passed or Acts previously passed to amend even earlier Acts. The result is extremely confusing. The Law Commission is engaged on a complex consolidation of all these statutory provisions. It is not a mechanical job: anomalies and inconsistencies have so far as possible to be ironed out. It is a skilled task which needs skilled draftsmen and the backup of the relevant government departments.[5]

However, most of the resources of the Law Commission at any one time are directed to law reform and I now return to that topic.

The aims of the Law Commission can be found in the Law Commissions Act 1965 and in its current programme of work.[6] The objective of the Law Commission is to recommend reform of the law to make it fairer, simpler, more modern, and in appropriate cases more cost-effective. As respects cost-effectiveness, there are areas of law where reform makes enforcement of the law cheaper for the citizen and also, in criminal cases, cheaper for the state. However, it is not possible to save costs in all cases. For instance, the Law Commission may feel that it is necessary to recommend a new remedy.

Under s 3(1) of the Law Commissions Act 1965 the Law Commission's primary function is 'to keep under review all the law with which [it is] concerned with a view to its systematic development and reform, including in particular the codification of such law, the elimination of anomalies, the repeal of obsolete and unnecessary enactments, the reduction of the number of separate enactments and generally the

---

[4] Law Commission and Scottish Law Commission, *The Chronological Table of Private and Personal Acts* (Law Com No 256, Scot Law Com No 170, 1999).

[5] This project, which involved both the Law Commission and the Scottish Law Commission, led to the enactment of the Powers of Criminal Courts (Sentencing) Act 2000. However, that Act has been heavily amended since it was enacted, causing a lack of coherence and clarity in sentencing law once again. The Law Commission's 12th Programme of Law Reform (HC 354), adopted in July 2014, contains a further project on sentencing procedure. The aim of this project is to produce a single sentencing statute, which would in future be the first and last port of call for sentencing tribunals.

[6] Now the 12th Programme of Law Reform (see n 5). The Law Commissions Act 1965 has been supplemented in the case of the Law Commission by the Law Commission Act 2009. Section 1 of the 1965 Act places an obligation on the Lord Chancellor to deliver an annual report to Parliament setting out the progress made by the government in implementing Law Commission reports. Section 2 of the Act provides that the Lord Chancellor and the Law Commission may agree a protocol about the Law Commission's method of selecting and carrying out projects, the assistance which government departments and the Law Commission are to give each other, and the way the Lord Chancellor is to deal with Law Commission reports. The Protocol introduced in March 2010 states that the Law Commission will not take on a project unless the relevant minister undertakes that there is a serious intention to take forward law reform in that area. It also requires the relevant minister to give an interim response within six months of the report being published and a final response within one year. The process for selecting projects has thus changed since that described in this chapter.

simplification and modernization of the law'. Projects may be included in a programme approved by the Lord Chancellor. In other cases projects may be referred to it by Ministers of State. The Law Commission has a separate and ancillary function to provide advice and information to government departments and other authorities, or bodies concerned at the instance of government with proposals for reform or amendment of any branch of the law.

The Law Commission has specific power to obtain information about other legal systems. This is a power which it exercises wherever possible, since the Law Commission's views are always better informed with this knowledge. In the past the Law Commission has tended to concentrate on other common law jurisdictions but in, for example, one consultation paper, published jointly with the Scottish Law Commission, *Company Directors: Regulating Conflicts of Interest and Formulating a Statement of Duties*,[7] the Law Commissions also looked at a relevant provision of the German Commercial Code.[8]

How Law Commission projects are selected

I now turn to the question: how are Law Commission projects selected? A law reform project has to be on a subject which is appropriate for review by the Law Commission, as an independent non-departmental body. This means that it has to be a subject calling for systematic and principled review and reform. It has to be an area of law which is not more appropriately left for development by the courts in the usual way. It also must not be a party political matter and thus the Law Commission does not get involved in, for example, revenue law, employment law, sentencing (as opposed to consolidation or codification of sentencing powers), or legal aid. Likewise it does not generally get involved in amending small areas of law or dealing with such matters as dangerous dogs or the law on stalking.

On the positive side, the project has got to have relevance to some perceived need in business or society. The Law Commission therefore looks to see whether the project is significant in practical terms.

The law must also be in need of review. This may be because it is arcane (for example the recent project on shareholder remedies[9] recommended partial abolition of the rule in *Foss v Harbottle*,[10] whose antiquity is well known to company lawyers). Or it may be that the law no longer fits social changes.

Thus, for instance, the Law Commission has a project on the property rights of home sharers. Where people are married, family law enables the fair distribution of

---

[7] *Company Directors: Regulating Conflicts of Interest and Formulating a Statement of Duties* (CP No 153, 1998). In 1999, the Law Commissions issued their final report on this project, *Company Directors: Regulating Conflicts of Interest and Formulating a Statement of Duties* (Law Com No 261, 1999; Scot Law Com No 173, 1999). The final report was published in 1999 and implemented by the Companies Act 2006.

[8] *Company Directors: Regulating Conflicts of Interest*, final report (n 7) paras 12.26–12.32.

[9] *Shareholder Remedies* (Law Com No 246, 1997), implemented by the Companies Act 2006.

[10] (1843) 2 Hare 461, (1843) 67 ER 189.

their property to be made on dissolution of the marriage. Where parties are not married but decide to part, they have to rely on the principles of our trust and property law. There is insufficient recognition of any financial or non-financial contribution which either party makes but which is not used in acquiring the home. Some people would say that there should be no special regime which equates the rights of unmarried people to those of married couples. There is a debate about devaluing the institution of marriage and about the importance of marriage as a social institution. Accordingly this is likely to be a difficult area on which there are numerous views.[11] The question is whether the existing law should be changed to deal with the situation. But it is not for lawyers to impose solutions on matters of social policy. Nevertheless, it is often necessary when modernizing the law to reflect generally accepted social policy.

Another example of the need to keep pace with social change is the law on corruption. Some of the offences relating to corruption are confined to public bodies, but with the growth in the number of privatized bodies, this seems an unnecessary restriction. Accordingly the Law Commission has recommended reform which would abolish this distinction.[12]

When the Law Commission has doubts about whether a subject is suitable for a law reform project by it, it conducts a feasibility study, as it did in its study in joint and several liability of defendants sued for negligence.[13]

Methodology

I now wish to say a little about the Law Commission's method of working. This is largely consensus-based. The Law Commission does not desire to impose solutions on an unwilling society. When the Law Commission undertakes a law reform

---

[11] The Law Commission published *Sharing Homes: A Discussion Paper* in July 2002 (Law Com No 278, 2002), which considered a broad range of relationships, including friends and relatives. The Law Commission was unable to devise a scheme for the distribution of property which it considered would be an improvement on the existing law but it did recommend that parties consider coming to an agreement about the position and the possibility of civil partnerships. After the Civil Partnerships Act 2004 was passed the Law Commission was asked by Lord Filkin, then Parliamentary Secretary to the Department for Constitutional Affairs, to review cohabitation law. In 2006, this led to the Law Commission's consultation paper, *Cohabitation: The Financial Consequences of Relationship Breakdown* (CP No 179, 2006), followed by its report under the same title in 2007 (Law Com No 7182, 2007). This provided for a new scheme of financial relief on relationship breakdown based on contributions made to the relationship rather than need (as in divorce). It is limited to persons living together as couples in an intimate relationship, whether married or not. This report has not yet been implemented. On 6 September 2011, the Parliamentary Under-Secretary of State for Justice (Mr Jonathan Djanogly) made a written ministerial statement that the recommendations would not be taken forward in the then current Parliament as the findings of research into similar new Scottish legislation did not provide a sufficient basis for change and the family justice reforms were about to be implemented in England Wales (Hansard, HC vol 730, col 16WS (6 September 2011)).

[12] *Legislating the Criminal Code: Corruption* (Law Com No 248, 1998) para 4.78. The government presented a bill to Parliament to implement this report but it emerged that further changes were needed. In 2008, the Law Commission published its revised recommendations in *Reforming Bribery* (Law Com No 313, 2008), which was implemented by the Bribery Act 2010.

[13] Department of Trade and Industry, 'Feasibility Investigation of Joint and Several Liability by the Common Law Team of the Law Commission' (1996). For current project selection process, see n 6.

project it starts by conducting a thorough study into the area of law in question; it then conducts a pre-consultation exercise with users of the law in question and with government departments. Enquiries are made not simply of lawyers but also of people who use the law or who are affected by it. The Commission then issues its consultation paper (its equivalent of a government green paper) in which it seeks to obtain views from as wide a spectrum of users as possible. In the consultation document, the Law Commission will, where possible, express provisional views. The object of this is to expose the issues and get better responses. However, the Law Commission may not be able to express a provisional view. A graphic example of this is the Law Commission's work on legitimacy in 1982.[14] The Law Commission's work showed that there was an increasing number of illegitimate children and a decrease in the number of children being legitimated by adoption or subsequent marriage. Moreover, at that time an illegitimate child was subject to disadvantages. The Law Commission's consultation paper on illegitimacy said that there was a choice to be made as a matter of fundamental policy. One could either take the view that the discrimination was justified and that the disadvantages should be continued, or one could take the view that the discrimination was not justified in principle and that it should be removed.

The Law Commission then allows the period for consultation. The views that are expressed by consultees are carefully analysed and considered. The Law Commission then formulates its final recommendations. These are published in its final report. However, these are only recommendations, because the Law Commission is only an advisory body.

The Law Commission's final report is made to Parliament. It would generally contain a draft Bill which shows Parliament how the law would be changed to make the recommendations which the Law Commission puts forward. It is a great privilege to have Parliamentary Counsel assigned to the Law Commission and the addition of a Bill drafted by Parliamentary Counsel makes sure that the Law Commission does not produce theoretical reports and recommendations which could not easily be implemented. This obviously eases the passage towards ultimate implementation if the report is accepted by Parliament.

The draft Bill enables readers of Law Commission reports to focus on the precise changes recommended. Moreover, it should mean that by the time the Bill comes before Parliament any problems which the Bill will cause have been brought to light. This can be contrasted with, for instance, the government's Insolvency Bill in 1985, which was a government Bill to which over 1,000 amendments were ultimately proposed. The fact that there is a draft Bill also means that, if a member of either House of Parliament wishes to present a Private Member's Bill, there is a ready drafted Bill to enable him or her to do so.

The Law Commission also makes an Annual Report to Parliament. The fact that the Law Commission reports to Parliament in all these various ways shows the importance which Parliament attaches to law reform and the way in which it was

---

[14] *Family Law: Illegitimacy* (Law Com No 118, 1982), implemented by the Family Law Reform Act 1987.

intended by the architects of the 1965 Act that the Law Commission should be accountable to it. But I stress that the Law Commission's role is advisory not determinative. If the Law Commission could determine the law, there would obviously be what is sometimes called a democratic deficit. The Law Commission is not, of course, an elected body.

The Law Commission's relationships with government departments

There is scope at many stages in the process for a close working relationship with the government department involved in the administration of the law in question. The government department can draw the Law Commission's attention to the problems of which it is aware and to policy considerations in its view. However, it is important to note that at the end of the day it is up to the Law Commission as an independent body to produce its own independent view as to the changes of the law it considers should be adopted. This, in my view, is where the true value of the Law Commission lies.

Over the thirty-four years of its existence the Law Commission has produced over a hundred reports. The record year was in 1995 when ten reports were dusted down and implemented in whole or part. In 1996 there were six Law Commission reports which became Acts of Parliament. But implementation of the Law Commission's reports tends to be cyclical. In 1991, for instance, no Law Commission reports at all were implemented. In the 1997–98 session of Parliament, no Law Commission Bills were implemented. However, over the entire period of the Law Commission's existence, over 70% of its reports have been implemented in whole or part.[15] It is important also to stress that implementation by Parliament is not the only means of assessing the success of the Law Commission. The Law Commission is to be valued for the contribution it makes to the development of law in general, and this could be either through Parliament or through the courts or in some other way. In 1998, for instance, there were two important decisions of the House of Lords which relied on Law Commission reports: *Kleinwort Benson v Lincoln City Council*[16] on mistake of law, which implemented principal recommendations in the Law Commission's report on Mistake of Law; and a decision on Chinese Walls,[17] which drew heavily on the views expressed in the Law Commission's consultation paper on fiduciary duties and regulatory rules.[18]

---

[15] *Annual Report of the Law Commission for 1998* (Law Com No 258, 1999) para. 1.8. In *The Work of the Law Commission incorporating the Twelfth Programme*, published by the Law Commission in February 2015, this figure was revised slightly downwards to 69%.

[16] [1998] 3 WLR 1095.

[17] *Prince Jefri Bolkiah v KPMG* [1999] 1 All ER 517.

[18] *Fiduciary Duties and Regulatory Rules* (CP No 124, 1992). The government rejected the ensuing report (Law Com 236), but in July 2014 the Law Commission made recommendations on the *Fiduciary Duties of Investment Intermediaries* (Law Com No 350, 2014), which the government has accepted.

There is, however, a bottleneck in Parliament. There is always more work for Parliament than Parliament can cope with. The Law Commission therefore presses for improvements in Parliamentary procedure. In the last Parliament, there were a number of improvements so far as the Law Commission was concerned. There was a statement in the Queen's Speech for several years that the government might bring forward other measures of law reform, and this enabled Law Commission Bills to be introduced as part of the government's programme for the session when Parliamentary time allowed. In addition, in 1995, the 'Jellicoe' procedure was introduced. This is a special public Bill procedure in the House of Lords. It enables the House of Lords to consider detailed Bills, such as law reform bills, on the main floor of the House. The Committee can take evidence from experts and can make amendments and then report back to the House.[19] This was particularly helpful in the last government as one of the principal difficulties was, as I have mentioned, lack of Parliamentary time. It enables Parliament to give detailed scrutiny to Bills without reducing the time which the government needs for its own programme.

In this Parliament, there have been further improvements in Parliamentary procedure. The House of Commons has set up the Select Committee on Modernization of the House of Commons. This has recommended increased use of Select Committees, and the carry-over of Bills from one session to another in appropriate cases, and it has encouraged the publication of draft Bills for consultation. Most recently, it has invited the views of Members of Parliament on the question of a 'Main Committee', which would be a forum off the floor of the House for discussing uncontroversial measures. Many Law Commission reports would fall within the category of 'uncontroversial' for this purpose.[20]

In the 1998–99 session there were two Law Commission Bills before Parliament:[21] the Law Commission's Bill on privity of contract[22] and the Law Commission's Bill on trustee delegation.[23]

I would now like to say a little about some of the current and recent projects of the Law Commission.[24]

[19] For the up to date position as regards Parliamentary procedure for non-controversial Law Commission Bills, see Preface to Section B by the Rt Hon Lord Mackay of Clashfern, Author's Notes on Law Commission Bills, n 1.

[20] For the results of the consultation on the 'Main Committee' see the *Annual Report of the Law Commission for 1998* (Law Com No 258, 1999) paras 1.29–1.30, and also the *Annual Report of the Law Commission for 1999* (Law Com No 265, 2000) paras 1.27–1.29.

[21] In the 1999–2000 session there is a further Law Commission Bill before Parliament, namely the Trustee Bill. This will implement recommendations in *Trustees' Powers and Duties* (Law Com No 260, Scot Law Com No 172, 1999).

[22] Contracts (Rights of Third Parties) Bill implementing with minor modifications *Privity of Contract: Contracts for the Benefit of Third Parties* (Law Com No 242, 1996). This Bill became the Contracts (Rights of Third Parties) Act 1999.

[23] Trustee Delegation Bill implementing *The Law of Trusts: Delegation by Individual Trustees* (Law Com No 220, 1994). This Bill became the Trustee Delegation Act 1999.

[24] Some of the projects originally referred to in the speech on which this chapter is based have been omitted in order to confine the text to those of most interest at the date of publication of this work.

Land registration

This is an ambitious project to replace the whole of the Land Registration Act 1925. A consultative document issued jointly by the Law Commission and the Land Registry in September 1998 made proposals for making land registration legislation more accessible and introducing some improvements, for example by clarifying the classes of overriding interests, and making the doctrine of adverse possession more consistent with a registration system.[25] It also proposes that legislative provision should be made for electronic conveyancing. The consultation period has closed and it is expected that a final report will be published in 2000.[26]

Limitation of actions

The present law on limitation lacks coherence and has developed in an ad hoc way over time. The traditional rules for actions in tort now apply only to a minority of tort actions because so many exceptions have been grafted on to them. For example, actions for personal injury, defamation, and consumer protection, among others, are all governed by different and separate regimes. Deliberate concealment can stop a period running but cannot suspend it once it has started to run. The provisions, for example, on breach of trust and date of knowledge in personal injury and latent damage under the Consumer Protection Act 1997 are very complicated. Moreover, whilst there has been a move towards protecting claimants who have suffered 'latent damage' from losing their cause of action before they could reasonably have known of it, these provisions are confined (outside the sphere of non-deliberate personal injuries) to the tort of negligence and to claims under the Consumer Protection Act 1997. They do not extend to other torts or the breach of contract. The following example is given in the consultation paper:[27]

Fred has an extension built to his home. Several years later, it starts to crack because some of the materials used were inadequate. If he sues his builder for breach of contract in using inadequate materials his action is barred 6 years after the house was built even though he could not reasonably have known of the breach of contract by then. Had the contract been made by deed, the limitation period would be 12 years.[28]

---

[25] *Land Registration for the Twenty-First Century: A Consultative Document* (Law Com No 254, 1998).

[26] *Land Registration for the Twenty-First Century* (Joint report of the Law Commission and HM Land Registry) (Law Com No 271, 2001). The draft Bill attached to this report was presented to Parliament on 1 June 2001 and with a few amendments became the Land Registration Act 2002. In 2015, the Law Commission was asked to carry out a wide-ranging review of this Act with a view to amendment where elements of it could be improved in light of experience with its operation.

[27] *Limitations of Actions* (CP No 151, 1998). A report and draft Bill were published in 2001: Limitation of Actions (Law Com No 270, 2001). It seemed at first that the government were minded to implement this reform but in 2009 Bridget Prentice, then Parliamentary Under-Secretary for the Ministry of Justice, announced that the report would no longer be pursued.

[28] *Limitations of Actions* (n 27) para 1.1.

Furthermore, the lack of a long stop in personal injury actions may be regarded as unfair to defendants, who can never be sure that they are free of claims. They must retain records for years for fear they may be exposed to claims many years after the act or omission.

From the practitioners' point of view it is clear that there is a considerable lack of clarity in this area and this makes it difficult to advise clients accurately. While, no doubt, specialist lawyers have got used to this complexity, the law is undoubtedly unsystematic and high street solicitors approach the law of limitations with a considerable degree of trepidation. Moreover, if the law is difficult to understand for practitioners, it must be incomprehensible for members of the public. This is unacceptable, especially since the consequences of misunderstanding the law can be to eliminate valid claims. Furthermore, the reliance on a judicial discretion to override a limitation period (as in an action for personal injuries and defamation or malicious prosecution) renders the law too uncertain. These matters need to be resolved in expensive litigation which is subsidiary to the claimant's main claim, an expensive process for both the plaintiff (or the legal aid fund) and the defendant. There have been over 115 appellate decisions on s 33 of the Limitation Act 1980 reported on LEXIS.

In summary, the present law does not provide an even balance between the interest of claimants in having sufficient time to identify and pursue their claim, and the interest of defendants in having the certainty that, after the expiry of a fixed period of time, they are no longer exposed to liability. The interests of the state are in ensuring that there is an end to litigation and that resources are efficiently used.

The Law Commission has produced a large consultation paper on this matter seeking views. It provisionally recommended a core regime. Essential features of the core regime were as follows:

(1) There would be an initial limitation period of three years that would run from when the plaintiff knows or ought reasonably to know that he or she has a cause of action....

(2) There would be a long-stop limitation period of 10 years, or in personal injury claims 30 years that would run from the date of the act or omission which gives a rise to the claim.

(3) The plaintiff's disability (including supervening disability) would extend the initial limitation period (unless, possibly, there is a representative adult other than the defendant). Adult disability would not extend the long-stop limitation period.... Deliberate concealment (initial and subsequent) would extend the long-stop.... Acknowledgements and part-payments should start time running again but not once the initial long-stop limitation period has expired.

(4) The courts would *not* have a discretion to displace the limitation period.[29]

This core regime would apply without qualification to the following actions: 'the majority of tort actions including negligence, trespass to the person, including sexual abuse, defamation and malicious falsehood, contract claims, restitution, breach of trust, actions on a statute and actions on a judgment or arbitration

---

[29] *Limitations of Actions* (n 27) para 11.16.

awards'.[30] Subject to the normal rules in the validity of contractual terms, the parties would be free to alter the length of the starting date of the initial limitation period by contract. The plaintiffs would also be able to add new claims in existing actions where they were sufficiently related to the original cause of action, even where the limitation period had expired since the proceedings were started.[31]

While a move to discoverability may be regarded as having the principal merit of producing greater justice for claimants by overcoming the latent damage problem, it might be thought to carry the disadvantage of uncertainty. This may be most keenly felt in contractual disputes where there is a danger of adding to the factual issues in dispute, increasing satellite litigation, and increasing legal costs. The date of breach is usually clear. Why therefore should there be a change? While certainty should be an important goal it can be argued a better way of achieving this is by combining an initial limitation period running from discoverability with an overall long-stop.

Then there is the question of when time should start to run. The Law Commission's provisional view was that time should generally start to run from the date of discoverability. This would focus on the following: 'that the claimant has a cause of action against the defendant which is significant'.[32] Actual knowledge would be treated as a straightforward concept. Constructive knowledge should include a large subjective element so that it should be defined as 'what the claimant in his circumstances and with his ability ought to have known had he acted reasonably'.[33]

The situation of corporate claimants is obviously a more complicated area. The Commission has proposed that specific statutory provisions should be laid down on how discoverability should apply to corporate claimants. Actual knowledge in this situation would be triggered where an employee or officer has that knowledge, but this would be disapplied where the employee did not have authority to act on the information, did not in fact communicate to a superior with the requisite authority, and would not be expected to communicate that information to such a superior. The company would have constructive knowledge of any fact relevant to its cause of action of which one of its employees or officers had constructive knowledge, namely knowledge that he would have obtained if he had made reasonable enquiries. This would be disapplied where the employee would not have been expected to act on the information, or to communicate that information to anyone else within the company with authority to act on the information.[34]

Certain factors would extend the limitation period. As regards disability, as under our present law, the Law Commission's provisional view was that disability[35] should extend an initial limitation period so that it started only when the claimant's disability had ceased. The Commission proposed that adult disability should not

---

[30] *Limitations of Actions* (n 27) para 11.17.   [31] *Limitations of Actions* (n 27) para 11.20.
[32] *Limitations of Actions* (n 27) para 12.44.
[33] *Limitations of Actions* (n 27) paras 12.45–12.57.
[34] *Limitations of Actions* (n 27) paras 12.70–12.87.
[35] Disability in general means under the age of majority or of unsound mind.

override the long-stop where there was no necessary end to the disability. This is in contrast to the position on minority.[36]

As regards deliberate concealment, the Commission's provisional view was that a long-stop limitation period should be inapplicable where the defendant had deliberately concealed from the claimant the facts relevant to the discoverability test under the core regime, that is, the facts concerning the cause of action, the identity of the defendant, and the significance of the cause of action. Concealment subsequent to the act or omission giving rise to the cause of action should suspend the running of the long-stop. As under the present law for deliberate concealment, the defendant must conceal the relevant facts intending the claimant not to discover the truth or be reckless as to whether the claimant discovers the truth or not.[37] As regards acknowledgement and part-payment, the Law Commission's provisional recommendation was that acknowledgement or part-payment should continue to restart the limitation period in relation to, at least, the same actions for which this is currently the law.[38]

The consultation period ended in April 1998 and the responses have been analysed. It is expected that a final report containing the Law Commission's recommendations will be published in 2000–01.

Fraud

The Home Office has referred to the Law Commission the law of fraud, including a question whether a general offence of fraud is desirable.[39] There are doubts about whether a general offence of fraud would comply with the European Convention on Human Rights. The matter is under active consideration.[40]

Mental incapacity

The Law Commission published its report on mental incapacity in 1995 following considerable work, including the issue of full consultation papers.[41] It made important recommendations in a field of great relevance to modern society, where people are living longer and many incapable adults are cared for in the community. The report recommended the introduction of a single comprehensive

---

[36] *Limitations of Actions* (n 27) paras 12.115–12.145.
[37] *Limitations of Actions* (n 27) paras 12.146–12.154.
[38] *Limitations of Actions* (n 27) paras 12.155–12.156.
[39] Hansard, HL vol 588 WA, col 176 (7 April 1998).
[40] See the Law Commission consultation paper, *Legislating the Criminal Code: Fraud and Deception* (CP No 155, 1999) and see the *Annual Report of the Law Commission for 1999* (Law Com No 265, 2000) para 4.9. In 2002, the Law Commission published its report on *Fraud* (Law Com No 276, 2002). The recommendations included the abolition of the offence of conspiracy to defraud and the introduction of a new general offence of fraud. The recommendations in this report were substantially implemented by the Fraud Act 2006.
[41] *Mental Incapacity* (Law Com No 231, 1995).

piece of legislation to make new provision in respect of the personal welfare, health care, and financial affairs of people who lack mental capacity. In December 1997, the government published a green paper[42] inviting comments on a wide range of questions relating to mental incapacity. Most of the green paper was based on the Law Commission's report.

As regards the test of capacity, the Law Commission recommended a new statutory definition of capacity that would apply for the purposes of the legislation it recommended, as the existing tests were neither clear nor widely understood. The Law Commission considered a number of possible approaches, including the 'functional approach', which is currently the main method used in common law. Following consultation, the functional approach was widely favoured. This was no surprise as it had been the most frequently adopted in English law. In essence, it asks whether an individual is able, at the time when a particular and specific decision has to be made, to understand its nature and effects. This approach emphasizes the fluctuating nature of capacity. Its aim has been to provide a degree of certainty and clarity for practitioners in this area of law. It arises, for instance, when a client wants to make a will.

It should be noted that the Law Commission's draft Bill made no attempt to alter the definition at common law. The report considered that, after implementation of the new statutory definition, it was likely that the courts would consider it and then adopt it for the purposes of the common law if they saw fit. The new definition expands upon rather than contradicting the terms of the existing common law tests, with the only difference in the provision being a requirement for an explanation of the relevant information to have been made, if a finding of incapacity is to have prospective effect.[43] It is to be noted that the government accepted this definition but invited further views.

What is the effect of the functional test in practice? If the Law Commission takes the case of testamentary capacity, the leading case is *Banks v Goodfellow*.[44] The Lord Chief Justice set out the following criteria for a testamentary capacity:

It is essential . . . that a testator shall understand the nature of the Act and its effects; shall understand the extent of the property of which he is disposing; shall be able to comprehend and appreciate the claims to which he ought to give effect; and with a view to the latter object, that no disorder of mind should poison his affections, pervert his sense of right or prevent the exercise of his natural faculties—that no insane illusion shall influence his will in disposing of his property and bring about a disposal of it which, if the mind had been sound, would not have been made.

Thus a testator is not only required to pass the test of understanding the nature of his act, and its broad effects, but he must also pass a memory test of recalling the extent of his property and the moral test of awareness of the obligations owed to others. A valid will may be made by a person, including a patient of the Court of Protection who is frequently subject to delusions, or whose condition fluctuates,

---

[42] *Who Decides? Making Decisions on Behalf of Mentally Incapacitated Adults* (Cmd 3803, 1997).
[43] *Mental Incapacity* (n 41) para 3.23.   [44] (1870) LR 5 QB 549.

provided that it is executed during a lucid spell, or his particular delusions have not influenced the disposition of this property. The Law Society and the British Medical Association have produced a useful booklet entitled *Assessment of Mental Capacity.*[45] It contains a checklist which although not intended to be authoritative is nonetheless valuable.

People making a will should understand that they will die, that the will then comes into effect, and that they can change the will if they have capacity to do so. They should also understand who the executor is, who gets what out of the will, whether the beneficiary's gift is outright or conditional, that the beneficiaries might lose out if they spend their money during their lifetime, that a beneficiary might die before them, and whether they have already made a will.[46]

The proposed functional approach focuses on the particular type of decision and the capability of the person concerned to understand, at the time it is made, the nature of the decision required and its implication.

How does the definition apply? What would follow under the Law Commission's recommendations if a person was without capacity on the Law Commission test?

The decisions for a person without capacity should be taken in that person's interests. To decide what is in a person's best interests one has to have regard to:

... the ascertainable past and present wishes and feelings of the person concerned, and the factors that person would consider if able to do so; the need to permit and encourage the person to participate, or to improve his or her ability to participate, as fully as possible in anything done in any decision affecting him or her; the views of other people whom it is appropriate and practical to consult about the person's wishes and feelings and what would be in his or her best interests; and whether the purpose for which any action or decision is required can be effectively achieved in a manner less restrictive of a person's freedom of action.[47]

Then the Law Commission recommended that there should be a general authority in certain circumstances to do anything for the personal welfare or health care of a person who is, or is reasonably believed to be, without capacity in relation to the matter in question. For this to apply, it must in all the circumstances be reasonable for the matter to be done by the person who does it.[48]

It is obvious that there are some matters to which the Law Commission recommendation does not apply. No person should be able to make decisions about, for instance, consent to marriage or consent to a divorce petition on behalf of a person without capacity.[49]

The Law Commission's recommendations on mental incapacity also covered advanced statements about health care. These are sometimes called 'living wills'.

---

[45] 'Assessment of Mental Capacity Guidance for Doctors and Lawyers A report by the British Medical Association and the Law Society', London (1995).
[46] 'Assessment of Mental Capacity Guidance' (n 45) para 4.4.
[47] *Mental Incapacity* (n 41) para 3.28 and draft Bill, cl 3(2).
[48] *Mental Incapacity* (n 41) para. 4.4 and draft Bill, cl 4(1).
[49] *Mental Incapacity* (n 41) para. 4.29 and draft Bill, cl 30.

The Law Commission examined the common law here. At common law, certain forms of advanced statement already have full effect. A patient who is conscious and of sound mind is at liberty to decline to undergo treatment, even where death would be the result. This extends the situation where a person, in anticipation of his incapacity, gives clear instructions that in a particular event he is not to be given medical care, including a caesarean section or artificial feeding to keep him or her alive.

Special care is necessary to ensure that prior refusal of consent is still properly to be regarded as applicable in all the circumstances which have subsequently occurred. A doctor may be put in a more difficult position where the decision to refuse treatment is against his or her professional judgment. However, the present situation is that a mentally competent patient has a right to refuse medical treatment for any reason, even where that decision could lead to death, and indeed in that situation physically invasive medical treatment is a criminal or tortious assault.[50] The situation is more complicated in relation to advance statements on future health care since it is necessary to consider both the state of mind of the person at the time of making the statement and at the time for which the statement is made to take effect.

The Law Commission recommended that an 'advance refusal of treatment' should be defined as a refusal, made by a person aged 18 or over with the necessary capacity, of any medical, surgical, or dental treatment or other procedure and intended to have effect at any subsequent time when he or she may be without capacity to give or refuse consent.[51] The recommendations stated that the general authority should not authorize any treatment or procedure if an advance refusal of treatment by the person concerned applies to that treatment or procedure in the circumstances of the case.[52] However, the Law Commission recommended that there should be a rebuttable presumption that an advance refusal of treatment does not apply in circumstances where those having the care of the person who made it considered that refusal endangers (a) that person's life or (b) if that person is a woman who is pregnant, the life of the foetus.[53] In addition, it recommended that no person should incur liability (i) for the consequences of withholding any treatment or procedure if he has reasonable grounds for believing that an advance refusal of treatment applies or (ii) for carrying out any treatment or procedure to which an advance refusal applies unless he knows or has reasonable grounds for believing that an advance refusal applies.[54] In the absence of any indication to the contrary it was to be presumed that an advance refusal was validly made if it was made in writing, signed, and witnessed.[55] An advance refusal of treatment might at

---

[50] *Who Decides?* (n 42) para 4.12.
[51] *Mental Incapacity* (n 41) para 5.16 and draft Bill, cl 9(1).
[52] *Mental Incapacity* (n 41) para 5.21.
[53] *Mental Incapacity* (n 41) para 5.26 and draft Bill, cl 9(3).
[54] *Mental Incapacity* (n 41) para 5.27 and draft Bill, cl 9(4).
[55] *Mental Incapacity* (n 41) para 5.30 and draft Bill, cl 9(5).

any time be withdrawn or altered by the person who made it if he or she has capacity to do so.[56]

An advance refusal of treatment should not preclude the provision of 'basic care', namely care to maintain bodily cleanliness and to alleviate severe pain, as well as the provision of direct oral nutrition and hydration.[57]

What is clear is that solicitors are now preparing advance statements on their clients' instruction. Advance statements cannot require or allow a doctor to participate in mercy killing. This may involve commission of the offence of murder and the government has no plans to change this position.[58]

As regards the liability of health providers, the Law Commission recommended that the legal position be clarified where they either withhold treatment when they understand that this would accord with a patient's wishes, or where they proceed with treatment, only to find that, unknown to them, the patient did not wish this. The recommendations make it clear that no person should incur liability in either of these circumstances. It would be the responsibility of the person making an advance refusal to ensure that the existence of the refusal comes to the notice of the treatment provider.[59]

The Law Commission's Report on Mental Incapacity also made recommendations about powers of attorney.[60] At the present time a power of attorney can only deal with financial affairs and is revoked upon the donor becoming mentally incapable. An enduring power of attorney[61] enables a person to decide who should look after their property or financial affairs when they become incapable.

The Law Commission recommended a new concept, that of a continuing power of attorney which should be capable of extending to matters regarding personal welfare as well as property and affairs (including the conduct of legal proceedings).[62] These proposals were unanimously supported on consultation. There would have to be safeguards.[63] An attorney could not override a patient where the patient was able to make the decision,[64] or consent to the patient's admission to hospital for assessment or treatment for mental disorder against their will.[65] Moreover, an attorney would not be able to consent to treatment where the patient had made an advance refusal unless expressly authorized to do so. A person would be able to revoke a continuing power of attorney whilst they still had capacity to do so. One important issue for practitioners is whether a continuing power of attorney should be registered by a solicitor. The Law Commission, following consultation, rejected certification. The government considered that a system for certification by

[56] *Mental Incapacity* (n 41) para 5.32 and draft Bill, cl 9(6).
[57] *Mental Incapacity* (n 41) para 5.34 and draft Bill, cl 9(7)(a) and (8).
[58] *Who Decides?* (n 42) para 4.15.
[59] *Mental Incapacity* (n 41) para 5.27 and draft Bill, cl 9(4).
[60] A power of attorney is an authority which a person (the donor) gives to another (his attorney) to act on his behalf.
[61] Under the Enduring Powers of Attorney Act 1985.
[62] *Mental Incapacity* (n 41) para 7.7 and draft Bill, cl 16(1).
[63] *Mental Incapacity* (n 41) paras 7.12 et seq and see draft Bill, cl 16(3)–(5).
[64] *Mental Incapacity* (n 41) para 7.14 and draft Bill, cl 16(3)(a).
[65] *Mental Incapacity* (n 41) para 7.15 and draft Bill, cl 16(3)(b).

a solicitor and a medical practitioner might help unnecessary abuse of these powers.[66]

The Law Commission's report on mental incapacity also dealt with reform of the Court of Protection.[67] The Law Commission identified three possible options: first, a jurisdiction integrating the Court of Protection and exercised by ordinary courts; second and alternatively, a jurisdiction exercised by administrative tribunals; and third, a hybrid system with medical issues decided by tribunals and courts deciding all other issues. Ultimately, the Law Commission recommended that the new jurisdiction be operated by the courts, particularly as an informal and inquisitorial approach is adopted by the Court of Protection in any event.[68] These conclusions were supported by the House of Lords Select Committee.[69] The Law Commission recommended the establishment of a new superior court of record called the Court of Protection in place of the office of the Supreme Court also known as the Court of Protection.[70] The Law Commission had suggested that some applicants for private law orders[71] should be able to apply as of right while others would require leave. The government is minded to reject this recommendation as there is no evidence that the current system is being abused. A requirement for leave would increase delay and cost and there would be an increased sense of formality.[72]

In October 1999 the government published its plans to reform the law on making decisions on behalf of mentally incapacitated adults. The government accepted most of the Law Commission's recommendations but there are no proposals to legislate on advance statements about health care.[73]

Privity of contract: contracts for the benefit of third parties

The common law doctrine of privity of contract means that, as a general rule, a contract cannot confer rights or impose obligations on any person except the parties to it. So, third parties cannot acquire or enforce rights under contracts, even contracts which have been made for the express purpose of conferring rights upon them. The non-recognition of third party rights has been much criticized by the judiciary, academics, and law reform bodies. The Law Commission

[66] *Who Decides?* (n 42) para 6.40.
[67] At the time of the Law Commission's report, the Court of Protection made decisions only about the financial affairs of those who could not look after their own property.
[68] *Mental Incapacity* (n 41) para 10.24.
[69] 'Report of the Select Committee on Medical Ethics', London (1993–94) HL 21-I, para 248.
[70] *Mental Incapacity* (n 41) para 10.9 and draft Bill, cl 46(1).
[71] Application for public law orders may only be made by authorized officers of a local authority: see *Mental Incapacity* (n 41) para 10.20.
[72] *Who Decides?* (n 42) para 9.21.
[73] *Making decisions* (Cmd 4465, 1999). Likewise the White Paper contained no proposals to legislate on the Law Commission's recommendations on public law protection for vulnerable adults. However, the Mental Capacity Act 2005 subsequently implemented most of the Law Commission's other recommendations, including those about advance decisions to refuse treatment (see ss 24–26).

produced a report[74] and a draft Bill entitled the Contracts (Rights of Third Parties) Bill. This Bill with certain amendments was enacted in the 1999–2000 session of Parliament as the Contracts (Rights of Third Parties) Act 1999.

Pursuant to the 1999 Act's provisions, a third party now has a right to enforce a term of the contract, both when the contract expressly provides that he should have that right and also where there is no such express provision but where there is a contractual term which purports to confer a benefit, unless it appears on a true construction of the contract that the contracting parties did not intend the third party to have a right to enforce it.[75] In order to acquire that right, the third party must be expressly identified in the contract but need not be identified by name. It is sufficient if he or she is identified as a member of a class or answers a particular description.[76] The remedies available to the third party are the same as those available to a party to a contract bringing an action for breach.[77]

Once a third party has the right under the Contracts (Rights of Third Parties) Act 1999 to enforce a term of a contract, then pursuant to the provisions of the Act there are circumstances in which the parties to the contract may only cancel or vary it in a way which affects the third party's entitlement, if he consents.[78] In keeping with the preservation of the contracting parties' freedom to agree their own terms, these rules are displaced by an express term of the contract providing that the contract can be cancelled or varied without the third party's consent or that the third party's consent is to be required in different specified circumstances.[79]

The differences between the 1999 Act and the Bill attached to the Law Commission's report are mostly minor. There are variations to the exceptions, and the Act refers to 'a term of a contract' whereas the Bill attached to the report referred to the contract as a whole and then in cl 7 made reference to the 'term'.

The new Act now prevents a third party from suing an employee for breach of his contract of employment. This was not in the Law Commission's Bill. Without this exception it was thought that there was a risk that the rights of workers to take lawful industrial action might be restricted in unexpected ways.

Another exception introduced prevents third party rights arising from the 'deemed' contracts under s 14(1) of the Companies Act 1985 under which the registered memorandum and articles of the company constitute a contract between the company and its members in respect of their rights as such.[80] The peculiar nature of these deemed contracts makes them unsuitable for enforcement by a third party under a general reform aimed at giving effect to the parties' intentions.

The Bill as introduced also clarifies that in relation to contracts 'for the carriage of goods by sea'[81] it was intended to exclude from the Bill not only those contracts

---

[74] *Privity of Contract: Contracts for the Benefit of Third Parties* (Law Com No 242, 1996).
[75] Contracts (Rights of Third Parties) Act 1999, s 1(1)–(2) and see *Privity of Contract* (n 74) para 7.6.
[76] Section 1(3) and see *Privity of Contract* (n 74) para 7.6.
[77] Section 1(5) and see *Privity of Contract* (n 74) para 3.32.
[78] Section 2(1), (2) and see *Privity of Contract* (n 74) paras 9.26, 9.30.
[79] Section 2(3) and see *Privity of Contract* (n 74) paras 9.40, 9.42.
[80] Section 6(2).   [81] Section 6(6).

already covered by the Carriage of Goods by Sea Act 1992 but also those to which the 1992 Act could be applied by virtue of regulations made under s 1(5) of that Act (for example a contract for the carriage of goods by sea evidenced by an electronic bill of lading).[82]

Shareholder remedies

Shareholders are concerned with their remedies to enforce their personal rights and also their remedies to enforce rights belonging to the company. Shareholder remedies[83] have a key role to play in any question of company law reform. One cannot have an effective law on directors' duties unless shareholders can effectively enforce them if a company fails to do so. The importance of that is increased if criminal sanctions are removed or special rules, such as rules on the maintenance of capital, are also dismantled. The law of directors' duties then has greater importance.

Another drive towards making shareholder remedies more efficient is the process of civil justice reform. The principal aim of such reform is to cut cost and delay. Civil justice reform is strongly supported by the senior judges.

Among the shareholders' armoury of remedies is the statutory remedy for relief from unfair prejudice under ss 459 and 461 of the Companies Act 1985. These proceedings have been compared to old-fashioned matrimonial cruelty petitions, because of their complexity and length.[84] All sorts of allegations are made, from diverting the company's business to throwing the teapot out of the window. The research done by the Law Commission showed that the remedy was mainly used by shareholders of private companies in circumstances where a director had been excluded from managing the company and that director wanted a buy-out of his shares.[85] The Law Commission recommended that the Companies Act 1985 should be amended so as to add a presumption of unfair prejudice in owner-managed companies where a director was excluded.[86] If the court decided to make a buy-out order, it would be further presumed that the valuation should be on a pro rata basis, not on a discounted minority shareholder valuation.[87] The value of such

---

[82] Section 6(5)–(8).

[83] *Shareholder Remedies* (Law Com No 246, 1997), implemented by the Companies Act 2006.

[84] In one of the most extreme examples, *Re Freudiana Music Co Ltd*, 24 March 1993 (unreported), Jonathan Parker J, the hearing lasted for a year and extended over some 165 court days. The judgment stretched to some 499 pages in length and the costs awarded in favour of the respondent alone were £2m. The relevant sections are now the Companies Act 2006, ss 994–996.

[85] *Shareholder Remedies* (n 83) para 1.5, App J.

[86] *Shareholder Remedies* (n 83) paras 3.30, 3.38 et seq and draft Bill, cl 3.

[87] *Shareholder Remedies* (n 83) paras 3.30, 3.57 et seq and draft Bill, cl 4. In the event it was unnecessary to proceed with the recommendations in the text to which nn 86 and 87 relate because subsequently the House of Lords made it clear that these recommendations reflected the existing law: *O'Neill v Phillips* [1999] 1 WLR 1092, 1107–8 per Lord Hoffmann, with whom the remainder of the House agreed.

a provision is that it would encourage settlement and reduce costly litigation. The Law Commission also recommended increased case management by the court.[88]

As regards the shareholders' derivative action, the Law Commission recommended a new rule of court setting out clearly how a derivative action was to be conducted.[89] This would enable a derivative action to be brought where directors were negligent. This is not at present possible under the exceptions to the rule in *Foss v Harbottle*.[90] The main recommendations in this report have now been provisionally accepted by the relevant government departments.[91]

Conclusion

Finally I turn to the question: why have a Law Commission at all? In my view, there are three principal reasons:

(1) the Law Commission is independent;

(2) the Law Commission is an ongoing institution, not one that has to learn how to do law reform in a specific context and for the purpose of a specific exercise only;

(3) the Law Commission's methodology is very thorough and its practice is to promote systematic and principled law reform.

The Law Commission has built up a considerable reputation over thirty-five years. Lord Mackay of Clashfern, when Lord Chancellor in 1995, said that, when it came to considering a report which fell within his responsibilities as Lord Chancellor, his normal assumption is that one would wish to give effect to the Law Commission's proposals.[92]

In my view the Law Commission has an essential role to play in improving access to justice. This is echoed in the passage from the White Paper *Modernising Justice* which I quoted earlier. As Lord Mackay said on one occasion 'litigation is quite hazardous enough already without having to pursue it through a fog of ill-defined or conflicting law.'[93]

Having a law reform commission then means that there is a body devoted to law reform. If law reform was exclusively left to government departments, it would be subject to delay as it would always be put behind matters which needed an urgent

---

[88] *Shareholder Remedies* (n 83) Pt 2.

[89] *Shareholder Remedies* (n 83) Pt 6. The Law Commission recommended that the right to bring a derivative action should be set out in the Companies Acts, but that the details of the procedure should be set out in rules of court: para 6.111.

[90] (1843) 2 Hare 461, (1843) 67 ER 189.

[91] Department of Trade and Industry, 'Shareholder Remedies, A Consultative Document' (1998). Note: the Law Commission's recommendations on derivative actions were in due course reflected in the Companies Act 2006, Pt 11.

[92] *Annual Report of the Law Commission for 1995* (Law Com No 239, 1996) para 1.2.

[93] 'Civil Justice: choice and Responsibility', Paper given by the Lord Chancellor at All Souls College, Oxford, 14 June 1996.

solution. The Law Commission is not subject to those distractions and is able to get on with difficult and time-consuming law reform.

Undoubtedly, someone has to do the job of regular ongoing, non-party-political law reform. Over the years the Law Commission has demonstrated that having an independent Law Commission is the best way of achieving this.

10

Improving the Statute Book 1

A Law Reformer's Viewpoint

This chapter is based on the first part of an address given to the Annual General Meeting of the Statute Law Society, held in London on 19 May 1997.*

The role of the Law Commission Chairman

Now that I have held my office for seventeen months I can see that the Chairman of the Law Commission has rather a privileged position from which to espy what progress, if any, is being made to improve statute law. This is because the duty of the Law Commission, which is to review the law of England and Wales, extends not merely to making recommendations for the reform of the law in a particular area—the task for which it is best known—but also specifically to reviewing statute law with a view to its reform by a reduction in the number of separate enactments and the repeal of obsolete and unnecessary enactments. These tasks of the Law Commission rarely hit the headlines but they are as essential to good government in a developed democratic society as regular servicing is to one's motor car.

In the light of the functions of the Law Commission, the Chairman is a member of the Advisory Committee on Statute Law.[1] This body is perhaps not well known but it succeeded the Statute Law Committee and advises the Lord Chancellor as and when required on all matters which relate to the publication of the statute book. This widens the Chairman's horizons on statute law work, and has brought me into contact with others, such as the Clerk of the Parliaments and the Clerk of the House of Commons, who are of course closely involved with the statute book.

---

* This lecture was first published in (1997) 18(3) Statute Law Review 169. The next chapter, Ch 11, is based on the second part of this lecture, and offers some ideas about how to make statute law more accessible to users. Both parts of the lecture are reproduced here with the kind permission of Oxford University Press.

[1] The Advisory Committee on Statute Law has since ceased to exist, but it was closely involved in the setting up of the computerized database of statutes which members of the public can now use: <http://www.legislation.gov.uk>. This took many years' work on the part of those directly involved.

Consolidation of statutes

As regards the consolidation of statutes, the Chairman receives regular reports on the work being done by parliamentary counsel at the Law Commission to prepare consolidation Bills. Consolidation is a highly skilled task, requiring painstaking care by counsel and support from the government departments involved. This part of the work of the Commission has its fair share of problems. One of the major stumbling blocks often turns out to be the decision by the department to devote its resources to something else. Save in the most exceptional case we learn about this before work on the consolidation begins.

But the fact remains that there are relatively few statutes which, for one reason or another, departments want consolidated. This is just as well because the Commission's resources for this work are limited. Thus consolidation will take place, we would hope at a steady rate, but consolidation alone will not transform the statute book.

Revision of statutes

Similarly unglamorous to most people, but essential, is the Commission's work on statute law revision.[2] This is the work of preparing statute law revision bills for the repeal of enactments which no longer serve any useful purpose. This, too, is painstaking work because of all the investigations and checks that have to be made. I do not have time to give a fuller account of this work, but anyone who would like to know more should look at the information on the work of statute law revision included in our Annual Reports.[3]

The synergy between statute law and law reform

Statute law is the science which makes law reform by legislation possible. Thanks to the work of parliamentary counsel assigned to the Law Commission, the Law Commission's final report on a law reform project has the enormous advantage that it will usually include a draft Bill ready to be laid before Parliament. The Law Commission Chairman can follow the intricate drafting process involved in the preparation of this Bill, and is likely to become involved in the discussions with the department responsible for the relevant area of law, especially after publication of the report. At that stage the Law Commission's Bill may be amended by counsel instructed by the department to meet some problem which it feels has not been adequately dealt with in the draft Bill. The Chairman may also be involved, even if

---

[2] See also Ch 12 for more on statute law revision.
[3] See for example Law Com No 244 (HC (1996–97) 305).

only as an observer, when a Law Commission Bill is introduced into Parliament and makes its way through the legislative process.

The wider picture

So it can be seen that the Chairman of the Law Commission works closely with statute law and sees it 'from the inside'. However, there are many other bodies which are consulted about law reform or which press for law reform. I sit on two such bodies, the Financial Law Panel[4] and the Law Society's Company Law Committee. These are within the term 'law reformer' for present purposes, although they are *consumers* of law reform whereas the Law Commission is a *producer* of law reform. Consumers as well as producers have a valid interest in the improvement of the statute book. In the next chapter (Chapter 11), I put forward a number of ideas designed to make the task of understanding statutes more easy. These ideas are the product of my experience on these bodies as well as at the Law Commission.

[4] Now the Financial Markets Law Committee.

PART IV

MAKING STATUTE LAW MORE ACCESSIBLE

The function of legislation is to make law. Legislation constitutes an increasingly large part of the law affecting people's daily lives, yet receives relatively little attention from scholars or practitioners.

Legislation must be as clear as humanly possible. The key question is how to make statutes easier to understand. It would be tempting to think that this can always be achieved by putting more into the legislation but the risk is that it will in that event become less, rather than more, clear. In Chapter 11, *Improving the Statute Book 2: Particular Ways to Help the User*,[1] I offered two proposals for making the statute book more user-friendly. The first was a proposal that Bills should be published with an authoritative guide. In fact, Parliament now publishes official Explanatory Notes with a new Bill, and indeed Explanatory Notes on the Act when the Bill receives Royal Assent. This is an important development as Explanatory Notes can provide insights into the reasons for having various provisions. Judges can refer to them in case of doubt as to what a statute means.

My second proposal was for the publication of draft Bills to improve their quality. This practice has now been established and a relatively small, but increasing, number of Bills (or parts of Bills) are now published in draft before introduction into Parliament. Some of those Bills are also the subject of scrutiny by a Parliamentary committee before introduction.

Finally the paper points out the 'snare' of simplicity in statutory drafting: people often call for greater simplicity but it can lead to undesirable uncertainty in the law. What is needed is not simplicity but clarity.

In Chapter 12, *Modernizing Legislation: Signposts Along the Path*, I trace a number of developments designed to improve the statute book in the United Kingdom and in the Commonwealth. These developments included the project for simplifying UK tax law known as the Tax Law Rewrite, which led to the modernization of the statutory provisions dealing with direct tax.

---

[1] Ch 10 (*Improving the Statute Book 1: A Law Reformer's Viewpoint*) and Ch 11 are both based on an address given to the Statute Law Society.

In anticipation of the Human Rights Act 1998, Chapter 12 also examines cases about interpreting constitutional rights. Many of these cases were from the Judicial Committee of the Privy Council.[2] In these cases, the courts had given particular weight to the need to make constitutional rights effective. This case law remains relevant to constitutional legislation,[3] such as devolution legislation.[4]

---

[2] A senior UK court which heard final appeals from countries in the British Empire and which some newly independent Commonwealth countries have retained as their final court of appeal.

[3] That is, legislation of a kind that would be found in a written constitution, such as legislation setting out fundamental rights. It has been held that constitutional legislation can only be amended or repealed by unambiguous provisions in later legislation.

[4] This is discussed further in Ch 8, *What is the Safeguard for Welsh Devolution?* See especially pp 126–8.

11

Improving the Statute Book 2

Particular Ways to Help the User

This chapter is based on the second part of an address given to the Annual General Meeting of the Statute Law Society, held in London on 19 May 1997.*

Complexity and unwieldiness of the statute book

To a large extent the problems in statute law are caused not by any deficiency in technique as such but by the fact that there is simply so much legislation. The Companies Act 1985 is a case in point. It was painstakingly consolidated in 1985, but the consolidated statute was radically altered the following year by repeals and amendments effected by the Insolvency Act 1986, itself a consolidating statute. Since then there has been a steady stream of amendments which have added dozens of new sections to the 1985 Act, often by statutory instrument and often for the purpose of implementing the requirements of EC directives.

There is no further consolidation on the horizon, and the untidy mess that results is left to commercial publishers to sort out.

Over the years there have been many studies of the problems of statute law. The Law Commission and the Scottish Law Commission produced a report entitled *The Interpretation of Statutes* in 1969.[1] We have not been alone in this, for the Law Commissions in Victoria,[2] New Zealand,[3] and Hong Kong[4] have also published reports on interpretation and legislative drafting. There has also been other important work on the subject in the United Kingdom. In 1975, a committee appointed by the Lord President of the Council published a report, *The Preparation of Legislation*,[5] commonly styled the Renton report, since Lord Renton, President of the Statute Law Society, was its Chairman. The Hansard Society Commission on

---

* This lecture was first published in (1997) 18(3) Statute Law Review 169. It is reproduced with the kind permission of Oxford University Press. The previous chapter, Ch 10, is based on the first part of this lecture.

[1] Law Com No 21, Scot Law Com No 11 (HC (1968–69) 256).
[2] 'Plain English and the Law' (1990); 'The Structure and Format of Legislation' (1990).
[3] 'A New Interpretation Act: to Avoid "Prolixity and Tautology"' (1990); 'The Format of Legislation' (1993); 'Legislation Manual: Structure and Style' (1996).
[4] 'Report on Extrinsic Materials as an Aid to Statutory Interpretation' (1996).
[5] *The Preparation of Legislation* (Cmd 6053, 1975) (the Renton Report).

the Legislative Process published a report, *Making the Law*, often referred to as the Rippon Report after its Chairman, the late Lord Rippon. More recently there has been the Tax Law Rewrite initiative.[6] This is a potentially revolutionary force which could have a profound effect outside the narrow confines of revenue law. It aims in particular to rewrite tax law using shorter sentences, modern language, improved drafting, and a reordering of material. Many of these things are being done already, but less dramatically, in other less extensive legislative drafting, including the Commission's own draft Bills. Finally, one must not forget the contribution made by pressure groups such as Clarity and Lucid Law.

But it seems to me that yet more could be done to improve statutes both *internally*, by which I mean within a statute, and *externally*, by which I mean outside the statute. Improvement must be judged from different points of view. As I see it, statute law is improved if a statute is more easily used or accessed, or more susceptible to accurate interpretation. These are all valid ways of measuring the success of statute law. Space permits mention of only some things that can be done.

Possible internal improvements

Conveyances of unregistered land use language and conventions perfected over several centuries. They are usually effective for their purpose but their style and manner of expression hardly lend themselves to ready understanding, unless the reader happens to be a conveyancer. A visitor from Mars might feel much the same about the presentation of material in a statute. Take, for instance, the short title in the Companies Act 1985: 'An act to consolidate the greater part of the Companies Acts'. That is short and no doubt fulfils all the conventions of a short title. It conveys one vital piece of information, that the Act is a consolidating statute to which of course certain canons of construction generally apply. But it does not provide certain other information which these days is essential for the purposes of construction, namely, that much of the legislation is based on EC directives. It would be helpful if, as the Renton Report recommended,[7] there could be some reference to this, and, where the statute implements several different community instruments, if there could be a schedule giving the references to the EC legislation which the provisions of the statute were designed to implement.

Nor does the statute tell you at any point where all the relevant parliamentary debates are to be found. As these are scattered in Hansard, it would help the consumer of statutes considerably if there were a schedule which set out the relevant

---

[6] See Board of Inland Revenue, 'The Path to Tax Simplification: a Report under Section 160, Finance Act 1995' (HMSO, 1995); 'Tax Law Rewrite: The Way Forward' (Inland Revenue, July 1996); 'Tax Law Rewrite: Examples of Rewritten Legislation' (Inland Revenue, October 1996); 'Tax Law Rewrite: Plans for 1997' (Inland Revenue, December 1996); 'Tax Law Rewrite: First Exposure Draft—Trading Income of Individuals' (Inland Revenue, July 1997). See also, 'Second Report, House of Commons Select Committee on Procedure, Legislative Procedure for Tax Simplification Bills', HC (1996–97) 126. See further Ch 12, pp 179–81.

[7] The Renton Report (n 5) para 19.39.

references. As I understand it, this is already done in Australia, and the New Zealand Law Commission has recommended that the same be done in New Zealand.[8] Likewise, if the Act implements recommendations of the Law Commission or a similar body, there should be some reference to the relevant report. This would be especially useful where the statute does not legislate in precisely the same terms as the body in question recommended—some method could be found of making this clear in relation to the provisions in question. All this information would be additional to tables of derivations and destinations published with consolidated Bills.

Again, it would be helpful if in substantial legislation we could have a table of contents (as well as the arrangement of sections) and an index of the main subject-matter.

Now of course these changes would require some additional resources but the information in question is surely collated in any event, and, in the case of the index, this could probably be done quite efficiently using modern technology. Accordingly, I would hope that the resources we are talking about would not be significant. It seems to me that they would be well justified by reference to the convenience of consumers of statute law.

Possible external improvements

In the interests of brevity I make two assumptions here: (1) that the courts will look at any authoritative material produced before or at the same time that a statute was passed which shows clearly what the aim and the genesis of the legislation was understood by the legislators to be (although I do not exclude the possibility that post-legislative material may also be of use on questions of interpretation); and (2) that the courts will look at all such material for the purpose of resolving ambiguities, and abandon the hermetic distinction between the use of extrinsic material to resolve ambiguities and the use of such material for the purpose only of finding out the mischief to which the statute was directed.

These are large assumptions, as a digression back to the statutory reform of company law will illustrate.

In company law it is a fundamental concept that a company's assets should be used for the purposes of carrying on its business and not, for instance, for conferring a financial benefit on shareholders except in one of the ways which company law specifically permits, such as dividends paid out of profits. It follows from this that a company is not permitted to apply assets to help to fund the acquisition of shares in itself. Indeed successive Companies Acts have backed up that prohibition with a criminal offence. The prohibition was, however, created in such wide terms that it was, in the words of a report by a committee chaired by the Rt Hon Lord Justice Jenkins as long ago as 1962, 'an occasional embarrassment to the honest without being a serious inconvenience to the unscrupulous'.[9] Parliament did nothing until the Companies Bill 1981 was introduced.

---

[8] See 'Legislation Manual: Structure and Style' (n 3) para 122.
[9] Cmd 1749, para 176.

By that time the provisions of the then existing section had been considered by the Court of Appeal in *Belmont Finance Corporation Ltd v Williams Furniture Ltd (No 2)*.[10] In the course of the majority judgment in that case doubts were expressed as to whether the prohibition made unlawful a transaction into which the company entered partly with a genuine view to its own commercial interests and partly with a view to putting a purchaser of shares in funds to complete his purchase. For instance a company which is taken over may buy an asset of its new parent for the purposes of its business, but knowing that the new parent will use the cash proceeds to reduce monies borrowed to acquire the company.

Now the acquisition of one company by another is very common and almost inevitably it is followed by a reconstruction of some kind so that the companies can get the full benefits of the merger. The dicta in *Belmont* almost paralysed corporate acquisitions for a time and the government was anxious to clear the doubt while at the same time jumping agilely between certain inflexible restrictions which EC legislation, designed to harmonize company law, had laid down since the prohibition was originally introduced. The end product was a new defence available (in summary) where the financial assistance given by the company was incidental to some larger purpose of the company.[11] Hansard shows quite clearly that Parliament's purpose was merely to resolve the doubts raised in *Belmont*. There was no debate about what might or might not be a larger purpose of the company.

In 1988 the House of Lords had to consider that issue in a case called *Brady v Brady*.[12] This was before *Pepper v Hart*.[13] The House correctly divined that the purpose of the provision was to dispel the doubts raised by *Belmont*. But they went on to hold that the word 'purpose' was capable of several meanings. They held that in the context of the prohibition in question it had to mean something other than a reason. It followed that merely to give financial assistance with a view to achieving the benefits of being acquired by the new parent company was not enough. There had to be some independent purpose, such as the purchase of an asset. The distinction is difficult to explain and difficult to apply. In practice the new defence is little used and the Department of Trade and Industry had to consider very carefully how (if at all) it could be amended so that it had an effect more like that which it was originally thought to have prior to the distinction imposed by the House of Lords.[14]

What is evident from looking at Hansard in that case is that the parliamentary material was of no help. This meant that it was left to the judges to work out what the policy should be where the statute gave potentially too wide a defence. This case

---

[10] [1980] 1 All ER 393.
[11] See the Companies Act 1981, s 42 which became the Companies Act 1985, s 153.
[12] [1989] AC 755.   [13] [1993] AC 593.
[14] In the end no change was made and an alternative solution of restricting the prohibition was adopted. Thus, in the Companies Act 2006, following the recommendations of the DTI's Company Law Review Steering Group (of which I was a member) (see Final Report, 'Modern Company law for a Competitive Economy', DTI (2001), para 2.30), the provisions have been amended principally so that they apply only to financial assistance with a view to the acquisition of shares in a public company: Companies Act 2006, ss 678 and 679.

is therefore an interesting illustration of the limitations of parliamentary material and, in a rather stark way, the role of the courts in refining and defining the scope of statutes.

That said, external material should not be ignored. It should, where relevant, be considered for such help as it can give, but the weight to be attached to it in any circumstances involves judgment. The issue must have been directly addressed and answered. The answer must be a considered one and not merely a response given in the cut and thrust of debate at some late hour of the night.

With that health warning about the limitations on material extrinsic to the statute itself, I return to the steps that may be taken externally to improve the quality of statute law. I have two specific suggestions to make.

Two proposals

The first suggestion is that where a Bill is known from the start to be a substantial one, the Bill should be published with an authoritative guide. Very often this guide would simply be helpful background reading for anyone who has to study the Bill or, in due course, the Act. In my experience words that might, if read in isolation, appear to be ambiguous often cease to be ambiguous if they are read in context. This would happen in many cases if the background to the legislation were more widely known. The guide to which I refer would be the same, or much the same, as notes on a clause at present.

I do not exclude the possibility that on occasions the guide might also be used as an aid to resolving ambiguities.[15] The guide which I propose could not, however, alter the meaning of any provision. This is a fine line but in my view it is essential to maintain the supremacy of the enacted word over any extrinsic material. I emphasize that the guide must be available with the Bill when the Bill is introduced. This will enable Members of Parliament to raise questions on it, and it will also enable professional bodies and others who are monitoring the legislation from outside Parliament to consider the legislative proposals in their full context.

If the government or private member responsible for the Bill introduces significant amendments, there should likewise be a guide to the amendments in question.

In short, Parliament may have much to learn from the courts' experience in skeleton arguments. It could save a considerable amount of time in the long run and I think lead to a higher standard of legislation if there were some guide which showed Members of Parliament and the public alike what in essence was proposed. Scrutiny then becomes more focused.

Of course one would need some safeguards against the inclusion of material in the guide which went beyond merely explaining in an objective way the content of the legislative proposals. I envisage that, if there were to be some such guide as I have suggested, Parliament would have some procedure for regulating the preparation of

---

[15] See n 6, and compare the position in relation to Hansard, discussed at pp 182–3.

the guide. This is necessary to preserve the integrity of the legislative process and, as I have said, the supremacy of the written word as enacted by Parliament.

The guide would only reflect the provisions of the Bill as it goes through Parliament. There is some concern that what is really needed is not notes on clauses but notes on sections. I do not think that this needs to be the concern of Parliament or the executive. Notes on sections can be done by commercial publishers pulling together the guide that I propose, any notes on amendments, and any material that passes the *Pepper v Hart* test[16] in the Parliamentary debates themselves.

The second suggestion which I would make is not new. To some extent it is already being done or proposed to be done; one example was the statement in the Queen's Speech on 14 May 1997 that the government would publish in draft for public consultation a number of Bills which it intends to introduce in subsequent sessions.[17] I propose that *all substantial legislation* should be published in draft for public comment first. This would give the public a proper chance to see what is happening. It would facilitate the production of the guide which I have suggested. It would enable professional bodies, like the Law Society's Company Law Committee on which I sit, to give full and considered comments on legislative proposals. What often happens at present is that because time is short a professional body has to make a point which, if it had had longer to think about it, it would have realized did not need to be reflected or should not be dealt with in the manner that they suggest. This has a consequential effect on the use of parliamentary time on the floor of the House since, in desperation as much as anything else, the professional body will sometimes ask a Member of Parliament to raise the point on its behalf. Moreover the standard of our legislation will improve if more draft legislation is made available for public comment. I hope that this proposal may be sympathetically examined in the course of the current consideration by the House of Commons Select Committee on a modernization of its procedure.[18]

Of course, so far as the Law Commission is concerned, its proposals are generally the subject of extensive public consultation but in many cases there is, as yet, no formal consultation on the Bill. An analysis of the appropriate mechanics of such consultation is, however, beyond the scope of this chapter.

Clarity over simplicity

Finally something should be said about the snare of simplicity. I doubt if we really want legislation to be simpler. That would in many cases make the legislation more uncertain and less likely to be effective. It would also inevitably remove rights and remedies and protections currently given. Where legislation increases the power of the state in relation to the individual, the legislation must be very clearly expressed if it is to achieve its purpose, and it is no doubt healthy that Parliament should

[16] See Ch 12, under '4. Changes in the courts' approach to interpreting statutes'.
[17] Hansard, HC vol 294, cols 41–44 (14 May 1997).
[18] For the current position, see Ch 12, under '5. Modernization of House of Commons procedure'.

expressly consider this aspect. Likewise, commercial lawyers do not want simple legislation. They want to know precisely what is or is not allowed so that they can advise their clients how to proceed. It is too late to wait to see what the court decides in a few years' time. Again, in criminal law and fiscal law the law must not leave gaps; no one can be taxed or punished without express provision.

What is needed in my view is not simplicity but clarity. Perhaps I may illustrate this by something which I learnt on a recent visit to Japan. As you may know, in Japan there are many fewer lawyers than in this country. When I asked how conveyancing was done I was told that you did not need a lawyer; the law was clear enough so that all you needed was a scrivener to draw up the document that had to be registered. The Japanese law of conveyancing is thus in a state that it would be highly desirable for our law to be in as well. Perhaps we need so many lawyers because our laws are obscure. What we need to do is to make them clearer. Of course that is one of the reasons why we have Law Commissions in this country but unfortunately there is a limit to what they, alone, can achieve. Clarity generally can in my view be assisted by making the sort of internal and external improvements to statutes that I have proposed here.

12

Modernizing Legislation

Signposts Along the Path

This chapter is based on the Harry Street lecture delivered at the University of Manchester on 22 October 1997.*

Increasing recognition of the importance of statute law

The legal world is rapidly becoming divided into two camps: statute lawyers and common lawyers. Legislation has been prolific in recent years so that there are several areas of law which now have a substantial statutory base. Some years ago, in 1983, the first Chairman of the Law Commission, Lord Scarman, said: 'The Common Law is delightful but is now of marginal importance only.'[1] That was something of an exaggeration but it is a clear reminder of the increasing importance of legislation.

As we saw in Chapter 10, the Law Commission's responsibilities extend to the statute book. We have a duty under the Law Commissions Act 1965 to review the law with a view to its systematic development and reform.[2] Our best known activity is the production of law reform reports with draft Bills annexed, but the duty of the Commission also extends to codifying the law. We have sought to codify the law of contract and the criminal law, going even so far as publishing a report and draft criminal code in 1989, but as yet the Commission's efforts at codification of the whole or a substantial part of a subject have not borne fruit. We also produce consolidation Bills, whose purpose is to reduce the number of separate Acts on the statute book. As we saw in Chapter 10, we have another team engaged on statute law revision. This is a skilled and arcane process which eventually leads to spent enactments which can safely be repealed by being removed from the statute book.

Parliamentary counsel are assigned to the Law Commission to enable it to do its consolidation work and also to assist it to prepare draft law reform Bills, as the Law Commission generally annexes draft Bills to its reports on law reform. I have heard it said by more than one commissioner that the process of working with parliamentary counsel is one of the most instructive experiences because of their

---

* This paper was first published as Mary Arden, 'Modernizing Legislation: Signposts Along the Path' in [1998] Public Law 65, © Sweet & Maxwell Ltd. It is reproduced here with the kind permission of the publisher Sweet & Maxwell Ltd.

[1] See Hansard, HL vol 437, col 634 (15 December 1982).
[2] This chapter was written during my period of office as Chairman of the Law Commission.

exacting approach. The involvement of parliamentary counsel is one of the reasons in my view why the recommendations of the Law Commission for law reform have historically been of such a high standard.

So the Law Commission has a particular interest in statutes. Some years ago it produced a report on statutory interpretation.[3] This did not lead to any legislation itself but it was a useful exercise in analysing the issues which arise in that field.

Meanwhile, slowly but surely, a number of developments have been occurring in statute law, and the purpose of this chapter is to give an insight into the types of changes that have taken place or are going to take place in this field of law and to draw them together. It is not possible to describe them all.[4] This chapter can only give six principal signposts to change.

Signposts on the path of reform of statute law

1. Reports on the legislative process

The story for the purpose of this chapter begins in 1975, when the first intensive study of the drafting of legislation and of the legislative process in recent times was completed. This was the report of the Renton Committee on the preparation of legislation.[5] It made detailed recommendations on the drafting of statutes and parliamentary procedures, and the interpretation of statutes. There was another report covering a similar field published much later, in 1992. This was the Report of the Hansard Society Commission on the Legislative Process,[6] which was chaired by the late Lord Rippon. This, too, contained a large number of suggestions as to what might be done to improve the comprehensibility of statutes and as to Parliamentary procedure. These reports have earned their place in the history of statute law.

2. Developments in the Commonwealth

The second signpost is marked 'developments in the Commonwealth'. I will mention just four of these developments.[7]

The first was the report[8] published in 1987 by the Law Reform Commission of Victoria in Australia. This stated that legislation suffered from 'excessive sentence

---

[3] *The Interpretation of Statutes* (Law Com No 21, Scots Law Com No 11, 1969).

[4] Other developments, not mentioned in this chapter, include: the work of the Deregulation Task Force, now the Better Regulation Task Force; developments in the European Community such as the Report of the Group of Independent Experts on Legislative and Administrative Simplification; the SLIM initiative (Simpler Legislation for the Internal Market); the introduction of the government's Statute Law Database; and the possibility of statute law in electronic form having hypertext links: see for example Richard Susskind, *The Future of the Law: Facing the Challenges of Information Technology* (Clarendon Press, 1996) 166.

[5] *The Preparation of Legislation* (Cmd 6053, 1975).

[6] Published by the Hansard Society in 1992.

[7] There have been other Commonwealth initiatives including the Report of the Law Reform Commission of Hong Kong, 'Intrinsic Materials as an aid to Statutory Interpretation' (March 1997).

[8] 'Plain English and the Law', Law Reform Commission of Victoria Report No 9 (1987).

length, the creation and use of unnecessary concepts, poor organization of material and unattractive layout'. It said that such legislation created a number of problems: (a) unintelligible legislation encouraged litigation and was, therefore, expensive; (b) if legislation was not clear, the power to determine the law was transferred from an elected legislature to the courts; and (c) it is a fundamental civil liberty that people should be able to know and understand the laws that govern them. The Commission made various suggestions as to how legislative drafting could be improved.

Second, there have been various developments in the Commonwealth with respect to the style of companies legislation. In 1993, the Commonwealth of Australia adopted the Corporate Law Simplification Programme spear-headed by a Task Force whose members consisted of an experienced lawyer from the private sector, an expert in plain language, a senior legislative drafter, and a senior policy adviser from the Attorney-General's Department. The Task Force was assisted in its work by a Steering Group comprising lawyers and accountants in private practice, representatives of large and small business, and other representatives of the investor and business community. Its ambitious aims included: (a) creating a law that works as opposed to a law that was unnecessarily complicated and inefficient; (b) making the law accessible, especially to the non-professional user; (c) ensuring that it was as easy as possible to comply with; (d) eliminating unnecessary requirements; and (e) converting complex companies legislation into plain English.

Making statutes intelligible to the non-professional user of the law is a high ideal in commercial law. In his second reading speech on the First Corporate Law Simplification Bill, the Australian Attorney-General, Michael Lavararch MP said that simple laws promote economic efficiency and that a particular aim was to produce a law which allows its users to obtain a clear understanding of their rights and responsibilities without the need for costly legal advice.

It must be questionable, however, whether simple law always does promote efficiency. It can also promote uncertainty and all the direct and indirect costs that that involves. Sometimes simplification of complex technical law can only be at the cost of precision and concision. This may not be true of other types of legislation. We can also see that the Australian Corporate Law Simplification Programme was very much user-orientated, as if the statute law was about to become a best-seller. However, there is no logical reason why legislation should necessarily be written for the lay user. Complex planning legislation, for example, might be best if written in a style that would be understood by professionals, leaving it to be turned into layman's language by commercial publishers.

In addition there is always the risk, whatever the drafter thought he had written, that the courts will say that it has some different meaning. The Attorney-General was clearly concerned about this as he went on in his second reading speech to say:

I hope that the legal profession in general, and the courts in particular, will show support for this initiative by striving to apply the provisions in a straightforward and accessible fashion, and rejecting arguments based on unlikely construction or excessively fine distinctions. The problem of complex laws is one that must be tackled by all those involved in the legal system. This bill, once enacted, will be a major contribution by the law makers in this parliament. But those who use and apply the law must also play their part.

I was hoping that we would see the results of this programme and in particular whether it was possible to reproduce company law in words of one syllable and yet retain the degree of precision necessary for commercial law; but the programme has been cut short due to a desire to revise the underlying law before simplifying it further, and a new corporate law economic reform programme has been set up.

In Hong Kong an important recent report[9] has also stated that it should be one of the aims of company law to be written 'in clear concise language so as to be accessible to business people as well as lawyers and accountants'.

Another development in the Commonwealth which should be mentioned is the publication in 1996 by the New Zealand Law Commission of a 'Legislation Manual: Structure and Style'.[10] This, inter alia, recommended that explanatory material should be incorporated into statutes, where it would be useful. The report suggested including notes outlining the legislative history of a section, identifying which provisions implement international law obligations, listing those elements of a statute that delegate legislative power, and making cross-references in statutes to reports of law reform bodies upon which the recommendations are based. The report also suggested providing flow charts giving an overview of the statute, and answering questions of entitlement and liability.

Finally, work has been done in the United Kingdom too, by the Plain English Campaign and Clarity, to promote the use of clearer, simpler language in Acts of Parliament and other documents.[11]

3. The Tax Law Rewrite

The third signpost along the way of modernizing legislation is the Tax Law Rewrite, as it has come to be called.[12] This is the name given to a programme of rewriting tax legislation initiated by the Inland Revenue.

Tax law has developed over some 200 years. Income taxes were first levied in the late 1790s. For instance, s 198(1) of the Income and Corporation Taxes Act 1988, which sets out the circumstances in which a person in employment may deduct expenses, and which is derived from a much older provision, quaintly provides that:

If the holder of an office or employment is necessarily obliged to incur and defray out of the emoluments of that office or employment the expenses . . . of keeping and maintaining a horse to enable him to perform those duties . . . there may be deducted . . . the expenses so necessarily incurred and defrayed.

[9] Consultancy Report, 'Review of the Hong Kong Companies Ordinance' (March 1997). App 10 to this report contains a sample of model legislation.

[10] Law Commission of New Zealand Report NZLC R35 (1996).

[11] See for example Martin Cutts, *Lucid Law* (Plain English Campaign, 1994).

[12] HM Customs and Excise is also now engaged on a programme of rewriting VAT legislation in more user-friendly language, but this exercise is a much less public one.

The Tax Simplification Programme was memorably described thus by the Chancellor of the Exchequer, the Rt Hon Kenneth Clarke MP: 'The project is as ambitious as translating the whole of "War and Peace" into lucid Swahili. In fact it is more ambitious. I am told that "War and Peace" is only 1,500 pages long. Inland Revenue tax law is 6,000 pages long and was not written by a Tolstoy.'[13]

The Inland Revenue has issued a number of reports and papers.[14] Significantly they have engaged in public consultation on the issues of principle for legislative technique thrown up by the simplification of tax law. In 1995 the Revenue issued *The Path to Tax Simplification* and *The Path to Tax Simplification—A Background Paper*. In the first of these documents, the Revenue listed the criticisms of tax legislation. These criticisms are also often heard in relation to other legislation. They were:

(1) The legislation has 'complicated syntax, long sentences and archaic or ambiguous language'.[15]

(2) The principles underlying the rules are not apparent. The courts are, therefore, forced to interpret strictly by reference to the wording of the law, which may not correspond to the legislators' purpose.

(3) The legislation contains too much detail, with legislators drafting statutes to deal with 'every conceivable situation'.[16]

(4) Many sections of legislation cannot be understood in isolation. The resulting need for a holistic approach makes statutory interpretation much more complex.

(5) Some rules, especially anti-avoidance rules, are drafted widely and this makes their interpretation uncertain.

(6) It can be difficult to establish where all the tax rules on a particular area are found. Many topics are spread across different statutes.

(7) Definitions, some of which are inconsistent, are spread throughout different statutes.

(8) There has been criticism of the balance between primary and secondary legislation. Some argue that more detail should be moved from the former to the latter, to make the primary legislation shorter and simpler. Others argue that most of the rules should be in primary legislation to make the rules themselves more accessible.

(9) There has been criticism of the lack of consultation and openness in the drafting of statutes.

---

[13] Budget Statement, November 1996.

[14] Pursuant to the Finance Act 1995, s 160 which provided for the Inland Revenue to prepare and present to Treasury Ministers a report on the deficiencies of tax legislation and on the process whereby it could be simplified. Important papers were also issued by the Tax Law Review Committee of the Institute of Fiscal Studies: 'Interim Report on Tax Legislation' (1995) and 'Financial Report on Tax Simplification' (1996). The Tax Law Committee has played a vital role in the tax simplification process.

[15] Inland Revenue Report (n 14) 24.   [16] Inland Revenue Report (n 14) 24.

The Revenue looked at various solutions. They of course concluded that if the policy behind tax law was simpler the legislation would be simpler too.[17] But that was not possible. They also considered that changes in Parliamentary procedures would lead to improvements in the legislation, particularly if there was more time for scrutiny during the course of the Bill's passage through Parliament.[18] There is a lot of truth in Pascal's remark: 'I am sorry that this letter is so long but I did not have time to write a shorter one!'[19]

The Revenue rejected the idea that it would be possible to produce less detailed legislation, but they did conclude that there would be great benefits from a plain English rewrite of the tax code utilizing a number of modern techniques, for example in design and layout.

It is notable that the process selected for the rewrite was not a Royal Commission but rather a project led by the Revenue on the basis of full consultation with the representative bodies and taxpayers generally. It has been estimated that the project will take at least five years.[20] It occupies, I am told, a staff of some forty lawyers so that it is not much smaller than the Law Commission.

The Revenue have consulted about how the rewritten law should look[21] and have published examples of how existing UK tax law could be rewritten.[22] They announced the results of the consultation and published a plan[23] for work leading to the preparation of the first tax simplification Bill, which will be ready for enactment in the present session of Parliament. In addition, a small joint private sector/Revenue steering group has now been appointed to oversee the project and a larger consultative committee has also been announced.[24]

In July 1997 the Revenue issued their first exposure draft containing initial drafts of clauses covering the income tax treatment of the trading income of individuals. These drafts use modern language and techniques, such as shorter sentences. The draft also canvasses the question whether it would be helpful if the legislation set out examples.

The rewritten legislation will not be any shorter than the existing legislation. Indeed it is estimated that there will ultimately be more than 6,000 pages of new legislation when the rewritten legislation becomes law. Clearly Parliament would not have time to consider such a mass of technical legislation and so a procedure off the floor of the House of Commons has been devised which will enable the Bills to be scrutinized by a joint committee of the House of Commons and the House of Lords.[25]

---

[17] Inland Revenue Report (n 14) 4–5.   [18] Inland Revenue Report (n 14) 27.

[19] Blaise Pascal, *Lettres Provinciales* (1657) xvi.

[20] 'Tax Law Rewrite—the Way Forward', a consultative document published by the Inland Revenue in 1996.

[21] 'Tax Law Rewrite—the Way Forward'.   [22] 'Tax Law Rewrite—Examples'.

[23] 'Tax Law Rewrite—Plans for 1997'.

[24] A consultative committee was set up to ensure continuous consultation on the rewritten text with the main interested private sector bodies.

[25] See 'Second Report of the Select Committee on Procedure', 30 January 1997 (1996–97) HC 126, and see House of Commons Standing Order No 60. The Tax Law Rewrite Project continued for some 14 years. In this time, it produced, following consultation, seven draft enactments, including the

4. Changes in the courts' approach to interpreting statutes

There are two particular items to mention here: the decision of the House of Lords in *Pepper v Hart*[26] to admit Hansard for the purpose of construing an Act of Parliament; and the move towards purposive interpretation.

I turn first to *Pepper v Hart*. A breakthrough was made in that case when the House of Lords looked at Hansard for the purpose of resolving an ambiguity in the Finance Act 1976. This may only be done if there are clear statements by the minister or promoter of the Bill directed to the very point in issue in the litigation and Parliament has passed legislation on the basis of the ministerial statement.[27]

This case is bound to lead to consideration of allied issues: for instance should the court also use as an aid to construction the notes on clauses which are prepared by the executive and parliamentary counsel to accompany the Bill so as to explain its purpose to busy MPs? These are only very brief summaries of the purpose of the clauses but they may contain relevant material.[28]

The principle in *Pepper v Hart* undoubtedly has a logical ring about it. In statutory construction what the court is endeavouring to do is to find the meaning of the Act of Parliament, and what more logical step to take than to see from the parliamentary debate what was actually said. But unless the principle is kept within strict bounds, and the conditions for its application strictly observed, there are great dangers in it. In particular, ministers may prefer to have draft Bills which are expressed in general terms and avoid the difficulties which would become apparent if they were more precisely drafted, and hope to make the deficiency good by an appropriate speech in Parliament. Alternatively the executive may try to take short

---

Bills for what became the Income Tax Act 2007 and the Corporation Tax Acts 2009 and 2010. The rewrite process sought to restructure the statute into a more logical order, add navigational aids and introductory texts, use clearer language, and adopt harmonized definitions, without making substantive changes except for occasional minor changes to clarify the law or remove obsolete provisions. The Project was brought to an end in 2010. This may possibly have been due to a loss of professional support. The major legislation which it did not cover was the capital gains tax and inheritance tax legislation, which were not rewritten. Surveys were done to assess the benefits of the rewritten legislation but it proved difficult to quantify those benefits. The result of the Tax Law Rewrite was a considerable increase in the length of tax statutes. The UK tax statutes have been said to be the longest in the world. But the conclusion of the subsequently established Office for Tax Simplification, set up in 2010 to provide the government with independent advice on simplifying the UK tax system, was that, while length was a factor in complexity, longer tax statutes could be clearer and easier to use. Tax practitioners did not think that the increase in length was an improvement, while those who were not experts found the presentation in the rewritten statutes helpful: Office for Tax Simplification, 'Length of Tax Legislation as a Measure of Complexity', 16 April 2012.

[26] [1993] AC 593. Subsequent case law shows that, while Hansard will sometimes provide support for a judge's conclusion on the meaning of a statute, the occasions when the rule in *Pepper v Hart* will assist will be rare: see per Lord Nicholls in *R (o/a Spath Holme Ltd) v Secretary of State for the Environment, Transport and the Regions* [2001] 2 AC 349, 398 and per Lord Neuberger in *Cadogan v Pitts* [2010] 1 AC 226, [113].

[27] See *Melluish v BMI (No 3) Ltd* [1996] AC 454.

[28] A similar purpose is now achieved by Explanatory Notes, which Parliament introduced in 1999. The courts may refer to these as setting out the context of the Bill but as Parliament does not approve them the courts cannot rely on them as setting out the intention of Parliament: see *R (Westminster City Council) v National Asylum Support Service* [2002] UKHL 38, [2002] 1 WLR 2956, paras 2–6 per Lord Steyn.

cuts by failing to get the legislation accurate and relying instead on some statement in (say) the notes on clauses. In this situation, far from the principle in *Pepper v Hart* strengthening the authority of Parliament, it would be strengthening the power of the executive, for which of course there is no democratic mandate.

Parliament is aware of these dangers. In a written answer given on 3 February 1997 the Chancellor of the Duchy of Lancaster assured the House of Commons as follows:

> ... administrative procedures are in place for avoiding or correcting any errors or ambiguities arising out [of] ministerial statements during the passage of legislation. In particular, speeches and speaking notes will generally be reviewed by departmental legal advisers for possible influence on interpretation; the *Hansard* record of Ministers' contributions to debates on legislation will similarly be reviewed to consider whether there is any inaccuracy; and, where it seems sensible to do so, Ministers may more frequently offer to reflect and take further advice on points of interpretation that are raised in debate.
>
> If it does prove necessary to correct a ministerial statement, the aim will be to do this as promptly as possible at an appropriate point during the further consideration of the Bill.[29]

I now turn to purposive interpretation. In recent years the courts have been increasingly inclined to apply the purposive approach to the construction of statute rather than a literal one. This can be illustrated by referring to the recent case of *IRC v McGuckian*,[30] in which Lord Steyn said:

> Towards the end of the last century Pollock characterised the approach of the judges to statutory construction as follows: 'Parliament generally changes the law for the worse, and ... the business of the judge is to keep the mischief of its interference within the narrowest possible bounds ...' Whatever the merits of this observation may have been when it was made, or even earlier in this century, it is demonstrably no longer true. During the last 30 years there has been a shift away from the literalist approach to purposive methods of construction. When there is no obvious meaning of a statutory provision the modern emphasis is on a contextual approach designed to identify the purpose of a statute and to give effect to it.

The courts, however, can only apply a purposive approach where the purpose is sufficiently clear. This has led some to believe that it would be best to state the statutory objective expressly in some provisions, but the danger of that approach is that the general provisions will conflict with the operative provisions in some situations. For instance in *Page (HM Inspector of Taxes) v Lowther*,[31] the Court of Appeal held that, if there was a conflict between a purpose provision and an operative provision, the latter should prevail.

5. Modernization of House of Commons procedure

Parliament has set up a Select Committee on modernization of the House of Commons. In July 1997 this Committee delivered an interim report.[32] There are

---

[29] Hansard, HC vol 289, col 469 (3 February 1997). [30] [1997] 1 WLR 991.
[31] [1983] STC 799. [32] (1997–98) HC 190.

a large number of recommendations, in particular recommendations on the time-tabling of parliamentary debates, so that Parliament can deal with more legislation and the consideration of draft Bills in committee before they are presented to Parliament. The Select Committee also recommended that the government should consider publishing with each Bill a simple explanatory guide to be distributed via the internet. This select committee report is only an interim report so it is hoped that the Select Committee will produce more suggestions for streamlining the parliamentary process.

Normally it is the hope of the Law Commission that improvements in parliamentary procedure will one day lead to more time being available for Law Commission Bills. With the exception of the Family Law Bill, these Bills have historically taken very little time on the floor of the House, but there is still rarely parliamentary time allocated to them under the present system. Some years ago, a new special public bill procedure was introduced by the House of Lords which enabled Bills to be considered in detail off the floor of the House by a committee which was able to receive oral or written evidence. However, the procedure has not worked quite as had been hoped as it makes heavy demands on the time of members of the committee and of ministers and their officials.[33]

6. European influences

The sixth signpost is the contribution from Brussels.[34] I had some doubts as to whether one could say that this was a modernizing force, given that often European legislation is not welcome and merely adds an additional layer of complexity to an already overcrowded statute book. European legislation is frequently drafted to a less rigorous standard than our own primary legislation, sometimes deliberately, as where the member states have been unable to reach agreement but are content to allow the European Court of Justice to fill the gap by interpretation. However, like it or not, European directives are a feature of the modern 'statute book'. They can be implemented either literally without changing their provisions or by rewriting their provisions in the language typical of an English statute. Both methods have difficulties.

Signposts within sight on the road ahead: lessons from abroad

Thus far I have been dealing with some comparatively technical aspects of statute law. There is a commonly-held feeling that a statute ossifies the law and that once a matter is the subject of legislation the scope for organic growth of the law is necessarily lost. This prejudice against statute law is almost always relied upon by

---

[33] For the up to date position, see Preface to Section B by The Rt Hon Lord Mackay of Clashfern, Author's Notes on Law Commission Bills, n 1.

[34] References to 'European' law in this section are, as the case requires, to the law of the European Community and of the European Union.

opponents of the Law Commission's work of codification. The truth is that when it is enacting legislation, Parliament has a choice: it can either make the law detailed and exact and thereby give precise guidance to lawyers and users and limit the court's freedom to enlarge the statute by a process of interpretation; or it can decide that it wants the detail of the policy in the statute to be worked out by the courts on a case-by-case basis and use words that are not exact but rather require to be explained and applied. Accordingly, there are statutes which permit organic growth of the law by the process of judicial interpretation.

Examples of the first type of statute (setting out detailed requirements and thus limiting the scope for intepretation) are a tax statute or a companies statute or a criminal statute. Another example might be a statute which gives the court a discretion but requires it to be exercised only according to a specified list of factors. This is often called a structured discretion. An example of the latter type of provision is s 33 of the Limitations Act 1980 which confers on the court a discretion to disapply the limitation period applicable to actions for personal injuries.

These are to be contrasted with legislative provisions in wide terms. There is probably no better example of this sort of legislation than legislation which confers rights and freedoms. Thus far the English courts have really only had an opportunity to consider statutes of this nature in the case of Commonwealth constitutions; but in view of the government's proposal for the incorporation of the European Convention on Human Rights ('the Convention')[35] it is appropriate to look at some of these decisions. The courts are not, at this stage at least, to be given the power to strike down statutes. But the courts will be intimately concerned with the Convention. This may be in criminal trials where the defendant claims that the use of some evidence is in breach of the Convention; or judicial review cases or other civil proceedings where the claimant claims, for example, an injunction or a declaration.

The Commonwealth constitution cases show that the courts may take a vigorous approach to the construction of provisions conferring human rights. In *Ministry of Home Affairs v Fisher*[36] the Privy Council had to decide whether the word 'child' as used in the Constitution of Bermuda included an illegitimate child, so that the child would be entitled to Bermudan status. It was argued on the basis of a long line of reported cases that it was a principle of statutory interpretation that 'child' meant legitimate child. The Privy Council expressed the view that it had two routes to reach the conclusion that illegitimate children were included. It could either accept that the correct starting point was to say that there was a presumption that child in a statute meant legitimate child, and then to conclude that there was room for applying the presumption with less rigidity where one was dealing with a constitution, as opposed to, say, a statute dealing with property or succession.

---

[35] This led in due course to the enactment of the Human Rights Act 1998, which enabled Convention rights to be enforced in English courts for the first time.

[36] [1980] AC 319.

The other route was the bolder course of treating the Constitution as *sui generis*, calling for principles of interpretation of its own, suitable for the fact that the purpose of the constitution was to protect fundamental rights and freedoms. This would mean that not all the presumptions applicable to other legislation dealing with private law would be relevant. Lord Wilberforce giving the judgment of the Privy Council said:

It is possible that as regards the question now for decision either method would lead to the same result. But their Lordships prefer the second. This is in no way to say that there are no rules of law which should apply to the interpretation of a Constitution. A Constitution is a legal instrument giving rise, among other things, to individual rights capable of enforcement in a court of law. Respect must be paid to the language which has been used and to the traditions and usages which have given meaning to that language. It is quite consistent with this, and with the recognition that rules of interpretation may apply, to take as a point of departure for the process of interpretation a recognition of the character and origin of the instrument, and to be guided by the principle of giving full recognition and effect to those fundamental rights and freedoms with a statement of which the Constitution commences. In their Lordships opinion this must mean approaching the question what is meant by 'child' with an open mind.

The Privy Council found that the Constitution recognized the unity of the family group and acceptance that young children should not be separated from a group which as a whole belongs to Bermuda. In the instant case the illegitimate children of a Jamaican woman who had married a Bermudan were 'children' for the purpose of the Bermudan Constitution and therefore had the right to stay in Bermuda with their mother and their stepfather, who had accepted them into the family.

This approach to interpretation was endorsed by a later judgment of the Privy Council in *Attorney-General of the Gambia v Jobe*,[37] in which Lord Diplock, delivering the judgment of the Privy Council, said that: 'A constitution, and in particular that part of it which protects and entrenches fundamental rights and freedoms to which all persons in the state are to be entitled, is to be given a generous and purposive construction.'

In another Privy Council case, *Maharaj v Attorney-General of Trinidad and Tobago (No 2)*[38] the question arose as to whether there was a right of redress for a breach of human rights. The breach occurred when the claimant, a barrister, was committed to prison for seven days without being told the grounds on which the Court considered that he had been guilty of contempt, before being sentenced, so that he could offer an explanation or apology. There had therefore been a breach of the rules of natural justice and an infringement of the claimant's right to liberty. The finding of contempt was set aside on appeal, but the claimant wanted compensation under provisions of the Constitution of Trinidad and Tobago entitling persons to 'redress' if there was a breach of human rights. It was held that this provision enabled the Court to grant damages in public law for the infringement. The claim was against the state, which was directly liable for the acts of the judge, not on the basis of vicarious liability.

---

[37] [1984] AC 689, 700H.   [38] [1979] AC 385.

These cases are already in our jurisprudence and they will be pressed into service when the courts are asked to apply a bold and innovative approach to the application of the Convention.

The *Maharaj* case was applied in *Simpson v Attorney-General (Baigent's case)*,[39] a decision of the Court of Appeal of New Zealand. In that case the question at issue was whether a claim for compensation could be made against the New Zealand government under the New Zealand Bill of Rights Act even though there was no provision for this in the Bill of Rights Act itself. The Court of Appeal of New Zealand held by a majority that such a claim could be made. Cooke P noted that one of the purposes of the legislation was to affirm New Zealand's commitment to the International Covenant on Civil and Political Rights. This imposes an obligation on states which are parties to ensure an effective remedy for violation. Cooke P said: 'we would fail in our duty if we did not give an effective remedy to a person whose legitimately affirmed rights have been infringed'.

Another case which shows that a different and more liberal approach to interpretation may apply to cases where the statute lays down fundamental or constitutional rights is the decision of the Western Samoan Court of Appeal in *Attorney-General v Sapa'ai Olomalu*.[40] There the question was whether the constitution guaranteed suffrage only to certain members of the population or whether it conferred universal suffrage. This very question had been considered by the convention which led to the Constitution, and universal suffrage had been rejected. The Court held that it would be artificial to ignore this material. However, it had already reached the same conclusion without reference to it. This case indicates that in interpreting constitutional rights the courts may be able to go beyond the terms of the constitution or legislation in question to determine its meaning.

The Convention will of itself bring a number of changes. Among the rights it contains is Art 7 which requires criminal offences to be defined with reasonable precision to enable the citizen to regulate his conduct.[41] This is to be contrasted with the approach in English law exemplified by the dictum of Lord Morris in *Knuller (Publishing Printing and Promotions) Ltd v Director of Public Prosecutions*[42] that 'those who skate on thin ice can hardly expect to find a sign which will denote the precise spot where they will fall in'. This throws into doubt whether the court can rely on a residual power such as was used in *Shaw v DPP*[43] to prosecute the compiler of the *Ladies' Directory*, a directory of prostitutes, which was outside the criminal offences in relation to obscenity, for conspiracy to corrupt public morals. One consequence of incorporating the Convention may be to alter the way in which common law offences are developed and statutory offences are construed.

---

[39] [1994] 3 LRC 202.
[40] Decision of 26 August 1982; see 'Symposium on Statutory Interpretation' (Australian Government Publishing Service, 1983) App 3.
[41] *G v Federal Republic of Germany* (1989) 60 DR 256, 6 March 1989.
[42] [1972] 2 All ER 898, 908.   [43] [1962] AC 220.

Conclusion

So statute law might sound dull and seem to be an unimportant corner of the law but it is much more important than we think. First, it is important as a matter of principle because it is an area of law of constitutional importance. Legislation defines the relationship between citizen and state. One of the main reasons which the Law Commission advances for the codification of the criminal law is that criminal law is part of that relationship and it therefore ought to be clearly set out in a comprehensible and accessible form. Second, a state which does not have a developed tradition of legislative drafting stands to see the rights of the individual taken away without proper scrutiny and a shift of power from citizen to state. Third, slowly but surely, steps are being taken to improve the state of statute law in this country. The Tax Law Rewrite should produce some general lessons that can be learnt in other parts of the statute law. And lastly, the courts have already the beginnings of a principled approach to the judicial interpretation of the rights conferred by the Convention. That is a good start to the enormous challenges that lie in that direction in the future.

PART V

CODIFICATION

Once a reformer, always a reformer. The experience of law reform has given me a particular interest in making the law as clear, accessible, and up to date as possible. In Chapters 11 and 12, I discussed various ways in which statute law could be improved. Codification is another way in which law, including but not limited to statute law, can be made more accessible. The code which results from the process of codification will benefit from the type of improvements already discussed, such as a clearer method of drafting, publication as a draft Bill and explanatory notes. What codification additionally does, with a certain amount of labour and skill, is to bring the different strands of law on the same topic together.

Chapters 13, 14, and 15 concern codification in three very different areas of law: commercial, criminal, and company law. From these examples, one thing becomes apparent: it can take a very long time to achieve consensus on codification.

Codification of commercial law, discussed in Chapter 13, *Time for an English Commercial Code?*, has not come about as yet due to the size of the task and concerns about it making the law less flexible. The pendulum may yet swing the other way. The European Commission has for some years been attempting a harmonization of the contract law of member states,[1] but many member states, including the United Kingdom, are opposed. There seems to be little prospect of such a measure in the foreseeable future. The Scottish Law Commission has started a project on the EU proposal, so there may be pressure within the United Kingdom again for a contract code applying to the United Kingdom. As the chapter explains, the Law Commissions started work on such a code some years ago but the project was not brought to fruition.

In Chapter 14, *Criminal Law at the Crossroads: The Need for a Code*, I describe the Law Commission's work in trying to achieve a codification of the criminal law. The arguments for codification of the criminal law are really arguments of constitutional law. Criminal law profoundly affects the relationship between the individual and the state; it therefore ought to be clearly set out in statute law.[2] However,

---

[1] The development of the EU Commission's proposals is described in B Zeller, 'Anatomy of EU Contract Harmonisation: Where Do We Stand?' (2015) 21 International Trade Law and Regulation 41.

[2] For a recent discussion of the arguments in favour and against codification, see Ian Dennis, 'Codifying the Law of Criminal Evidence' (2014) 35 Statute Law Review 107.

there are considerable political problems in legislating for a criminal code. The Law Commission recognized this and, until recently, took the pragmatic view that it would work on a block-by-block approach with discrete topics within the field of criminal law.

Such a process will take a very long time to complete, which is hardly a satisfactory state of affairs, but it is probably the best that can be done. It is loyal to the principle of codification at the end of the day. In recent years, the Law Commission has preferred to work on simplifying the criminal law on the footing that this could ultimately assist in a process of codification. This involves, as I see it, a departure from the principle of ultimate codification. However, there are some signs that the Law Commission may revert to that principle. The Law Commission's latest programme of work includes the codification of sentencing powers. That might suggest that it will give stronger support for codification of the criminal law in the future—a very welcome development.

The Companies Act 2006: A New Approach to Directors' Duties, Chapter 15, deals with the codification of directors' duties and explains new codifying provisions in the Companies Act 2006. Before codification, directors' duties had been developed by the courts through numerous cases, which made it difficult for directors to know what the law was without legal advice. In addition, the codified statement of duties was intended to encourage directors to take a longer-term view of their company's best interests when making their decisions. That reflected changed expectations of directors' conduct within the business community and the community at large.

The Companies Act 2006[3] implemented the recommendation of the Law Commission and the Scottish Law Commission[4] that there should be a codified statement of directors' duties. At the same time, it implemented most of the recommendations of the wide-ranging review of company law carried out by the Department of Trade and Industry's Company Law Review.[5] The new provisions implementing the Law Commissions' recommendation appear to be working well in practice.

The United Kingdom never adopted the great civil codes that emerged in continental Europe in the nineteenth century. But, as Chapters 13, 14 and 15 show, a judicious use of codes may sometimes be to our benefit as a means of making the law more manageable and accessible. The rule of law surely requires that the state should provide a means whereby people can find a comprehensible statement of the laws that are relevant to them.

---

[3] Sections 170–177.

[4] *Company Directors: Regulating Conflicts of Interests and Formulating a Statement of Duties* (Law Com No 261, Scot Law Com No 173, 1999).

[5] I was also a member of the Steering Group of that Review.

13

Time for an English Commercial Code?

This chapter is based on a lecture given to the Commercial Bar Association (COMBAR) in February 1997.*

Understanding the meaning of codification

Parliament has imposed on the Law Commission the duty to review the law of England and Wales 'with a view to its systematic development and reform, including in particular the codification of [the] law . . . and generally the simplification and modernisation of the law'.[1] There are a number of points which flow from this. First, as a body which reviews great swathes of the common law to see if they require to be modernized or simplified, the Law Commission has a unique standpoint from which to view the strengths and weaknesses of the common law method. Second, it has unique experience of law reform and the Parliamentary process. Third, in discharge of its functions, it has an interest in seeing that, if codification is appropriate, a recommendation to that effect is made to the Lord Chancellor. It need not be the Law Commission which carries out the recommendation, and indeed the Law Commission could not carry out a project purely on its own initiative.

Parliament has not, however, vouchsafed us a definition of codification, and English law is not exactly replete with examples of written laws called 'codes'. What then is codification? In its most extreme form, codification is the process of expressing the whole of the law on a particular topic so that any development of that law has in general to be by way of interpretation of it or deduction from it. The principal difference between a code and, for example, the Unfair Contract Terms Act 1977 is that the whole of the law on a recognizable division of law, such as obligations or contract law, is put into the code. The French Code Napoleon or the German Commercial Code are examples of codes of this kind. So far as I am aware there are no codes of this kind in English law. Even if all the companies legislation was to be consolidated into a single statute, there would still not be a

---

* The COMBAR lecture 1997 was delivered in Lincoln's Inn, London, and subsequently published with permission in (1997) 56(3) Cambridge Law Journal 516. Reproduced here by kind permission of Cambridge University Press.

[1] Law Commissions Act 1965, s 3(1). Over the years several learned articles have been written on the topic of codifying commercial law: see for example Roy Goode, 'The Codification of Commercial Law' (1986) 14 Monash Law Review 135, and the literature cited therein.

comprehensive companies code because there are substantial areas of the law, such as the duties of directors, which have not been put into the legislation[2] and which are not simply a matter of deduction from it. Then there are the less comprehensive codes—the Consumer Credit Act 1974, the Sale of Goods Act 1893, the Bills of Exchange Act 1882, the Married Women's Property Act 1882, and the Marine Insurance Act 1906. These codes satisfy the dictionary definition of code, even though they cover a relatively limited area, because they nonetheless constitute a set of systematic rules on a particular subject.[3] The Children Act 1989, which, inter alia, implemented a Law Commission report, brings together all the law on children apart from adoption, and is therefore a form of code. An Act which is the principal source of law on a particular topic is a code in this wider sense.

All these different types of codes have statutory force, but in some jurisdictions there are also authoritative non-binding statements of the law. In the United States, for example, the American Law Institute was set up in 1923 in response to a call by prominent legal professionals for improvements in the legal system through the clarification and simplification of the law. In the 1930s to 1950s, the American Institute produced restatements on agency, contract, conflict of laws, property, restitution, security, judgments, torts, trusts, and landlord and tenant law. Restatements are not primary sources of law but systematic compilations of American common law. The examples given did not therefore achieve any reform, and they do not have the status of a code. However, they are often relied on by the courts, and in general carry more weight than other treatises. The completion of the restatements was a remarkable achievement of leading academic and other lawyers in the United States, to whom tribute is due.

Also to be mentioned in this context is the Uniform Commercial Code which was a joint project of the American Law Institute and the National Conference on Uniform State Laws. The Uniform Commercial Code is a model law covering many aspects of commercial transactions, including sale, negotiable instruments, secured transactions, letters of credit, bills of lading, and so on. It was first produced in 1951 and it has been revised on several occasions since. Many practitioners, judges, and academics were involved in the drafting, and the original version took some ten years to produce. The Uniform Commercial Code has formed the basis of state law on some at least of the areas covered in nearly all of the states of the United States. The provisions of the code are explained in an accompanying commentary. This is not enacted as part of the state law but forms an authoritative source for assistance in interpreting the code. Again the drafting of the Uniform Commercial Code has been a remarkable achievement, and it has been particularly valuable as a means of ensuring uniformity of commercial law in the various states of the United States.

---

[2] But see now in relation to directors' duties, Ch 15, *Companies Act 2006: A New Approach to Directors' Duties*.

[3] *The Concise Oxford Dictionary* (8th edn, Oxford University Press, 1990) defines a code as 'a systematic collection of statutes, a body of laws so arranged as to avoid inconsistency and overlapping: a set of rules on any subject . . .'.

Codes can be classified not only according to their status and coverage, but also according to the type of law reform they seek to achieve. It is often thought that a code has to be a piece of substantially new law but there is no reason why that need be so. The Bills of Exchange Act 1882, for instance, to very large extent makes a statutory statement of the common law and alters the underlying law only in a very minor way. There is therefore no need to assume that the adoption of a code must be accompanied by some radical change in the law. Likewise, what is effectively a code may be achieved by enlightened consolidation of several different statutes already in force on the same topic. Alternatively a code could be a hybrid—part new law, part restatement of the common law, and part consolidation of existing statute law.

The history of the codification of English commercial law

There would probably be little to say on this part of the subject, were it not for three things: first, the remarkable work on codification which took place in the nine-teenth century, principally by Sir Mackenzie Chalmers; second, the drafting of the Indian Contract Code which also took place in the nineteenth century, at a time when India was a colony and applied English contract law; third, the work which has been done by the Law Commission in producing draft codes.

1. Sir Mackenzie Chalmers

Chalmers was born in 1847. In 1875 he joined the Chambers of Farrer Herschell, later Lord Herschell. Herschell encouraged Chalmers to produce a digest on the law of bills of exchange, which involved the study of some 2,500 cases and some seventeen statutes. Chalmers set out the law in a number of propositions which he supported with commentary. He published his work in 1878. In 1880 he read a paper on codification to the Institute of Bankers. The idea was an instant success and the Institute instructed him to draft a Bill. The Bill was introduced into Parliament and considered by a committee chaired by Lord Herschell. No doubt with the help of Herschell's strong support, the Bill was passed in 1882.

In 1884 Chalmers became a county court judge in Birmingham. While he was a judge there he set about the task of codifying the law of the sale of goods. This is how he described the common law of sale as he found it:

[The] rules [of the law of sale] are to be found embodied in judicial decisions ranging from the time of Edward III down to the present year of Her Majesty's reign. Lord Blackburn in his text-book on the *Law of Sale*, devotes seven pages to the discussion of a case decided in the seventeenth year of Edward IV's reign (A.D. 1487). On some points there is a plethora of authority, and as regards them, the reported decisions have become so numerous as to tend to obscure the general principles which underlie them, just as when a tree is in full foliage the numbers of its leaves frequently hide from view the form and development of the trunk and branches which support them. The last edition of Mr Benjamin's work on *Sale* contains 1,013 pages, and cites nearly 2,000 English cases. On other questions there is a curious dearth of authority. The important point which was settled in *Glyn Mills Currie & Co v The East and West India Dock Company*[4] was the subject of a *nisi prius* ruling in 1753, but it did not arise again for authoritative decision until 129 years had elapsed. For some elementary principles authority seems to be altogether wanting. Mr Benjamin lays it down, and no doubt correctly, that in the absence of any different agreement, the place of delivery is the place where the goods are at the time when the contract of sale is made. But he can cite no decision in support of that proposition, and is driven to rely on the authority of Pothier. Now Pothier was an admirable exponent of legal principles, but it is strange that a modern English text-book, re-edited last year, should cite as an authority for an elementary principle a French lawyer who died in 1773, and who was primarily treating of French law, as modified by the custom of Orleans, before the Code Napoleon. The statutory enactments relating to the law of sale are fragmentary in character, and deal only with isolated points . . .[5]

Chalmers added: 'The law of sale is in pretty much the same condition as other branches of the common law regulating our everyday life.'[6]

In 1888, Chalmers produced a draft of the Bill which he settled in consultation with Herschell. Herschell introduced it in the Lords, not to press it, but to get criticisms on it. In 1891 it was introduced again and it was referred to a distinguished select committee consisting of Lords Herschell, Halsbury, Bramwell, and Watson. Delay followed while Scots law was taken into account so that the Act when passed could apply to the whole of the United Kingdom.[7] The Bill as so modified was again introduced and it became law in 1893.

Nothing daunted, Chalmers went on to tackle his third great contribution to English commercial law, namely the Marine Insurance Act 1906. In 1894 he completed a draft Bill synthesizing the effect of numerous cases. It was introduced into the Lords where it was considered by a committee consisting of lawyers, shipowners, and average-adjusters appointed by Lord Herschell. In 1900 it was again introduced into the Lords and Lord Chancellor Halsbury had it considered by a similar committee, but it was blocked in the Commons until 1906 when Lord Chancellor Loreburn took it up, and it became law.

Before this develops into a panegyric for Chalmers, it should be pointed out that some criticisms can be made of his work, but they are not major ones. For instance, Chalmers' use of the terms 'condition' and 'warranty' can be criticized. He uses the word 'warranty' in the Sale of Goods Act 1893 to mean a subsidiary term of a contract of sale, breach of which gives rise to the right to claim damages but not the right to reject the goods.[8] In the Marine Insurance Act 1906, however, the term 'warranty' is used to mean a promissory warranty, breach of which discharges the insurer.[9] But, as the notes he included in his work on the Sale of

[4] (1881) 7 App Cas 591.

[5] Mackenzie Chalmers, 'The Codification of the Law of Sale' (1891) 12 Journal of the Institute of Bankers II, 12.

[6] Chalmers, 'Codification of the Law of Sale' (n 5) 12.

[7] For an account of the Scottish approach to the codification of commercial law in the UK, see Alan Rodger, 'The Codification of Commercial Law in Victorian Britain' (1992) 109 LQR 570.

[8] Sale of Goods Act 1890, s 62(1).   [9] See Marine Insurance Act 1906, s 33.

Goods Act 1893[10] make clear, Chalmers was following the common law as he found it. The term 'warranty' had always had a special meaning in insurance. Likewise in these notes he explained why he had used the term 'condition' to mean a term of the contract, breach of which gives rise to the right to treat the contract as repudiated. This was the sense in which the expression 'condition' was used in conveyancing. It was not there limited to conditions precedent.[11]

There is a further issue with the Sale of Goods Act 1893, albeit not a fatal one. The Act refers only to conditions and warranties and not to intermediate or innominate terms.[12] Breach of innominate terms can give rise either to the right to repudiate the contract or the right to claim damages, depending on the seriousness of the breach.[13] As the Sale of Goods Act 1893 was only a codifying Act, and the common law before 1893 had recognized innominate terms, the Court of Appeal was able to hold in *The Hansa Nord*[14] that contracts for the sale of goods can contain innominate terms like any other contract.

It has been said that Chalmers' intentions in undertaking these codifications were two-fold. First, it is said that his purpose was to assure the commercial community greater certainty in the law, in order to avoid litigation, even if this meant an inconvenient rule. Second, it is said that he considered that codification would simplify the process of legal reasoning by clearly stating the existing principles of commercial law which hitherto might require to await distillation from the mass of case law.[15] The effect of his work was to transform English commercial law from a mainly common law subject to one which had a very significant codified element.[16] And to a large extent Chalmers' work has stood the test of time. One only has to think how time consuming it would have been to learn the law of sale of goods or the law on bills of exchange without the Sale of Goods Act or the Bills of Exchange Act to realize just what a major and permanent contribution Chalmers made to the codification of commercial law in this country.

Sir Mackenzie Chalmers was the most notable of the codifiers, but there were others, including Sir Frederick Pollock, who prepared the original draft of the Bill that became the Partnership Act 1890. According to the long title, the purpose of the Act was 'to declare and amend the Law of Partnership'. After it was passed, Pollock wrote: 'It may be doubted whether the Act will add much to the knowledge of the law possessed by practising members of the Chancery Bar . . . [but] Possibly

[10] See for example Mackenzie Chalmers, *The Sale of Goods Act 1893* (2nd edn, W Clowes & Sons, 1894) 168–9.

[11] A condition precedent is a term which must be performed before the provision to which it is attached (for example a promise to make a gift) will take effect.

[12] A term of a contract which is neither a condition nor a warranty. The remedies for breach of an innominate term will depend on the seriousness of the breach and may therefore be the same as either those for a breach of a condition or those for breach of warranty.

[13] See *Hong Kong Fir Shipping Co Ltd v Kawasaki Kisen Kaisha Ltd* [1962] 2 QB 26 (CA).

[14] *Cehave NV v Bremer Handelsgesellschaft GmbH* [1976] 1 QB 44.

[15] AW Brian Simpson (ed), *Simpson's Biographical Dictionary of the Common Law* (Butterworths, 1984) 108.

[16] So far as I have been able to ascertain, the Acts drafted by Chalmers are the only three English Acts of Parliament which include the words 'to codify' in their long title.

members of the Common Law Bar . . . will be thankful for the Act . . .'[17] The
Partnership Act has also stood the test of time. It sets out in clear terms the
fundamentals of partnership law for the great benefit of the commercial community.
It was only in 1997, over a century later, that it was decided by the government that
the law on partnerships should be reviewed. On 24 February 1997, the Corporate
and Consumer Affairs Minister, Mr John Taylor MP, announced that the Department of Trade and Industry had asked the Law Commission and the Scottish Law
Commission to carry out a review of the law on partnerships.[18]

   Not all of Parliament's attempts at codifying commercial law were as successful
as those drafted by Sir Mackenzie Chalmers or Sir Frederick Pollock. In 1882,
Parliament tried to simplify the law of personal security over chattels in the Bills of
Sale Act 1878. The aim was to make the law easier for the debtor and creditor alike
by introducing a requirement for a bill of sale to be in accordance with a particular
form, if given by way of security for the payment of money.[19] There was a vast
amount of litigation on such issues as to whether the inclusion of additional clauses,
which creditors wanted to protect their security, was permitted.[20]

2. The Indian Codes

In the nineteenth century, a series of codes were drafted for India on contract,
criminal law, trusts, property, evidence, procedure, limitation, and other subjects.
Work on these Codes started in about 1833 and finished some forty years later. Those
who worked on the Codes included men who became distinguished lawyers of the
period, including Lord Macaulay, Sir Barnes Peacock, Sir Henry Maine, Sir Fitzjames
Stephen, Lord Hobhouse, Lord Chief Justice Erle, Mr Justice Willes, Lord Justice
James, Lord Justice Lush, and Sir John Jervis. Sir Frederick Pollock said they were 'the
best models yet produced'.[21] The Indian Codes in part codified rules of English law
already received in India, and in part created new law. They were adopted for India,
with exclusions on certain points for certain parts of India where they would be
inappropriate. Previously a variety of different laws had applied in India, including
religious laws, such as Hindu and Mohammedan law. The principal draftsman was a
hard-working and gifted man by the name of Whitley Stokes, who began his career as
a pupil of Lord Cairns. But the results of his work were not perfect, and several
amendments had to be made. However, all the most important branches of English
law applicable to India except for the law of torts were codified.[22]

---

[17] Sir Frederick Pollock, *A Digest of the Law of Partnership incorporating the Partnership Act 1890*
(5th edn, Stevens, 1890) vi.
   [18] DTI Press Notice, 24 February 1997. The recommendations in the Law Commissions' report,
Partnership Law (Law Com No 283, Scot Law Com No 192, 2003), were accepted only as regards
limited partnerships. Those recommendations have as yet only been partially implemented.
   [19] The Bill of Sale Act (1878) Amendment Act 1882, s 9. In 2014, the Law Commission started a
project on this subject.
   [20] See for example Lord Hailsham (ed), *Halsbury's Laws of England* (4th edn, LexisNexis, 1992) Vol
4(1), paras 692–720.
   [21] Sir Frederick Pollock, *Digest of the Law of Partnership* (1st edn, Stevens, 1877) xi.
   [22] See CP Ilbert, 'Indian Codification' (1889) 5 LQR 347.

The Indian Contract Act 1872 was far more extensive than its title suggests. It covered not only the general principles of the law of contract, but also agency, bailment, partnership, the sale of goods, and the law of indemnity and guarantee. It was an early commercial code. Its drafting conventions were in most respects similar to those of an English statute, but there were notable departures. For instance, notes of 'explanation' and illustrations were included, for example s 113 provides:

Where goods are sold as being of a certain denomination, there is an implied warranty that they are such goods as are commercially known by that denomination, although the buyer may have bought them by sample, or after inspection of the bulk,

Explanation—But if the contract specifically states that the goods, though sold as of a certain denomination, are not warranted to be of that denomination, there is no implied warranty. Illustrations . . .

  (b) A buys, by sample and after having inspected the bulk, 100 bales of 'Fair Bengal' cotton. The cotton proves not to be such as is known in the market as 'Fair Bengal'; there is a breach of warranty.

As already mentioned, the Uniform Commercial Code also has explanatory material, although this is not incorporated into state statutes.

3. Codification work done by the Law Commission

The Law Commission has done a significant amount of work on two code projects. In the case of the second, it worked jointly with the Scottish Law Commission. Neither of these codes has reached the statute book.

The Criminal Code

The criminal law of England is fragmented. Some offences are governed by the common law, and some are statutory.[23] The law is not only fragmented; it is also in many respects unclear and there are inconsistencies between various offences. As long ago as 1879, a Royal Commission recommended the adoption of a draft criminal code containing over 550 clauses.[24] Penal codes were adopted for many of the colonies, but not in England itself.

It would seem almost axiomatic that criminal law should be accessible and certain, but this is not so in English law. With these points in mind, a distinguished Criminal Code team, whose members included Professor Sir John Smith and the late Professor Edmund Griew, produced a draft Criminal Code which was

---

[23] Codification of the criminal law is explored more fully in Ch 14, *Criminal Law at the Crossroads*.
[24] *Report of the Royal Commission Appointed to Consider the Law Relating to Indictable Offences* (C 2345, 1879). The Commissioners were Lord Blackburn, Barry J, Lush J, and Mr Fitzjames Stephen.

published by the Law Commission in 1985.[25] This draft Code was revised and expanded in cooperation with the Commission and republished in 1989.[26] It was a substantial document running to 220 clauses. It was not a complete code.[27]

And what happened to this Code? It became apparent that there was no prospect of Parliament finding time to deal with such a major measure. Accordingly the Commission decided not to press for the whole code but rather to proceed to work on specific offences[28] and to do further work on the general principles.[29] This meant that the Law Commission would be making recommendations in specific areas rather than creating a complete code. But the Law Commission's preference during my Chairmanship remained for a comprehensive code, even if it had to be put together by consolidating a number of enactments on specific areas, including those implementing Law Commission reports. It remained the view of the Commission that in the interests of fairness, certainty, accessibility, coherence, and consistency there is an urgent need for a criminal code.[30] That can now only be achieved by codification. It cannot be done by the courts alone.[31]

The Contract Code

Codification of the law of contract was included in the first programme of law reform.[32] The project was a joint one with the Scottish Law Commission. Harvey McGregor QC was engaged as a consultant and produced numerous drafts with commentary. His drafts reformed the law rather than restated it. One can get a glimpse of the approach of the draft contract code by looking at some of its provisions. We have already seen how in the Sale of Goods Act 1893, Chalmers had distinguished between conditions and warranties. This is how the draft code would have dealt with that issue:

106. Gradations of promises and obligations

Obligations of the contracting parties are of varying importance but the importance of an obligation is of no practical significance until breach or alleged breach and therefore falls to be ascertained only at that point in time.

---

[25] *Criminal Law: Codification of the Criminal Law. A Report to the Law Commission* (Law Com No 143, 1985).

[26] *Criminal Law: A Criminal Code for England and Wales*, Vols 1 and 2 (Law Com 177, 1989).

[27] A description of the contents of the Law Commission's Criminal Code appears in Ch 14, and so has been removed from this chapter.

[28] The first such report to be published was *Legislating the Criminal Code: Offences Against the Person and General Principles* (Law Com No 218, 1993).

[29] See the Law Commission *Twenty-Fifth Annual Report 1990* (Law Com No 195, 1991).

[30] There are many other jurisdictions which have criminal codes, including Queensland, Western Australia, Tasmania, New Zealand, and Canada.

[31] See Peter Glazebrook, 'Still No Code! English Criminal Law 1894–1994', in Martin Dockray (ed), *City University Centenary Lectures* (Blackstone Press, 1996) 1.

[32] Law Com No 1. As to codification of the law of contract, see generally Diamond, 'Codification of the Law of Contract' (1960) 31 MLR 861. A draft of a much shorter contract code than the McGregor Code was prepared by the Law Reform Commission of Victoria: see 'An Australian Contract Code', Discussion Paper No 27 (1992).

This section is designed to harmonise English and Scottish law by removing from the former the tendency to categorise obligations at the formation stage, as opposed to the stage of performance, and to distinguish between 'conditions', 'warranties' and 'fundamental terms'. Under the Code the vital issue is not whether the broken promise is an important promise but whether the breach of any obligation is an important breach. Accordingly, no categorising of obligations according to their apparent weight and importance is to be made before breach and in particular no technical significance is to be attached to the words 'condition' and 'warranty' or to the expression 'fundamental term' in relation to obligations. The consequence of this radical approach is seen when we reach the issue of breach of contract.

. . .

306. Substantial breach: relevance and definition

(1) The effect of breach of contract depends upon whether it is substantial or not.

(2) A breach of contract is substantial either where there is total non-performance by a contracting party or where there is such other failure to perform as to make it unreasonable to require the other party to continue with his own performance.

(1) It is undoubtedly true, as the law stands today, that certain breaches of contract entitle the victim of the breach to invoke more drastic remedies than others. The distinction between the two categories turns upon the nature of the breach—in effect upon whether the breach is or is not substantial—and is an important and useful one, accepted by most legal systems, and one from which there is no reason to depart. But what does need departing from is the bewildering superstructure of conceptual analysis which has grown around this comparatively simple concept. Thus we find that the victim of a breach may invoke the more drastic remedies available for substantial breach—

(1) if what he has promised is 'dependent' upon the other party's promise but not if their promises are 'independent';

(2) if performance by the other party is a 'condition precedent' of his own obligation to perform;

(3) if the contract is an 'entire' one but not if it is 'severable';

(4) if the breach goes to the 'root' of the contract but not if it does not;

(5) if the breach is of a 'condition' but not if it is of a 'warranty'.

These are at base really variations upon the same theme and the Code therefore proposes to effect a drastic amalgamation of all of them. Indeed the concepts of 'dependent promises' and 'entire contracts', unknown in many legal systems, are best totally discarded.

Moreover, there is a second line of terminology which has also led to confusion: the victim of the breach who invokes the more drastic remedies is sometimes said to reject, sometimes to repudiate, and sometimes to rescind. These variants reflect the difference between the sale of goods—where goods are rejected—and contracts in general, and between law and equity—repudiation being the legal term and rescission the term adopted by equity. It seems best to eliminate all three terms from the Code in this connection, particularly as repudiation on account of breach is liable to be confused with wrongful repudiation which, if accepted, itself constitutes a breach (see section 303), and rescission on account of breach is liable to be confused with rescission of defective contracts (see section 501 et seq).[33]

(2) Of course the difficult question remains: what constitutes a substantial breach? It is questionable whether a more exact definition can be afforded than the one attempted here. In any event it is thought that, for the moment, the important task is to ensure that the

---

[33] Lord Wilberforce deals with the potential confusion from using rescission in these two senses in *Johnson v Agnew* [1980] AC 367, 393.

technical distinctions of the past and present are consigned to oblivion . . . [W]ith 'conditions' and 'warranties' little progress has been made until *Hong Kong Fir Shipping Co v. Kawasaki Kishen Kaisha* [1962] 2 Q.B. 26 (C.A) and *Harbutt's 'Plasticine' v. Wayne Tank and Pump Co* [1970] 1 Q.B. 447 (C.A).[34] Following their lead, the Code takes the view that the test whether a breach is substantial depends on the nature and effect of the breach, not on the nature of the provision broken, and cannot be applied until the breach occurs. This is not to say that the terms of the contract will be wholly irrelevant; they may be material in so far as they indicate the relative importance which the parties place on its various provisions. Clearly a breach of a provision which they have indicated is vital is more likely to be a substantial breach. Nor are parties precluded from providing that in certain circumstances one or other shall be entitled to bring the contract to an end (*c.f.* section 212): in that event the contract is ended in accordance with its terms and there is no breach. All that is being said is that the nature and effect of the breach is decisive and that the parties cannot prejudge the issue by introducing into their agreements expressions such as 'condition precedent' or 'time of the essence'. This may indicate that they regard the provision as an important one; but a trivial breach of an important provision may not necessarily amount to a substantial breach whereas a grave breach of an important provision may, particularly if the party in breach refuses to perform it at all.[35]

If this approach to definition of substantial breach is adopted it will clearly be desirable to revise existing statutes such as the Sale of Goods Act 1893[36] . . . so as to remove the 'condition'—'warranty' dichotomy . . . see, for example, sections 11(1), 11(2) and 53(5), and the definitions of 'warranty' and 'breach of warranty' in section 62, of the Sale of Goods Act.[37]

The McGregor Code was only a draft. Current Law Commission methodology involves extensive public consultation. There is room for considerable difference of opinion on such matters as the effect of conditions precedent, and clauses expressly making time of the essence of a contract. It may very well be that the draft Code would have been amended after consultation. It is important to consider the passages cited in the round. They are striking examples of what can be achieved by codification. Complexities and distinctions which were introduced into the common law as a necessary part of its development, but which may safely be dispensed with, are stripped away. The core principles are extracted and clearly stated—made bright in the crucible of carefully-calibrated codification.

The intention was that the contract code, when completed, should apply to Scotland as well as England and Wales, but there were fundamental differences of opinion between the two Commissions. In 1971 the Scottish Law Commission withdrew from the project.[38] As a result, the Law Commission had to reassess its plan to produce a contract code. In 1972 it suspended work on the code and

---

[34] *Harbutt's 'Plasticine'* has been overruled by *Photo Production v Securicor Transport* [1980] AC 827 but on the different issue of whether the particular breach prevented reliance on an exemption clause.

[35] The law, however, has not developed along these lines: the cases start with *Maredelanto Compania Naviera SA v Bergbau-Handel GmbH (The Mihalis Angelos)* [1971] 1 QB 164 (CA).

[36] Now the Sales of Goods Act 1979.

[37] Provisions now in, respectively, Sale of Goods Act 1979, s 11(2)–(4) (for England), s 11(5) (for Scotland), s 53(5), s 61(1) (for England), and s 61(2) (for Scotland).

[38] See the *Scottish Law Commission, Seventh Annual Report 1971/2* (Scot Law Com No 28, 1973) para 16.

decided to adopt a topic-by-topic approach.[39] This would enable the Commission to issue consultation papers on more limited areas of contract law. The Law Commission has gone on to consider such specific areas as exemption clauses,[40] minors' contracts,[41] the sale and supply of goods,[42] sale of goods forming part of a bulk,[43] and contracts for the benefit of third parties.[44] The Law Commission never reached the stage where it could publish the contract code, although Parliamentary Counsel at the Commission spent considerable time casting it into a form that might ultimately be suitable for a Bill. Harvey McGregor's draft and commentaries have very recently been published,[45] though not by the Law Commission.

Modern developments

The stimulus for the great codifications of English commercial law that took place in the nineteenth century was the production of the Indian and other colonial codes. These were needed so that the vast continent of India and other then colonies could have a uniform and easily accessible statement of developed law.

In recent times there has also has been an interest in the codification of commercial law provoked by different stimuli. In particular technological advances in communications have led to an increase in the number of international transactions and that has contributed to the globalization of the law and commercial practices of the dominant trading nations, often expressed in model laws or international conventions. Added to this has been the growth of the European Union. An increase in the competence of the European Union is intended to be achieved in part by EU legislative measures which eliminate the differences in the law of the member states or harmonize them. The desire for a single European legal fabric has in turn reinforced the trend towards codification.

On the international front, there have, for example, been conventions on the carriage of goods by road,[46] rail,[47] sea,[48] and air[49] which have been incorporated

[39] See *Law Commission Eighth Annual Report, 1972–1973* (Law Com No 58, 1973) paras 3–5.

[40] *Exemption clauses in Contracts, First Report: Amendments to the Sale of Goods Act 1893* (Law Com No 24, Scot Law Com No 12, 1969) which was implemented by the Supply of Goods (Implied Terms) Act 1973; *Exemption Clauses: Second Report by the two Commissions* (Law Com No 69, Scot Law Com No 39, 1975), which led to the Unfair Contract Terms Act 1977.

[41] *Law of Contract: Minors' Contracts* (Law Com No 134, 1984), which led to the Minors' Contracts Act 1987.

[42] *Sale and Supply of Goods* (Law Com No 160, Scot Law Com No 104, 1987), which led to the Sale and Supply of Goods Act 1994.

[43] *Sale of Goods forming Part of a Bulk* (Law Com No 215, Scots Law Com No 173, 1999). This joint report was implemented by the Sale of Goods (Amendment) Act 1995.

[44] *Privity of Contract: Contracts for the Benefit of Third Parties* (Law Com No 242, 1996).

[45] Harvey McGregor, *Contract Code Drawn Up on Behalf of the English Law Commission* (Milan: Giuffrè Editore; London: Sweet & Maxwell, 1993).

[46] See the Convention on the Contract for the International Carriage of Goods by Road, to which effect is given in the UK by the Carriage of Goods Road Act 1965.

[47] See now the Convention concerning International Carriage of Rail, to which effect is given in the UK by the International Transport Conventions Act 1983.

[48] See now the Carriage of Goods by Sea Act 1971.

[49] See now the Carriage by Air Act 1961.

into the law of the United Kingdom. There has also been the 1980 United Nations Convention on Contracts for the International Sale of Goods (the Vienna Convention) produced by UNCITRAL (the United Nations Committee on Trade Law), which has not been ratified by the United Kingdom. On the European front, there has been, for example, the Rome Convention on the Law Applicable to Contractual Obligations,[50] and the ill-fated European Community Convention on Insolvency Proceedings[51] which has not yet been adopted. Moreover, the European Community has been one of the main sponsors of the Commission on European Contract Law, which was established to provide principles of contract law for the European Community. The members of the Commission in its work to date have included Professor Roy Goode of St John's College Oxford and Professor Hugh Beale of Warwick University. One of the Commission's objectives is that at some point in the future the principles identified by the Commission will serve as a draft for a future European Code. In 1995 the Commission published the first part of the principles, covering performance, non-performance, and remedies.[52] Work is proceeding now on the authority of agents and the formation, validity, and content of contracts.

There has also been a resurgence of interest in codification north of the Tweed. On 7 February 1997, the Scottish Law Commission published its *Fifth Programme of Law Reform*.[53] Item No 2 in that programme is headed Codification. It refers to unsuccessful projects in the 1960s and 1970s to codify the law of evidence and the law of obligations, and states that one possible reason why these projects foundered is that they were too ambitious for the time. It refers to later incremental statutory reform as a form of codification. Paragraph 2.16 then states:

We continue to believe, however, that there may also be a place for codification in the wider traditional sense; that is, a comprehensive legislative restatement of the general principles underlying some unified area of the common law. We therefore propose, as a long-term project, to carry out a feasibility study of codification, focusing on a restricted area of the law as a pilot exercise. We have in mind as possible candidates selected topics in the law of property or in the law of obligations, for example, servitudes, contract or unjustified enrichment.

Then, yet more boldly, paragraph 2.29 states:

In a recent discussion paper,[54] . . . we invited comments on a proposal to publish a further discussion paper setting out a 'non-binding' statement (or 'restatement') of the existing law on unjustified enrichment and seeking views on whether comprehensive statutory codification or further piecemeal statutory reforms are desirable. In an appendix, we also published

---

[50] Made applicable to the UK by the Contracts (Applicable Law) Act 1990.

[51] The Convention can be found in App 3 to the Seventh Report of the House of Commons Select Committee on the European Communities, HL Paper 59, 29 March 1996. The Convention was not ratified by the UK, and as a result it failed to achieve the requisite number of signatories.

[52] Ole Lando and Hugh Beale (eds), *Principles of European Contract Law. Part 1: Performance, Non-Performance and Remedies* (Martinus Nijhoff, 1995), prepared by the Commission on European Contract Law.

[53] *Fifth Programme of Law Reform* (Scot Law Com No 159, 1997).

[54] 'Judicial Abolition of the Error of Law Rule and its Aftermath', Discussion Paper No 99 (1996).

Draft Rules on Unjustified Enrichment and Commentary which had been prepared by Dr E M Clive to test the feasibility of codification.[55] While opinion was divided, there was considerable support for such a discussion paper—hence our present proposal to undertake a further long-term project on the topic, possibly including an exercise in codification.[56]

On our own domestic front, too, there has recently been an extremely important example of the codification of commercial law—the Arbitration Act 1996. The Departmental Advisory Committee on Arbitration, under the chairmanship of Lord Mustill, had earlier recommended a statutory statement of the more important principles of common law and statute law applicable to arbitration, which is as I see it a form of codification of the law. The Arbitration Act 1996 achieves this codification in a number of ways: it restates existing statute law. For example, s 1 of the Arbitration Act 1979 as construed in *Nema*[57] and *Antaios*[58] is restated in s 69 of the Arbitration Act 1996 (appeal on a point of law). The 1996 Act also resolves uncertainty in the case law, for example on the question of the arbitrator's immunity.[59] The 1996 Act reverses case law, for example the rule established in *Hiscox v Outhwaite*[60] that an award is to be treated as made where it is signed. In addition, the 1996 Act alters arbitration law by introducing some of the provisions of the UNCITRAL Model Law, for example it enables a party to agree to apply 'equity clauses' to the substance of their dispute.[61]

The Arbitration Act 1996 is expressed in clear terms. The purpose of the Act was to update and modernize arbitration law and at the same time to make London an attractive venue for international arbitration. The Bill was drafted under the auspices of the Departmental Advisory Committee on Arbitration, chaired by Lord Justice Saville.

The 1996 Act is a striking example of how the need for codification can arise in commercial law, and how codification can be carried through to the statute book. It is early days yet, but it seems likely that the Act will, in relation to the particular matters which it covers,[62] constitute an invaluable code of law for arbitrators and lawyers.

The reasons for and against codifying commercial law

No one doubts, of course, the genius of the common law. It is an invaluable method of developing law to meet proven need and it has the advantage that it is tested against real life situations. But there are limits on its ability to develop the law. For instance, the common law process is restricted by the doctrine of precedent

---

[55] The rules represented Dr Clive's personal views and not necessarily those of the Scottish Law Commission. The Appendix was published as a separate document.

[56] See *Fifth Programme of Law Reform* (n 53).

[57] *Pioneer Shipping Ltd v BTP Tioxide Ltd (The Nema)* [1982] AC 724.

[58] *Antaios Compania Naviera SA v Salen Rederierna AB* [1985] AC 191.

[59] Section 29.   [60] [1992] 1 AC 562.   [61] Section 46.

[62] There are aspects of arbitration law with which the 1996 Act does not deal, for example confidentiality.

and by the unwritten limits on judicial legislation. The limitations on the common law method are one of the reasons why a developed modern society like ours needs a Law Commission which can undertake extensive reviews of large areas of outdated law. However, these limitations, though real, do not materially detract from the value of the common law method.

The next question is what should be done when, as a result of the common law process, principles of law on any particular subject have started to emerge in a recognizable and reasonably solid form from the miasmic stew of the case law. It is important to emphasize that it is not being suggested that codification should be attempted where the law on a particular topic is still in a fluid form to a significant extent.

My predecessor, Lord Scarman, the Law Commission's first Chairman, expressed the view in 1983 that: 'The Common Law is delightful but it is now of marginal importance only.'[63] That is a rather more extreme view then I would seek to urge. There is a vastly increased amount of legislation these days, but much of it is hasty and ill-considered. Every lawyer can think of situations where Parliament's intervention has been ineffective or counter-productive. One example is s 153 of the Companies Act 1985 which contains a defence to s 151 of that Act, which prohibits a company from giving financial assistance for the purpose of an acquisition of its shares.[64] The Court of Appeal suggested that the predecessor prohibition might apply where the giving of financial assistance was a subsidiary object of the transaction.[65] Parliament responded by creating a defence where the principal purpose was not to give assistance for the purpose of a share acquisition. A later House of Lords decision[66] deprived the defence of any utility in practice by drawing a new and difficult distinction between reason and purpose.[67] It was not enough that the principal reason for giving the assistance was not to facilitate a share acquisition.

To obtain the benefit of the defence, the company's objective in entering into the transaction had to be to achieve an object independent of the giving of financial assistance and not merely a consequence, or by-product, of it. The government has recently engaged in consultation on a proposal to amend the legislation to achieve what was originally intended, hopefully with more success. Section 151 of the 1985 Act apart it is remarkable how little suggestion one hears that English company law is restrictive of commercial enterprise despite its significant codified element.

The deep-seated fears of common lawyers about the effect of codification have been clearly expressed by my fellow Law Commissioner, Professor Andrew Burrows, in a recent article in the Edinburgh Law Review:[68]

I should explain that, perhaps oddly for a Law Commissioner, I am not a great fan of legislative reform of the non-criminal common law. I have too much faith in the judiciary,

---

[63] See Hansard, HL vol 437, p 634 (15 December 1982).
[64] Also discussed in Ch 11 under the heading 'Possible external improvements'
[65] *Belmont Finance Corp v Williams Furniture Ltd (No 2)* [1980] 1 All ER 393 (CA).
[66] *Brady v Brady* [1989] AC 755.   [67] See further Ch 11.
[68] Andrew Burrows, 'Legislative Reform of Remedies for Breach of Contract: The English Perspective' [1997] Edinburgh Law Review 155, 156.

and too much love of the deductive technique of common law development to wish to see the law frozen by widespread legislative intervention. In my view legislative reform of the law of obligations ought normally to be confined to situations where the law is either already based on statute (e.g. the law of limitation periods or the Fatal Accidents Act 1976) or where the common law has plainly taken a wrong turn so that, short of waiting for an enlightened decision of the House of Lords, there is no other way of getting the law back on the right track (e.g. the law on restitution of payments under a mistake of law or on contracts for the benefit of third parties).

This passage expresses concern about statute law stifling the ability of judges to develop the law. But in the field of common law I am considering, the principles have already emerged. In that situation, the judge's room for manoeuvre is already limited. The judge must follow the principles that have already been established where the doctrine of precedent applies. The longer a principle has been established the less likely it is that the courts will depart from it, particularly in commercial law where certainty and consistency are recognized as important. In addition, there are limits on the extent to which the courts are able to create new principles of law.[69] Moreover, the courts will still have an important role in interpreting the code.

The limited loss of judicial flexibility must be compared with the positive advantages that can come from codification.

First, codification makes the law more accessible. A code of law, written in modern language, can be read by the non-lawyer, whereas case law is largely inaccessible to him except through textbooks. Pollock wrote in one of his letters to Oliver Wendell Holmes:

I . . . admit that the consideration of case law as a pure science tends to make one look on codes as a kind of brutal interference with the natural process of legal reason . . . But Stephen met the supposed scientific objection with (as I think) the right answer: that laws exist not for the scientific satisfaction of the legal mind but for the convenience of lay people who sue or be sued.[70]

Law should be expressed, where possible, in the manner in which it will be most easily understood by the user. Codified law is more intelligible to the layman than case law and so codification can enhance accessibility to law.

Second, it is in most situations quicker and easier to find the answer to a legal problem in a code. The majority of legal problems do not raise new and interesting points of law but can be solved by applying existing well-established principle. Dispensing with encrustations of case law will make it easier to find the answer in many cases. This should reduce the costs of litigation and the costs of taking legal advice and reduce the cost to the taxpayer of the justice system. The approach to the interpretation of codifying statutes adopted by the courts does not favour recourse to the pre-existing law[71] and this assists in the process of dispensing with encrustations of authority.

---

[69] See for example *Rhone v Stephens* [1994] 2 AC 310, 321 (restrictive covenants); and *Kaye v Robertson* [1991] FSR 62 (no tort of privacy).
[70] *The Pollock-Holmes Letters*, Vol 1 (Cambridge University Press, 1942) 7–8.
[71] See *Bank of England v Vagliano Bros* [1891] AC 107.

Third, the process of codification enables the law to be updated and modernized as part of the process. Take, for instance, the doctrine of consideration in contract. In its opening pages, the commentary on the McGregor Code criticized the doctrine of consideration in these terms:

The doctrine of consideration never succeeded in drawing a clear distinction between agreements which were bargains and agreements which were gratuitous. From the moment that it was accepted that consideration need not be adequate, all chance of carving out a satisfactory division along these lines disappeared. That no attention should be paid to the adequacy of the consideration was of course a perfectly legitimate and necessary rule designed to protect the person who had made a good bargain and to hold to his promises the person who had made a bad one. But it also gave a simple means for the evasion of the consideration doctrine: a nominal consideration could be used to make a gratuitous promise binding. It therefore cannot truthfully be said that the doctrine acts in any real sense as a sieve through which only bargains can pass.

It is hardly necessary to state what the McGregor Code did about the doctrine of consideration: it proposed the removal of it. But suppose it had set the Rule in *Pinnel's* case.[72] It would have to have said words to this effect:

Where a person is owed a sum of money by another person that person cannot accept a lesser sum in satisfaction of that debt but may accept a smaller sum together with a peppercorn or other chattel instead.

Such a rule has only to be formulated to be shown to be ridiculous, and one potential advantage of codification would be to enable obvious blots on the law like this to be removed. As the commentary to s 306 of the McGregor Code indicates, technical distinctions can in the course of codification be 'consigned to oblivion'.

Fourth, revision and development of the law through codification avoids the need to wait and see if a point on which the law is uncertain ever comes up for decision. The courts may not be given the chance to resolve an ambiguity, either because the point does not arise in litigation or because counsel fail to argue it. For these reasons, the development of the law through the common law system can be haphazard. I have already quoted a passage from Chalmers in which he said that the important point decided in *Glyn Mills v The East and West India Docks Company* about the liability of a warehouseman in conversion had originally arisen on a *nisi prius* ruling in 1753 but then not again until 129 years later.

Fifth, the process of codification can be used to resolve the uncertainty that arises where there is a conflict on the authorities or where there is no authority on a particular point.

Sixth, and not least, there is in many areas an excessive amount of case law. A hundred years ago, as we have seen, Chalmers compared the common law of sale with a tree in full foliage the number of whose leaves 'frequently hide from view the form and development of the trunk and branches which support them'. Skeleton arguments are often overburdened with case law. The introduction of

[72] (1602) 5 Co Rep 117a; 77 ER 237.

the CD-ROM, a powerful research tool for the common lawyer, is sometimes used to inflate skeleton arguments by inserting long extracts obtained from a CD. Valuable court time is spent trying to synthesize the effect of numerous cases. Codification, on the other hand, enables the law to have a clean break with the past. The new, clearly-formulated, and (where appropriate) updated provision becomes a springboard for further development of the law.[73] Chalmers put this point graphically. He said that developing the law by the common law method was like putting new wine into old bottles. The process of codifying established law, on the other hand, was like putting old wine into new bottles. Now, he said, 'I leave it to your commercial experience to decide which plan is best'.[74]

The process of codification

Do the right procedures and technical skills exist to codify the law? It is not a question of whether the right software is available or whether the product is suitable for user-friendly electronic publishing. Those questions today apply to all forms of expression of the law. The real question is whether the production of a code requires a different process from that by which statute law is generally produced. In my view, codification does have certain special needs if it is to be successful.

Codification of commercial law has, as I see it, the following special requirements, at the least, if it is to be successfully achieved:

(1) Codification of the area of commercial law in question must be identified by the commercial community as meeting a real commercial need.

(2) The basic work must be done using experts, and with the benefit of extensive research, and experts must include those with practical experience.

(3) The proposals must be developed in consultation with the government department having responsibility for the area in question.

(4) Parliamentary counsel, when instructed to put the proposals into legislative form, should work in cooperation with experts in the field. The language chosen must be clear and at the same time permit creative interpretation by the courts.

(5) The proposals and the draft legislation should be subject to extensive public consultation before the Bill is presented to Parliament.

(6) Consideration must be given to the appropriate drafting conventions. For example it may be appropriate to use illustrations in a code although it would not be appropriate to use them in other forms of legislation. It may

---

[73] It can help to strengthen the common law system, which Professor Birks advocates in 'Equity in the Modern Law: An Exercise in Taxonomy' [1996] Western Australian Law Review 1, though Professor Birks argues that this can be achieved by a more analytical approach to the common law rather than codification.

[74] Chalmers, 'Codification of the Law of Sale' (n 5) 15.

also be appropriate to have an authoritative commentary contained in or referred to in the legislation.[75]

(7) Where possible, the Committee of the House of Parliament responsible for scrutinizing the draft legislation must be able to receive oral and written evidence from experts, as under the House of Lords' special public bill procedure.[76]

(8) There should probably also be some means of monitoring the operation of the code in practice and there must be a method of implementing any amendments which are found to be necessary. Amendment may be necessary to deal with a new situation that has arisen or to alter the effect of the code or to reflect case law that has built up around the code.

Conclusions

Although I am the Chairman of the Law Commission, I stress that the views that I have expressed are my own, and not those of the Commission.

It may well be that the Law Commission has neither the human resources, nor the financial resources, required to complete a project on the codification of commercial law. Moreover, even if the Commission does such a project, there is no guarantee that Parliament would enact it. Those problems should not be underestimated. It is very disappointing, for instance, that the government has not shown more support for the idea of a criminal code. The case for a criminal code is virtually unanswerable: it would make criminal law more coherent, fairer and simpler, and cheaper to administer. The case for the codification of commercial law is a different one, and is best judged in my view by reference to the question whether it has become desirable in any field of commercial law to formulate in a single statute principles established by the common law method, and to have some law reform 'at the margins'. Codification can be seen, for example, in the Sale of Goods Act 1893 and the Arbitration Act 1996. It has worked well in the past, and there is reason to believe that, with the help of commercial lawyers and the commercial community, and the support of the government and Parliament, it could be successfully achieved in the future and bring benefits to all. A start could be made on an English Commercial Code to which later generations could add.

---

[75] This problem was addressed in *The Interpretation of Statutes* (Law Com No 21, Scot Law Com No 11, 1969) paras 68–73.

[76] This is known as the Jellicoe procedure. It is described in Sir Henry Brooke, 'Special Public Bill Committees' [1995] Public Law 351; the *Law Commission Thirtieth Annual Report 1995* (Law Com No 239, 1996); and the Report of the House of Lords Procedure Committee, Hansard, HL, cols 554–556 (21 January 1997). See further Author's Notes on Law Commission Bills, n 1, which follows Lord Mackay's Preface on pp 137–8; and also n 16 on page 212.

14

Criminal Law at the Crossroads

The Need for a Code

This chapter is based on the Hardwicke Lecture given in 1998.*

The arguments for a criminal code

In July 1998 the Lord Chief Justice, Lord Bingham, made a powerful call for Parliament to set about the task of enacting a criminal code. He said:

The arguments in favour of codification are what they have always been. First, it would bring clarity and accessibility to the law. As the Attorney-General put it in the House of Commons 119 years ago:

'Surely, it is a desirable thing that anybody who may want to know the law on a particular subject should be able to turn to a chapter of the Code, and there find the law he is in search of explained in a few intelligible and well-constructed sentences; nor would he have to enter upon a long examination of *Russell on Crimes*, or *Archbold*, and other textbooks, because he would have a succinct and clear statement before him.'[1]

Secondly, a code would bring coherence to this branch of the law. Sir John Smith has expressed his general disbelief in codes—a disbelief which I for my part share—but he continued:

'The criminal law is entirely different. It is incoherent and inconsistent. State almost any general principle and you find one or more leading cases which contradict it. It is littered with distinctions which have no basis in reason but are mere historical accidents. I am in favour of codification of the criminal law because I see no other way of reducing a chaotic system to order, of eliminating irrational distinctions and of making the law reasonably comprehensible, accessible and certain. These are all practical objects. Irrational distinctions mean injustice. A is treated differently from B when there is no rational ground for treating him differently; and this is not justice.'[2]

Sir John has entertained generations of students, practitioners and judges by highlighting the anomalies in our present law. As the present Chairman of the Law Commission has

---

* The Hardwicke Lecture was given on 24 November 1998 in Lincoln's Inn Old Hall, London. It was chaired by The Rt Hon Lord Woolf MR and was given at the invitation of Hardwicke Chambers, Lincoln's Inn. The lecture was first published as Mary Arden, 'Criminal Law at the Crossroads: the Need for a Code' in [1999] Crim LR 439, © Sweet & Maxwell Ltd. It is in part reproduced here by kind permission of Thomson Reuters (Professional) Limited.

[1] Hansard, HC vol 245 (3rd series), col 316 (3 April 1879).
[2] 'Codification of the Criminal Law' (Child & Co, Lecture, 1986).

herself said, the cure now can only be achieved by codification; it cannot be provided by the courts alone.

Thirdly, a code would bring greater certainty to the law, and in this of all fields the law should be so far as possible certain. The arguments for incremental development of the law, persuasive elsewhere, have no application here. It is not just that a defendant should be held punishable for an act which would not have been thought criminal when he did it; and if he is held not liable for conduct which would at that time have been thought criminal, the almost inevitable consequence is that others have been unjustly punished. Incorporation of the European Convention reinforces the need for certainty if the principle of legality is to be observed. Even the most breathless admirer of the common law must regard it as a reproach that after 700 years of judicial decision-making our highest tribunal should have been called upon time and again in recent years to consider the mental ingredients of murder, the oldest and most serious of crimes.

. . .

One hopes that parliamentary time may yet be found to achieve something that has eluded our predecessors but would, I think, come to be recognised as an important milestone in our legal and public life.[3]

The Law Commission has for years encouraged the codification of the criminal law. The project had support from Roy Jenkins as Home Secretary in a previous Labour Government who said that the then government had 'now decided the time has come to have a complete criminal code':

There are too many archaic principles that have been handed down from precedent to precedent. As a result much of our criminal law is in many areas obscure, confused and uncertain. Yet no area of the law is of greater importance to the liberty of the individual and nowhere is it more important that the law should be stated in clear and certain terms to take account of modern conditions. It is almost impossible for the layman to consult the learned text books and commentaries on the criminal law. It should however be possible for the layman to grasp the broad outlines of his rights and obligations in one comprehensive document which states what the criminal law is.[4]

Shortly before the general election in 1997, Jack Straw, then Shadow Home Secretary, said:

. . . I should like to mention one further area of mutual concern—the current complexity of the criminal law. Some parts of the criminal law, such as the law on offences against the person are now over-complex and in need of revision. The Law Commission has done an enormous amount of work to update our law, but all too often their reports are left on the shelf collecting dust. I should like to see a codification of the law, implementing many of the Law Commission's proposals.[5]

This chapter argues that systematic reform of the criminal law is necessary and overdue and goes on to explain the Law Commission's strategy for codifying the criminal law, and argues that this strategy offers the only satisfactory way forward.

[3] Lord Bingham, 'A Criminal Code: Must We Wait For Ever?' [1998] Crim LR 694.
[4] *Codification of the Criminal Law* (Law Com No 143, 1985) para 7.
[5] 'Reforming the Criminal Justice System' (1997) 165 The Justices' Clerk 163, 167.

Systematic reform of the criminal law overdue

Morris Cohen said that criminal law was 'the pathology' of civilization.[6] It is society's expression of what conduct is so socially undesirable or harmful that it requires to be punished. It is therefore important that the criminal law is kept up to date. For example, and perhaps most obviously, there is a need for the law to keep pace with technological change: thus in 1989 the Law Commission published a report on computer misuse[7] which recommended the introduction of new offences: unauthorized access to computer material; unauthorized access to computer material with intent to facilitate the commission of a serious crime; and unauthorized modification of computer material. The recommendations in this report became, with immaterial modification, the Computer Misuse Act 1990.

A further problem to which the Commission had to respond quickly concerned money transfers. On 10 July 1996 the House of Lords had unanimously allowed the appeals in *Preddy*.[8] The basis of the decision was that the borrowers, who had been charged with mortgage fraud under s 15(1) of the Theft Act 1968, had not 'obtained property belonging to another', as required by s 15, when they obtained advances which were credited to a bank account. As a result of the decision in *Preddy*, it became difficult to prosecute an individual who obtained by deception any form of payment by any form of banking transfer. The Law Commission undertook a brief consultation process and published its report, *Legislating the Criminal Code: Offences of Dishonesty (Money Transfers)*,[9] on 15 October 1996. It recommended, inter alia, the creation of an offence of dishonestly obtaining a money transfer by deception. This offence would extend to payments made by cheque as well as those made electronically. Within hours of publishing the report the Home Secretary announced that the government accepted its recommendation. The Theft (Amendment) Bill was introduced, and became law on 18 December 1996.

There is also a need to keep the law up to date with changing social values, as illustrated by the Law Commission's report, *Rape within Marriage*.[10] Normally, the Law Commission undertakes a project because it is suggested that the courts are unable to adapt the law to modern circumstances, but in this project the courts and the Law Commission were both actively considering the subject during the currency of the project. In 1992, the House of Lords held that marital immunity no longer existed.[11] Within a month of the decision the final report of the Commission was published. Lord Lester subsequently moved an amendment to the Criminal Justice and Public Order Bill which gave effect to the most important draft clause in the report. That clause, now s 142 of the Criminal Justice and Public Order Act 1994, placed the House of Lords decision on a statutory basis.[12]

---

[6] Morris L Cohen, 'Moral Aspects of the Criminal Law' (1940) 49 Yale LJ 987, 1025.
[7] *Computer Misuse* (Law Com No 186, 1989).   [8] [1996] AC 815.
[9] Law Com No 243, 1996.   [10] *Rape within Marriage* (Law Com No 205, 1992).
[11] *R v R* [1992] 1 AC 599.
[12] In a subsequent case, *SW v United Kingdom* [1995] 21 EHRR 363, the husband complained to the Strasbourg Court that his conviction and sentence for attempted rape of his wife constituted

Both *Money Transfers* and *Rape within Marriage* were promptly implemented by Parliament. There are other reports which have not been implemented, despite their importance. The work which the Law Commission has done on non-fatal offences against the person is a good example of this. This is a much used area of the law, but very out of date. In 1993 the Law Commission published its report on offences against the person[13] and recommended that the present law should be replaced by three offences: intentionally causing serious injury, recklessly causing serious injury, and intentionally or recklessly causing injury. The recommendations would replace the archaic language and conflicting concepts in the Offences Against the Person Act 1861, a consolidating Act, with clearly stated offences:[14]

... Our criminal law is a mixed system of statutory provisions and common law. The judges can within limits keep the common law up to date. Statute law, however, has to be kept up to date by Parliament. For many years there has been legislative inertia. The situation is that there is an accumulated backlog of work for Parliament leaving large areas of criminal statutes needing reform.

One of the problems impeding reform is the difficulty of obtaining Parliamentary time. Our research, however, shows that our Bills take very little time on either floor of the House.[15] There is, however, always a concern that they will do so. We consider that this risk would be diminished if more Bills, including at least some of our criminal law Bills, were considered by a select committee or other procedure off the main floor of the House of Commons. The Law Commission engages in extensive consultation before its recommendations reach Parliament.[16] We have pressed for changes in Parliamentary procedure to speed up law reform. . . . [17]

---

retrospective punishment in breach of Art 7 of the European Convention on Human Rights. The Court rejected this argument. The Court referred to the Law Commission's work in this area (at 400). The Court noted that 'there were strong indications that still wider interpretation by the courts of the inroads on the immunity was probable' (at 401). It was satisfied that the essentially debasing character of rape was so manifest that the Court of Appeal and House of Lords decision could not be said to be at variance with the objects and purpose of Art 7 of the Convention (at 402).

[13] *Legislating the Criminal Code: Offences against the Person and General Principles* (Law Com No 218, 1993). Part II of this report dealt with defences of general application: see n 41.

[14] *Offences against the Person* (n 13) was implemented, in certain respects only, by the Domestic Violence Crime and Victims Act 2004. However, the Law Commission has now been requested by the Ministry of Justice to carry out a scoping exercise as a first step towards a new project to reform the law in this area (see Law Commission, *Annual Report 2013–14* (2014) 17–18). On 12 November 2014 the Law Commission issued a scoping consultation paper (*Reform of Offences against the Person A Scoping Consultation Paper* (CP No 217, 2014)).

[15] See memorandum submitted by the Law Commission, First Report of the Select Committee on Modernisation of the House of Commons (HC 190) published in the 1997–98 session, App 3; and see Philippa Hopkins, 'Parliamentary Procedures and the Law Commission. A Research Study' (Law Commission, 1994).

[16] There have been improvements in Parliamentary procedure in recent years, in particular the institution of the special public bill procedure (or Jellicoe Committee) in the House of Lords and the adoption of standing order 59 in the House of Commons, under which Law Commission Bills are remitted to a committee for their second reading, but there is still a backlog of Law Commission Bills awaiting implementation. See further Preface to Section B by The Rt Hon Lord Mackay of Clashfern, Author's Notes on Law Commission Bills, n 1.

[17] The next part of the article on which this chapter is based has been omitted. It focused on the potential impact on the criminal law of the Human Rights Act 1998, which had not then come into

The Law Commission's strategy for codifying the criminal law offers the only satisfactory way forward

The Law Commission has devoted a considerable amount of effort to codification of the criminal law. In its Second Programme of Law Reform, published in 1968, the Law Commission set out its objective of a comprehensive examination of the criminal law with a view to its codification.[18] The first stage of that examination was to include consideration of certain specific offences and, with the assistance of a working party, the general principles of the criminal law.[19] While no specific mention of work on criminal procedure and evidence was made in the Second Programme, it was envisaged that this would find a place within a complete criminal code and that such work would in due course be undertaken. In the years following the Second Programme, the Commission made substantial progress in the examination of specific offences. It published many working papers and reports[20] and some of the reports were implemented by legislation.[21]

Some progress was also made on the general principles of liability to be incorporated in a code of the substantive criminal law. Several working papers[22] and reports were published.[23] Again, some of these reports were implemented by

force. It concluded that there were many aspects of criminal law which might undergo change once the 1998 Act had come into force. There have been significant developments in the case law since the article was written. The arguments for codification of the criminal law are not affected by the detailed effect of the Convention on any particular offence. The overarching point is that the Convention would be an important factor in any future codification. Any future criminal code or building block in creating such a code would, like any other statute, have to be considered for its compatibility with the Convention. This is confirmed by Human Rights Act 1998, s 19 which requires a minister presenting a Bill to Parliament to file a statement of compatibility with the Convention, stating that it is compatible, or that, although he is unable to make the statement, the government wishes the Bill to proceed. The Law Commission took account of the Convention even before the passing of the Human Rights Act 1998.

[18] (Law Com No 14, 1968) Item XVIII.

[19] Work on specific offences was to be undertaken by both the Commission and the Criminal Law Revision Committee, particular items being allocated to each body.

[20] See Reports on *Offences of Damage to Property* (Law Com No 29, 1970); *Forgery and Counterfeit Currency* (Law Com No 55, 1973); *Offences relating to Interference with the Course of Justice* (Law Com No 96, 1979); *Offences relating to Public Order* (Law Com No 123, 1983); *Offences against Religion and Public Worship* (Law Com No 145, 1985); *Poison-Pen Letters* (Law Com No 147, 1985); *Criminal Libel* (Law Com No 149, 1985), (Cmd 9618). See also Working Papers Nos 72, *Treason, Sedition and Allied Offences* (1977); and 104, *Conspiracy to defraud* (1987). Much work has also been done by the Criminal Law Revision Committee, for example their *Fourteenth Report: Offences against the Person* (Cmd 7844, 1980); and *Fifteenth Report: Sexual Offences* (Cmd 9213, 1984).

[21] See the Criminal Damage Act 1971; Forgery and Counterfeiting Act 1981; Public Order Act 1986, Part I; Malicious Communications Act 1988.

[22] Working Papers Nos 31, *The Mental Element in Crime* (1970); 43, *Parties, Complicity and Liability for the Acts of Another* (1972); 44, *Criminal Liability of Corporations* (1972); 50, *Inchoate Offences: Conspiracy, Attempt and Incitement* (1973); 55, *Defences of General Application* (1974).

[23] See Reports on *Conspiracy and Criminal Law Reform* (Law Com No 76, 1976); *Defences of General Application* (Law Com No 83, 1977); *Mental Element in Crime* (Law Com No 89, 1978); *Territorial and Extraterritorial Extent of the Criminal Law* (Law Com No 91, 1978); *Attempt, and Impossibility in relation to Attempt, Conspiracy and Incitement* (Law Com No 102, 1980).

legislation.[24] Eventually, however, the Commission realized that its limited resources prevented it from making as much progress as it wished in this area.[25]

In 1980 the Criminal Law Sub-Committee of the Society of Public Teachers of Law proposed that a team drawn from its members should consider and make proposals to the Commission in relation to a criminal code. The Law Commission welcomed this initiative. The Law Commission invited Professor Sir John Smith to chair the project. In consultation with the Commission, he chose as the other members of his team Professor Edward Griew, Mr Peter Glazebrook,[26] and Professor Ian Dennis.

The Code team submitted its report to the Law Commission in November 1984. The Law Commission published it in March 1985 as *Criminal Law: Codification of the Criminal Law, A Report to the Law Commission.*[27] The report contained a draft Criminal Code Bill consisting of fifty-five clauses covering such matters as jurisdiction, proof, external elements of offences, fault, parties to offences, mental disorder and incapacity, defences and preliminary offences, and twenty-six clauses setting out the offences against the person (derived from recommendations made in the Fourteenth Report of the Criminal Law Revision Committee),[28] and nine clauses relating to offences of damage to property (derived from the Criminal Damage Act 1971). The publication of the draft Code stimulated a great deal of debate by way of lectures, conferences, articles, and legal journals.

In 1989 the Law Commission published a revised and expanded Criminal Code.[29] This was a substantial document running to some 220 clauses, although it was not a complete code. There were a number of offences with which it did not deal. However, it contained extensive provisions on the general principles of liability and on a number of substantive offences, including offences against the person, sexual offences, theft, fraud, and related offences. The code largely restated the existing law with limited changes, such as provisions to implement the recommendations of the Butler Committee on Mentally Abnormal Offenders and provisions to resolve existing inconsistencies and anomalies. The code brought many areas of our criminal law into one enactment and removed anomalies. It was drafted in modern language to make it as accessible as possible.

Unfortunately it became apparent that the criminal code would not be implemented. Accordingly the Commission decided not to press for the whole code but rather to work on specific offences and to do further work on the general principles. In pursuance of this policy, the Law Commission published first its report, *Offences against the Person,*[30] followed, inter alia, by its reports *Involuntary Manslaughter,*[31]

---

[24] See the Criminal Law Act 1977, Pts I and II; and the Criminal Attempts Act 1981.

[25] See *Fifteenth Annual Report 1979–80* (Law Com No 107, 1981) para 1.4.

[26] Mr Glazebrook withdrew from the Code team in January 1984.

[27] Law Com No 143, 1985.

[28] *Offences against the Person* (Cmd 7844, 1980).

[29] *Criminal Law: A Criminal Code for England and Wales* (two volumes) (HC 299).

[30] *Legislating the Criminal Code: Offences against the Person and General Principles* (Law Com No 218, 1993). Part only of this Report has been implemented (by the Domestic Violence, Crime and Victims Act 2004).

[31] *Legislating the Criminal Code: Involuntary Manslaughter* (Law Com No 237, 1996).

and *Corruption*.[32] However, it remained the view of the Commission that in the interests of fairness, certainty, accessibility, coherence, and consistency there was an urgent need for a criminal code.

If a criminal code is ever to be achieved in this country, it is clear that it is necessary to focus on the attainable, even though the result might not be as comprehensive as would be desirable in an ideal world. This is because the process of producing a code will take time and resources, and require a significant amount of Parliamentary time in particular. Therefore as a practical matter it has to be confined to the key areas of criminal law. Thus the first step is to identify those key areas.

The next step is to consider whether the law in those areas needs review, and if so to proceed with the review in an appropriate way. This will often, but not always, involve a law reform project by the Law Commission. A major advantage of review, by whomever it is undertaken, is that there will be an opportunity to check that the offence is adequately defined, that the fault element is appropriate, and that the law complies with the European Convention on Human Rights ('the Convention'). Review will also provide an opportunity for wide public consultation on the issues. If it is decided to change the law as a result of such a review, there will have to be an amending statute.

When all the key areas have been identified and any change in the law thought necessary has been made, the resulting statute law can be consolidated into a single statute. At this stage, the special streamlined Parliamentary procedures for consolidation Bills can be used.

A criminal code produced as a result of this process would look very like any other large consolidating Act. It would not require any new rules of statutory construction: the legislative style would remain as now, and the courts would retain their important responsibility for interpreting the code. The courts would also retain their role in relation to the common law in the key areas which is not made statutory. Certain defences would continue to be governed by the common law, and it may be very desirable that they are not made statutory in case they lose some of their valuable flexibility.

Scope of a criminal code

I now turn to consider the scope of the code. In my view, ultimately it would be likely to consist of four separate codes dealing with sentencing, substantive law, evidence, and procedure respectively. This sounds like an ambitious scheme, but, as explained later, much of the work that is needed has already been done or is now under way. For example, in relation to sentencing, the Law Commission is already engaged on a consolidation of the sentencing powers of the courts. This is a complex task.[33] When it becomes law, it will in effect be the sentencing code.

---

[32] *Legislating the Criminal Code: Corruption* (Law Com No 248, 1998).
[33] As stated in n 14 the Law Commission now has a new project on this subject.

When, after its enactment, Parliament amends the law on sentencing, it is to be hoped that it will do so by amending the sentencing code so that the value of the codification is not undermined.

In relation to substantive criminal law, the key areas to be contained in this code would be: offences against the person, dishonesty, corruption, offences against public order, and sexual offences. The part dealing with offences against the person would be principally based on the Law Commission's recommendations in the first part of its report on offences against the person,[34] and in its report on involuntary manslaughter.[35]

The part dealing with dishonesty would need to have regard to the Law Commission's work on money transfers,[36] which was implemented by the Theft (Amendment) Act 1996, as well as its current work on fraud pursuant to a reference by the Home Secretary.[37] The part dealing with corruption would take account of the Law Commission's recommendations in its recent report on corruption.[38] The part dealing with offences against public order would be based on the Public Order Act 1986 which implemented the Law Commission's recommendations in *Offences Relating to Public Order*.[39]

The last part of the code dealing with substantive criminal law would be concerned with sexual offences. The Law Commission does not have any current or completed work in this field, but in June 1998, the Home Office announced that it intended to review the law in this area and it has since published the terms of reference for this review.[40]

These, then, would be the parts of the code dealing with substantive law. Review of most of these areas has already been undertaken or is in hand. There are some areas which have not yet been considered but these could be phased into a carefully structured programme for the preparation of a code. Once all the key areas had been reviewed and if necessary amended, the code on substantive law could be created through consolidation. There would be nothing to prevent further areas of substantive law from being added to the new code as and when that was possible.

[34] *Legislating the Criminal Code: Offences against the Person and General Principles* (Law Com No 218, 1993). Originally, the government had accepted the first part of this report in principle, but on implementation see n 14 in this Chapter.
[35] *Legislating the Criminal Code: Involuntary Manslaughter* (n 31).
[36] *Offences of Dishonesty: Money Transfers* (Law Com No 243, 1996). The Law Commission issued its final report in July 2002: *Fraud* (Law Com No 271, 2002).
[37] The Law Commission issued a consultation paper on fraud in April 1999: *Legislating the Criminal Code: Fraud and Deception* (CP No 155 (1999)). For the terms of the reference by the Home Secretary, see Hansard, HL vol 588, col 119 WA (7 April 1998).
[38] *Legislating the Criminal Code: Corruption* (Law Com No 248, 1998). The government has not yet announced its response to this report.
[39] *Criminal Law: Offences Relating to Public Order* (HC 85, 1983).
[40] Hansard, HC vol 324, col WA 80–81 (25 January 1999). The Law Commission later contributed a policy paper, *Consent in Sex Offences* (2000), to this review, which led to the Sexual Offences Act 2003.

Those additional areas might include defences of general application,[41] jurisdiction,[42] and the liability of accessories.[43]

That leaves the law on evidence in criminal cases and the law of procedure. The main areas to be dealt with in any evidence code would be hearsay and previous misconduct. These two areas were referred to the Law Commission by the Home Secretary in the light of recommendations made by the Royal Commission on Criminal Justice.[44] The Law Commission has already published its report on hearsay,[45] and its recommendations have been accepted in full by the government.[46] It is expected that the Law Commission will publish its report *Evidence in Criminal Proceedings: Previous Misconduct of a Defendant* in the near future.[47] So far as procedure is concerned, there are a large number of statutory provisions, including the Police and Criminal Evidence Act 1984, which could be usefully drawn into a single code. One candidate for inclusion would be the Bail Act 1976. The Law Commission has recently begun a project on bail. The aim of the project is to see how far the principles which presently govern the grant of bail are compatible with Convention rights; the Law Commission expects to publish a consultation paper on this in 1999.[48]

Benefits of a criminal code

When the concept of the criminal code is examined in this way, it becomes clear that we have made progress towards achieving a criminal code. As noted by Lord Bingham, the Lord Chief Justice, in the speech cited at the beginning of this chapter, the chief advantages of a code are enhanced accessibility, clarity, coherence, and certainty. The Law Commission has also stressed the constitutional arguments in favour of a criminal code: 'The criminal law controls the exercise of state power against citizens, and the protection of citizens against unlawful behaviour, and it is

---

[41] See *Legislating the Criminal Code: Offences against the Person and General Principles* (Law Com No 218, 1993) Pt II, which was implemented but only in part by the Domestic Violence, Crime and Victims Act 2004. The Law Commission now has a new project on offences against the person. (see n 14 in this Chapter)

[42] As to which see the Criminal Justice Act 1999, Pt I which implemented the Law Commission's Report, *Criminal Law: Jurisdiction over Offences of Fraud and Dishonesty with a Foreign Element* (HC 318, 1989).

[43] The Law Commission has already issued a consultation paper, *Assisting and Encouraging Crime* (CP No 131, 1993), but the project has not yet been completed. In the course of the project, the House of Lords reconsidered the law on joint enterprise in *R v Powell; R v English* [1997] 3 WLR 959.

[44] *Report of the Royal Commission on Criminal Justice* (Cmd 2263, 1993) Ch 8, paras 26 and 30.

[45] *Evidence in Criminal Proceedings: Hearsay and Related Topics* (Law Com No 245, 1997).

[46] Hansard, HC vol 322, col 725W (17 December 1998). The report was implemented by the Criminal Justice Act 2003.

[47] The Law Commission issued both a consultation paper (CP No 141, 1996) and a final report (Cmd 5257). The title of the report was *Evidence of Bad Character in Criminal Proceedings*. Its recommendations were also implemented by the Criminal Justice Act 2003.

[48] The Law Commission issued a consultation paper (CP No 157, 1999) and on 20 June 2001 its final report, *Bail and the Human Rights Act 1998* (Law Com No 269, 2001), which was also implemented by the Criminal Justice Act 2003.

important that its rules should be determined by Parliament and not by the sometimes haphazard methods of the common law.'[49]

The position in England may be contrasted with that in Canada. A Canadian citizen can buy a copy of the Canadian Criminal Code in a bookshop for the modest sum of Can $25. The Code is republished annually to take account of any changes in the law. A policeman can carry it in his pocket. It even has specimen charges in it. The Canadian Criminal Code is also a useful precedent for any future criminal code for this country for another reason: it abolishes common law *offences*, but preserves common law *defences*,[50] and this should in my view be the approach in any new English criminal code.

A further advantage of having a criminal code is that it is likely to lead to savings in court time and this will reduce the cost of the criminal justice system for the state and the citizen. The court would need less time to consider the law and hear argument on it, and there should be fewer appeals. In addition, if there were a criminal code, it would be easier to keep it up to date than the present law. The law has to be kept up to date whether there is a criminal code or not, but once it is organized into a modern, carefully-considered and well-drafted code it will be easier to monitor and amend in future.

These are powerful arguments for a criminal code. In the last century, the Indian Penal Code was devised by distinguished lawyers from this country, including Lord Macaulay and Sir James Fitzjames Stephen. It has been amended from time to time but it otherwise remains in force today. It is encouraging to note how well this has worked: writing in 1966, MP Jain wrote:

The code has been very successful. It has stood the test of time very well. A proof of its intrinsic worth and merit may be found in the fact that during the last century that it has been in force it has not been found necessary to amend it except only a few times, and substantially the code subsists as it was enacted in 1860.[51]

Codification also offers a way of doing a systematic audit of substantive criminal law to ensure that it complies with the Human Rights Act 1998.

Conclusion

There continue to be serious delays in the acceptance and implementation of Law Commission reports on criminal law. The criminal law can be likened to a traveller who has been travelling for some time down the road and has now come to a crossroads. It has been a long journey and the road stretches a long way ahead into the distance. The road is in bad condition and little has been done to put it in order. The traveller passes a sign. It says: 'There are several major unimplemented Law

---

[49] 27th Annual Report 1992 (HC 518, 1993) para 2.15.
[50] Canadian Criminal Code, s 8.
[51] MP Jain, *Outlines of Indian Legal History* (2nd edn, Tripathi, 1966) xxiv, 'Codification of Law', 655–6, passage cited by Lord Bingham LCJ in 'A Criminal Code' (n 3).

Commission reports on criminal law.' With a heavy heart he gets to the crossroads. He can either take the path which starts with a little uphill climb and then brings him to a green and verdant land or he can take the road which leads downhill into the marshy land, beset with difficulty, where he will get bogged down. The criminal law faces a choice. The choice is between having a strategy and an overall vision of a well-considered, consistent, coherent, and modern criminal law on the one hand, and on the other hand patching up an area of law which is already seriously defective and out of date under a policy of mend and make do. The right choice is obvious: it is the former path which entails the adoption over time of a criminal code. But this needs courage and political will. It needs the support of the judiciary and the profession. It will also take time and effort, but, as I see it, it is the only course that will lead to the real improvement in the criminal law that many would like to see.

15

Companies Act 2006

A New Approach to Directors' Duties

This chapter is based on a lecture given at the University of Sydney in 2007.*

A radical departure

The United Kingdom enacted its first codified statement of the duties of directors in the Companies Act 2006 ('the 2006 Act'). This chapter explains the thinking behind this statutory statement and points out that it reflects the 'enlightened shareholder' model of directors' duties. This means that directors must promote the success of the company for the benefit of its members, rather than for the benefit of different interest groups, but at the same time they must have regard to the interests of other parties which contribute to the company's success. This chapter evaluates the new provisions.

The 2006 Act is the largest UK Act ever, having over 1,300 sections and seventeen Schedules. Its size, however, is not the only thing that makes this Act remarkable. For, although much is not new, and merely consolidates earlier legislation, the new Act does make significant changes in some areas. In particular, for the first time, there is a codified statement of the general fiduciary duties of directors. Previously, the general law, not the Companies Acts, governed the fiduciary duties of directors. The case law is extensive. Given the quantity of case law on the subject, the codification of directors' duties is ambitious and can to some degree be compared with the codifications of commercial law in the nineteenth century.[1] So the codification of directors' duties is a new radical departure for UK company law, but it is debatable to what extent the content of the codified statement does more than merely reflect existing good practice.

* Published in (2007) 81 Australian Law Journal 159 and reprinted with the kind permission of Thomson Reuters (Professional) Australia Ltd.

[1] See generally, Ch 13, *Time for an English Commercial Code?*

History of the reforms

It has become traditional in the United Kingdom to have a new Companies Act about once every twenty years. In the second half of the twentieth century Parliament got into the habit of amending company law by a series of smaller Acts and then having a consolidation Act. Thus the Companies Act 1948 was amended in 1967, 1980, 1981, and 1983 and the resulting Acts were then consolidated in 1985 by the Companies Act 1985. Over time it became clear that there were many shortcomings, particularly in relation to the statutory restrictions on transactions between directors and their companies (such as loans, service agreements, compensation for loss of office, and so on),[2] and the prohibition on a company providing financial assistance for the purpose of a purchase of its own shares.

The Department of Trade and Industry (DTI)—the UK government department with primary responsibility for company law—held a number of consultation exercises on particular areas that needed reform and built up a 'blood bank' of ideas for reform after the consolidation but these all came to naught. Then, in about 1995, the DTI conceived the idea that the Law Commission of England and Wales, together with the Scottish Law Commission, might be able to help. Unlike the Law Commission of New Zealand, the Law Commission of England and Wales had not previously been asked to make any recommendations in the field of company law. The first project on company law was one on shareholder remedies. In due course the DTI gave the Law Commissions a second project on company law. The terms of reference were to consider whether there should be a statutory statement of directors' duties and also whether there should be any amendments to the complex provisions on statutory restrictions on transactions between directors and their companies.

As Chairman of the Law Commission of England and Wales from January 1996 to the end of January 1999, I was involved in much of the work on both projects. The reports of the Law Commissions on shareholder remedies and directors' duties made a material contribution to the important changes to the law made by the 2006 Act.

The way the Law Commission dealt with the project on shareholder remedies[3] was to identify the principles that ought to underpin the law on shareholder remedies[4] and this approach was repeated when the question of codifying directors'

---

[2] Following a series of scandals in the 1970s and 1980s, Parliament introduced a whole raft of extra rules for directors designed to reinforce the normal fiduciary duties. They included prohibitions on substantial property transactions and long service contracts without the prior consent of the company in general meeting.

[3] *Shareholder Remedies* (Law Com No 246, 1997).

[4] The principal recommendation in the Law Commission's report, *Shareholder Remedies*, was that there should be a statutory derivative action in place of the rule in *Foss v Harbottle* (1843) Hare 461, (1843) 67 ER 189, which governed the circumstances in which a minority shareholder could sue on behalf of his company.

duties was considered.[5] The methodology was important because it made possible a review from first principles. The same approach was adopted in the project on directors' duties.

In 1998 the DTI decided to set up its own review of the whole of company law, known as the Company Law Review. That review was conducted by a Steering Group, of which I was also a member. The composition of the Steering Group was carefully chosen to ensure representation of the major interest groups in company law, including not only lawyers but also accountants, financial journalists, directors, and economists.

The Steering Group of the Company Law Review applied the same methodology as the Law Commission. It sought to identify the guiding principles for legislation on the relevant topic. It also made a practice of consulting widely on any problem that it discovered and any provisional recommendation that it made. All these factors put the Steering Group in a strong position to conduct a major rethink of company law from the bottom up.

The Company Law Review considered questions arising across the full width of company law, and its final report was presented to the Secretary of State for Trade and Industry in July 2001. In July 2002, the government published a White Paper accepting most of the recommendations. It then started preparing the new Companies Bill. This was finally introduced into Parliament in November 2005.

Why codify directors' duties?

The United Kingdom did not have even the most general statement of the duties of directors in its Companies Acts prior to the 2006 Act. Accordingly, it has gone in one move from a Companies Act with no statutory statement of directors' duties to one which has a comprehensive statement of the general duties of directors. The statement will apply in place of the equivalent duties imposed on directors under the general law.

The question whether the duties of directors should be codified has exercised the United Kingdom for over a hundred years. So why did it opt for a comprehensive codified statement at this stage? The answer is that the climate of opinion had changed. Codification of directors' duties had previously been seen as the search for the Holy Grail, on the grounds that it would be virtually impossible to express in the words of the statute all the intricacies and nuances of the general law. Today, however, the imperative is to improve corporate governance, and the codification of directors' duties is seen as having a role to play in this process. If it reflects best practice, it will guide all directors towards higher standards. Codification should also make the law more accessible to directors and their advisers. Empirical research done for the Law Commissions showed widespread support among serving directors for

---

[5] In their joint report, _Company Directors: Regulating Conflicts of interests and Formulating a Statement of Duties_ (Law Com No 261, Scot Law Com No 173, 1999), the Law Commissions recommended that there should be statutory statement of directors' duties.

a statutory statement of directors' duties. This was particularly the case among private companies, where the directors often did not have access to legal advice. Thus the current approach towards codification of directors' duties is that it is not just a question of lawyers' law but can play an essential part in making positive improvements in corporate governance. It is important to note that the Law Commissions were not concerned with the question whether there should be any change to the content of directors' duties.

Guiding principles of company law

As I have said, the Company Law Review followed the approach of the Law Commission in identifying the principles on which any new legislation should be based. It came to the conclusion that there were certain high level general principles that ought to apply to company law. I will merely mention those which are relevant to the codification of directors' duties. First, the Steering Group considered that the law on directors' duties should be accessible and clear. Second, the Steering Group took the view that company law generally had to be enabling rather than prescriptive in its approach. In other words all aspects of regulation had to be justified. Third, the Steering Group identified the need for company law to be efficient in its operation and to enhance international competitiveness, which has always been a major issue for British company law. Fourth, the Steering Group emphasized that any new companies legislation had to recognize the modern asset mix of companies. In the past, companies had in the main had tangible assets such as mining gear, or railway rolling stock. The modern company's assets often consist of human resources and intellectual property.

This last point may seem mundane, but in my view is more important than it appears. In effect the Steering Group of the Company Law Review was saying that times had changed. The attitude of well-run companies to those groups which were essential for the success of the company had changed. This is so, for instance, in relation to employees. In Victorian times, when the first Companies Act was passed, company law treated employees rather like tangible assets and companies generally did not seek to foster their relationships with them. These days, running a company is seen much more as a collaborative exercise between employees and management. Thus the reference here to the change in asset mix is a reference to a much more fundamental change in the approach that good businesses adopt to their relationships with employees and indeed all the other groups involved in the business, such as suppliers, the community, and so on.

When the Steering Group of the Company Law Review issued its final report, it made three major recommendations. First, it recommended that company law be rebased around the private company, treating the rules for public companies as exceptions to the general rule. This contrasts with the normal approach in the Companies Act of treating the public company as the norm and the private company as the exception. Today, the number of private companies vastly exceeds the number of public limited companies. The second main recommendation was to improve corporate governance. This was to be done in a number of ways but principally by defining directors' duties. The third major recommendation was for institutional structures to keep company law up to date. The government did not accept this recommendation, and I need say no more about it.

The stakeholder question

The decision that directors' duties should be codified immediately led to a debate as to what has become known as the stakeholder question. In other words, before you can codify directors' duties, it is necessary to decide in whose interest companies should be run. Should they be run in the interests of employees or in the interests of shareholders or in the interests of the community? There were two principal schools of thought about the answer to this question:

(1) The school of thought known as pluralism: the company is to serve the interests of many different interest groups or stakeholders: shareholders, employees, the community, and so on. People who adopt this way of thinking consider that the duties of directors should be widened so that they are owed to a wider group of people than the shareholders.

(2) The school of thought known as enlightened self-interest: namely the purpose of the company is to create value for the benefit of shareholders but this should be done by taking a long-term view of the company, and thus the relationships which the company has with suppliers, employees, the community, and so on have to be fostered.

The Company Law Review preferred the enlightened shareholder value approach. This acknowledges that at the end of the day it is the interests of shareholders which count. It is the interests of shareholders which give motivation to investors and directors to maximize profits for the benefit of the nation's economy. However, the approach is said to be enlightened when it proceeds on the basis that a company's potential for success can best be realized through maximizing the relationships which the company enjoys with stakeholder groups. What tends to happen in practice is that some boards take the view that their duty to act in the best interests of shareholders under the existing law requires them to take short-term decisions to obtain short-term profits. This view is undesirable for a number of reasons, not least because the brunt of these decisions is often borne by other groups who have also contributed to the success of the company. Well-run companies today appreciate the role of these groups.

The Company Law Review therefore took the view that directors' duties should be stated in statutory form in a manner which reflected best practice, that is to say which reflected both the need to make profits for shareholders but also the need to consider the interests of other stakeholder groups. In this way, the time horizons for decision-making would be improved and the directors guided towards a more enlightened approach to relationships with third parties, such as employees and suppliers.

Technical difficulties of codification

Opponents of codification argue that the process of codification will inadvertently alter the law, and more importantly that it stultifies development. They contend that codification also leads to higher transaction costs as there is an increased need for directors to take advice, at least when the restatement is first enacted. They also make the point that codifying statutes become less accessible over time once the courts have started interpreting them.

As against these points, however, it has to be borne in mind that at the present time the duties of directors have to be deduced from large quantities of case law. Codification of directors' duties makes the law clearer and more accessible to directors and their advisers at least to some degree. This should help directors in practice because directors are frequently called upon to make speedy decisions. Yet it must also be recognized that the codification of directors' duties presented a unique challenge to those responsible for the drafting. The statement had on the one hand to be clear and accessible and to make the law more predictable, and yet on the other hand not to be such that fiduciary duties would lose their flexibility or that the codified statement should hinder the development of the law by the courts.

The other potential advantage of codification was that it would provide an opportunity to correct minor defects in the present law. There were certain situations in which fiduciary duties no longer corresponded to accepted norms of modern business behaviour. Accordingly, there are two areas where the statutory statement of directors' duties departs from the existing law. Both concern corporate opportunities and will be examined in the context of the relevant clause.

New provisions

The principal provisions on directors' duties are found in ss 178 to 191 of the Companies Act 2006. In the following paragraphs I shall explain some of the features of the new sections.

1. Shareholder orientation

The general duties of directors[6] are stated to be owed to the company. Therefore codification of the directors' duties by the 2006 Act does not open up the prospect of the duties being enforced by persons other than the company or members acting on its behalf.

---

[6] These are: the duty to act within powers; the duty to promote the success of the company; the duty to exercise independent judgment; the duty of reasonable care, skill, and diligence; the duty not to accept benefits from third parties; and the duty to declare an interest in a proposed transaction or arrangement.

2. To whom do the duties apply?

There are three categories of directors to whom the duties apply in different ways:

(1) Directors in office are subject to all the duties.

(2) Former directors are subject to certain aspects of the fiduciary duties even after they have ceased to be directors. These duties include the duty not to exploit opportunities of which a director became aware while he was a director. The statutory statement thus applies to a former director with necessary modifications.[7]

(3) Shadow directors[8] are subject to some of the duties as if they were directors formally appointed. The statutory statement of directors' duties provides for this to continue to be the position.[9]

3. Extensive substitution but codification not exclusive

Some seven duties are codified,[10] making the statement of directors' duties an extensive one.

Section 170(3) of the 2006 Act provides that the codified duties take the place of the common law rules and equitable principles as regards the duties owed to a company by a director.[11] This means that the codified duties are to be substituted for the equivalent duties under the general law. However, the codified statement of directors' duties does not exclude the possibility that there may be a duty which has not been codified. Such a duty will continue to exist.

4. Interpretation

There is a very important provision in s 170(4) of the 2006 Act:

The general duties set out in the statutory statement shall be interpreted and applied in the same way as common rules or equitable principles, and regard shall be had to the corresponding common law rules and equitable principles in interpreting and applying the general duties.

It will be extremely interesting to see how the courts deal with this novel provision. Statutory interpretation in the United Kingdom has moved on considerably in recent years due to the doctrine of primacy of EU law (which requires UK courts to disapply legislation which is inconsistent with EU law) and due also to the statutory obligation in s 3 of the Human Rights Act 1998 to interpret legislation so far as

---

[7] Section 170(2).
[8] A shadow director is defined in s 251 as 'a person in accordance with whose directions or instructions the directors of the company are accustomed to act'.
[9] See s 170(5).   [10] See n 6.
[11] Section 170(3) provides: '(3) The general duties are based on certain common law rules and equitable principles as they apply in relation to directors and have effect in place of those rules and principles as regards the duties owed to a company by a director.'

possible in conformity with the rights conferred by the European Convention on Human Rights ('the Convention') . These methods of interpretation may result in the court adopting a strained interpretation.

The first task of the court when faced with a problem of interpreting the newly codified duties will be to identify the relevant common law rule or equitable principle. These are rules and principles developed by the courts. It could be said that the court should have regard only to the common law rules and equitable principles as developed by the courts prior to the enactment of the 2006 Act. It seems unlikely that such a result was intended, since in theory the courts do not change the law by their later decisions but merely declare it. In those circumstances it is doubtful whether the courts will be limited to the law as it stood prior to the 2006 Act. Of course, the general law on directors' duties codified by the 2006 Act will be replaced by the Act and will therefore not itself develop further in the courts of England and Wales, but many of the fiduciary duties owed by company directors are owed by other fiduciaries, and the general law formerly applying to directors may therefore be said to have developed as part of the development of the law regarding the duties owed by agents in similar positions. Moreover, the courts may decide that the way that the general law on the fiduciary duties of directors is developed in other common law jurisdictions also represents the law of England and Wales. These are some of the questions which the courts may in due course have to decide under this section.[12]

The remedies which flow from breach of a fiduciary duty under the general law often differ from those available for other breaches. The remedies available for breach of fiduciary duty are preserved by s 178 of the 2006 Act. Accordingly the rule that the evidential burden of proof shifts to the defaulting fiduciary when an account of profits is ordered would seem to be preserved.[13]

5. Duty to act within powers

Section 171 of the 2006 Act imposes the familiar duty that directors should act within their powers and that they should use their powers for purposes for which they were conferred.[14] The main authority in England on the latter point is *Howard Smith Ltd v Ampol Petroleum Ltd*,[15] a decision of the Privy Council on appeal from the Supreme Court of New South Wales.

---

[12] See Bennion, *Statutory Interpretation* (4th edn, Butterworths, 2002) 762 et seq. The recent case of *Harding v Wealands* [2006] UKHL 32, [2007] 2 AC 1 is an interesting example of a case where the House of Lords declined to apply an updating interpretation. In that case the words were 'questions of procedure' appearing in a statute in the field of private international law.

[13] See generally *Murad v Al Saraj* [2005] EWCA Civ 959, (2006) 65 Camb LJ 278, (2006) 122 LQR 11, applying the decision of the High Court of Australia in *Warman International v Dwyer* (1995) CLR 544.

[14] Section 171 provides: 'A director of a company must—(a) act in accordance with the company's constitution, and (b) only exercise powers for the purposes for which they are conferred.'

[15] [1974] AC 821.

6. The duty to promote the success of the company

The duty to promote the success of the company in s 172[16] of the 2006 Act replaces the fiduciary duty to act in what the director in good faith considers to be in the interests of the company. The duty remains a duty owed to the company and the company alone.

Section 172 enshrines the principle of enlightened shareholder value. The directors must have particular regard to the factors listed. The list is not exhaustive but highlights areas of particular importance.

The weight to be given to particular matters will remain a matter for the judgment of the directors. It seems unlikely that the courts would be required to substitute their views on such matters for those of the directors. In identifying the relevant considerations, the directors will be expected to act with reasonable skill and care in accordance with the further duty considered next.

Section 172 states that a director must 'have regard' to relevant matters. This does not mean that a director must act with the aim of furthering those matters, for example the interests of the company's employees. They must give these matters appropriate weight. However, lip service is unlikely to constitute appropriate consideration. A director must genuinely take the relevant matters into account, but his decision need not be dictated by them if that is not, in his good faith opinion, appropriate for the purpose of promoting the success of the company as a whole. The relevant matters are often set out in the papers presented to the board of directors, and directors will generally be able to rely on such papers having been properly prepared. Board minutes are always important, and it would be sensible for directors to ensure that the minutes identify the relevant considerations for the purpose of section 172(2). However, where there are board papers, the minutes can often do this by reference to the board papers.

The existing fiduciary duty of loyalty is capable of adaptation and application in many situations. For example, in *Item Software v Fassihi*,[17] the facts were that one director advised the other on negotiations with a major supplier with whom he had already been in negotiations privately and personally with a view to setting up his own business and taking that supplier with him. He advised his fellow director to insist on terms which he knew the supplier would not anticipate in the expectation

---

[16] The main provision is s 172(1):

> (1) A director of a company must act in the way he considers, in good faith, would be most likely to promote the success of the company for the benefit of its members as a whole, and in doing so have regard (amongst other matters) to—
> (a) the likely consequences of any decision in the long term,
> (b) the interests of the company's employees,
> (c) the need to foster the company's business relationships with suppliers, customers and others,
> (d) the impact of the company's operations on the community and the environment,
> (e) the desirability of the company maintaining a reputation for high standards of business conduct, and
> (f) the need to act fairly as between members of the company.

[17] [2005] 2 BCLC 91.

that those negotiations would fail and he would be able to set up his company and obtain the source of supply for his own benefit. He did not succeed in obtaining any benefit for himself so that all the company could sue him for was his failure to disclose his own breach of duty to the company. It was held that the director was in breach of the duty to act in the best interests of the company when he gave advice without disclosing his conflict of interest and breach of duty. So it was unnecessary to find that there was a so far unknown duty owed by a fiduciary to disclose his own wrong doing. The answer was found by explicating the traditional duty of loyalty.

7. Duty to exercise independent judgment

Section 173 of the 2006 Act requires a director to exercise independent judgment, but this does not prevent him from entering into an agreement which fetters his discretion or from delegating his powers in accordance with the company's constitution.[18]

8. Duty to exercise reasonable care and diligence

Historically the duty owed by directors was treated as predominantly subjective. The relevant test was how much skill should a person with this particular director's knowledge and experience show. If the company chose an incompetent director, the company had no remedy. However, the courts developed the law. Section 174 of the 2006 Act reflects the law as it has now evolved:

(1) A director of a company must exercise reasonable care, skill and diligence.
(2) This means the care, skill and diligence that would be exercised by a reasonably diligent person with—
    (a) the general knowledge, skill and experience that may reasonably be expected of a person carrying out the functions carried out by the director in relation to the company, and
    (b) the general knowledge, skill and experience that the director has.

It will be noted that s 174 of the 2006 Act does not provide for a business judgment rule as in Australia. Under s 180(2) of the Australian Corporations Act 2001, the business judgment rule provides a safe harbour for directors who take decisions acting in good faith and for a proper purpose, having properly informed themselves of the matter in advance, having no conflict of interest, and rationally believing that the transaction is in the corporation's best interests. When the business judgment rule applies, the director is deemed not to have committed a breach of his statutory duty of care and diligence.

---

[18] Section 173 provides:
    (1) A director of a company must exercise independent judgment.
    (2) This duty is not infringed by his acting—
        (a) in accordance with an agreement duly entered into by the company that restricts the future exercise of discretion by its directors, or
        (b) in a way authorised by the company's constitution.

However, like the Australian courts, the UK courts now appreciate that in large modern corporations, there is a distinction between oversight and management. A director may very well be in the position simply of making decisions on the basis of information provided by other people. Every company must have a system of control to ensure that full and accurate information is disclosed. Only in that way can directors inform themselves about the company's affairs. This means that the nature and extent of the duty of skill, care, and diligence will depend on such factors as the size, location, and complexity of a company's business and the urgency of any decision.

Some directors have special skills. For example, they may have special knowledge or professional qualifications. The formulation in s 174 takes account of the special background, qualifications, and management responsibilities of a particular director. The standard of skill and care expected from such a person is correspondingly greater. On the other hand, a director is not excused because he lacks the basic attributes that a director should have.

Directors hold different types of responsibilities, for example non-executive directors will have less burdensome duties than those imposed on financial or other executive directors. The formulation in s 174 accepts this differentiation and takes account of it by relating the knowledge, skill, and experience that may be expected of a director to the functions which he performs.

9. Duty to avoid conflicts of interest

Section 175[19] of the 2006 Act deals with conflicts of interest. It is to be noted that the general law about liability to account for secret profits has been converted into a

---

[19] Section 175 provides:

(1) A director of a company must avoid a situation in which he has, or can have, a direct or indirect interest that conflicts, or possibly may conflict, with the interests of the company.

(2) This applies in particular to the exploitation of any property, information or opportunity (and it is immaterial whether the company could take advantage of the property, information or opportunity).

(3) This duty does not apply to a conflict of interest arising in relation to a transaction or arrangement with the company.

(4) This duty is not infringed—
  (a) if the situation cannot reasonably be regarded as likely to give rise to a conflict of interest; or
  (b) if the matter has been authorised by the directors.

(5) Authorisation may be given by the directors—
  (a) where the company is a private company and nothing in the company's constitution invalidates such authorisation, by the matter being proposed to and authorised by the directors; or
  (b) where the company is a public company and its constitution includes provision enabling the directors to authorise the matter, by the matter being proposed to and authorised by them in accordance with the constitution.

(6) The authorisation is effective only if—
  (a) any requirement as to the quorum at the meeting at which the matter is considered is met without counting the director in question or any other interested director, and
  (b) the matter was agreed to without their voting or would have been agreed to if their votes had not been counted.

(7) Any reference in this section to a conflict of interest includes a conflict of interest and duty and a conflict of duties.

duty. Hitherto a director had not owed a company a duty not to become a director of a company with a competing business, provided always that he did not disclose confidential information or misappropriate property of the company. However, s 170(4) may require s 175 to be interpreted in accordance with the pre-existing law.

The duty is not infringed if the situation cannot be regarded as likely to give rise to a conflict of interest.[20] This reflects the better view of the law expressed by Lord Upjohn in *Boardman v Phipps*.[21]

Contrary to the existing law, transactions or arrangements in which a director is interested will not always have to be approved by the company in general meeting. There are two new exceptions to this rule in s 175(5), and these are the two respects in which the law of directors' duties has been expressly changed by the codified statement of their duties. In a private company, unless the articles otherwise require, the board of directors will be able to give the necessary approval. This will also be possible in a public company if its constitution enables directors to give approval in these circumstances. These changes were made to facilitate the exploitation of corporate opportunities which might otherwise be left to waste because of the expense of convening a general meeting of shareholders.

10. Duty not to accept benefits from third parties

This is covered by s 176 of the 2006 Act.[22] Unlike the duty covered by the previous section, this duty is not subject to any provision for board authorization. The duty is not infringed if the benefit is unlikely to result in a conflict of interest.

11. Duty to declare interest in proposed transaction or arrangement

Section 177 of the 2006 Act replaces the familiar rule.[23] Companies may impose additional requirements for approval in their articles. There must be proper disclosure of the nature and extent of the interest, but a director is not required to make disclosure if his fellow directors already know of his interest.[24] These provisions reflect recent case law. Nor is the director in breach if he could not reasonably have been aware of the matters requiring disclosure.[25] The extent to which an interested director may participate in decision-making with regard to a transaction in which he has an interest depends on the articles.

[20] Section 175(4). [21] [1967] 2 AC 46.
[22] Section 176(1) provides: '(1) A director of a company must not accept a benefit from a third party conferred by reason of—(a) his being a director, or (b) his doing (or not doing) anything as director.'
[23] Section 177(1) provides: 'If a director of a company is in any way, directly or indirectly, interested in a proposed transaction or arrangement with the company, he must declare the nature and extent of that interest to the other directors.'
[24] Section 177(6)(b). [25] Section 177(5).

12. Breach

The consequences of a breach of duty are the same as under an existing law.[26]

13. Prior sanction

The current law on prior authorization of what would have been a breach of duty is preserved.[27]

14. Insolvency

Section 172(3) of the 2006 Act states that the new duty of loyalty 'has effect subject to any enactment or rule of law requiring directors, in certain circumstances, to consider or act in the interests of creditors of the company'. Thus, s 172(3) recognizes that the duty of loyalty may be displaced when the company becomes insolvent. The 2006 Act does not deal with the obligations of directors when a company is approaching insolvency because the law in this area is unclear and the decision was taken to leave the law to develop in this area. Once a company becomes insolvent, certain acts of a director may not only be in breach of his fiduciary duties. He may also in a serious case incur liability for wrongful trading under s 214 of the Insolvency Act 1986.

In its final report, the Company Law Review referred to two approaches. The first is that, as the company became insolvent, the directors should consider the interest of creditors and not just those members. Thus directors would need to have regard to creditors as the company approached insolvency and not just when the company actually became insolvent. Supporters of this approach point to authorities such as *Nicholson v Permakraft*,[28] a decision of the Court of Appeal of New Zealand where Cooke J held that, as a matter of business ethics, directors should consider whether what they do would prejudice their company's practical ability to discharge promptly debts owed to current and likely continuing creditors. This is not so much a duty to creditors as a duty to the company itself. The second approach is that such a rule would lead to great uncertainty and have a chilling effect on decision-making by directors. As I have said, the 2006 Act leaves the general law to develop on this point.

15. Cumulative effect

In any given situation more than one duty may apply.

---

[26] Section 178.   [27] Section 180.   [28] [1985] 1 NZLR 242.

16. Ratification

The general law is preserved by s 239 of the 2006 Act,[29] save that the votes of the directors involved and their connected persons are disregarded unless the resolution is passed by unanimous consent. Previously directors could vote on any resolution for ratification of their own acts amounting to breach of duty unless the passing of the resolution by use of their votes amounted to what was called a fraud on the minority. Under this exception, a member who sought to challenge such a resolution would have to show that the wrongdoers controlled the company and that the resolution gave the majority some benefit of which the minority were deprived. These rules have now been changed. However, the rule that there must be full and frank disclosure before any resolution is put to the company in general meeting is not affected. Nor is the rule that ratification is not possible when the company is insolvent or is nearing insolvency.

Concluding points

1. Process challenges

Some people have expressed concern that the new duty to promote the success of the company will encourage people to challenge board decisions on the grounds that the board has failed to take into account all relevant considerations. Alternatively, they say that the new duty to have regard to a number of matters will lead to a 'compliance driven' approach which is equally damaging because it leads to a slowing down of the process of decision-making and to a concentration on form rather than substance.

It is likely that at least when the 2006 Act is first brought into force there will be a number of challenges to decisions made by boards of companies in circumstances where such challenges would not previously have lain. That is only natural. Moreover, process challenges are familiar in public law or when the exercise by a

---

[29] The material parts of s 239 provide:

(1) This section applies to the ratification by a company of conduct by a director amounting to negligence, default, breach of duty or breach of trust in relation to the company.

(2) The decision of the company to ratify such conduct must be made by resolution of the members of the company

. . .

(4) Where the resolution is proposed at a meeting, it is passed only if the necessary majority is obtained disregarding votes in favour of the resolution by the director (if a member of the company) and any member connected with him. This does not prevent the director or any such member from attending, being counted towards the quorum and taking part in the proceedings at any meeting at which the decision is considered . . .

. . .

(6) Nothing in this section affects—
(a) the validity of a decision taken by unanimous consent of the members of the company, or
(b) any power of the directors to agree not to sue, or to settle or release a claim made by them on behalf of the company.

judge of his or her discretion is challenged. However, company law is different. First, there is no basis on which one party to a transaction could seek to assert that a decision was not binding on the other party, simply because the board of directors of that other party had failed in the proper performance of their duties to consider the interests of some group or other. If directors come to a decision which is in breach of duty, the decision is voidable at the instance only of the company to whom the duties are owed. Thus the counterparty to a transaction will not be in a position to challenge the transaction on the grounds of a breach of duty by the directors.

The only persons who can challenge a breach of duty by directors of a company are the company itself, or its liquidator, or a member suing on behalf of the company and using the new derivative action procedure discussed later, or using relief granted by the court in unfair prejudice proceedings. If there has been no change of management or insolvency, the company itself is unlikely to want to sue, even if the directors negligently fail to take into account the interests of some particular group. Likewise, a liquidator is unlikely to sue unless there is a reasonable prospect of damages. Under the 2006 Act, the ability of a member to sue on behalf of the company will be heavily circumscribed by the new derivative action procedure.

2. Link between the codification of directors' duties and the new derivative action

So far as the members are concerned, any legal proceedings which they bring on behalf of the company against the directors will have to be brought within the very strict rules on derivative actions introduced by other provisions of the 2006 Act. So far as the law of England and Wales is concerned, the original purpose of the new statutory derivative action procedure was simply to implement the recommendation of the Law Commission that there should be a statutory procedure to replace the old rule in *Foss v Harbottle*.[30] It will be recalled that members wishing to bring derivative actions had to bring themselves within the exceptions to that ancient rule and that the exceptions were not available where it was alleged that a director had acted negligently. In addition the meaning of wrongdoer control (which had to be established if the member relied on the exception for fraud on the minority) was unclear. The Law Commission recommended that it should be possible to bring a derivative action for negligence against a director as well as an action for breach of fiduciary duty, provided that certain conditions were fulfilled. That situation will now be capable of being the subject of a derivative action.

However, when the Bill which became the 2006 Act was introduced there was much discussion as to whether the new statutory statement of directors' duties and the new derivative action procedure would lead to an increase in litigation against company directors. There have been some large settlements in cases brought against

---

[30] (1843) Hare 461, (1843) 67 ER 189.

directors in the United States, for example in cases involving Enron, WorldCom, and Global Crossing. To meet this concern, the new provisions were strengthened to make it unlikely that the new statutory derivative action would result in an increase of shareholder litigation in the United Kingdom.

Section 260 of the 2006 Act defines what is meant by a derivative claim. It has to involve a claim against a director under s 260(3). Section 261 deals with the procedure for obtaining the court's permission to continue a derivative action. Permission of the court is required under the existing procedure in England and Wales.[31] Section 261 provides that the court must dismiss the application if there is no prima facie case for granting permission. If that hurdle is crossed, the court goes on to consider whether to grant permission. Section 263 sets out the criteria to be applied by the court in deciding whether to give permission. This section was inserted to allay the fears of some business people that the new statutory derivative action would lead to US-style class actions. In particular the court must not give permission if a person acting in performance of his duty of loyalty as a director would not seek to continue the action on behalf of the company; and the court must have particular regard to any evidence before it as to the views of members of the company who have no personal interest, direct or indirect, in the matter. In addition the court must not give permission if the action has been authorized or ratified by the company. When giving permission, the court can impose conditions. The Secretary of State is given power to specify further criteria.

Accordingly, where what has occurred is merely a failure in the process of decision-making by directors required by s 172 of the 2006 Act, with no adverse financial effect on the company, it is difficult to see that any court would give permission for a derivative action to be brought.

3. Evaluation of the new codification

The codification of directors' duties in the 2006 Act is extremely ambitious. However, it has been carefully considered over many years. The work in this field began with the inception in 1998 of the Law Commissions' project, *Company Directors: Regulating Conflicts of Interests and Formulating a Statement of Duties.* The Company Law Review took the matter forward and investigated the difficulties with great care. The DTI, too, on receiving the report of the Company Law Review, consulted very widely and considered all the available options. The approach of all three bodies was to seek to obtain consensus among the various groups interested in company law. The process has been long and drawn out and required much stamina.

The corporate vehicle is an ingenious institution for the creation of wealth, but opinion on how wealth should be created has changed in the period since its first creation. The codification of directors' duties in the 2006 Act serves to bring about the reconnection of the corporate vehicle with the society in which it operates. It is

---

[31] As of 2015, Civil Procedure Rules 19.9–19.9F, as supplemented by Practice Direction 19C—Derivative Claims.

likely to improve the quality of corporate decision-making with benefits for the rest of society. Over time it is also likely to lead to a much greater consciousness on the part of companies of the debt they owe to the other groups who contribute to their success, in particular employees and the communities in which they operate.

The codification of directors' duties in the 2006 Act could present an immense challenge to the courts if it gave rise to a great deal of litigation. The courts will have to ensure that the codified statement operates in accordance with the provisions of the 2006 Act. They will have to give effect to the direction in s 170(4) of the Act that the duties are to be interpreted and applied in the same way as common law rules or equitable principles. They will have to have regard to the corresponding common law rules and principles in that process. But the very existence of this direction may make it easier for the courts to make a transition from a set of duties based solely on a substantial body of case law to a codified set of duties with a more focused approach to case law.[32]

---

[32] As of 2015, the codification of directors' duties in the Companies Act 2006 appears to be working well in practice. The new provisions in ss 170–180 of the 2006 Act came into force in October 2007, save for ss 175–177 which came into force in October 2008. So far, there has been very little litigation about the interpretation of the new provisions.

SECTION C

TOMORROW'S JUDICIARY

So far, we have seen a range of ways in which the law has evolved in response to social change. But the judiciary itself needs to stay up to date too. One area I consider especially important is the quality of judgment writing: concise and clear judgments make the law more accessible and save the time of those whose job it is to interpret the law. Another priority is the need for judges to have social awareness, which would be helped if there were greater diversity in the judiciary. Diverse views and approaches also make for better decision-making by the courts. In addition, senior judges today need to have some knowledge of the laws outside the United Kingdom.

This volume concludes with two short pieces, Chapters 20 and 21, offering advice and encouragement to young barristers and women lawyers.

Preface by The Rt Hon Jack Straw

Lady Justice Arden has lost none of that enthusiasm for the law which fired her determination in the early 1970s to make a career at the almost-exclusively male world of the Bar.

In the years since, she has combined that enthusiasm with great distinction as a jurist, and a readiness to challenge those areas of the practice of the law which need it.

Mary Arden's concern better to connect the judiciary with the public it serves shines through in the first theme of this Part—about the prolixity and inaccessibility of many judgments of our higher courts. 'In my view', she says 'judgment writing... should to some degree serve the community in general, not simply the legal profession'. Hurrah to that. Unless the legal profession's prime purpose is to envelop the meaning of the law in dense text impenetrable to those outside the priesthood, the laity need to be able themselves to understand what the courts are handing down. As Mary Arden elegantly brings out, there's a paradox here: the internet has made the judgments of the courts available to all, but it has contributed to their being less accessible to all, through a near-tripling in the length of judgments, compared with Appeal Cases reports of a century ago. She makes many practical suggestions as to how judgments could be made shorter, and sweeter.

Next, Mary Arden takes us on a *tour d'horizon* from Magna Carta to the second decade of this century, to make the case for today's judiciary to be more socially aware, and better reflect the society it serves.

Not the least of the challenges, she rightly shows, is for the proportion of women in the senior judiciary to be raised from its lamentably low level today. Her arguments, which she advances with great passion and forensic skill, will not go away.

The Rt Hon Jack Straw

PART VI

THE FUTURE OF JUDGMENT WRITING

Judges have always in general been expected to give reasons for their decisions but in my view there is a case to be made for making judicial reasoning more accessible. I discuss this topic in *Are Shorter Judgments Achievable?* and *A Matter of Style*, Chapters 16 and 17 of this work.

At the appellate level at least, judgment writing is not just for the immediate parties but also, depending on the type of case, for a much wider audience, including the media and interested non-lawyers. The essence of a good appellate judgment is the same as the essence of a good appellate judge: breadth of thought, exactness of language, cohesion, courage, concision, and good sense. The danger in judgment writing is that judges may write in a 'watch me think' style. By that I mean that the reader is bound to follow the writer's process of thought without the conclusions being made clear at an early enough stage and without the ideas being structured for clarity, emphasis, and coherence. One thing I have tried in recent years is to summarize the issue and my conclusions near the start of the judgment, to help readers, including lawyers, to navigate easily and quickly round the document. Judgments of the appellate courts are often very long.

Are Shorter Judgments Achievable? has sparked off an ongoing debate within the judiciary in this country and elsewhere. Even though it was first published three years ago, we seem to be a long way from finding any consensus on a solution. The key requirement is, of course, that judgments should be clear, but that means that there should be enough but not too much explanation of the points. Another requirement, given the constitutional importance of independence of the judiciary, is that judges should still be able to express themselves in precisely the way that they consider best conveys their legal conclusions, using where appropriate metaphors, analogies, or quotations from outside the usual range of legal authorities.

Judgment writing can in my view still be improved even within these constraints. I suggest priority is given to three steps:

(1) Identification—before the drafting process starts—of the *central* issue. This will enable the subsidiary issues to be dealt with more economically. Complex issues, on close analysis, often turn on a single question, and the skill lies

in defining that issue. The central issue acts as a pivot upon which everything else rests.

(2) Logical ordering of the points so that they flow with the minimum number of words. The best order is likely to be the one which someone coming to the matter afresh would find most helpful.

(3) Ruthless editing so that unnecessary circumlocution and repetition is avoided.

By taking these three simple steps, judgments could often, in my view, be made both clearer and shorter. I accept that changes are not always easy to make. Practice is needed, and practice requires time, but with practice improvements become easier and quicker to implement.

16

Are Shorter Judgments Achievable?

This chapter is based on an article first published in the Law Quarterly Review.*

Increasing length of judgments

Many pages of the Law Quarterly Review are devoted to valuable criticism of the content of judgments of the higher courts of England and Wales. Very little is said about their form. I would like to raise one aspect of their form: their ever-growing length.

This ever-growing length can be seen by comparing judgments in the 1890s with those for any year since the start of the twenty-first century. Without a shadow of a doubt, they have got much longer: they have almost trebled.[1] Many judgments are wholly admirable, but some are longer than they need to be. And the length of a judgment is not a necessary ingredient of its excellence.

In his famous essay in 1925, 'Law and Literature',[2] Benjamin N Cardozo, then Chief Judge of New York State's Court of Appeals, wrote that there were six types of judgments. The first five types were the magisterial, the sententious, the conversational, the refined, and the persuasive. Each of these had their place. Well-written judgments come in many styles. The sixth type was 'the tonsorial or agglutinative, so called from the shears and the paste pot which are its implements and emblem'. Cardozo accepted that that category was happily already rare by the time he wrote. It is clear, however, from reading his article as a whole that he admired judgments that were succinct. Had he known about the photocopier and the word processor he would, I think, have included a powerful passage or two on the dangers of too much quotation or detail.

---

* Published as Mary Arden, 'Judgment Writing: Are Shorter Judgments Achievable?' in (2012) 128 LQR 515, © Sweet & Maxwell Ltd. Reproduced here with the kind permission of the publisher Sweet & Maxwell Ltd.

[1] In the years 1891–1901 inclusive, there were 632 cases reported in the Appeal Cases reports (AC). From a sample of 10% of these, the average number of pages was 12.1. In the AC reports between 2001 and 2011 inclusive, there were 444 reported cases. A sample of 10% of these reveals the average number of pages had almost trebled to 33.8. The true figure for the page-length of judgments in the 1890s is probably smaller even than the above, given the convention at that time of reporting the arguments of Counsel much more extensively than at present.

[2] Reprinted in (1939) 48(3) Yale LJ 489, 493.

What I want to do here is to address the following questions: 'Is there any way to achieve succinctness as well as excellence?' and 'What could judges and others in the profession do in practice?' But first, let us take a look at what lies behind the trend towards more expansive judgments.

Why are judgments getting longer?

First, the sheer complexity of the issues arising in modern litigation and technology seem to me to bear much of the responsibility for the length of modern judgments. There have also been changes in the way litigation is conducted. The move in many cases from a largely oral process of trial to a mainly paper-based one, coupled with more efficient databases, has led to far more issues being argued. If the issues raised in a skeleton argument are not expressly or implicitly abandoned at the hearing, the usual view is that the judgment must deal with them. Thanks to modern technology, there may also be substantially more documents referred to in a case than previously, and judges can incorporate with ease large quotations from other judgments as well as swathes of lengthy written arguments and witness statements. In addition, the legal issues themselves have become more complex. There may also be an element of 'defensive' judgment writing: the inclusion of citations and other material to display knowledge to gain praise—or at least ward off criticism—on appeal. But does length matter?

Should we be concerned about the length of judgments?

Are long judgments inevitable? Some cases require long and complex judgments, but in my view we should be concerned if this course is taken in cases that do *not* require long judgments. There are significant social and economic costs if the higher courts produce judgments that are longer than required for deciding the case and establishing the law. As Lord Bingham said, there comes a point when a judgment is so long that it becomes inaccessible and threatens the rule of law.[3] I do not consider that we have reached that point but, the longer judgments are, the more time lawyers and others have to spending reading and analysing them to work out what the law is. This expenditure of time and money makes legal services more expensive, and the cost of legal advice in this country is already high by international standards. As judgments get longer, more time is inevitably spent in distilling the law at almost every level of the legal system.

Added to the cost of lengthy judgments is the international dimension. In many fields, courts all over the world look to English law. In addition, it is used as the preferred legal system for many international contracts. To maintain that position, judgments of the English courts have to be clear and accessible. Moreover, the

---

[3] Lord Bingham, *The Rule of Law* (Allen Lane, 2010) 42.

clearer the judgment the more likely it is that it will be influential in the European supranational courts in Strasbourg and Luxembourg. It stands to reason that the easier judgments are to read the more others will read them.[4]

Interestingly, other leading courts of the world have been working on ways to make their judgments more accessible. The Conseil d'Etat in France, for example, has recently engaged in a public consultation on how its judgments, which are written more in a civilian tradition and tend to be short relative to judgments of the higher courts in England and Wales, could be made more accessible to readers inside and outside France.[5] The Federal Constitutional Court of Germany produces English summaries and versions of judgments of some of its leading cases to ensure that they are more widely read.

In short, I conclude that anyone concerned about the development of English law must also be concerned with finding out what can be done about long judgments.

What could judges do about the problem?

Could steps be taken in England and Wales to reduce the length of judgments in the higher courts? That is a very large question and I propose at this stage to concentrate on just one possible solution: the contribution that judges can make themselves. (I am not, incidentally, claiming any prerogative for my own judgments, still less that they are free from fault. I am, however, interested in seeing whether solutions can be found.)

There is no doubt that judgment writing is a highly individual process and that writing style is accordingly likely to vary. Judges should be able to write judgments in the style that they consider best expresses what needs to be conveyed, but I would expect them to welcome suggestions from other leading judges. They would be disappointed, however, if they expected to find much guidance from that source. With a few notable exceptions, such as Lord Denning,[6] Lord Macmillan,[7] Kitto J,[8] and Lord Hope of Craighead,[9] there is little guidance to be found. Cardozo, in his other well-known work, *The Nature of the Judicial Process*, provides useful insights on how common law judges reason, but, as he suggested in relation to judicial

---

[4] Lundmark makes the additional point that judgments should be written with an eye to their being useful to national courts of other member states of the EU when interpreting European legislation: Thomas Lundmark, '"Soft" *stare decisis*: the Common Law Doctrine Retooled for Europe' in R Schulze and U Seif (eds), *Richterrecht und Rechtsfortbildung in der Europäischen Rechtsgemeinschaft* (Mohr Siebeck, 2003) 161.

[5] 'Groupe de Travail sur la Rédaction des Décisions de la Jurisdiction Administrative' (April 2012). The project is continuing: see 'Comité d'évaluation de l'expérimentation d'une nouvelle rédaction des décisions de la juridiction administrative, Rapport d'évaluation', 29 January 2014.

[6] Lord Denning, *The Family Story* (Butterworths, 1981) 206–8.

[7] Lord Macmillan, 'The Writing of Judgments' (1948) 26 Canadian Bar Review 491.

[8] Frank Kitto, 'Why write judgments?' in Ruth Sheard (ed), *A Matter of Judgment* (Judicial Commission of New South Wales, 2003) 69.

[9] Lord Hope, Speech (unpublished) given to the Judicial Studies Board of Hong Kong, 26 September 2011.

reasoning, every judge has to work out their own style for themselves by dint of practice.[10]

Common sense suggests, however, that some valuable things might be learnt from pooling ideas and experience and I think that some focused judicial training in this field might usefully be developed. In the meantime I am going to suggest some basic steps that individual judges can take.

The first step in my view is to *recognize that there is a problem*. The form of judgments needs to be considered with fresh eyes because life has moved on. In particular, the speed of communication means that it is time to revisit, if not revise, thinking on some of the basic questions. For example, to whom are the judgments of the higher courts addressed? That raises a wider debate about the purpose of the legal system and whom it serves. To my mind, judgment writing in the higher courts should to some degree serve the community in general, not simply the legal profession. In other words, judgments are addressed not just to the parties but also to all those who have to use them thereafter, and those persons are not limited to fellow experts in the law. Some might argue that long judgments are a boon to academic readers, but judgments are not solely directed to them.

In short, judgments of the higher courts are, I suggest, directed to the parties and *all* those who may subsequently wish to find out the law applied in the case, including students of the law and readers who are not lawyers at all. Yet the length and complexity of judgments makes this difficult in many cases.

Not everyone would agree with my view. They might say that it is the function of the head note appearing in the published report to provide any explanation that a layperson needs. That view, however, assumes that a head note will be available to the layperson. But head notes are produced by commercial publishers: they are only available to subscribers to that service. The copy of the judgment that the layperson is likely to read will be the copy published on the internet. This will not contain a head note. It may be accompanied by an executive summary. Judgments of the Supreme Court are always published with a press release containing a summary of the issues and principal reasoning in the judgment. However, this rarely happens with judgments of the Court of Appeal or the High Court in England and Wales. In any event, head notes and press releases do not form part of the judgment. A layperson who wishes to read what a judge has written would have to read the judgment.

If I am right to define the readership as including laypersons, it follows that, to achieve effective communication, judgments should aim for simplicity of expression. This cannot always be achieved. What I intend is that, as Einstein is reported to have said, 'everything should be as simple as it can be but not simpler'.[11] In particular, judgments should so far as possible avoid using words that have a

---

[10] Benjamin N Cardozo, *The Nature of the Judicial Process* (Yale University Press, 1921) 162.

[11] This remark is commonly attributed to Einstein but appears to be what the composer Robert Sessions and others have interpreted him as saying (for the remark by Sessions, see 'How a "Difficult" Composer Gets That Way', *New York Times*, 8 January 1950). The remark is consistent with Occam's Razor, sometimes called the law of succinctness, under which no more should be stated than necessary.

specialized legal meaning without making that meaning clear. They should also contain a clear statement of the issues and a summary of the main points that have been decided. This leads me to my next point.

The next step, in my view, is *more refining of judgments* in order to achieve maximum clarity and reasonable accessibility. Judgments already commonly go through several drafts before reaching their approved versions. It is important to step away from the process of writing, even if only briefly, and to re-read the text critically. As Wittgenstein said, 'Light dawns gradually over the whole'.[12] The time spent re-reading after the completion of a judgment is one of the best guarantees of the *coherence* of judicial reasoning. And it may become clear as a result of a rigorous edit that a judge has set out a great deal of evidence and argument without making it clear which points are accepted and which rejected.

And to return to the central issue of this chapter, refining judgments can also be an opportunity to reduce their *length*. Professor Zimmermann has pointed out that Aulus Gellius' advice on dialectics is well worth heeding in legal life. 'A discussion will become endless and hopelessly involved,' commented the author of *Attic Nights*, 'unless it is confined to simple questions and answers'.[13] While the substantive law that has to be dealt with in judgments often cannot be reduced to such simplicity, savings in length can be achieved by rigorous editing. Moreover, once text that unnecessarily strays from the issues is eliminated, a more penetrating analysis of the real issues can be achieved.

Often judgment writing stimulates new thinking in the writer. This is a good thing, but it can increase the length of the text and make the structure more complicated. This makes it all the more necessary to refine the writing. As Cardozo said, more important than a turn of phrase was what he called the 'architectonics' of a judgment:

The groupings of fact and argument and illustration so as to produce a cumulative and mass effect; these, after all, are the things that count above all others . . . Often clarity is gained by a brief and almost sententious statement at the outset of the problem to be attacked. Then may come a fuller statement of the facts, rigidly pared down, however, in almost every case, to those that are truly essential as opposed to those that are decorative and adventitious. If these are presented with due proportion and selection, our conclusion ought to follow so naturally and inevitably as almost to prove itself.[14]

The practical problems of judgment writing must not, however, be underestimated. Pascal remarked of a letter he was writing that it was very long, simply because he had no leisure to make it shorter.[15] Effective editing has a high time cost, and judgments are usually written under considerable pressure of time. By the time a judge has reached the end of a judgment on a substantial case, there may be insufficient time to revise it. There is usually no time, alas, to put it on one side

---

[12] Ludwig Wittgenstein, *On Certainty*, GEM Anscombe and von Wright (eds), Dennis Paul and GEM Anscombe (trans) (Blackwell, 1969) para 141.

[13] John C Rolfe, *The Attic Nights of Aulus Gellius*, Vol III (Heinemann, 1928) 133.

[14] Benjamin N Cardozo, *The Nature of the Judicial Process* (n 10) 503–4.

[15] Blaise Pascal, *Lettres Provinciales* (1657) xvi.

and come back to it with a fresh mind. Nevertheless, in my view there is room for some experimentation. And we should not assume that just because judgments have always been written in a particular way they need to be written in that way in the future.

Other measures?

It is not only the efforts of individual hard-pressed judges that are needed to achieve change. There are other steps that advocates can also take. The introduction of skeleton arguments has in general been of great value to the despatch of justice. Those who write them, however, could usefully remember that a skeleton argument is also not to be judged by its length. It is the analysis of the relevant issues that matters. The best writer of a skeleton argument is one who, like the pearl diver, dives as far into the ocean as is necessary to bring up pearls of great price. The pearl diver avoids the flotsam and jetsam lying near the surface. Similar observations could be made about lengthy witness statements.

There are also no doubt actions which appellate judges can take collectively, for instance, by having, where it is possible to do so, a single majority judgment rather than a succession of individual judgments. There is in general no reason why single majority judgments should not be supplemented by concurring judgments. There will, of course, always have to be separate judgments where there is dissent. In days when there was less material to read, and more time for reading it, it was possible to say that separate judgments from each member of the appellate court enabled the reader to obtain a rounder and richer picture of the law.[16] What I am suggesting is a departure from this approach. Here, in particular, events have moved on. Today, having several judgments to read may simply distract readers and confuse them as to what has actually been decided. It may also make our judgments less competitive internationally.

The international theme is an important one. Different legal systems approach judgment writing in different ways and we could enrich our own judgment-writing ideas by looking to see how judgments are written in other systems. As in other areas, comparative law is likely to give us a wider perspective on the issues and their solution.[17]

My aim in this chapter has been to stimulate discussion about the form of judgments. If the points I have made provoke further response and ideas, I will have achieved my intention.[18]

---

[16] See *Broome v Cassell* [1972] AC 1027, 1085B per Lord Reid.

[17] See, for instance, Mitchel Lasser, *Judicial Deliberations—A Comparative Analysis of Judicial Legitimacy and Transparency* (Oxford University Press, 2004).

[18] I gratefully acknowledge the assistance I have received from my senior colleagues and others with whom I have discussed this somewhat provocative topic, but the views expressed remain solely my own.

17

A Matter of Style

This chapter is based on a paper given in honour of Lord Bingham in Oxford in 2009.

Finding the best way to convey the message

The quality and accessibility of Lord Bingham's judgments is justly famous and one can only marvel at the riches of his judicial legacy. This is a good moment to reflect on judgment writing more generally, because our new United Kingdom Supreme Court will shortly be in operation. The more I thought about the form of written judgments, the more I realized that there were many different benchmarks that could be applied. There are certainly different forms of judgment. I consider that, at the end of the day, the judge, if free to choose between the different forms, should aim to follow the form that will best enable the message in the judgment to be conveyed, not for any formalistic reason. In this contribution, I shall mainly be discussing judgments of appellate courts.

I will pose a number of questions:

(1) Why does the form of judgments matter?
(2) What is wrong with judgments?
(3) What are the options?
(4) What is the solution?

Why does the form of judgments matter?

Judgments are the cornerstone of the common law. The common law is judge-made law and gradually evolved as more cases had to be decided. The judges did not portray themselves as making new law. They had no right or power to do that. Instead, they were declaring what the law had always been.

There are records of decisions dating back to 1194. The reports from that date are extremely brief but bit by bit a comprehensive jurisprudence evolved. The work of producing the law never ceases because new problems arise and new conditions require old solutions to be adapted or replaced. The practice of the judge giving a reasoned judgment developed comparatively recently. In earlier times, the reasoning had to be found in the record of the argument between the advocates and the bench.

So much for the history. The subject of the form of judgments plumbs the very depths of the common law. In judgments lawyers have to find the reasoning that will tell them whether the same result will apply in another situation or whether there are sufficient distinguishing features. Cases are rarely the same. Since the nineteenth century, the courts of England and Wales have applied a relatively strict doctrine of precedent. In general, the *ratio decidendi* of decisions of the higher courts are binding on lower courts and the higher courts are bound by their own decisions, but there are exceptions. So, English lawyers have to find the *ratio decidendi* of a judgment. Reasoning in a judgment is thus crucial to finding out what the law is. The art is to use precedent wisely. As Lord Nicholls has said, one of the well-known ailments of lawyers, meaning common lawyers, is a hardening of the categories.[1] But that is a problem for another day.

The great advantage of the common law is that it enables judges to develop it, though there are limits which they must observe. Cockburn CJ, in *Wason v Walter*,[2] described this advantage in these terms:

> Whatever disadvantages attach to a system of unwritten law, and of these we are fully sensible, it has at least this advantage, that its elasticity enables those who administer it to adapt it to the varying conditions of society, and to the requirements and habits of the age in which we live, so as to avoid the inconsistencies and injustice which arise when the law is no longer in harmony with the wants and usages and interests of the generation to which it is immediately applied.

So a judgment in a common law system is likely to be different from a judgment in a civil system. For example, in Germany as I understand it, the emphasis is on finding the norm and on deciding the case by reference to that norm. Moreover, in many jurisdictions, there is much more use of scholarly texts than in England and Wales.

So what are the problems?

I should make clear that in trial courts many judgments are given orally and *ex tempore*, but this does not happen in the Appellate Committee of the House of Lords and happens only in a minority of cases in the Court of Appeal.

There is a concern about prolixity. Judgments before the age of the word-processor and databases of case law were often much shorter. We can take as an example the opening lines of the judgment of Lord Atkin in *Donoghue v Stevenson*[3] as a model of brevity for setting out the problem, and also for doing so at the start of the judgment, where it is most conveniently placed:

---

[1] *Attorney General v Blake* [2001] 1 AC 258, 284. [2] (1868) LR 4 QB 73, 93.
[3] [1932] AC 562, 578.

My Lords, the sole question for determination in this case is legal: Do the averments made by the pursuer in her pleading, if true, disclose a cause of action? I need not restate the particular facts. The question is whether the manufacturer of an article of drink sold by him to a distributor, in circumstances which prevent the distributor or the ultimate purchaser or consumer from discovering by inspection any defect, is under any legal duty to the ultimate purchaser or consumer to take reasonable care that the article is free from defect likely to cause injury to health.

Another example of brevity is the statement of facts by Blackburn J in *Rylands v Fletcher*,[4] which is less than 300 words:

It appears from the statement in the case, that the plaintiff was damaged by his property being flooded by water, which, without any fault on his part, broke out of a reservoir constructed on the defendants' land by the defendants' orders, and maintained by the defendants.

It appears from the statement in the case . . . , that the coal under the defendants' land had, at some remote period, been worked out; but this was unknown at the time when the defendants gave directions to erect the reservoir, and the water in the reservoir would not have escaped from the defendants' land, and no mischief would have been done to the plaintiff, but for this latent defect in the defendants' subsoil. And it further appears, . . . that the defendants selected competent engineers and contractors to make their reservoir, and themselves personally continued in total ignorance of what we have called the latent defect in the subsoil; but that these persons employed by them in the course of the work became aware of the existence of the ancient shafts filled up with soil, though they did not know or suspect that they were shafts communicating with old workings.

It is found that the defendants, personally, were free from all blame, but that in fact proper care and skill was not used by the persons employed by them, to provide for the sufficiency of the reservoir with reference to these shafts. The consequence was, that the reservoir when filled with water burst into the shafts, the water flowed down through them into the old workings, and thence into the plaintiff's mine, and there did the mischief.

This would be a convenient place to try to identify what makes a good judgment. The first quality is, of course, that it should get to the right answer, preferably for the right reasons. It should deal with all the points that need to be dealt with. It should not gloss over difficulties but fairly confront them. It should be bold, where necessary, and authoritative. It should be relevantly expressed. As for other qualities, concision, if it can be achieved, is one of them. There also needs to be a logical flow of argument. This greatly helps accessibility. It is one of the great features of the speeches of Lord Bingham. It has made his judgments accessible to a wider audience. Another quality is this: from time to time what is needed is to go back and identify the principle as it has been developed and to restate it in terms that are appropriate for modern conditions. It is also often necessary to discuss whether, and, if so, how far and in what terms, to develop the law. Lord Bingham has also been a shining example in this regard. A good appellate judge is always looking for ways to improve the law or move it on, and there are usually many opportunities to do this with the jigsaw that is the common law. It is in the nature of the common

[4] (1866) LR 1 Exch 265, 279.

law system that there may not be an opportunity to deal with the same issue again at appellate level for a very long time.

In recent times, appellate judgments have become longer and, of course, merit is not proportionate to length. The problem is exacerbated in the appellate courts where in theory, and often in practice, more than one judge will give a full judgment. The problem of prolixity leads to a problem of accessibility: it becomes harder and harder for lawyers to keep up with the law and for the public, if ever minded to read a judgment, to understand it.

Accessibility would probably not have been regarded by earlier generations as very important. But judgments are becoming more and more important because more and more political questions are being left to judges. Judgments are therefore reaching a wider audience than just the parties.

That is what prompted the Court of Appeal recently in *Birmingham City Council v Doherty*[5] to bemoan the fact that they had had to work through six full judgments of the Appellate Committee of the House of Lords in a previous case, and to argue in favour of a single, or single majority, judgment in that case.

Prolixity makes a judgment less accessible. That means, of course, less accessible to lawyers, scholars, students, the public, the courts, and lawyers abroad.

I am glad to say that it is not a problem unique to England and Wales. It is said that it is so rare for the High Court of Australia to have a single judgment that when, on the centenary of the Court, there was a fly past (which impressed the visiting judges greatly), a leading advocate turned to the visitors and said: 'Why, they do this every time there is a joint judgment!'

What are the options?

Broadly speaking, there are three main forms of judgments in appellate courts:

(1) *Single (or sole) judgment*—for example (generally speaking) at the Criminal Division of the Court of Appeal of England and Wales, and historically the Privy Council, (uniformly) at the Court of Justice of the European Communities (the Luxembourg Court) and some civilian courts, such as the Federal Supreme Court of Germany (but not, for example, the Federal Constitutional Court of Germany).

(2) *Seriatim judgments*—for example at the Court of Appeal of England and Wales and the Appellate Committee of the House of Lords.[6]

(3) *Single majority and separate dissenting/concurring judgments*—for example at the Supreme Court of the United States and the European Court of Human Rights (the Strasbourg Court).

---

[5] [2007] LGR 165, paras 62–65.

[6] This expression applies when there are two or more judges sitting on a case. They then usually give their judgments in turn. The first judgment will in general deal with all the issues, and concurring judgments may be quite short.

All of these forms of judgment will be familiar. I do not propose to go into them. Adjudication is a complex process and none of these models is a pure form. The English style is seriatim judgments. There are, of course, many variations on these basic models but the purpose of setting out the models is to show the *spectrum* of forms of judgment available. A single or sole judgment may be one in which different judges have written different parts. Such a judgment may be called 'a composite judgment'. However, in my experience, that is rare because of the difficulties of editing the various parts to produce a consistent whole. The three models just listed show the range of options available to judges when writing their judgments in collegiate courts.

The practice of the Supreme Court of the United States was developed by Chief Justice Marshall. He encouraged the court to deliver an oracular single opinion or a single majority opinion. The process continued after his departure, although since the 1940s judgments have been more fragmented. Nonetheless, while the Supreme Court of the United States did have the practice of seriatim judgments, in its earliest days, it did not continue it.[7] Perhaps, as Lord Devlin said: 'The US Supreme Court like the vines of France is not for transplantation.'[8]

I turn next to the very important question of the dissenting judgment. Some dissenting judgments are useful; some are not. But there is no serious suggestion in England and Wales (save in the courts I have mentioned) that judges should not be able to write dissenting judgments. It is sufficient that they can be useful. They plant the seed for future development. They can point out difficulties and other solutions, and other courts not bound by the decision of the majority under the doctrine of precedent may in time decide on the course advocated by the minority. They demonstrate a judge's independence of thought.

I would add that obiter dicta are also valuable: as Lord Devlin said, these are 'rumblings from Olympus' which 'give warning of uncertain weather'.[9]

Let us consider for a moment the reasons for adopting the single or single majority judgment. I would summarize the main reasons as follows. First, it is said that a single or single majority judgment should make law more certain, coherent, and accessible. Second, in certain special cases, such as constitutional courts in developing democracies, there may be a need for collective rather than individual responsibility. This may be the case in some common law jurisdictions, but not in the United Kingdom. Third, in civil systems, there is a less rigid approach to precedent and so there may be less need to set out the full reasoning. However, the reason generally advanced for a single or single majority judgment is that it should make the law more certain, coherent, and accessible. I stress the features of coherence and accessibility, to which I return later.

---

[7] I am grateful to Justice Ginsburg for pointing out that the US Supreme Court did have the practice of seriatim judgments in its earliest days, until the fourth Chief Justice, John Marshall, instituted the practice of an 'Opinion of the Court'. On dissenting opinions, Justice Ginsburg provides an illuminating description of her practice of choosing when to deliver such an opinion—see 'The Role of Dissenting Opinions' (2010) 95 Minnesota Law Review 1.

[8] Patrick Devlin, *The Judge* (Oxford University Press, 1979) 7.

[9] Devlin, *The Judge* (n 8) 11.

By contrast, the reasons for adopting seriatim judgments include:

(1) *Judicial independence.* Judicial independence is fundamental to the common law. It is of two kinds, decisional and institutional. Most relevant at this stage is decisional judicial independence: judges must be at liberty to decide the case as they think fit and to express their reasons fully and freely. If there are different perspectives on the legal issue or different routes for reaching the solution, each individual judge has to be free to write those reasons in his own words. For example, in a case concerning a woman's ability to have fertility treatment, I decided that it would not be right for my judgment to become the judgment of the court. I had written it in part from a woman's perspective and wanted it to be seen as such, especially as the decision was to reject the woman's case. I would add that some judges say that they cannot be sure that they do agree with another's judgment until they have worked a judgment out on paper for themselves, though that is not logically a reason why they should publish all that they write. The real reason for seriatim judgments is judicial independence.

(2) *Accountability of judges.* It is by their judgments that judges are made accountable for the decisions, which can in general be appealed. Therefore, in principle, they ought to be free to express their reasons as they think fit.

(3) *The practice of seriatim judgments avoids any risk of adjustment of reasoning.* It is often the experience of judges on courts which only issue single judgments that judges have to modify their reasoning in order that the judgment should obtain the largest majority. This means that the reasons are not fully stated. This can hold back the development of the law. The effect of having a single or single majority judgment may be that it lacks the style of an individual justice. In addition, it may also mean that some judges have to compromise on reasoning and that the judgment as published may not set out the real reasons why the judges came to their conclusion.

There are other factors influencing the form of judgments, such as personalities, resources, and institutional factors. As to personalities, members of the judiciary have unparalleled independence of action and thought. Therefore personalities are bound to matter. Justice Scalia, for instance, is very outspoken and is frequently critical of his colleagues in his judgments. Justice Sandra Day O'Connor by contrast made a practice of trying to bring different judges together. The individual makeup of court is bound to make a difference to its ethos and to its output.

Individual judges have different ways of expression. Some of them use literary quotations or historical explanations or metaphors or examples to explain the point that they are making. The quotations and so on are often the things which people remember. Therefore, they can assist accessibility and can be used within reason for this purpose. Lord Denning was particularly known for some of the opening words of his judgments, for example: 'A gigantic ship was used for a gigantic fraud. She was the Salem, a supertanker';[10] or 'Broadchalke is one of the most pleasing villages

---

[10] [1982] QB 946, 982.

in England. Old Herbert Bundy, the defendant, was a farmer there. His home was at Yew Tree Farm. It went back for nearly 300 years. His family had been there for generations. It was his only asset but he did a very foolish thing';[11] or 'It happened on 19 April 1964. It was blue bell time in Kent.'[12]

As to resources, some courts have more funds for lawyers or judicial assistants than others, meaning that more research can be done. As a result, it has been said that some judges' function may have been reduced to the function of editors, rather than writers, of judgments. This is not only regrettable, but, as I see it, also wrong in principle.

Institutional arrangements to facilitate engagement are very important and influential. Sometimes judges have special meeting rooms, or a fixed series of meetings. But, to be effective, internal discussion need not be formal. There can be useful informal meetings over the telephone or in one another's rooms. I will return to that point.

So what do we have to do to solve the problems of accessibility and prolixity?

1. Accessibility

I would make the following suggestions to improve the accessibility of appellate judgments:

- *'Roadmaps' in judgments.* Here I have in mind some indication at the start of the judgment of the organization of material within it, or alternatively, in a very long judgment, an index.

- *Shorter judgments.* This is self-explanatory. It is too easy to add in citations that are not strictly necessary. It may also help if the judgment contains its own summary.

- *Press summaries.* In a case that attracts public attention, the court can also usefully publish a press summary. This often helps accuracy in press reporting.

- *Fuller headnotes.* If judgments cannot be shortened or simplified, it may help if law reporters develop a way of providing fuller headnotes. Obviously, they are only concerned with what was actually decided by a case. But, if individual judges have expressed views on important issues and their views are not part of the *ratio* of the case, it would facilitate accessibility if the headnote could go on to summarize those views.

2. Prolixity

I would make two suggestions for reducing prolixity in judgments:

---

[11] [1975] QB 326, 334.   [12] [1970] 2 QB 40, 42.

First, I would stress the value of *internal engagement.*[13] It does not have to be lengthy; it does not have to be formal. It can occur at any stage. If it takes place before a hearing, the issues to be heard can be reduced. If it takes place immediately after the hearing, the judges can give their immediate reactions to the arguments while these are fresh in their minds. Another useful time to have a discussion is after the leading judgment has been produced and the other judges have had a chance to study it and to map out any points which they would want to make in a separate judgment. If the case breaks new ground, the internal engagement to which I refer is not simply about deciding the case. It is bound to cover how far the court should develop the law and in which direction, how far earlier cases should be overruled, and so on. Those issues are relevant to ensuring coherence in the law. To obtain coherence you need collaboration.

Second, I would suggest regular consideration of the option of a *single majority judgment.* There may be good reasons for not having a single majority judgment, but equally there may be good reasons to do so, as where the point calls for a firm response from all members of the court.

Third, good judgment writing in an appellate court will also call for good leadership. If there are separate judgments, the presiding judge should facilitate a discussion, even over the telephone, to make sure that the implications of any different or additional view are fully worked out. Leadership in this sense is not inconsistent with the importance attached to judicial independence.

Of these suggestions, it is internal engagement which will ensure that the court has judgments that are lasting and of the highest quality. Independence is not compromised in any way by discussing a point.

Drawing the threads together

We have had the present system of seriatim judgments for many years. In fact there is a whole spectrum of forms of judgment from seriatim judgments to composite judgments. But there is a bias to seriatim judgments. The creation of the UK Supreme Court is an opportunity which will never recur and so this is a logical time to think about the practice of forms of judgment. Leading Supreme Courts across the world have considered the system of seriatim judgments and have adopted different ones. I have already mentioned the practice of the Supreme Court of the United States. By way of further example, in Canada, in response to criticism from the profession about prolix judgments, the Supreme Court decided some years ago to strive for a single judgment of the court wherever possible and for a single dissenting judgment if there were opposing views. The change has, I understand, been well received.

I should make one thing clear. A single majority judgment does not mean that you cannot also have concurring judgments, just as they do in Strasbourg. But the

---

[13] By this I mean an exchange of views between the judges which reaches as deeply as possible into the issues or problems raised by the case.

main reasoning will be in one place and expressed in the same terms in the single majority judgment. It is also theoretically possible to say in a single majority judgment, 'One of us, X LJ, thinks as follows'. A single majority judgment is not inconsistent with judicial independence.

Society is increasingly heterogeneous. The judiciary of the United Kingdom is also a little less homogenous than it used to be. Both of these factors mean that there will be more and more perspectives to be taken into account in deciding some cases. These perspectives will enrich judicial decision-making. I anticipate therefore that, even if there are more single majority judgments in the future, there are likely to be concurring judgments too. One advantage, however, of the single majority opinion is that it would appear first in the law reports, so that the reader would know at the outset what the decision of the majority was.

It should be noted that writing a single majority judgment may not be easy. Temperamentally, judges in a common law system have very independent lines of thought. Nearly all judges in the higher courts in England and Wales come from the self-employed Bar and have never acted in partnership, as solicitors have. If there are more single majority judgments, that may lead to delay in writing judgments, which is not desirable.

I would start the process of change by having more regular consideration of the various options as to form of judgment. Of course, if the court decides to have a single substantive judgment, the adage may apply that it takes longer to write short than to write long. It is, as so often, a question of balancing priorities. The value of having a coherent and certain statement of the law covering all the points the judges wish to raise may sometimes be greater than that of every single judge expressing the reasoning in his or her own words. What the court has to balance is judicial independence versus risk to coherence and collaboration in the law.

In practical terms my proposal would often involve an early decision that one person is going to write the lead judgment, and who that person is, and an understanding that the other members of the court will not generally circulate their own judgments until they have seen the lead judgment. If that practice is observed, overlap and inconsistencies can be minimized.

So my suggestions for England and Wales are as follows:

(1) Whenever an appellate court has to prepare a judgment after hearing a case, it should consider the form its judgment should take.

(2) It should consider whether in that instance judicial independence requires a series of separate judgments or whether the view of either the majority or the minority can be expressed in a single set of reasons.

(3) Whenever there is a concurring or dissenting judgment, the author of the judgment should (a) make it clear with what reasoning or propositions in the main judgment the author agrees or disagrees and (b) avoid if possible repeating the facts or citations of authority already set out in the main judgment. As a supplement to that, it does not meet this proposition merely to say: 'My judgment is in substantial agreement with that of the lead

judgment.' But that is I suppose better than nothing, and there may be circumstances where that is an appropriate course.

(4) There should be internal engagement at appropriate stages in the preparation of judgments.

Finally, I would reiterate that the decision between a single majority judgment and seriatim judgments is likely to involve a balance between judicial independence on the one hand, and, on the other hand, collaboration and the risk to coherence in the law. Those are the principles primarily at stake when a decision is made as between the forms of judgment generally used in a common law system.

PART VII

THE JUDICIARY IN THE TWENTY-FIRST CENTURY: THE OLD ORDER CHANGETH

Following the 800th Anniversary of Magna Carta in 2015, this Part celebrates the historical development of the independent judiciary. But history did not stop in 2015. I therefore set out to identify some of the different ways in which the judiciary may be evolving today. I address two areas of potential changes: the composition of the judiciary and the notion of judicial accountability.

The title to this Part is taken from *Morte d'Arthur* by Alfred Lord Tennyson. It reflects the need for institutions to change over time without losing their core values. Such change may not be immediately apparent, or indeed immediately accepted. But some change is inevitable and we should recognize that change will not necessarily be welcomed at first and that it will need time to bed in.

When I originally wrote the lecture on which Chapter 18, *Magna Carta and the Judges: Realizing the Vision*, is based, I put the role of the judiciary into its historical context in the United Kingdom, showing that fundamental concepts such as independence of the judiciary may be traced back to Magna Carta. That led on to a discussion of the qualities required of judges today, particularly social awareness and an understanding of jurisprudence from the European supranational courts. Discussion of social awareness led to discussion of the need for change in the composition of the judiciary.[1]

In Chapter 18, I argue that the vision today should be one of greater judicial diversity in order to keep pace with modern society. The percentage of women in the workforce, for instance, had grown from 31% in 1950–51 to 65% in 2010–14.[2] The judiciary should reflect the make-up of society, so far as it can consistently with maintaining the principle of appointment on merit.

---

[1] Ch 18 thus examines Magna Carta in the specific context of the development of the principle of an independent judiciary. Ch 6, by contrast, considered more generally how Magna Carta contributed to the development of constitutional principles in the UK and the part it played in the drafting of the US and French bills of rights and international rights instruments.

[2] David Butler, 'The Changing Face of Britain', *Prospect*, May 2015, 33.

Importantly, Parliament has approved that principle in at least four ways. First, it has imposed a duty on both the Lord Chancellor and the Lord Chief Justice to take such steps as they consider appropriate for the purpose of encouraging judicial diversity.[3] Second, Parliament has imposed a duty on the Judicial Appointments Commission, the independent judicial selection body for England and Wales, to have regard to the need to encourage diversity in the range of persons available for selection for judicial appointments.[4] Third, Parliament has not sought to define it, and so it has left room for merit to be defined in practice by the independent selection bodies in a way that is inclusive of the merits of candidates with different talents and backgrounds. Fourth, Parliament has enacted a 'tie-break' provision, which may give an under-represented group an advantage if the candidates are found to be of equal merit.[5] Fourth, the Report of the Select Committee of the House of Lords on the Constitution in 2011,[6] to which I gave written evidence,[7] supported judicial diversity and considered that, if there was no improvement within five years, the government should consider setting non-mandatory targets for the Judicial Appointments Commission.[8] No doubt everyone hopes that it will not come to that. It might lead to immediate gains but may not produce a real change in the end.

I do not limit diversity to the cases of women and ethnic minorities. Diversity can also be the product of other differences. As one great American judge put it, 'out of the attrition of diverse minds there is beaten something which has a constancy and uniformity and average value greater than its component elements'.[9]

Diversity is particularly important where decisions are taken not just by one judge but by several sitting together, as in an appellate court. The reason for greater judicial diversity is not just so that the judiciary can be more reflective of the society

---

[3] Constitutional Reform Act 2005, as amended, s 137A.

[4] Constitutional Reform Act 2005, s 64.

[5] Constitutional Reform Act 2005, as amended, s 63(4), which is to be read with s 63(2). Section 63(2) and (4) provides:

> (2) Selection must be solely on merit.
> . . .
> (4) Neither 'solely' in subsection (2), nor Part 5 of the Equality Act 2010 (public appointments etc), prevents the selecting body, where two persons are of equal merit, from preferring one of them over the other for the purpose of increasing diversity within—
>   (a) the group of persons who hold offices for which there is selection under this Part, or
>   (b) a sub-group of that group.

Slightly different provisions apply to the Supreme Court. Equality Act 2010, Part 5 includes s 159, referred to on p 273.

[6] 'Report on Judicial Appointments', House of Lords, Select Committee on the Constitution, HL 272, 28 March 2012.

[7] See 'Report on Judicial Appointments' (n 6) 70.

[8] There is a form of non-mandatory target for the selection of judges of the European Court of Human Rights (the Strasbourg Court). Those judges are elected by the Parliamentary Assembly of the Council of Europe (PACE). Resolution 1366 of PACE, as amended by Resolutions 1426 and 1627, requires contracting states generally to present a list of three candidates, which must have at least one candidate of each sex. There are two exceptions: first, all three candidates may belong to a sex which is under-represented, that is, the sex to which under 40% of the total number of judges belong; the second exception is where the state has taken all necessary steps to find a candidate of the under-represented sex but has not been able to do so. The percentage of women judges at 1 June 2015 was about 40%.

[9] Benjamin N Cardozo, 'The Nature of the Judicial Process' (Yale University Press, 1921) 177.

which it serves. It is well-known in other walks of life that diversity of thought can lead to deeper and richer reasoning than if the decision is taken by those whose personalities, interests, and backgrounds are all very similar.[10] So diversity is not inconsistent with selection on merit but is an essential way of achieving it.[11] If the existing selection process is not securing diversity, we need to know why. It may be that it is the system, not the pool of candidates, which has to be more closely scrutinized.

Since I wrote the original 'Magna Carta and the Judges: Realising the Vision', there has been some remarkable improvement in the position as regards women.[12] In particular the percentage of women judges in the Court of Appeal is now over 21%. It is important that the progress where it is occurring is ongoing, which indicates that there is a lasting change and not simply the appointment of the non-dominant group up to a certain threshold.

But a number of problems remain.

First, there still needs to be more progress in relation to ethnic minorities. Taking the figures for the higher courts, as at 30 July 2015,[13] there were no BAME (black and minority ethnic) judges in the Court of Appeal or above and only 3% in the High Court.

Second, while the appointments system has been successful in achieving a judiciary which is reflective of the society it serves in terms of gender at most levels, it has not done so at the highest levels.[14] Indeed there has been some regression. The achievement of Lady Justice Butler-Sloss[15] in being appointed as one of the Heads of Division, that is, as the President of the Family Division, and thus one of the top five judges in England and Wales, from 1999 to 2005, has not been repeated.

---

[10] It does not matter whether women judges approach some issues differently. A recent experiment suggests that they do not write judgments differently: see Erika Rackley, 'The Neuberger Experiment' (2013) 163(7573) New Law Journal 13. Nevertheless, women judges may have an influence on the approach of the rest of the panel. See, for example, Ruth Bader Ginsburg, 'The Role of Dissenting Opinions' (2010) 95 Minnesota Law Review 1.

[11] I have cited in the footnotes to Ch 18, *Magna Carta and the Judges: Realizing the Vision*; Lord Reid's famous article, 'The Judge as Lawmaker' (1972) 12 Journal of the Society of Public Teachers of Law 22. In that article, written over 40 years ago, he saw the need for judges to have wider experience of life, and (even though he omitted to mention the possibility of women judges and referred only to prior experience in public service) he said:

> If the law is to keep in step with movements of public opinion then judges must know how ordinary people of all grades of society think and live. You cannot get that from books or courses of study. You must have mixed with all kinds of people and got to know them. If you only listen to those who hit the headlines you get quite the wrong impression. If we are to remain a democratic people those who try to be guided by public opinion must go to the grass roots. That is why it is so valuable for a judge to have given public service of some kinds in his earlier days. I sincerely hope that the 'rat race' of today will not prevent our young men from acquiring the breadth of mind that comes from widespread personal contacts in different strata of society.

[12] The most up to date figures are given in Ch 18, at n 28. The overall percentage of women judges (including both fee-paid and salaried judges) rose from 24.5% to 25.2% between 1 April 2014 and 1 April 2015: see Judicial Diversity Statistics 2015 published by the Lord Chief Justice and Senior President of Tribunals on 30 July 2015. This is welcome news and suggests that the overall percentage of women judges will increase over time. However, that does not mean that there is nothing to be done, still less that the progress is occurring at all levels of the judiciary.

[13] See Judicial Diversity Statistics 2015, n 12.   [14] See the statistics in Ch 18, at n 28.

[15] Now Baroness Butler-Sloss of Marsh Green.

Third, England and Wales have simply not kept pace with the rest of the world. The progress made by visible minorities on the Bench in this country is far less than that made in other, comparable jurisdictions. In Chapter 19, *Women Judges: Britain's Place in the World*, which is based on an address given to the Association of Women Barristers as long ago as 2007, I sought to encourage women to apply for the High Court Bench. This chapter shows among other things how far behind England and Wales are in relation to the rest of the world. The comparative position has changed little since then.

What is to be done? I do not doubt that many people have thought about this problem. It may be that something could be learnt from the recent experience in Parliament or the City. In the May 2015 general election, the percentage of women MPs went up from 23% to 29%, the largest increase since 1997. The number of women directors on boards of top companies—the FTSE 100 companies—likewise increased from 12.5% to 23.5% between 2011 and 2015.[16]

It is vital that women are encouraged to apply for judicial appointments so that there is a reservoir of women in the ranks of the judiciary who can assume the mantle of high office. As so often happens in public life, once people acquire the mantle of office, they grow in stature. The world will wonder why more women were not appointed before. By their presence in leading positions, they in turn encourage others to seek progression.

In short, we must celebrate the progress to date, but be mindful that it also needs to be sustained and real. We must not think that, because some progress has been made, the future is assured. Assumptions can be hard to shift, and things can move backwards as well as forwards. So the pace of change must be maintained. We need to move quickly to a world where diversity ceases to be a matter of debate.

The debate on judicial diversity demonstrates that the boundaries of the accountability of the legal system and judges have been shifting. Parliament, the media, and academics (among others) have expressed views on the composition of the bench and what ought to be done about it.

More generally, the legal system, which holds others to account, is now being expected to account for itself by making changes in its practices or giving explanations for its actions. Today there is rising interest in what happens in the courtroom: hence, for example, the increase in the televising of judicial proceedings, particularly in the Supreme Court, and to a lesser extent, in the Court of Appeal.

Access to justice

There are many issues which will need to be thought of afresh in the future. In the introduction to this book (*Why a Second Volume?*) I mentioned access to justice for civil claims, now beyond the reach of so many because of its cost and cuts in public

---

[16] 'Women on Boards: Davies Review Annual Report 2015'.

funding. Different methods of adjudication must be considered, both by judges within court proceedings and by other suitably qualified persons outside the court system. There must be an appropriate way in which justice can be made available even to those who cannot now afford to litigate. I see this as one of the most important problems to be solved in the interests of the future health of society and the legal system.

In conclusion, as the title of this Part puts it, *The Old Order Changeth*: today's judiciary is the product of a long historical development which we celebrate in 2015 with the 800th Anniversary of Magna Carta. But it is destined to continue to evolve in response to the needs of society. I have highlighted two issues: judicial diversity and access to justice. There are many others. Today's judiciary will have to find ways of responding to the changes that society properly requires of it without imperilling that essential core value of the justice system: independent and highly skilled judges, achieving justice for all, in accordance with the law and the constitution of this country.

18

Magna Carta and the Judges
Realizing the Vision

This lecture was given in 2011 at the Royal Holloway College, University of London, as part of its Magna Carta series of annual lectures between 2005 and 2015.*

Early recognition of the role of judges

This chapter discusses the significance of Magna Carta from the point of view of the judiciary and the legal system.[1] Magna Carta laid the corner stones of England's unwritten constitution. It placed great trust and authority in the judges. Furthermore Magna Carta cast a spotlight on the appointment and identity of judges. Clause 45 provided: 'We will appoint as justices . . . only such as know the law of the realm and mean to observe it well.'

Thus, Magna Carta identified the qualities that it was important for judges to have: knowledge of domestic law and loyalty to the rule of law. But what other qualities are needed today? This chapter discusses two qualities in particular: (1) the need for social awareness; and (2) the need for an understanding of the case law of courts outside the United Kingdom, particularly elsewhere in Europe. It is no longer enough that judges know 'the law of the realm' in the sense of purely domestic law. They may also be required to apply law developed outside the realm—such as law under the European Convention on Human Rights ('the Convention').

In this study of Magna Carta, I wish to focus on the role of the judges, the vision which Magna Carta had for them and how it is to be realized today—800 years on. This is a topical subject because, since the last centenary of Magna Carta in 1915, we have had, all within the last half century, at least three statutes of great significance to the constitutional framework of the United Kingdom—the

---

* This lecture was published in Australia by the Judicial Commission of New South Wales, and the first part was published by the Library of Congress of the United States of America in Randy J Holland (ed), *Magna Carta Muse & Mentor* (Thomson Reuters, in association with the Library of Congress, 2014) as part of the 800th Anniversary celebrations for Magna Carta in 2015. It is published here by kind permission of the Judicial Commission of New South Wales.

[1] In Ch 6, *Magna Carta and the Hidden Wiring of the Common Law*, I focused more on the constitutional implications of Magna Carta.

European Communities Act 1972, the Human Rights Act 1998, and the Constitutional Reform Act 2005. In addition, we currently have two major high-level inquiries of particular interest and importance in relation to the judicial function, namely, the Commission on a UK Bill of Rights and the inquiry of the House of Lords Constitution Committee into the judicial appointments process. I do not propose to discuss what these two inquiries may show or may recommend. What I wish to examine is the context in which these inquiries arise. They are building on the foundations which Magna Carta laid.

Magna Carta then and now

In 1215, King John, acceding to the demands of the Barons, set the Great Seal of England on the Charter of Liberties we now call Magna Carta 'in the meadow which is called Runnymede, between Windsor and Staines'.

In the years which followed, Magna Carta was confirmed over thirty times by royal charter; it was directed to be read out twice yearly in the great cathedrals of the land; archbishops and bishops were directed to pronounce sentences of excommunication on those who by word, deed, or counsel went against Magna Carta; and Kings were expected to confirm Magna Carta at the start of their reigns. This gives us some idea of Magna Carta's importance in mediaeval England. Not all of the provisions of the document signed by King John were reconfirmed but most were and indeed some of the clauses remain the law of the land today.

In this chapter, I propose to examine an aspect of Magna Carta which, so far as I know, has not been considered before, namely the role which Magna Carta assigned to the judges, and to ask whether the features of the judicial role envisaged by Magna Carta have changed and how they are being realized today.

To do this, I have to start by exploring the significance of Magna Carta from the point of view of the law and the administration of justice by the judges. I propose to concentrate on the following clauses from the 1215 version of Magna Carta:

(17) Ordinary lawsuits shall not follow the royal court around, but shall be held in a fixed place.
. . .

(39) No free man shall be seized or imprisoned, or stripped of his rights or possessions, or outlawed or exiled, or deprived of his standing in any other way, nor will we proceed with force against him, or send others to do so, except by the lawful judgment of his equals or by the law of the land.

(40) To no one will we sell, to no one deny or delay right or justice.
. . .

(45) We will appoint as justices, constables, sheriffs, or other officials, only men that know the law of the realm and are minded to keep it well.

Clause 45 did not appear in later versions of Magna Carta after 1215, and cl 40 was renumbered as cl 29 in at least one later version, but nothing turns on these points for present purposes. Clauses 39 and 40 are still in force today by virtue of the Charter of 1225.

How significant were the provisions of Magna Carta?

Magna Carta is a monumental affirmation of the rule of law. It proceeds on the all-important assumption that disputes are to be decided in accordance with the law. This was not a new idea but an important confirmation of it. As Lord Irvine LC put it: 'The primary importance of Magna Carta is that it is a beacon of the rule of law.'[2] Laws LJ has described Magna Carta as a 'proclamation of the rule of law'.[3] The King was not above the law and he could not displace the due application of the law by his judges. Moreover, by providing for the judicial determination of disputes according to the law of the land, Magna Carta laid the foundations of what we know today as due process of law. It also gave judges what has been their traditional and vital role of acting as a bulwark for the individual against arbitrary action by the state. The concept of due process is an element within the concept of the rule of law.

This is not the place for a detailed exposition of the concept of the rule of law, which may be found instead in Lord Bingham's remarkable book, *The Rule of Law*.[4] In a speech which he gave on Magna Carta,[5] Lord Bingham summed up its achievements in these terms:

Conditioned as we are today by our own knowledge of political and constitutional development over the last nine centuries, it calls for the exercise of real historical imagination to appreciate the enormity, the grandeur of what was done at Runnymede. King John entered the meadow as a ruler acknowledging no secular superior, whose word was law. He left the meadow as a ruler who had acknowledged, in the most solemn manner imaginable, that there were some things even he could not do, at any rate without breaking his promise. This, then, is the enduring legacy of Magna Carta: the lesson that no power is absolute; that all power, however elevated, is subject to constraint; that, as was to be said by Dr. Thomas Fuller some centuries later, 'Be you never so high, the law is above you'.

In addition, there is significance in the fact that cl 17 provided that the judges were to sit in a fixed place. This court became the Court of Common Pleas, as opposed to the Court of the King's Bench, which followed the King around the country, and as opposed to the Court of Chancery. The Court of Common Pleas existed down to the end of the nineteenth century. The fact was that, before Magna Carta, the King often took the decisions in disputes between his subjects as he went around the country, without involving his judges, or his judges made the decisions but applied the *lex regni*.

Putting the judges into a fixed place, away from the King, achieved two ends in particular. First, it laid the foundation for the doctrine of separation of powers.

---

[2] Lord Irvine, 'The Spirit of Magna Carta Continues to Resonate in Modern Law' (2003) 119 LQR 227.

[3] *R (Bancoult) v Secretary of State for Foreign and Commonwealth Affairs* [2001] QB 1067, para 36.

[4] Tom Bingham, *The Rule of Law* (Allen Lane, 2010).

[5] Tom Bingham, *Lives of the Law, Selected Essays and Speeches 2000–2010* (Oxford University Press, 2011) 5.

Judges were to be separate from the King, who made laws by royal decree. The doctrine of separation of powers has been much debated and developed in the eight centuries since Magna Carta. The separation was only gradual: at least until the end of the eighteenth century judges could be members of Parliament as well as holding judicial office. Most recently, the doctrine was invoked as the principal reason for setting up the new Supreme Court of the United Kingdom pursuant to the Constitutional Reform Act 2005. The Supreme Court replaced the House of Lords, which had been the highest court in the land since 1399, although the concept of the Lords of Appeal in Ordinary only came about pursuant to the Appellate Jurisdiction Act 1876. Second, the separation of judges from the King's court made clear that judges were to operate independently of the King. This led to the development of the concept of judicial independence.

Clause 45 provides that the judges were to apply the law of the realm. What was the significance of that? It was the law of the realm as opposed to the law of the King, canon law, or local law. I have already explained that some judges were attached to the royal court. Other judges were people in the locality who were trusted by the local inhabitants to try disputes or to hear criminal cases. There were, of course, no professional judges. The judges were often priests and so they were very familiar with canon law, which was derived from Roman law.[6] The significance of requiring judges to apply the law of the realm was that they would have to apply the law that was built up by tradition and accepted by the population. So the law of the realm was the law of England, including the law applied by local custom in different areas of England. Significantly, the law of the realm was the law of the people or, as it was and is called, the common law. As it was put in a work known as *The Mirror of the Justices*, published in about 1290, it is called common law 'because it is given to all in common'.[7] This emphasis on commonality suggests that the common law is a system of law in which all members of society are to have a share.

Moreover, Magna Carta, by requiring judges to apply the law of the realm, authorized the judges to apply the common law. This was an enormous shift of power away from the King and to the judges. In the fullness of time, the authority to apply the common law was taken to include the authority to develop the common law, but the judges had to exercise restraint. They adopted a theory known as the declaratory theory of the common law. They were loath to admit that they were developing the common law, and instead expressed themselves as simply declaring common law which had previously lain hidden. This theory continued for many hundreds of years: only comparatively recently has it been said that judges 'do not believe in fairy tales anymore, so we must accept that for better or worse judges do make law'.[8] It is, therefore, no longer denied that judges are developing the law but this is always subject to Parliamentary sovereignty. The judges cannot

---

[6] Roman law and canon law may also have had an influence on the drafting of Magna Carta: see RM Helmholz, 'Magna Carta and the Ius Commune' (1999) 66 University of Chicago Law Review 297.

[7] Book I (*Of Sins Against The Holy Peace*), ch 1, 'Of the Generation of Holy Law'.

[8] Lord Reid, 'The Judge as Lawmaker' (1972) 12 Journal of the Society of Public Teachers of Law 22.

develop the law so that it contradicts a statute; nor do they develop the law in an area that ought properly to be left to Parliament, for example, because to lay down the law needs more than the judges can do by judicial decision in a particular case.

Furthermore, by providing that any interference with an individual's liberty had to be authorized by the law of the land,[9] which was to be applied by the judges, Magna Carta expressly recognized something that it is today easy to take for granted but which is utterly fundamental, namely that every person should have the right not to have his liberty taken away other than in accordance with a decision of a court and due process of law. Clause 39 outlawed detention by order of the King or, in more modern terms, mere executive detention, not prescribed by law, for whatever reason.

And, by providing for the judicial determination of disputes, Magna Carta laid the foundations of certainty and consistency in the law and for the law to be administered in a public place, thus laying the foundations of open justice for all.

The provision in cl 40 that justice would not be sold or delayed was also a vitally important guarantee in all courts, even in the King's Bench and the Court of Chancery. However, in parenthesis, it should be noted that this clause was never applied to the sale of writs, which was an important source of revenue for many Kings. This is an opportunity which has not escaped elected governments in recent times, as court fees have been substantially increased for the Treasury's benefit. However, court fees cannot be of such an amount as to bar a person from obtaining access to a court.[10]

As to the barons who caused King John to apply the Great Seal to Magna Carta, it is of course impossible to believe that they had any idea of the epic nature of the act on which they were engaged. They were, almost certainly, seeking to protect their own rights and interests against excessive royal power, and possibly even to put themselves above the law. It is now generally accepted that when cl 39 refers to the judgment of a person by his peers, it is in fact referring to the judgment of the barons by the barons, and not to trial by jury. But once it became accepted, as it did, that it was not just the barons but every free person who was entitled to the protection of Magna Carta, the parallel with trial by jury was obvious. It is also to be noted that cl 40 was not the source of *habeas corpus*, which was a remedy developed by the judges.

Magna Carta acquired its name, not because of its contents, but to distinguish it from a shorter document called the Charter of the Forest with which it was reissued in 1217. Its execution did not mean that all was sweetness and light afterwards. Kings continued to err. In addition, the legal system did not meet all the high ideals which Magna Carta suggested that it should. Thus, for instance, the Tudors established the Court of Star Chamber,[11] which acted as an immediate agent of the King's prerogative.[12] The tyrannical proceedings of the Star Chamber

---

[9] The only exception in cl 39 was for 'the lawful judgment of his equals', which is considered later.
[10] *R (Witham) v Lord Chancellor* [1998] QB 575.
[11] Established by the Act of 1487 (3 Henry VII CI), the Act of Pro Camera Stellata.
[12] Sir William Holdsworth, *A History of English Law*, Vol 1 (7th edn, Sweet & Maxwell, 1956) 495.

under the Stuarts, especially Charles I, in political cases led to its abolition in 1641 by an Act of Parliament that referred to Magna Carta and stated that cases 'ought to be tried and determined in the ordinary courts of justice, and by the ordinary course of law'.[13] Trial methods in ordinary courts did not meet modern standards either, since trial by ordeal and trial by battle were for many years the order of the day. But, over time, the ideals of Magna Carta became embedded.

Of course, no mention is made of the relationship of the common law to statute law. That Great Council of the nation, known as Parliament, had not yet been convened.[14] When it was, it became accepted that the common law should be subject to the will of Parliament. The doctrine of Parliamentary sovereignty, as it is now known, is explored by Lord Bingham in a speech which he gave in King's College, London in October 2007.[15]

Constitutional and Individual Liberty Themes

I pose the question: why was Magna Carta so significant for the role of judges and the administration of justice in England? Quite simply, the Magna Carta laid the foundations for some of the most fundamental concepts of our legal system. These concepts echo two major themes, which overlap. The first theme may be called the constitutional theme, and it involves:

(1) the separation of powers;
(2) the birth of the judiciary as a separate arm of the constitution of England;
(3) the independence of the judiciary;
(4) the incorruptibility of the judiciary; and
(5) the development of the common law, based in theory on long tradition but in reality representing judge-made law.

There is a second, equally important, theme based on the liberty of the individual in relation to the state, involving:

(1) the judiciary as the bulwark of individual liberty against arbitrary action by the state;
(2) the rule of law;
(3) equality before the law;
(4) due process;
(5) open justice; and
(6) certainty and consistency in the law.

[13] 16 Charles I C ss 4 and 5.
[14] This occurred later in the 13th century, particularly with the convening by Simon de Montfort of Parliaments in 1264 and 1265: see generally Kenneth Mackenzie, *The English Parliament* (Pelican, 1950).
[15] Lord Bingham of Cornhill, 'The Rule of Law and the Sovereignty of Parliament', King's College, London, 31 October 2007, at <http://www.kcl.ac.uk/news/news_details.php?news_id=672&year=2007>.

The second theme, then, is all about liberty and, it might be said, the first theme is the framework which allows the second theme to flourish. Liberty begins historically with liberty of the person in the sense of freedom from arbitrary arrest. It has been developed over the centuries to include other freedoms, such as freedom of expression and freedom of self-realization. Most recently, it has been developed in terms of respect for one's home and private life.

Magna Carta thus gave us fundamental law. It is little wonder that we call this the Great Charter of our Liberties.

It is not within the scope of this study to explore the ways in which the provisions of Magna Carta, which I have set out, have found their way into the written constitutions of many democracies around the world but I will give one example where it finds particularly clear expression: the Fourteenth Amendment of the Constitution of the United States, which reads:

XIV. Section 1.... nor shall any State deprive any person of life, liberty, or property, without due process of law; nor deny to any person within its jurisdiction the equal protection of the laws.

Magna Carta also finds clear reflection in the International Convention on Civil and Political Rights,[16] the Universal Declaration of Human Rights,[17] and the European Convention on Human Rights.[18] Magna Carta belongs today, not only to England, but to the world.

However, Magna Carta's high ideals depend on there being a plentiful supply of persons capable of acting as judges and enforcing the rights which it guaranteed, including the rights conferred by the common law. That leads naturally to the question to which I next turn, which is: what are the qualities required of judges?

Qualities required of judges today

To start with a very basic point, the office of judge is a public office, which must be discharged in the public interest. It is thus important continually to review the qualities that judges require in order to discharge their role.

It is obvious that certain qualities are required of all judges. These include utter integrity, legal skill and knowledge, sound judgment, courage, an independent cast of mind, and an ability to act fairly.

---

[16] See for example Art 9(1), which provides: 'Everyone has the right to liberty and security of person. No one shall be subjected to arbitrary arrest or detention. No one shall be deprived of his liberty except on such grounds and in accordance with such procedure as are established by law.'

[17] See for example Art 9, which provides: 'No one shall be subjected to arbitrary arrest, detention or exile.'

[18] See for example Art 5(1), which provides: 'Everyone has the right to liberty and security of person. No one shall be deprived of his liberty save in the following cases and in accordance with a procedure prescribed by law: (a) the lawful detention of a person after conviction by a competent court...'

There are also additional qualities required of judges according to the nature of their case load. Criminal judges, for example, need to be able to sum up to juries clearly and correctly, and to deal with problems arising within a jury trial. Nowadays, many judges also need to have administrative skills. Others have responsibilities in connection with the organization of the legal system and keeping the rules of procedure under review, dealing with judicial discipline, and so on. Judges play an important part in ensuring the efficient delivery of justice, at a reasonable price, to litigants and society. But not all judges are required to have administrative and organizational skills. Some will be thinkers and concentrate on developing the law and seeing the big picture.

These are judicial qualities that are well understood and regularly discussed. The Judicial Appointments Commission website sets out many of the important qualities. But there are two other qualities which are not so often mentioned and which, it seems to me, need to be brought to the fore:

(1) the need for judges to have an awareness of the background to the problems they are likely to have to deal with, which one might term 'social awareness'; and

(2) The need for senior judges to have an understanding of the case law of courts outside the United Kingdom, particularly elsewhere within Europe.

Additional quality one: social awareness

The first additional judicial quality I wish to discuss is consciousness of the social context in which decisions have to be made today. This is often said to be necessary because of the Human Rights Act 1998 and the fact that, to determine rights such as the right to respect for private and family life, courts need to make value-laden judgments. As I pointed out in a judgment in 2011, however, this sort of decision may need to be made in other contexts where the court is required by an Act of Parliament to form a view as to whether an act was, or was not, reasonable. In that case, the question was whether a testatrix had not made reasonable financial provision for her adult child in her will.[19] A decision as to what constitutes reasonable financial provision cannot be taken in a social vacuum.

The need for social awareness arises for reasons independent of the changes in the law wrought by the Human Rights Act 1998. It is required because society has itself changed. There has been a substantial increase in the number of women earning and contributing to the economy. The percentage of women active economically has grown from 56% in 1971 to 70% at the end of 2008, while the percentage of men active economically has decreased over a similar period from 92% to 78%.[20] Women have achieved success in many areas: in 2010, in both Houses of

---

[19] *Ilott v Mitson* [2011] 2 FCR 1. The court's finding, upheld on appeal, was that on the evidence the testatrix's will had not made reasonable provision for her adult child. As to the determination of the amount which the court should order, see *Ilott v Mitson* [2015] EWCA Civ 797.

[20] Office of National Statistics, 'Women in the Labour Market', March 2009; and Office of National Statistics, 'Labour Market Trends', March 2002.

Parliament, approximately 22% of the members were women, and 34% of the Senior Civil Service.[21] There has also been an increase in the percentage of the population who belong to ethnic minorities. The 2001 census showed that 8.7% of the population of England and Wales was composed of ethnic minorities, a 53% increase from the 1991 census figures. Approximately 13% of businesses in London alone are Asian-owned[22] and, despite accounting for only 4% of the population, persons of Asian origin account for approximately 10% of the UK's economic output.[23]

Equally, changes in the commonly-accepted meaning of the family mean that we have moved away from the traditional idea of a nuclear family. Relationships are now much more varied and complex. There have also been immense technological developments and advances in medical and other sciences. There have been numerous other changes as well.

Many decisions, especially those made by the High Court and above, resolve issues which have consequences far beyond the particular case in which the judgment is given. At the appellate levels there are many cases in which 'the law runs out' and the judges have to exercise their judgement as to how far, if at all, to extend the law. The law has an important function to play in society, and law should, in general, be developed to meet changing conditions. In other words, it must connect with society. Legal developments must, obviously, be in accordance with the law but they should not focus on the theoretical at the expense of the socially relevant.

Changes in society increase the complexity in decision-making. Judges must be able to explain the reasons for their decisions in accessible language so that the important parts can be read and understood by laypeople, and not just by other lawyers. Judges have to balance their technical or theoretical reasoning with the practical so that the law can be applied without difficulty. What I am saying here chimes in with a point made by Justice Kate O' Regan, formerly a Justice of the Constitutional Court of South Africa.[24] In the context of constitutional law, her thesis is that, as a matter of judicial craftsmanship, judges must balance functional factors against normative factors. By 'functional factors' she means the considerations surrounding the question how the public office can be discharged if a particular remedy is given, and by 'normative factors' she refers to the values contained in the provisions of the Constitution of South Africa. A judge must balance those two sets of factors, one against the other, to come to a properly calibrated decision. Otherwise, put bluntly, there is a risk that the law will not respond to society's needs or that it will be unworkable in practice. An awkward judgment can block what may be socially desirable progress.

---

[21] Civil Service Statistics Bulletin, November 2010.

[22] That is, owned by a majority of persons of Asian origin: 'Spotlight on Asian Business—Their contribution to London', December 2007, published by the Mayor of London's Office.

[23] Speech of Sir Edward George, Governor of the Bank of England, 19 March 2002.

[24] 'Political Questions, the Social Question and other Quandaries', Chorley Lecture, London School of Economics, 14 June 2011.

Judges must be able to demonstrate that they understand the context in which their decisions are being made. The judiciary, therefore, needs to understand people in different walks of life and in different cultures. Where possible, they should have an understanding of what solutions are likely to work best. This is an aspect of developing the law with which I am very familiar in a different context, having been the Chairman of the Law Commission of England and Wales for three years, and having been thus involved in making recommendations as to how best to reform the law.

The judiciary also needs to have an awareness of social concerns so that their judgments can respond to them. To some extent, of course, social awareness may be gained by reading up about these issues, but awareness gained in this way is rarely a substitute for that obtained by experience, and so it is most likely to be found in those who have different backgrounds. I am not suggesting that judges should decide cases other than according to law, but they do need to know about social issues so as to be able to respond to them. In the past the judiciary has been able to decide issues using its own inner resources but there is presently very little diversity in the judiciary, and to compensate for this, greater weight needs to be given to this sort of awareness. The Report of the Advisory Panel on Judicial Diversity, chaired by Baroness Neuberger DBE ('the Neuberger Report') proposed that there should be a requirement within the merit criterion for judges to show that they have social awareness.[25]

The view has been expressed over several decades that there ought to be a more diverse judiciary, that is, a judiciary which is more diverse in terms of gender, ethnicity, and sexual orientation.[26] No one suggests that the judiciary should be precisely representative of the population but people are bound to have more confidence that their concerns have been properly and fully considered if the judiciary includes people from their section of society among its own members and the judiciary's own composition reflects the fact that those groups play an important role in society. This is consistent with the ancient idea to which I have previously referred that the common law is something common to all, and is thus something in which all members of society have a share.

Additionally, if the judiciary is more diverse, it is obvious that different ideas will be brought to bear on the development of the law. This will inevitably lead to a richer body of case law with more voices heard in the development of the law. Diversity of contributions in judicial deliberations tends to act like grit in the oyster

[25] 'Report of the Advisory Panel on Judicial Diversity', 2010, announced by the Lord Chancellor in April 2009 and chaired by Baroness Neuberger, DBE, see Recommendation 20. The Judicial Appointments Commission accepted this recommendation and has since included within the qualities and abilities required for appointment an awareness of the diversities of the communities which the courts and tribunals serve and an understanding of differing needs.

[26] The Report of the Judicial Diversity Taskforce, established pursuant to the Report of the Advisory Panel on Judicial Diversity, published its first report, 'Improving Judicial Diversity', in May 2011, in which it states that as at 31 March 2010 the percentage of women and BAME (that is, black and minority ethnic persons) in the courts-based judiciary was 20.6% and 4.8% respectively. This figure includes both salaried and fee-paid members of the judiciary, and the equivalent figures for the salaried judiciary were lower, namely 18.9% and 2.8% respectively.

which can produce a pearl of great price. In addition, diversity brings with it the added advantage of enhancing everyone's self-awareness and knowledge of their own subconscious prejudices.

One of the objectives of the Constitutional Reform Act 2005 was to promote diversity in the judiciary, so far as consistent with appointment on merit. Thus, the Act imposes a duty on the Judicial Appointments Commission, the new independent body set up to make selections of candidates to be judges in the courts of England and Wales, as follows:

64 Encouragement of diversity
　(1) The Commission, in performing its functions under this Part, must have regard to the
　need to encourage diversity in the range of persons available for selection for appointments.
　(2) This section is subject to section 63.

Section 63 of the 2005 Act provides that selection must be solely on merit. But is merit a criterion which means that no weight is to be given to diversity? As I see it, there is little point in Parliament imposing a duty on the Judicial Appointments Commission to encourage diversity in the pool of persons eligible for appointment if it did not also intend that the selection criteria should be suitable to ensure that a diverse group of candidates achieved the selection on merit. The new 'tie-breaker' provision in the Equality Act 2010 supports this conclusion since it appears to provide that where the representation in public office of a particular section of society is disproportionately low, and two candidates are equally well qualified, the selecting body may select the candidate from the under-represented group.[27]

Nevertheless, the pace of change has been very slow. The composition of the senior judiciary has not changed significantly even in recent years. In the High Court, the approximate percentage of women is 15.5%, in the Court of Appeal it is 7.9%, in the Supreme Court it is 8.3%, and there are no women heads of division.[28]

---

[27] Equality Act 2010, s 159. This provision has been replaced by section 63(4) of the Constitutional Reform Act 2005, s 63(4) as explained on page 256.

[28] *Author's Note:* these statements were about the position at the time. As indicated earlier (n 12 in the introduction to Part VII, *The Judiciary in the Twenty-First Century: The Old Order Changeth*), there has since been some welcome improvement in the overall percentage of women in the judiciary. There has also been particular progress in relation to the Court of Appeal and High Court. However, more remains to be done. The information in this footnote proceeds in three stages:

　(1) *Statistics showing the slow pace of change between 2000 and 2011*: The percentages of
　women and ethnic minority judges in post in the High Court and in the Court of
　Appeal of England and Wales as a percentage of the posts available were as follows as at
　1 June 2011 (figures for 2000 are given in brackets): High Court: Women—15.5%
　(7.7%), BAME—4.5% (0%); Court of Appeal (calculated on the basis that the Lord
　Chief Justice and the Heads of Division are excluded): Women—7.9% (8.6%),
　BAME—0% (0%); Heads of Division (excluding Lord Chief Justice): Women—0%
　(25%), BAME—0% (0%).
　(2) *Latest published statistics showing considerable progress in certain respects at the higher levels,*
　notably in the Court of Appeal, since 2011 (figures for 2011 are given in brackets): As at 1
　April 2015, the latest date for which published statistics are available (the Judicial
　Diversity Statistics 2015), the figures for women had increased to 19% (15.5%) for
　the High Court and to 21% (7.9%) for the Court of Appeal (calculated on the basis that
　the Lord Chief Justice and Heads of Division are excluded). However, the figure for
　BAME on the High Court remains low: 3% (formerly 3.3%). There has been no change

As a result, England and Wales lag behind other countries in terms of judicial diversity, especially at the higher levels. In particular, the figures for England and Wales do not compare well with those in other common law apex courts: in the United States of America Supreme Court it is now 33%, in the case of the High Court of Australia it is now 42%, and in the Supreme Court of Canada it is now 44%.[29] So the achievement of greater diversity may also be relevant to the courts' international standing. It may be that the Constitution Committee will reach a conclusion as to why the courts of England and Wales should have achieved so little in terms of judicial diversity. One of the reasons may be that, at the higher levels, the existing judiciary has a strong influence over the system of appointments, and that the judiciary is not well equipped to apply what have been the traditional criteria for judicial appointment to the task of diversifying itself. If this is right, then the provisions of the Constitutional Reform Act 2005 may need to be strengthened to produce the results that were envisaged.

> in the Supreme Court or with respect to the Lord Chief Justice or Heads of Division. In 2007, the new post of Senior President of Tribunals was created to head the Tribunals judiciary. This post can be held by a member of the Court of Appeal and has not been held by a member of any under-represented group.
>
> (3) *Other statistical information*: Statistics on the gender and ethnicity of applicants for judicial appointments serve the important purpose of enabling the public to see, for example, whether applications were drawn from a broad range of candidates and what proportion of applications succeeds. The Lord Chancellor, the Lord Chief Justice of England and Wales, and the Judicial Appointments Commission (JAC) are all under statutory duties to encourage diversity. (The Lord Chancellor and the Lord Chief Justice of England and Wales are under a duty to take appropriate steps for this purpose and the JAC must have regard to the need to encourage diversity in the range of persons available for selection: see Constitutional Reform Act 2005, ss 64 and 137A as amended in 2013.)

The statistics reveal trends over time, the extent to which any change in composition has been achieved in substance and, conversely, whether any particular group requires encouragement or support. However, there are certain gaps in the statistics which make it difficult to assess the position at higher levels (for instance, the level of applicants from under-represented groups). This is because, although statistics are generally published showing the number of women and BAME candidates for each judicial selection exercise and the number of such candidates who are successful (see, for example, Judicial Selection and Recommendations for Appointment Statistics, October 2014 to March 2015), a number of exceptions are made: (a) to maintain confidentiality and to ensure that candidates may not be personally identified, exercises with fewer than 10 recommendations have been amalgamated and presented as a grouped exercise; (b) in the case of Heads of Division and the Supreme Court, no statistics are published for competitions on grounds that the information could lead to speculation about the identity of candidates and possibly discourage applicants: Hansard, vol 753, col 842 (1 April 2014); and (c) no statistics have been published for competitions for the Court of Appeal, Lord Chief Justice, or Senior President of Tribunals.

[29] The statistics given in the text were those available for the three courts mentioned in June 2011. The statistics have remained constant: as at June 2015, the figures were: US 33.3%; High Court of Australia 42.8%; and the Supreme Court of Canada 44.4%. In Europe, it should be noted that, of some 40 states, the UK has the smallest number of women judges apart from Armenia, Azerbaijan, and Israel (according to a table included in a report published by the Council of Europe, 'European judicial systems—Edition 2014 (2012 data): efficiency and quality of justice', 35).

A fundamental point to my mind is that the judiciary is appointed to administer justice and develop the law. One of the major driving forces in administering and developing the law is to give dignity to all individuals affected by the law. The public may not perceive that the best decisions are being made so long as the judiciary appears to be drawn almost exclusively from one group in society and so long as it appears that diversity is welcomed in principle but is not often found in practice.

I am pleased to see that there are a number of scholars examining how women judges approach judgment writing. They consider that women take a more contextualized approach.[30] It is early days yet, but this ground-breaking work opens up new vistas. It challenges our traditional view of what judgment writing involves and may provide some practical support for the view that a diverse Bench would produce more diverse reasoning and insights, and that the judgments of a diverse Bench in a particular case may produce a better balance of views.[31] Certainly at the appellate levels, a legal problem can often be solved in different ways, and by looking at those different ways we can get to a better answer. I know from my own experience that courts here and in other jurisdictions often face the same problems but adopt different, often equally legitimate, routes to resolving them. To find the best solutions to legal problems we need to look at as many different perspectives on problems as possible, and thus to have judges who can bring their different backgrounds, and their different understandings and experiences, to bear on the resolution of legal issues.

Additional quality two: understanding of non-UK jurisprudence

I propose to move now to the second additional quality which I suggest is relevant at the present time, that is, knowledge of the case law of other courts, particularly courts elsewhere in Europe. We need today to be familiar with the jurisprudence of the two supranational courts in Europe. The way in which other courts in Europe accommodate the case law of these two supranational courts into their own domestic legal system is an area of study in which I am particularly interested as, in my work as Head of International Judicial Relations for England and Wales, I have particular responsibility for relations between our courts and the supranational courts. The two European supranational courts are: the Court of Justice of the European Union ('Luxembourg Court'), which sits in Luxembourg, and the European Court of Human Rights ('Strasbourg Court'), which sits in Strasbourg. These courts are frequently confused in the press and by politicians.

An important point to note is, of course, that the Convention is not an instrument of the European Union, but of the Council of Europe. That is not to say that the European Union does not now have its own human rights instrument.

---

[30] Rosemary Hunter, Clare McGlynn, and Erika Rackley (eds), *Feminist Judgments: From Theory to Practice* (Hart, 2010).
[31] Note also the findings of Erika Rackley, 'The Neuberger Experiment' (see n 10 in the introduction to Part VII, *The Judiciary in the Twenty-First Century: The Old Order Changeth*).

Under the Lisbon Treaty the twenty-seven member states of the European Union have adopted the Charter of Fundamental Rights,[32] which is far more extensive than the Convention but only applies to acts governed by EU law. The Convention is, however, of far broader application in terms of the number of countries and people to which it applies. The Council of Europe has forty-seven contracting states whose populations total approximately 800 million people. The Lisbon Treaty now provides for the accession of the European Union itself (as differentiated from its individual member states) to the Convention, but this has not yet taken place and leads to a new complexity in the legal position between the Luxembourg Court and the Strasbourg Court.

Now, it is important to make it clear that the legal status of decisions of the Strasbourg Court is very different from that of decisions of the Court of Justice of the European Union. Whilst the latter are binding on the UK courts, the former are not, but must be taken into account, when interpreting the Convention.[33]

In short, there now needs to be real familiarity, not just with the law of the land, but with the legal systems of other countries in Europe and with the case law of the two supranational European courts. To varying degrees, the case law of those two courts can now properly be described as part of the law of the land.

The provisions of the Convention include the right to life, the right of access to court, the right to property, and so on. Like any rights document, the Convention is, in many respects, open-textured and the Strasbourg Court has to give its provisions meaning in concrete cases. Thus, it is principally in the case law of the Strasbourg Court that we find out what the rights mean in practice. These rights raise moral and social issues of wide dimensions. The English courts are not obliged to apply the case law as if it were the case law of some higher national court. But they are obliged to take that case law into account in interpreting the Convention rights for themselves. So the courts have a choice. No doubt in most cases they would exercise that choice in favour of applying Strasbourg jurisprudence, but there are cases where the Strasbourg case law seems to take no account of some particular provision of English law or its far-reaching consequences in English law.

How does the Strasbourg Court develop its jurisprudence without inviting unnecessary conflict with the legal systems of the contracting states to the Convention? Sometimes the Strasbourg Court applies a 'consensus' test. It considers whether the area is one on which there is consensus among the contracting states. If there is a sufficient consensus, that may embolden it to develop its jurisprudence into a new area. If there is no sufficient consensus, the Strasbourg Court often finds that the matter falls within the margin of appreciation[34] of the contracting states, leaving it to them to decide what view to take. In other cases, the problem may be resolved by dialogue between the courts—either informally through discussion of

---

[32] Treaty on European Union, Art 6. Art 6(2) provides for the accession of the EU to the Convention as stated in the text but the Luxembourg Court has concluded that the proposed accession agreement is not compatible with EU law: see *Opinion 2/13* [2015] 2 CMLR 571.

[33] Compare the European Communities Act 1972, s 2 and the Human Rights Act 1998, s 2.

[34] The concept of margin of appreciation (see Glossary) is discussed in several contexts (such as proportionality) in Vol I, which also looks in detail at the value of dialogue between national courts and the Strasbourg Court.

general issues in the sphere of human rights, or formally through judgments of the respective courts which discuss the difficulties and seek a rapprochement. There are many techniques for resolving this conflict and each system has to have respect for the other and a desire to reach a compromise.

Thus, there are occasions where there have been successive judgments by the Strasbourg Court and national courts leading to a modification by the Strasbourg Court of its position. I was involved in a case as an ad hoc judge of the Strasbourg Court where this occurred. The short point was that, under the common law, to sue a public authority or indeed anyone in negligence, it is necessary to show a duty of care. The English courts held that there was no duty of care on a public authority in certain circumstances. The Strasbourg Court held that this violated the Convention right of access to a court on the grounds that it conferred immunity from liability. However, the English courts made it clear that this was a misunderstanding of domestic law. The Strasbourg Court, in consequence, accepted that the duty of care requirement was simply a mechanism for defining the circumstances in which the tort of negligence applied. This sequence is an example of the dialogue that can occur between a national court and the Strasbourg Court through the judgments they give. National judges need to understand the viewpoint of the Strasbourg Court when they frame their reasoning in domestic cases.

There are many problems with the Convention system. For example, the Strasbourg Court is overburdened by many cases which it ought not to receive because (a) they raise issues on which it has already ruled and (b) the contracting states ought to have, but have not, changed their laws so as to make them Convention-compliant. There is also an issue as to how far the Strasbourg Court should advance human rights standards where there is a social, technical, bio-ethical, or other major change in today's world.

From the Strasbourg Court's point of view, it has the difficult task of deciding how fast to force change in human rights standards in Europe. Judge Angelika Nußberger, the German national judge at the Strasbourg Court, has compared the position in European human rights protection to that of a house with many rooms where each of the rooms represents the legal system of a contracting state. The rooms are connected: they are all within the curtilage of a single house because we share common legal and ethical values; and the Strasbourg Court is like a person wandering outside, deciding whether to enter and, if so, into which rooms.

By contrast, EU law is part of the law of the land in any event. That is the effect of the European Communities Act 1972. We do not have a choice whether to follow EU jurisprudence, but we do have to work at what the decisions of the Luxembourg Court actually mean. It is becoming increasingly important to know how to apply EU law. It does not simply affect abstruse areas of competition law and VAT but subjects such as immigration and asylum, employment law, and criminal law. It is very pervasive.

There are very real problems in the reception of EU law. The decisions of the Luxembourg Court express propositions in a very concise form more familiar to civil law jurisdictions, and the national court will have to be able to decipher how these are intended to be applied in other situations. In addition, the decisions often use concepts and conventions drawn from other legal systems within the EU, the majority of which have codes rather than the common law, and make assumptions which do not apply in our system. Accordingly, when English judges read a decision of the Luxembourg Court they often have to have a different mindset. They have to have some knowledge of other European systems and have an understanding of why the case seems to have been decided in the way it has. There is, therefore, an increasingly obvious need for education in EU law and, further than that, for skills and interest in comparative law. To interpret EU law, a judge needs an ability to move easily within different legal cultures.

These skills are, in any event, needed for English law to develop, taking advantage of the best legal concepts and practices developed abroad. When it comes to law, we have one of the best legal systems in the world but that does not mean that we have a monopoly of wisdom. Take, for example, the principles of proportionality. Under the core principle of proportionality, a state measure can be justified if it is suitable and necessary to achieve the state's legitimate aim notwithstanding that it interferes with an individual's fundamental right. To be suitable and necessary, the measure must be a proportionate way of achieving that aim. In our purely domestic law, it is said that a measure is only proportionate if it achieves its legitimate aim by the least intrusive means of interfering with the individual's right. Under the jurisprudence of the Luxembourg Court, the test of proportionality may be applied with differing levels of intensity of review, so that when, for instance, there is an issue of national security, the court may apply a less strict test than one which requires it to be shown that the measure involves the least intrusive means of interference with the individual's right. The principle of proportionality is applied in differing ways by the Luxembourg Court, the German Federal Constitutional Court, and the Strasbourg Court, and their ideas are being absorbed in this area by common law courts, such as the Constitutional Court of South Africa. Judges need to have open and inquiring minds about the benefits to be obtained from studying concepts developed by other systems and, where appropriate, putting them to use, with all necessary modifications, in the English context. Judges in the twenty-first century need to be aware that this is an increasingly globalized world and we need to make ourselves familiar with other legal systems and not just 'the law of the realm' in the sense of English domestic law.

Conclusions

The object of this study of Magna Carta has been to demonstrate that, viewed from the perspective of the role of the judges and the legal system, Magna Carta was truly visionary. It is the source of many fundamental concepts in English law, especially those related to constitutional matters and individual liberty.

Magna Carta envisioned a society governed by the rule of law, where everyone was equal before the law and his or her dispute was decided by a competent judge in accordance with the law. It laid the foundations of the judicial role and our system of law, for example, by insisting on the separation of powers and the independence of the judiciary and authorizing the application of the common law. These are all still relevant concepts, needed as much today as in the past.

But, to realize the vision of Magna Carta, we have to keep the qualities required of the judges under review and up to date, so that they include any additional qualities that are appropriate in today's world. We need to update our view of what is required of judges because of changes in society, constitutional reform, and the increased relevance of European law. We also need to take account of the need for judges to possess social awareness and knowledge of the case law of courts outside the United Kingdom.

Because of the complexity of society, and the range of situations that can arise in cases before the courts, different points of view need to be expressed on legal issues. A source of some of those different points of view will inevitably be a person's background, gender, and ethnicity. The broader the experiences of the judges, the deeper the understanding of the issues they are likely to bring to the court and, by extension, the greater the legitimacy of the courts.

Moreover, diversity cannot, by its nature, be achieved simply through the selection of a single individual. The selection process for judges needs to look at the portfolio of judges at a particular tier and consider the diversity of the skill sets and experiences of the persons who make up that portfolio, and the complementarity of their skills and experiences.

This study is not a stopping point in the debate. The task of realizing today the vision of the judiciary contained in Magna Carta is not at the end of the road. We are simply at a fork in the road. But it is an important fork because of the recent changes in society and in our constitutional structure. It is now time to augment our understanding of the judicial role and to make advances in its development. If we do so, it will surely have been in part because of the inspiration provided by that extraordinary foundational document—the document we rightly call Magna Carta.

19

Women Judges

Britain's Place in the World

This chapter is based on an address given at the Annual General Meeting of the Association of Women Barristers on 3 June 2008 in Lincoln's Inn, London.

Why we should persevere

In 2008, I was delighted to lend my support to the activities of the Association of Women Barristers at their Annual General Meeting, as I consider that the Association has a vital role to play in helping women in their professional lives at the Bar and in due course in seeking appointment to the judiciary. I am particularly concerned that there should be more women judges on the High Court Bench given the important role played by the High Court in our legal system and given that the succession to the appellate courts is through the High Court. I appreciate that women have done well on the circuit and district Bench, and I do not underestimate that achievement, or the work done by circuit and district judges. Nonetheless, it is important that women should also be appointed to the High Court. I want to address the question how this might be achieved.

In January 2007, I gave a speech to the Chancery Bar Association in Lincoln's Inn. I drew attention to the fact that since October 2005 no women had been appointed as High Court judges. In June 2007, the percentage of women on the High Court Bench was a mere 10%. It took until 4 April 2008 for there to be a new woman High Court judge, namely Mrs Justice Eleanor King.[1] She is the only woman to have been appointed to the High Court Bench since 3 October 2005. In the same period, twenty-nine male High Court judges were appointed. I have no doubt that Mrs Justice King's appointment was well-earned. However, since Mrs Justice Bracewell sadly passed away in January 2007, the appointment of Mrs Justice King simply brought the number of women judges on the High Court back to what it was in October 2005. In addition, since Mrs Justice King was assigned to the Family Division, no women at all have been appointed as judges of the Chancery or Queen's Bench Divisions of the High Court. So on 3 June 2008 we were in the same position as we were on 3 October 2005.

---

[1] Now Lady Justice King.

I find this result extremely disappointing. There are many reasons why it is desirable to appoint women judges. The judiciary needs to reflect more accurately the composition of society. When I spoke to the Chancery Bar Association in January 2007, I also referred (among other things) to the perspectives which women are able to bring to the Bench. But, when I said this, the response from some was that men could equally have social awareness through their activities, perhaps as school governors or in voluntary work, and that therefore there was no particular reason to appoint women as judges. Undoubtedly, it is essential that both men and women judges have a broad social awareness. However, the point I am making is that men and women often bring different perspectives to bear on a problem. The *Times Law Supplement* for 22 April 2008, in placing Baroness Hale of Richmond in sixth place in the top 100 most powerful lawyers, specifically commented on her bringing a different perspective to her rulings. It is that potential for different perspectives that men and women often have that in my view has the potential to enrich judicial decision-making. I am not saying that other under-represented groups do not have different perspectives too, but women are by far the largest group under-represented in the judiciary.

The value of women has been accepted in many other walks of life. For instance, 17% of ambassadors, 19% of Members of Parliament, 23% of permanent secretaries, and 61% of the Government Legal Service are women.[2]

There are far fewer women judges in England and Wales than in many other jurisdictions throughout the world. I have the privilege of meeting judges from far and wide as part of my responsibility, delegated by the Lord Chief Justice to me, as Head of International Judicial Relations for England and Wales. Even in developing countries, there are many more women judges than we have in this country. Here are some statistics: compared to the mere 10% of judges on the High Court in England who are women, women judges account for 17% of the judges of the European Court of Justice; 18% of the judges of the High Court of New Delhi, India; 19% of the judges of the Federal Constitutional Court of Germany; 27% of the judges of the Constitutional Court of South Africa; 29% of the judges of the High Court of Australia; 30% of the judges of the Court of Appeal of New South Wales; 31% of the judges of the European Court of Human Rights; 44% of the judges of the Supreme Court of Canada, and so on.[3] Of course, there are some courts where there are fewer women than on the High Court of England and Wales, but there are not many comparable courts in this position.

Given the overseas numbers, it would be extraordinary if the judiciary of England and Wales were left behind for long. Our judiciary, which is charged

---

[2] According to the latest available information as at July 2015, 21% of ambassadors (and High Commissioners), 29% of Members of Parliament, 19% of permanent secretaries (or equivalent), and 60% of the Government Legal Service (now the Government Legal Department) are women.

[3] As at June 2015, women judges accounted for 18% of the judges of the European Court of Justice; 22% of the judges of the High Court of New Delhi, India; 32% of the judges of the Federal Constitutional Court of Germany; 20% of the judges of the Constitutional Court of South Africa; 42.8% of the judges of the High Court of Australia; 23% of the judges of the Court of Appeal of New South Wales; 31% of the judges of the European Court of Human Rights (the Strasbourg Court).

with keeping the common law up to date, will surely keep its own composition up to date and in line with modern conditions, so far as it lies within its power and so long as there are appropriate candidates. But it will require effort.

Starting the flow of appointments

So how *is* the flow to be started? Since 2006, with the commencement of the new provisions for the selection of High Court judges by the independent Judicial Appointments Commission, we have had a new system for High Court appointments. This may not be the first time that public appointments for women have fallen in number when a new system of appointments has been introduced. But we need to find out why it is happening in High Court appointments. There needs to be research so that we can know why it has happened. We also have to make up for lost time. As I see it, the number of women on the High Court Bench will have to double for that number to reflect more accurately the percentage of women in the eligible pool.[4]

The expression 'diversity', for all its virtues, suggests that the reasons for the under-representation of women or any disadvantages that they have are exactly the same as for other under-represented groups. The problems of each under-represented group need to be addressed, but we should not assume that the reasons for the under-representation of women, or any disadvantages which they have, are necessarily the same as for other under-represented groups.

So far as the women candidates are concerned, while it is never possible to generalize, there is evidence that many women need encouragement to apply. Women must have the confidence to apply, and they must get as much relevant experience as they can so that they do well in the application process.

On the other side of the equation, there has to be constant vigilance to avoid any residual disadvantage for potential women applicants. Great care has to be taken to ensure that the approach to potential women candidates is not through inadvertence inappropriately influenced by the fact that most of the role models (except in the Family Division) are male or by the fact that women advocates may be less visible than male advocates. I am confident, however, that there will be more women judges and advocates in time. If, moreover, there were to be any residual feeling that women are in some way less suited for positions of authority, that should be dispelled.

There also has to be constant vigilance against the less visible factors that may act as a disincentive to women candidates. There are well-known societal reasons, lifestyle reasons, and reasons connected with the organization of the professions why there are relatively few women eligible for appointment. It is also interesting to me that a number of women prefer to be mediators rather than become members of the judiciary. It would be useful to know why this is the case. It may indicate that

---

[4] The pool of those who meet the statutory qualifications for appointment. Candidates may be in the eligible pool without being senior practitioners in independent practice.

some women prefer a less gladiatorial approach to civil litigation, and that this is one of the matters on which they have a different perspective and on which they could no doubt make a quite special contribution to the development of the civil justice system.

And now I come to the Association's role. There is a role for collective responsibility in the development of under-represented groups, which the Association of Women Barristers and associations like it can carry out. As I said at the outset, the work of the Association is important both in helping women to succeed at the Bar and in helping them to prepare for appointment to the Bench. The Association can be a vehicle for providing career development and encouraging all women to expand their capabilities. This will help to form a 'pipeline' of suitable women to apply for appointments. The Association already represents the views of women in the profession on such matters as judicial appointments, and it already helps to increase the confidence of women by providing support networks and mentoring. If promotion to the Bench were a natural progression within a single organization, no doubt the organization could provide all these things. However, that is not the case, and professional organizations must step into the breach. Suitable candidates in the pool may find it helpful to be guided as to how and when to swim to the top so that they can be fished out at the relevant time. Women must show that there are plenty of fish in the pool ready to be pulled out.

Opportunity to achieve a breakthrough

But so much for the present and the past. Let us think of the future that lies ahead. There is an old saying about two prisoners looking out from behind the bars: 'One saw mud, the other stars!' Women have not done as well as I for one would have expected in the last two and a half years or so. But we must try not to look at the mud and be discouraged. Even a little bit of progress now would represent a breakthrough. It would be hugely symbolic as an acceptance that women candidates have the requisite merit. But we want progress, real progress, and progress that we can believe in. Any progress also has to be maintained. The flow may start as a trickle, but it must become a regular stream.

We must also support the Judicial Appointments Commission. The appointments system is new and the JAC has had to hit the ground running. It has made enormous strides in improving the processes for judicial appointments. We must turn our backs on any non-constructive criticism and move forward with an eye to the future. We must press the JAC to look at every way of realistically fulfilling its special statutory responsibility of having regard to the need to encourage diversity in the range of persons available for appointment. We have never before had the opportunity to contribute to, and help to fashion, the appointments process as we do now. We must make use of that advantage. If we think that improvements can be made, we should put forward our views to the JAC.

Moreover, as it seems to me, the existence of a strong, forward-looking and independent JAC has important consequences for all the members of this

Association, whatever their seniority. The JAC will turn the spotlight on those factors which cause women to leave the profession in greater numbers than men, or which mean that a smaller proportion of women get to the top of the profession, so as to form part of the pool for appointment, than men. Those matters will have to be investigated and action taken, where action is needed.

I will end with a story that I hope will be encouraging despite difficulties that some may face in practice. My husband and I were recently in India. In a small Indian hill station, my husband asked the local Judicial Magistrate (male, of course) whether there were any women judges.

'Pardon, sir?' he asked.

My husband repeated his question.

'Why, sir, we have about 30% women judges here and I hope that there will be more!'

PART VIII

THE FUTURE IS IN THEIR HANDS

I want to encourage those who are interested in a legal career. The strength of our legal system and our judiciary in particular depends on its continuing to recruit candidates of high quality. Candidates for the judiciary are generally drawn from the independent practising legal professions,[1] but may be academics or lawyers in the government legal service, commerce, or industry. Those who want to be barristers will first have to do a 'pupillage', that is, a year of practical training with a barrister, as well as pass their examinations.

I am sometimes asked if I had any female role model for my own judicial career. I find it difficult to name any individual who has struck the path that I have taken, as shown by this book. In this position, as they say, it is by walking that we make the road.

I would particularly like to encourage women to become barristers and judges. Some years ago, when I was still a High Court judge, I wrote the paper which forms the basis of Chapter 20, as a short contribution to *The Woman Lawyer*. This contains some personal history up to 1998 and some general guidance for women considering a legal career. I relate further experiences in *How to Succeed as a Pupil Barrister* (Chapter 21), and give some advice to would-be pupils. The law is immensely interesting and stimulating. Every case is different, and even now I can say that I am constantly learning.

---

[1] Principally the Bar of England and Wales and the Law Society.

20

The Woman Lawyer

This paper first appeared in *The Woman Lawyer: Making the Difference*.*

When I was at school in the 1960s, we did not have careers departments and we were expected to find out for ourselves what careers we would enjoy. So I followed the best example that anyone could have: my parents. My father was a solicitor and my mother had worked with him prior to getting married. My father had learnt about the law from his father and had an instinctive feel for legal reasoning and the high standards attached to being a practising lawyer. I worked in his office sometimes in the school holidays. I liked what I saw of the law and decided that I too would be a lawyer. By a stroke of great good fortune, I obtained a place to read law at Cambridge, and indeed stayed there for four years.

In my final term, I decided that it seemed that barristers had all the fun of helping to make new law and that I would become one too. My father was initially sad at my decision. The organization of the profession is not suitable for women he said—rightly at the time. But in my home town of Liverpool, there were then some very distinguished and able women barristers, including Rose Heilbron QC, a truly great woman lawyer and advocate who subsequently became a High Court judge, and so my father knew it *could* be done.

I had a splendid year studying in the United States at Harvard Law School, later passing the Bar finals (now the BVC). I then began looking for a pupillage. Through the help of a friend of my father, I was found an extremely good pupil master. There was a very short hiatus between pupillage and finding a set in Chambers. I wanted to practise in an area of commercial law and those were the days when people turned you down with such phrases as 'we have a woman already' or 'commercial solicitors would never instruct a woman'. Those days are over.

Then followed twenty-two years of practice at the Bar, seven as a Queen's Counsel. I married another barrister in a similar field to my own and we have three children. That certainly made demands on the skills that we women are supposed to have for multi-tasking. The organization and structure of the legal profession have changed since women joined, but the pressures and demands of professional and family life on women are still substantial.

* Clare McGlynn, *The Woman Lawyer: Making the Difference* (Butterworths, 1998), reproduced by permission of Reed Elsevier (UK) Limited trading as LexisNexis.

My husband and I were one of the small number of barrister couples. We then became one of the few pairs of QCs and now we are the only married couple who are both High Court judges. I was the first woman to be appointed a Judge of the Chancery Division of the High Court. In 1996, I was appointed Chairman of the Law Commission.

I would offer the following general advice to women lawyers. First, be yourself. Think about what you would like to achieve in your personal and professional life and see how you can get closest to it. Don't push yourself out completely just to have a successful career, important though it is. Second, plan it. Find out what is involved, as far as you can, in the future. Try to see the upside and downside of the various courses open to you. Third, enjoy the law. The law is immensely interesting and stimulating and it has many different facets. There are many different fields of law and you do not have to be a lawyer in private practice to use your law: you could go into industry or government, to mention just two other options. Decide whether it is helping people with employment law, housing law, or similar problems which affect their personal lives that you do best, or solving problems related to business, such as banking. This will help you to choose a field of law that will bring out your gifts if you decide to specialize. Fourth, when you start your career, keep in touch with other women lawyers. Many of the problems that you face will be problems that other women have or have had too, and by discussing them together you will often find that what you took to be a real difficulty is something that can easily be overcome.

21

How to Succeed as a Pupil Barrister

This chapter was first published in 2013 as a Foreword to a book by Dr Daniel Sokol and Isabel McArdle.*

If you have started reading this chapter, it is likely that in your heart of hearts you have decided that you want to be a barrister. Therefore you will have to overcome all the personal and professional obstacles that lie between you and the completion of a successful pupillage. I have no recent experience of being a pupil, but I can offer some reassurance that the system today is not as bad as it used to be.

When I did pupillage light years ago (1970–71), there was no systematic application process. You hoped you knew someone who might know someone else who might be able to ask a clerk if there was anyone in 'his' set of chambers willing to take a pupil. You would then arrive at the set of chambers with a begging letter. (CVs and word processors were not generally used.) The clerk would stretch out a tired hand to receive it, while warming his back to the fire and saying discouragingly, 'No, I am afraid our Mr X is far too busy to see/consider/take a pupil.'

For someone without a London base, and practically no barrister contacts, the situation seemed pretty Dickensian. But thanks to a family friend, and a huge slice of good luck (one of the factors was that, following a fire, the Chambers had just been relocated to a place which had facilities for both sexes), I did get the pupillage I wanted. Once I got into the swing of it, I hugely enjoyed the experience. I found that people had different reasons for seeking pupillage and for taking pupils—I did pupillage with budding bankers, diplomats' wives, and future politicians, a real cross-section of eager young people wanting to see what life at the Bar was really like.

But I also found that life in Chambers was not always glamorous. There was a great deal of hard work and heartbreak, not to mention long hours. Pupillage really makes you feel like the caterpillar wrapped up in chrysalis. You don't quite know what is going on around you and what is expected of you. When you are given a set of papers, they seem to be written in some entirely different legal language from the one you knew from Bar school or university. You are expected to know about all those procedural points which are tricks of the trade. And you don't know enough

* First appeared as the Foreword to Sokol and McArdle, *Pupillage Inside Out - How to Succeed as a Pupil Barrister* (2013, Sweet & Maxwell, London). Kindly reproduced with the permission of the Publisher.

about the tenants personally or their work or the Chambers' traditions to be able to participate fully in conversations with them or to feel part of the system, still less to interrupt them and ask for a teeny bit of help.

So feelings of trepidation are inevitable.

Remember that this is a career for the curious, for the brave-hearted and independent-minded. You need courage to stand up for what is right. Being a barrister is not about aping the habits of others but about forging your own path and adding value with some good points of your own.

Be sensitive, therefore, to the way Chambers operates and its hidden wiring. Give time for working out how to fit in with tenants' working practices and become part of the team.

Most of all, remember that your generation is one of the best qualified that there has ever been. You have every reason to think of the Bar. The competition is intense. If, however, you have landed in the right place for you at the right point in time, they will want you to stay as a tenant. I hope that will be your good fortune at the end of the pupillage process.

Glossary

Access to justice Means by which a person may exercise legal rights, particularly through legal proceedings.

aemulatio vicini A principle of Scots law which may be infringed by an owner of land if within his own premises he does anything, otherwise lawful, in mere spite or malice against his neighbour for the purpose of injuring him and not for the purpose of benefitting his own property.

American law Judge-made law developed by courts in North America after the discovery of America.

Appellate Committee of the House of Lords Most senior appeal court of the United Kingdom, which was replaced by the Supreme Court of the United Kingdom set up by the Constitutional Reform Act 2005, with effect from 1 October 2009.

BAME (noun) Black minority ethnic person; (adjective) Black minority ethnic.

Canon law Law governing a church, particularly the Roman Catholic Church or the Church of England, derived from its canons. In the case of the Church of England, canon law is to be distinguished from ecclesiastical law, which extends to all law (including legislation) that applies to the religious activities or organization of the Church of England.

Charter of Fundamental Rights EU charter principally setting out fundamental rights recognized by EU law or the Convention. Adopted as part of the Lisbon Treaty and binding on the EU institutions and (when implementing EU law) national authorities.

Codification The process whereby all the law on a particular topic is collected into a single statute or code.

Common law Judge-made law.

Constitutional statute A statute or part of a statute containing provisions which would normally be found in a written constitution, such as fundamental rights.

Convention The European Convention for the Protection of Human Rights and Fundamental Freedoms 1950 (usually referred to as the European Convention on Human Rights) and the Protocols in force.

Convention rights Rights guaranteed by the Convention, such as the right to life (art.2) and the right to respect for private and family life (art.8).

Court of Appeal Court of Appeal of England and Wales.

Damnum sine injuria* or *damnum absque injuria Loss without legal injury or loss due to legitimate competition.

De minimis Too small or inconsequential for legal redress or intervention. From Latin maxim, *de minimis non curat lex* (the law does not regard trifles).

Derivative (noun) A contract, for example for the purchase of foreign currency at a future date at a fixed price, the value of which is accordingly derived from the value of that asset at the date of purchase.

Derivative action Legal proceedings which are permitted by statute or procedural rules to be brought on behalf of another person, such as a derivative action brought by a shareholder on behalf of his company to redress a wrong done to it.

Devolution The conferral by the UK Parliament of powers on another parliament in the United Kingdom or on ministers for a part of the United Kingdom. The devolved legislatures are the Scottish Parliament, the Welsh Assembly, and the Northern Ireland Assembly. The devolved executive bodies are the Scottish government, the Welsh government, and the Northern Ireland Executive.

Disability (1) A person is said to be under a disability if his capacity to do certain acts is restricted by law, as for example where he is under 18 years of age. (2) The term is also used by the Equality Act 2010 to refer to a long-term physical or mental impairment which entitles a person to be protected from unlawful discrimination.

Economic torts Torts which generally involve the intentional infliction of economic loss, often through the actions of a third party.

European Union The economic and political organization of currently twenty-eight European member states, formed by treaty, which can take measures within the competences conferred on it which are binding on member states. The EU is a product of a number of treaties which have expanded its competences over the years. It succeeded the European Economic Community following the Lisbon Treaty signed on 13 December 2007, which came into force on 1 December 2009.

Good faith An obligation to act honestly or to act fairly towards another person (precise meaning depends on context).

Hansard The official record of proceedings in Parliament.

High Court The higher trial court in England and Wales. It consists of three Divisions, the Queen's Bench Division, the Family Division, and the Chancery Division. The heads of these Divisions are respectively the President of the Queen's Bench Division, the President of the Family Division, and the Chancellor of the High Court. They, together with the Master of the Rolls, who is the head of the Court of Appeal, are frequently referred to together as the Heads of Division.

Injuria sine damno As for *damnum sine injuria*.

Innominate term A term of a contract which is neither a condition, that is, a stipulation going to the root of the contract, breach of which will give rise to a right to treat the contract as repudiated, nor a warranty, that is, a promise which is collateral to the main purpose of the contract. The remedy for breach of an innominate term will depend on the seriousness of the breach and can therefore be ascertained only after breach has occurred.

JAC Judicial Appointments Commission: an independent body established by the Constitutional Reform Act 2005 with statutory responsibility for the selection of judicial office-holders on merit, principally for courts and tribunals in England and Wales.

Judicial accountability The various ways in which the actions of an individual judge or the judiciary as a body may, so far as consistent with judicial independence, be reviewed or questioned. These ways may be formal or informal. The appeals process is the principal method by which the decisions of individual judges are formally reviewed. But they may also be questioned informally by the media or in Parliament or by academics and others in legal publications.

Judicial independence The ability of each individual judge and also of the judiciary as a body to act free from any improper influence.

LJ Lord/Lady Justice of Appeal Judge of the Court of Appeal of England and Wales.

LJJ Plural form of LJ.

Law Commission The Law Commission of England and Wales.

Law Commissions The Law Commission of England and Wales and the Scottish Law Commission.

Law reform The making of proposals for reform of the law, usually by new legislation but sometimes by codification of existing statute and/or common law, or by consolidation or revision of existing statute law.

Lisbon Treaty Treaty signed on 13 December 2007 and coming into force on 1 December 2009 which amended the Maastricht Treaty (renamed the Treaty on European Union or TEU) and the Rome Treaty (renamed the Treaty on the Functioning of the European Union or TFEU) and which established the constitutional basis of what is now the European Union.

Lord Chancellor A senior Cabinet minister who, until the Constitutional Reform Act 2005 came into force, was also the head of the judiciary. He now has statutory responsibility for upholding judicial independence. In recent years the Lord Chancellor has also been Secretary for State for Justice, and thus the government minister in charge of the Ministry of Justice, which is the government department responsible for courts, prisons, probation, and constitutional affairs.

Luxembourg Court The Court of Justice of the European Union (CJEU), which sits in Luxembourg, or its predecessor, the Court of Justice of the European Communities, known as the European Court of Justice (ECJ).

Luxembourg jurisprudence Case law of the Luxembourg Court.

Magna Carta Royal charter executed by King John at Runnymede on 15 June 1215 and guaranteeing certain rights to his subjects. Regarded by many as a defining moment in English constitutional history.

Margin of appreciation Margin of discretion or corridor within which the Strasbourg Court permits a national body to choose between acceptable options for a rule which engages Convention rights.

Power of attorney An instrument by which a person (the donor) gives authority to another (his attorney) to act on his behalf. A power of attorney must generally comply with the Powers of Attorney Act 1971.

Privity of contract Legal rule which prevents a person from enforcing a right conferred on him by a contract to which he is not a party or being subject to an obligation imposed by such a contract.

Privy Council Judicial Committee of the Privy Council which hears appeals from members of the Commonwealth whose constitutions provide for such appeals and other territories, and certain other appeals.

Public funding Funding by the state in whole or part of a party's costs of civil or criminal proceedings.

Publici juris Belonging to everyone.

Pupil barrister A person who is training to be a barrister and who, to complete his training, works generally with a barrister or barristers already in practice (traditionally known as pupil masters but now known as pupillage supervisors) for twelve months or more.

Res communis pl *res communes* Thing which belongs to everyone, such as running water or air.

Riparian doctrine or riparianism Legal doctrine whereby a riparian owner has the right to make reasonable use of the water flow.

Riparian water rights The rights of an owner of land abutting water (the riparian owner) to use that water (for drinking, irrigation, etc) or to protect his property from it.

Roman law Law applied in ancient Rome. Many continental European systems are derived from Roman law, and it was used in the Byzantine Empire until the fifteenth century.

Separation of powers Constitutional doctrine that no one person or body of persons should be able to control more than one of the three arms of the state, being the legislature, the executive, and the judiciary.

Statute law Law consisting purely of statutes.

Strasbourg Court The European Court of Human Rights, which sits in Strasbourg.

Strasbourg jurisprudence Case law of the Strasbourg Court.

UK Supreme Court The Supreme Court of the United Kingdom established in 2009 pursuant to the Constitutional Reform Act 2005 as the final court of appeal in succession to the Appellate Committee of the House of Lords.

General Index

Names Index